THE TALMUD OF BABYLONIA

Number 84

THE TALMUD OF BABYLONIA
An American Translation
XXIIIB: Tractate Sanhedrin
Chapters 4–8

translated by
Jacob Neusner

21.25

THE TALMUD OF BABYLONIA
An American Translation
XXIIIB: Tractate Sanhedrin
Chapters 4–8

translated by
Jacob Neusner

Scholars Press
Chico, California

11018

THE TALMUD OF BABYLONIA
An American Translation
XXIIIB: Tractate Sanhedrin
Chapters 4–8

translated by
Jacob Neusner

Library of Congress Cataloging in Publication Data

Talmud. Sanhedrin IV–VIII. English.
  Tractate Sanhedrin, chapters 4–8.

  (The Talmud of Babylonia ; 23B) (Brown Judaic studies ;
no. 84)
  Includes index.
  1. Neusner, Jacob, 1932– . II. Title. III. Series: Talmud.
English. 1984 ; 23B. IV. Series: Brown Judaic studies ; no. 84.
BM499.5.E4 1984   vol.23B 296.1'2505 s   84–23550
[BM506.S2E5]   [296.1'2505]
ISBN 0–89130–801–6 (alk. paper)
ISBN 0–89130–802–4 (pbk. : alk. paper)

Printed in the United States of America
on acid-free paper

For

ERIC and CAROL MEYERS

in friendship

Contents

INTRODUCTION

To place into proper context the chapters covered in the present volume of the translation of tractate Sanhedrin, we review the tractate as a whole.

This tractate deals with two subjects, first, the organization of the Israelite government and court-system, second, punishments administered to those convicted by the courts of having committed various crimes. The two topics are treated in sections of approximately equal length. The tractate has attracted interest out of all proportion to its intellectual merits. The reason is that it is supposed to tell us whether or not the diverse accounts of the trial of Jesus conform to the laws of "the Jews." Since the only available statement purporting to give those rules is in Mishnah-tractate Sanhedrin, it is natural for people to pay close attention to what they find here. But, self-evidently, we may be certain only that the tractate, for its part, records the state of opinion as it was at the time of its own redaction, which, it is generally supposed, is at A.D. 200. Whether its picture is accurate for the procedures of the Temple nearly two hundred years earlier remains to be demonstrated and surely cannot be taken for granted.

If, however, the tractate has to stand on its own, it is hardly so compelling. It provides a sizable repertoire of extremely well-organized facts, enlivened by narratives illustrating the workings of the courts and rules for conducting trials. But, unlike the three Babas, the tractate asks no important questions about its facts, hardly attempts to show their complex potentialities, and undertakes no strikingly fresh intellectual initiatives. The framers of the tractate are satisfied to paint a picture and tell a story. They may claim significant success only in the excellent way in which the tractate is organized, since it is still more cogent and follows an even more disciplined pattern than the three tractates which precede (compare above, pp. 00-00).

Part of the reason for the tractate's logical and orderly treatment of its topic is that the framers choose to ignore the way Scripture handles the same set of themes. The make ample use of the facts they find in the Mosiac law codes. But these they lay out and organize entirely in their own way. When "Moses" does not provide information which their scheme or order and substance requires, they do not hesitate to make things up for themselves. Once more we shall see that fact most clearly by comparing the substance and sequence of Scriptures, laid out in accord with Mishnah's plan (Albeck, pp. 159-161), with the topical unfolding of the Mishnah tractate itself. These are the relevant verses, in the order in which the tractate calls upon them or upon information contained in them.

Deut. 16:18-20:

> You shall appoint judges and officers in all your towns which the Lord your God gives you, according to your tribes; and they shall judge the people with righteous judgment. You shall not pervert justice; you shall not show partiality; and you shall not take a bribe, for a bribe blinds the eyes of the

wise and subverts the cause of the righteous. Justice, and only justice, you shall follow, that you may live and inherit the land which the Lord you God gives you.

Deut. 17:8-13:

If any case arises requiring decision between one kind of homicide and another, one kind of legal right and another, or one kind of assault and another, any case within your towns which is too difficult for you, then you shall arise and go up to he place which the Lord your God will choose, and coming to the Levitical priests, and to the judge who is in office in those days, you shall consult them, and they shall declare to you the decision. Then you shall do according to what they declare to you from that place which the Lord will choose; and you shall be careful to do according to all that they direct you, according to the instructions which they give you, and according to the decision which they pronounce to you, you shall do; you shall not turn aside from the verdict which they declare to you, either to the right hand or to the left. The man who acts presumptuously, by not obeying the priest who stands to minister there before the Lord your God, or the judge, that man shall die; so you shall purge the evil from Israel. And all the people shall hear, and fear, and not act presumptuously again.

Exodus 23:21:

Give heed to him and hearken to his voice, do not rebel against him, for he will not pardon your transgression; for my name is in him.

Numbers 35:30:

If any one kills a person, the murderer shall be put to death on the evidence of witnesses; but no person shall be put to death on the testimony of one witness.

Deut. 17:6-7:

On the evidence of two witnesses or of three witnesses he that is to die shall be put to death; a person shall not be put to death on the evidence of one witness. The hand of the witnesses shall be first against him to put him to death, and afterward the hand of all the people. So you shall purge the evil from the midst of you.

Lev. 21:10-12:

The priest who is chief among his brethren, upon whose head the anointing oil is poured, and who has been consecrated to wear the garments, shall not let the hair of his head hand loose, nor rend his clothes; he shall not go in to any dead body, nor defile himself, even for his father or for his mother; neither shall he go out of the sanctuary, nor profane the sanctuary of his god; for the consecration of the anointing oil of his God is upon him: I am the Lord.

Deut. 17:14-20:

When you come to the land which the Lord your God gives you, and you possess it and dwell in it, and then say, 'I will set a king over me, like all the nations that are round about me'; you may indeed set as king over you him whom the Lord your God will choose. One from among your brethren you shall set as king over you; you may not put a foreigner over you; who is not your brother. Only he must not multiply horses for himself, or cause the people to return to Egypt in order to multiply horses, since the Lord has said to you, 'You shall never return that way again.' And he shall not multiply wives for himself, lest his heart turn away; nor shall he greatly multiply for himself silver and gold.

And when he sits on the throne of his kingdom, he shall write for himself in a book a copy of this law, from that which is in charge of the Levitical priests; and it shall be with him, and he shall read in it all the days of his life, that he may learn to fear the Lord his God, by keeping all the words of this law and these statues, and doing them; that his heart may not be lifted up above his brethren, and that he may not turn aside from the commandment, either to the right hand or to the left; so that he may continue long in his kingdom, he and his children, in Israel.

Deut. 21:22-23:

And if a man has committed a crime punishable by death and he is put to death, and you hang him on a tree, his body shall not remain all night upon the tree, but you shall bury him the same day, for a hanged man is accursed by God; you shall not defile your land which the Lord your God gives you for an inheritance.

Deut. 21:18-21:

If a man has a stubborn and rebellious son, who will not obey the voice of his father or the voice of his mother, and, though they chastise him, will not give heed to them, then his father and his mother shall take hold of him and bring him out to the elders of his city at the gate of the place where he lives, and they shall say to the elders of his city, 'This our son is stubborn and rebellious, he will not obey our voice; he is a glutton and a drunkard.' Then all the men of the city shall tone him to death with stones; so you shall purge the evil from your midst; and all Israel shall hear, and fear.

Deut. 13:12-18:

If you hear in one of your cities, which the Lord you God gives you to dwell there, that certain base fellows have gone out among you and have drawn away the inhabitants of the city, saying, 'Let us go and serve other gods,' which you have not known, then you shall inquire and make search and ask diligently; and behold, if it be true and certain that such an abominable thing has been done among you, you shall surely put the inhabitants of that city to the sword, destroying it utterly, all who are in it and its cattle, with the edge of the sword. You shall gather all its spoil into the midst of its open square, and burn the city and all its spoil with fire, as a whole burnt offering to the Lord your God; it shall be a heap forever, it shall not be built again. None of the devoted things shall cleave to your hand; that the Lord may turn from the fierceness of his anger, and show you mercy, and have compassion on you, and multiply you, as he swore to your fathers, if you obey the voice of the Lord your God, keeping all his commandments which I command you this day, and doing what is right in the sight of the Lord your God.

The outline of the tractate is as follows:

I.   The Court-System. 1:1-5:5

A.   Various kinds of courts and their jurisdiction. 1:1-6

1:1   Property cases are decided by three judges.
1:2   Various other sorts of cases which are decided by a court of three judges.
1:3   Continuation of the foregoing.
1:4   Cases involving the death-penalty are judged by twenty-three judges.
1:5   Political crimes are judged by seventy-one judges, e.g., a tribe, a false prophet, a high priest.
1:6   The large court had seventy-one members, and the small one, twenty-three.

B.   The heads of the Israelite nations and the court-system. 2:1-5

2:1   The high priest judges and others judge him.
2:2   The king does not judge, and others do not judge him.
2:3   Continuation of the foregoing.
2:4-5 The prerogatives of the king.

C.   The procedures of the court-system: Progerty cases. 1:1-8

3:1-2 Choosing the judges for a property-case.
3:3   These are not valid to serve as judges or as witnesses.
3:4   These relatives are prohibited from serving as one's witnesses or judges.
3:5   Others who may not serve as judges or witnesses.
3:6   How do they examine the testimony of witnesses. Procedures for reaching a decision.
3:7   Procedures for reaching a decision, continued.
3:8   Avenues of appeal.

D.   The procedures of the court-system: Capital-cases. 4:1-5:5

4:1-2   The difference of capital cases and their procedures from property cases.

4:3-4   The layout of the sanhedrin, the places of the judges.

4:5   How they admonish witnesses in capital cases.

5:1   The points of interrogation of witnesses (in capital cases).

5:2   The more they interrogate witnesses, the more is one to be praised.

5:3   Contradictory testimony.

5:4   The foregoing continued. The discussion of the case. The possibility of appeal.

5:5   Reaching a decision. Voting procedures in capital cases.

II.   The death-penalty. 6:1-11:6

A.   Stoning. 6:1-6

6:1-4   When the trial is over, they take the convicted felon out and stone him. Description of the penalty.

6:5   Appended homily.

6:6   Disposition of the corpse of the felon.

B.   Four modes of execution lie in the power of the court and how they are administered. 7:1-3

7:1   Four modes of execution: stoning, burning, decapitation, and strangulation.

7:2   How burning is carried out.

7:3   How decapitation and strangulation are carried out.

C.   Those who are put to death by stoning. 7:4-8:7

7:4   These are the ones who are put to death by stoning.

7:5   Continuation of the foregoing list and its exegesis.

7:6   Continuation of the foregoing list and its exegesis.

7:7   Continuation of the foregoing list and its exegesis.

7:8   Continuation of the foregoing list and its exegesis.

7:9   Continuation of the foregoing list and its exegesis.

7:10   Continuation of the foregoing list and its exegesis.

7:11   Continuation of the foregoing list and its exegesis.

8:1-4   Continuation of the foregoing list and its exegesis.

8:5-7   Appended homiletical materials.

D.   <u>Those put to death through burning or decapitation.</u> 9:1-10:6

9:1   And these are the ones who are put to death through burning, decapitation.

9:2   Murderers.

9:3   Continuation of the foregoing.

9:4   He who is liable to be put to death through two different modes of execution
        is judged to be executed by the more severe.

9:5-6   Extra-judicial modes of punishment, e.g., of recidivists.

10:1-3 Homiletical expansion of M. 9:5-6: extra-judicial punishment, at the hands
        of Heaven. All Israelites share in the world to come except....

10:4-5 Exegesis of M. 9:1's list for decapitation.

10:6   Homiletical continuation of the foregoing.

E.   <u>Those put to death through strangulation.</u> 11:1-6

11:1   These are the ones who are to be strangled.

11:2   Continuation of the foregoing list and its exegesis.

11:3   Continuation of the foregoing list and its exegesis.

11:4   Continuation of the foregoing list and its exegesis.

11:5   Continuation of the foregoing list and its exegesis.

11:6   Continuation of the foregoing list and its exegesis.

Both units of the tractate are very carefully organized. There is, moreover, a careful and obvious effort to link the two, since M. 6:1ff. carry forward the narrative begun at M. 5:5, and it is only in the unfolding of the new materials that we realize a decisive shift in the topic has taken place. The tractate unpacks the opening topic, the court system, by describing, first, the several types of courts, I.A. (I.B. is important and can go nowhere else), then the procedures followed for the two distinct kinds of cases with which they deal, property litigation, I.C., and capital-cases, I.D. This latter has to have its present position, for it serves as a prologue to the second unit.

The important pericope in unit II is M. 7:1, which lays the foundations for all which follows. First, the four modes of execution are described. Then, still more important, those who are subjected to each of the four modes of execution are specified. The spelling out is at II.C, D, and E. As is clear, except for some inserted or appended homiletical materials, the entire construction systematically expounds the facts important for a full understanding of M. 7:1. I cannot imagine a more cogent or logically and formally coherent tractate than this one. As I said, the facts so elegantly put together are considerably less interesting than the way in which they are organized and given linguistic and syntactic form.

In addition to using my already-available translations of the Mishnah and the Tosefta, I made reference throughout to <u>Sanhedrin. Translated into English with notes,</u>

glossary, and indices. Chapters I-VI by Jacob Shachter. Chapters VII-XI by H. Freedman (London, 1948: Soncino). Where I have followed translations proposed by Shachter and Freedman, I have so indicated. From time to time I interpolate their footnotes verbatim (these commonly provide a precis of what Rashi says), and here too I have, of course, indicated that fact.

For the checking and revision of my translation of this volume, I express to my students Howard Eilberg-Schwartz, Paul V. Flesher and Judith Romney Wegner.

CHAPTER ONE
BAVLI SANHEDRIN CHAPTER FOUR

4:1-2

A. The same [laws] apply to property cases and capital cases with respect to examination and interrogation [of witnesses],

B. as it is said, "You will have one law" (Lev. 24:22).

C. What is the difference between property cases and capital cases?

D. Property cases [are tried] by three [judges], and capital cases by twenty-three.

E. In property cases they begin [argument] with the case either for acquittal or for conviction, while in capital cases they begin only with the case for acquittal, and not with the case for conviction.

F. In property cases they decide by a majority of one, whether for acquittal or for conviction, while in capital cases they decide by a majority of one for acquittal, but only with a majority of two [judges] for conviction.

G. In property cases they reverse the decision whether in favor of acquittal or in favor of conviction, while in capital cases they reverse the decision os as to favor acquittal, but they do not reverse the decision so as to favor conviction.

H. In property cases all [judges and even disciples] argue either for acquittal or conviction. In capital cases all argue for acquittal, but all do not argue for conviction.

I. In property cases one who argues for conviction may argue for acquittal, and one who argues for acquittal may also argue for conviction. In capital cases the one who argues for conviction may argue for acquittal, but the one who argues for acquittal has not got the power to retract and to argue for conviction.

J. In property cases they try the case by day and complete it by night. In capital cases they try the case by day and complete it [the following] day.

K. In property cases they come to a final decision on the same day [as the trial itself], whether it is for acquittal or conviction. In capital cases they come to a final decision for acquittal on the same day, but on the following day for conviction.

L. (Therefore they do not judge [capital cases] either on the eve of the Sabbath or on the eve of a festival.)

M. 4:1

A. In cases involving questions of [B. adds: property[uncleanness and cleanness they begin [voting] from the eldest. In capital cases they begin from the side [with the youngest].

B. All are valid to engage in the judgment of property cases, but all are not valid to engage in the judgment of capital cases,

C. except for priests, Levites, and Israelites who are suitable to marry into the priesthood.

M. 4:2

I.

A. Do property cases require examination and interrogation of witnesses?

B. An objection was raised [to that proposition]:

C. If the date was inscribed on the writ, "On the first of Nisan, in the year of release," and others came along and said to them [the witnesses to the writ], "How in the world can you have signed that writ, for lo, you were with us on that day in such and such a place,"

D. their testimony remains valid, and the writ remains valid,

E. for we take into account the possibility that they postdated the writ [wrote the writ earlier but] when they wrote it out" [T. Mak. 1:2G-I].

F. Now if you maintain that we require examination and interrogation of the witnesses, how can we take account of the possibility that they postdated the writ when they wrote it out? [That would have come out in the interrogation, and in any event if we accept such a claim, why interrogate the witnesses at all?]

G. And by your reasoning you should find a problem in the following passage of the Mishnah:

H. Antedated bonds are invalid. [By antedating the document, the creditor gains rights, to which he is not entitled, against the property of the debtor. But postdated bonds are valid. [By postdating the document, the creditor voluntarily restricts his own legal rights against his debtor's property] [M. Sheb. 10:5C-D, Newman, p. 206].

I. Now if you maintain that we require examination and interrogation of witnesses to the bond, why should postdated bonds be regarded as valid? [These too could be forgeries. Shachter p. 201, n. *: Hence even if the loan itself is attested as having taken place, it should rank as only a verbal loan, which cannot be collected from property sold even after it was incurred.]

J. [The fact that we raise the issue on the basis of the passage of the Tosefta, of secondary authority, rather than of the Mishnah, of primary authority] poses no problem, since we raise our objection on the basis of a stronger issue.

K. Specifically, even in the case of a date of the first of Nisan in the Sabbatical Year, on account of which it would not be common for people to make loans [which would be nullified in the Seventh Year] and so would not likely claim, "Perhaps they postdated it when they wrote it," for one would not want to weaken the force of his bond.

L. even in such a case, since the Seventh Year only at the end nullifies existing debts, we declare the bond valid [Shachter, p. 202, n. 3: by assuming its writing has been postponed to the Sabbatical Year. Thus, this assumption, since it is possible, is made in spite of its improbability, a loan in the Sabbatical Year still being rare. How much more so is the assumption to be made in normal cases. Why then should the witnesses be examined on the date, since even if it is disproved, their testimony holds good?]

M. In any event the cited passage presents a problem [to the rule of the Mishnah before us].

II.

A. Said R. Hanina, "As a matter of Torah-law, the same [rules] apply to property cases and capital cases with respect to the examination and interrogation of witnesses as it is said, 'You will have one law.' (Lev. 24:22) [M. 4:1A-B].

B. "Then on what account did they rule that property cases do not require examination and interrogation of witnesses?

C. "It is so that you will not shut the door before those who wish to take out loans [by making it difficult for the lender to collect."

D. But deal with the following: [32B] If the judges made an error in their verdict, they should not have to make restitution. [Why not make this rule too?]

E. All the more so will you turn out to shut the door before those who wish to take out loans.

III.

A. Raba said, "The rule at hand [which requires examination and interrogation of witnesses in property cases] deals with cases involving judicial penalties, while the other passages [which do not require examination of witnesses] deal with cases of admission that a debt exists and cases of transactions in loans. [In such cases the procedure would discourage creditors from lending money.]"

B. Said R. Pappa, "Both rules [that of the Mishnah, requiring interrogation, and the others cited, not requiring it] deal with matters of admissions of existing debts and transactions of loans.

C. "The former speak of a case involving suspicious circumstances, the latter does not."

D. That accords with the statement of R. Simeon b. Laquish.

F. For R. Simeon b. Laquish contrasted [apparently conflicting verses of Scripture]. It is written, 'In justice you shall judge your neighbor' (Lev. 19:15). And elsewhere it is written, 'Justice, justice shall you follow' (Deut. 16:20. [The repetition of 'justice' indicates that strict justice must be followed, hence rules such as interrogation of witnesses].

G. Why [does the word justice appear twice in one verse but only once in the other]? The verse [that repeats the word justice] refers to a case involving suspicious circumstances [therefore interrogation of witnesses is necessary]. The other verse refers to a case in which there are no suspicious circumstances [hence no interrogation is required].

H.   R. Ashi said, "The Mishnah-passage may be reconciled with the contradictions pointed out above as we have now explained.

I.   "As to the verses of Scripture, one refers to strict justice, the other to arbitration."

J.   So has it been taught on Tannaite authority:

K.   "Justice, justice shall you follow" (Deut. 16:20):

L.   One reference to "justice' speaks of the strict justice of a trial, the other of arbitration.

M.   How so? Two boats going on a river which meet — if both of them pass together, they will both sink. If they go one after another, they will both pass safely.

N.   So too two camels going up the ascent at Bet Horon which meet — if they both try to go onward together, they will both fall. If they go up one after the other, they both will make it safely.

O.   How [do they proceed]?

P.   If one of the asses was loaded and one of them was not loaded, the one that was not loaded gives way to the one that was loaded.

Q.   If one of the asses was nearer [its destination] and the other not near, the one that was nearer gives way before the one that was not near.

R.   If both of them were near or both far, they should make a compromise among them and the one will pay compensation to the next [for the loss]. [T. B.Q. 2:10B-I].

IV.

A.   Our rabbis have taught on Tannaite authority:

B.   "Justice, justice shall you follow" (Deut. 16:20):

C.   [This means] seek out a well-qualified court,

D.   [such as] R. Eliezer in Lydda, [or] Rabban Yohanan b. Zakkai in Beror Hayyil.

E.   It was taught on Tannaite authority:

F.   If you hear the sound of the grinding of the wheel in Boreni, it is a sign that the week following the birth of a son has been fulfilled [and the circumcision is at hand].

G.   [If you see] the light of a lamp in Beror Hayyil, it is the sign that there is a banquet there.

H.   Our rabbis have taught on Tannaite authority:

I.   "Justice, justice shall you follow" (Deut. 16:20):

J.   [This means] seek out sages in session,

K.   [such as] R. Eliezer in Lydda, Rabban Yohanan ben Zakkai in Beror Hayyil, R. Joshua in Peqiin, Rabban Gamaliel in Yabneh, R. Aqiba in Bene Beraq, R. Mattia in Romi, R. Hanania b. Teradion in Sikhni, R. Yose in Sepphoris, R. Judah b. Beterah in Nisibis, R. Joshua in the Exile, Rabbi in Bet Shearim, sages in the hewn-stone chamber.

V.

A.   In property cases they begin [argument with the case either for acquittal or for conviction, while in capital cases they begin only with the case for acquittal and not with the case for conviction] [M. 4:1E]:

B.   What do they say [for the defense]?

C.   Said R. Judah, "This is what we say [to the witnesses for the prosecution], 'Who will say that matters are as you claim?'"

D.   Said Ulla to him, "And lo, we should shut them up!"

E.   And let them be shut up! Has it not been taught on Tannaite authority:

F.   R. Simeon b. Eleazar says, "They move the witnesses from place to place to confuse them so that they will retract" [T. San. 9:1A]?

G.   Are the cases parallel? In that case the witnesses are put off in the natural course of events, while here, by our own act we put them off.

H.   Rather, said Ulla, "This is what we say to them, 'Do you [the defendant] have witnesses to prove that they form a conspiracy for perjury?'"

I.   Said Rabbah to him, "But do we open the trial with an argument for the acquittal for this party which also constitutes an argument for the conviction of the other party?"

J.   But does this encompass an argument for conviction? Have we not learned in the Mishnah: Witnesses who have conspired to commit perjury are not put to death [for their perjury] unless the court process has been completed [M. Mak. 1:6A]? [Here, by contrast, the trial is just beginning, and the perjured witnesses can go off free if the accused is not convicted.]

K.   This is the sense of my statement: If this one remains silent until the end of the court process and then brings witnesses and demonstrates that the witnesses against him form a conspiracy to commit perjury, it turns out to be the conviction of the other party!

L.   Rather, said Rabbah, "We say to him, 'Do you have witnesses to contradict [the witnesses against you]?'"

M.   R. Kahana said, "[We say], 'From what you have said, it would appear that the accused is innocent.' [Shachter, p. 206, n. 2: The judges start by pointing out the weak features of the prosecution, e.g., even if certain statements of the prosecution are proved true, they do not show the guilt of the accused.]"

N.   Both Abayye and Raba say, "We say to him, 'If you did not kill anyone, do not be afraid'"

O.   R. Ashi said, "Let anyone who has any information for the acquittal of this party come and present it in his behalf.'"

P.   It has been taught on Tannaite authority along the lines of the position of Abayye and Raba:

Q.   Rabbi says, "'If no man have lain with you and if you have not gone aside...' (Num. 5:19).

R.   "[33A] On the basis of this verse we learn that in capital trials the court begins first with arguments for acquittal."

VI.

A.   In property cases they reverse the decision [whether in favor of acquittal or in favor of conviction, while in capital cases they reverse the decision so as to favor acquittal but they do not reverse the decision so as to favor conviction] [M. 4:1G]:

B.   An objection was raised on the basis of the following:

C.   If one judged a case, declaring a liable person to be free of liability, declaring the
     person free of liability to be liable, declaring what is clean to be unclean, declaring
     what is unclean to be clean, what he has done is done. But he pays compensation
     from his own funds [M. Bekh. 4:4D-F]. [Why not retract the decision, in line with M.
     4:1G ?]

D.   Said R. Joseph, "There is no contradiction. Here [where the decision may be
     changed] we deal with the decision of an expert, and there [where the decision
     cannot be changed but the judge has to pay compensation for his error], it is the
     decision of one who was not an expert."

E.   But in the case of the decision of a judge who was an expert, do we retract the
     decision?

F.   And lo, it has been taught on Tannaite authority:

G.   But if he was an expert recognized by a court, he is free from the liability of paying
     [M. Bekh. 4:4G] [but the decision holds good. So the expert-judges's decision also
     cannot be reversed].

H.   Said R. Nahman, "In the one case [where the decision may be retracted] it is where
     there is a court superior in learning and in numbers, and where [the decision may not
     be retracted] it is where there is no superior court in wisdom and in numbers [to
     reverse the decision]."

I.   R. Sheshet said, "Here we speak of a case in which the error was in a teaching in the
     Mishnah [and the decision may be revoked], while there we deal with an error in
     critical reasoning [in which case the decision may not be revoked]."

J.   For R. Sheshet said R. Assi said, "If one has erred in a matter that is taught in the
     Mishnah, the decision is to be retracted. If the error lay in critical reasoning, the
     decision is not to be retracted."

K.   Said Rabina to R. Ashi, "Even if one has erred in a matter attributed to R. Hiyya
     and R. Oshaia [e.g., in materials assembled in collections of Tosefta imputed to
     their authorship]?"

L.   He said to him, "Yes".

M.   [He asked] "And even in a matter attributed to Rab and Samuel?"

N.   He said to him, "Yes."

O.   "And even in matters attributed to me and to you?"

P.   He said to him, "Are we hackers of swamp-reeds? [Of course!]"

VII.

A.   What is an example of "a matter of critical reasoning"?

B.   Said R. Pappa, "It would involve, for example, a case in which there is a dispute on
     an issue between two Tannaite authorities or two Amoraic authorities, in which a
     statement of the decided law in accord with one or the other of the authorities has
     not been laid down. The judge at hand happened to make a decision in accord with
     one of them, but the trend of discussion in point of fact follows the other. This
     would be the case of an error involving critical analysis."

C.   An objection was raised by R. Hamnuna to R. Sheshet:

D. "There was the precedent of the case of a cow which had had its womb removed. R. Tarfon had the cow fed to the dogs [as invalid for Israelite consumption]."

E. "The case came before sages, and they declared it permitted. Said Todos, the physician, 'Neither a cow nor a pig leaves Alexandria without their ripping out its womb, so that it will not bear offspring."

F. "Said R. Tarfon, 'There goes your ass, Tarfon' [since he assumed he would have to pay restitution]."

G. "Said to him R. Aqiba, 'R. Tarfon, you are exempt, for you are an expert recognized by a court, and any expert recognized by a court is free from the liability of paying' [M. Bekh. 4:4H-M]."

H. "Now is you were right [that an error in a Mishnah-law warrants retracting a decision], then he should have said to him, 'You have erred concerning a rule of the Mishnah, and one who errs in a rule of the Mishnah may simply retract his decision.'"

I. The sense of [Aqiba's statement] is to give two reasons [that Tarfon is exempt]: first, "You have erred in a law of the Mishnah and may retract;" and furthermore, moreover, "You have erred in a matter of critical reasoning, and you are an expert publicly acknowledged by the court, and whoever is an expert recognized by a court is free from the liability of paying."

J. Said R. Nahman bar Isaac to Raba, "How could R. Hamnuna raise an objection to R. Sheshet from the case of the cow? As to the cow, lo, he fed it to the dogs, and there is no possibility of giving it back!"

K. This is what he meant to say to him: "If you claim that if one has erred in the matter of a Mishnah-law, he may not retract, therefore the decision stands, that is why R. Tarfon was concerned. So [Aqiba] said to him, "You are exempt, for you are an expert recognized by a court, and any expert recognized by a court is free from the liability of paying [compensation]."

L. But if you maintained that if one errs in a matter of Mishnah-law, he may indeed retract the decision, he should have said to him, "If the cow were still available, your decision would not have stood, and you would have done nothing [demanding reparations], now too you have done nothing whatsoever. [Shachter, p. 208, n. 9: Seeing that Aqiba did not argue in that manner, it can be inferred that if one errs regarding a law cited in the Mishnah, the decision may not be reversed.]

M. [Dealing with the contradiction], said R. Hisda, "at that passage [M. Bekh. 4:4] we deal with the case in which a judge personally took the beast from one party and disposed of it [in which case the decision cannot be reversed], and in the present matter [the rule of M. San. 4:1G, in which, in a property case, we may retract the decision], we deal with a case in which the judge did not personally remove [property] from one party and hand it over to the other."

N. Now [that thesis poses no problem in the case in which] a judge declared one liable who in fact was exempt. For example, it would be a case in which he removed property from one party and personally handed it over to the other party.

O. But if one is supposed to have declared the liable party to be exempt, how can we find an equivalent case? [All the judge has done is to leave the property in the hands of the person who now has it.]

P.   It would be a case in which the judge said to him, "You are exempt [from having to make a payment]."

Q.   But in this case he has not personally taken from the one party and handed it over to the other party!

R.   Since he has said, "You are exempt," it is as if he took property from one party and handed it over to the other party.

S.   But what about our Mishnah-paragraph, in which it is taught: In property cases they reverse the decision whether in favor of acquittal or in favor of conviction [M. 4:1G]?

T.   Now in the matter of reversing the decision in a case of acquittal we could find such a case, for example, when the judge said to him, to begin with, 'You are liable," but he did not personally take property from the one and hand it over to the other.

U.   But if it was on the side of guild, how would you find such a case?

V.   It would be where the judge said to him, "You are exempt."

W.   But you have just said that once the judge has said to him, "You are exempt," it is as if he had taken property from one party and personally handed it over to the other party.

X.   The Mishnah-passage makes a single statement [not two]: In property cases they reverse the decision in exemption of the one party, which is a decision of liability to the other party.

Y.   Along these same lines, in respect to capital cases:

Z.   In capital cases they reverse the decision so as to favor acquittal [33B], but they do not reverse the decision so as to favor conviction [M. 4:1G].

AA. They retract the decision so as to favor acquittal -- acquittal alone.

BB. And they do not retract the decision to favor conviction -- acquittal for one which is conviction for another.

CC. Conviction for whom?

DD. That is no problem, it would be conviction [to the detriment of] the one who is to redeem the blood.

EE. On account of avoiding a decision detrimental to the one who redeems the blood, should we put this one to death?

FF. And moreover, what is the sense of the language, whether...whether... [which indicates that we deal with two statements, not one]?

GG. That is a problem.

HH. Rabina said, "[As to R. Hisda's statement that where the guilty party is found innocent, the decision cannot be reversed, since that would involve taking from one and giving to the other], it would be illustrated by a case in which the plaintiff held a pledge in his hand, and the judge took it from him.

II. "'If he declared the clean to be unclean' would be illustrated by a case in which a judge [personally made the object unclean himself] by bringing it in contact with a reptile.

JJ. "'If he declared the unclean to be clean' would be illustrated by a case in which the judge personally mixed [the fruit he had declared clean] with the fruit [of the one who had brought the question, in fact thereby rendering the entire lot unclean]."

VIII.

A. In capital cases they reverse the decision [so as to favor of acquittal but not so as to favor conviction] [M. 4:1G]:

B. How on the basis of Scripture do we know that, if someone goes forth from court having been declared guilty, and one [of the judges] said, "I have arguments to offer in behalf of a verdict of innocence," that we bring the convicted man back?

C. Scripture says, "You shall not kill the guiltless" (Ex. 23:7).

D. And how do we know on the basis of Scripture that one who goes forth from court having been declared innocent, and one of the judges said, "I have arguments to offer in behalf of a verdict of guilty," that we do not bring the man back?

E. Scripture says, "And the one who has been declared righteous you shall not slay" (Ex. 23:7).

F. Said R. Shimi bar Ashi, "And it is the opposite with one who incites [Israelites to commit idolatry].

G. "For it is written, 'You shall not spare nor shall you conceal him" (Deut. 13:9)."

H. R. Kahana derived the same lesson from the verse, "But you shall surely kill him" (Deut. 13:10).

I. R. Zera asked R. Sheshet, "What is the law [about bringing back to court someone who has been held] and sent into exile [for unintentional homicide]? [Can he be brought back to court if one of the judges said 'I have arguments to offer in behalf of a verdict of innocence'? Yes.]"

J. "For we establish an analogy between that case and the present one through the common use, in both instances, of the word 'murderer.'" [Just as a murderer can be brought back, so too can a person who committed unintentional homicide.]

K. "What is the law concerning those who are liable to be flogged?"

L. "It comes through establishing an analogy between the one and the other area of law through the use, in common, of the word 'wicked.'"

M. So too has it been taught on Tannaite authority:

N. How do we know that the same rule applies in cases of those liable to exile?

O. We establish an analogy through the common use of the word "murderer."

P. And how do we know that that is the law in the case of those liable to a flogging?

Q. From the use of the word "wicked" in both contexts.

IX.

A. But they do not reverse the decision so as to favor conviction [M. 4:1G]:

B. Said R. Hiyya bar Abba said R. Yohanan, "And that applies if one has made a mistake about a matter about which the Sadducees do not concur [something not in Scripture], but if one has erred in a matter about which the Sadducees concur [which is to say, something actually written out in Scripture], then it is something you learn in school [and there is no reason to reverse the conviction],"

C.   R. Hiyya bar Abba asked R. Yohanan, "If one made an error in a law about an adulterer or an adulteress, what is the law? [Shachter, p. 211, n. 12: Whereas other criminal cases lend themselves to mistakes in judgment, owing to the investigation of the manifold details accompanying the act, in cases of illicit intercourse, once the act is done, there is no room for error.]"

D.   He said to him, "While the fire is lit, go harvest your pumpkin and roast it."

E.   So too it has been stated on Amoraic authority:

F.   Said R. Ammi said R. Yohanan, "If one made an error in a case involving an adulterer, the decision is retracted."

G.   In what sort of cases do they not retract a decision?

H.   Said R. Abbahu said R. Yohanan, "In a case, for instance, in which one made an error about sodomy [for this would be something on which the Sadducees do not concur, Scripture not being explicit about it]."

X.

A.   In property cases all [argue either for acquittal or conviction, in capital cases all argue for acquittal, but all do not argue for conviction] [M. 4:1H]:

B.   All encompasses even the witnesses.

C.   May we say that the Mishnah-paragraph represents the view of R. Yose b. R. Judah and not rabbis?

D.   For it has been taught on Tannaite authority:

E.   "'But one witness shall not testify against any person'" (Num. 35:30) -- whether to testify for a verdict of innocence or for guilt.

F.   R. Yose b. R. Judah says, "One may testify for innocence, but may not testify for a verdict of guilt." [So Yose would concur with the statement of the Mishnah, as interpreted at B, and rabbis would not.]

G.   Said R. Pappa, "The Mishnah-paragraph refers to one of the disciples [not one of the witnesses], and it represents the view of all parties."

H.   [34A] What is the Scriptural basis for the view of R. Yose b. R. Judah?

I.   It is because Scripture has said, "But one witness shall not testify against any person that he die" (Num. 35:30).

J.   "So that he die" he may not testify, but so as to acquit the accused he may testify.

K.   And rabbis?

L.   Said R. Simeon b. Laqish, "It is because the witness would appear to have a personal interest in his testimony [for acquittal, to avoid being convicted as a part of a conspiracy for perjury, and that is why he changes his testimony]."

M.   And how do rabbis interpret the language, "...that he die"?

N.   They apply that verse to the case of testimony from one of the disciples.

O.   For it has been taught on Tannaite authority:

P.   If one of the witnesses said, "I have an argument to offer in favor of the defendant," how do we know that we pay no attention to him?

R.   And how do we know that if one of the disciples said, "I have an argument against the defendant," we do not pay attention to him?

S.   Scripture says, "One shall not testify against any person that he die" (Num. 35:30) [but he may do so for acquittal (Shachter)].

XI.

A.   In capital cases one who argues [for conviction may argue for acquittal, but the one who argues for acquittal has not got the power to retract and to argue for conviction] [M. 4:11]:

B.   Said Rab, "The rule applies only to the time of the give and take of argument in the case. But when the verdict has been reached, one who has argued in favor of innocence may retract and argue in favor of guilt."

C.   An objection was raised on the basis of the following: And the next day they would get up and come to court. The one who favors acquittal says, "I declared him innocent yesterday, and I stand my ground and declare him innocent today." And the one who declares him guilty says, "I declared him guilty yesterday, and I stand my ground and declare him guilty today." The one who argues in favor of guilt may now argue in favor of acquittal, but the one who argues in favor of innocence may not now go and argue in favor of guilt [M. 5:5C-F].

D.   Now "the next day" is the time at which the verdict has been reached [and the one who voted for innocence cannot then change his vote, contrary to Rab's statement].

E.   But according to your reasoning [and the position you have taken], on the next day is there no more give and take? In point of fact the rule before us speaks of a time of give and take.

F.   Come and take note: [If thirty-six vote for conviction and thrity-five vote for acquittal,] they debate the matter, until one of those who voted for conviction accepts the arguments of those who vote for acquittal [M. 5:5S].

G.   Now if it is the case [that even at the point of a verdict, one who favors innocence may change his mind], the passage should also repeat matters in the reverse [so that one of those who voted for innocence may then accept the arguments of those who vote for guilt].

H.   The Tannaite framer of the passage will go back and refer to a verdict of innocence while not doing so for a verdict of guilt.

I.   Come and take note of the following that was said by R. Yose bar Hanina, "If one of the disciples voted in favor of innocence and then died, they regard him as though he were still alive and standing in his place [taking the same position, and so they count his vote]." And why should this be the case? May we not claim that, if he were alive, he might have reversed himself?

J.   But now, at any rate, he has not reversed himself [so we could count his original vote].

K.   And lo, they have sent from there, "In accord with the view of R. Yose bar Hanina, the opinion of our master [Rab] is excluded. [Shachter, p. 214, n. 1: Therefore his ruling not to consider an eventual change of opinion is due to the fact that he holds that at the promulgation of the decision one cannot retract]."

L.   What was said was, "Do not exclude [the opinion of our master, Rab]."

M.   Come and take note: And two judges' clerks stand before them, one at the right and one at the left. And they write down the arguments of those who vote to acquit and of those who vote to convict [M. 4:3C].

N.   Now there is good reason to write down the premises of those who vote to convict, since the next day they may perceive a fresh argument and it may be necessary to postpone judgment over night [to give the judges a chance to change their minds. Hence the necessity of recording their statements to show that they have changed their grounds for conviction, so necessitating a further postponement (Shachter, p. 214, n. 4).

O.   But why write down the premises of those who vote to acquit? Is it not because, if they should perceive a fresh argument, we pay no attention to them at all?

P.   No, it is so that two judges should not give a single reason based on two different verses of Scripture.

Q.   That accords with what R. Assi asked R. Yohanan, "If two judges gave a single argument on the basis of two different verses of Scripture, what is the law?"

R.   He said to him, "They count them only as one [vote]."

S.   How do we know on the basis of Scripture that that is the fact?

T.   Said Abayye, "It is because Scripture has said, 'God has spoken once, but I have heard two [different things] because strength belongs to God' (Ps. 62:12).

U.   "One verse of Scripture may yield a number of arguments, but one argument cannot derive from a number of verses of Scripture."

V.   The house of R. Ishmael's Tannaite authority [taught as follows:] "'And like a hammer that breaks the rock in pieces' (Jer. 23:29). Just as a hammer splits a rock into many pieces, so a verse of Scripture may yield a number of arguments."

XII.

A.   What would be an example of how a single argument may emerge from two different verses of Scripture?

B.   Said R. Zebid, "It would be exemplified by that which we have learned in the Mishnah:

C.   "The altar sanctifies that which is appropriate to it."

D.   "R. Joshua says, 'Whatever is appropriate to the altar-fires, if it has gone up on to the fires, should not go down, since it is said, "This is the burnt-offering, that which goes up on the hearth on the altar" (Lev. 6:9). Just as the burnt-offering, which is appropriate to the altar-fires, if it has gone up, should not go donw, so whatever is appropriate to the altar-fires, if it has gone up, should not go down.'

E.   "Rabban Gamaliel says, 'Whatever is appropriate to the altar, if it has gone up, should not go down, as it is said, "This is the burnt-offering on the hearth on the altar" (Lev. 6:2). Just as the burnt-offering, which is appropriate to the altar, if it has gone up, should not go down, so whatever is a appropriate to the altar, if it has gone up, should not go down.' [M. Zeb. 9:1A-C].

F.   "Now what is it that both authorities include [among things not to be removed from the altar]? It is invalid objects.

G. "One authority [Joshua] brings proof of that fact from the word 'firewood' and the other [Gamaliel] proves it from the word 'altar.' [Shachter, p. 215, n. 10: Now at this stage it is assumed that since both deduce the same general principle from two different verses, there is not real disagreement between them. This affords an illustration of 'one law drawn from two different verses.']"

H. But in the case at hand, do the two authorities differ at all? Note the concluding part of the same Mishnah-paragraph:

I. <u>Rabban Gamaliel and R. Joshua differ only on the matter of the blood and the drink offerings. For Rabban Gamaliel says, "They should not [having been placed on the altar] be taken down," and R. Joshua says, "They should be taken down" [M. Zeb. 9:1D-F].</u>

J. Rather, said R. Pappa, "[The example derives from a Tannaite teaching."

K. For it has been taught on Tannaite authority:

L. R. Yose the Galilean says, "Since it is said, [34B] 'Whatever touches the altar shall be holy' (Ex. 29:37), I might draw the inference that that is the case whether the substance is suitable for the altar or not suitable for the altar.

M. "Scripture then says, '[Now this is what you shall offer on the altar: two] lambs' (Ex. 29:37).

N. "This implies that just as lambs are suitable for the altar, so everything suitable [for the altar goes up and is not removed."

O. R. Aqiba says, "'...burnt-offering...' (Ex. 29:38). Just as a burnt-offering is suitable, so anything that is suitable [goes up and does not come down]."

P. What is it that both then exclude? It is invalid substances.

Q. One authority derives proof from the reference to "lambs," and the other authority derives proof from the reference to "burnt-offering."

R. But has not R. Adda bar Ahba stated, "At issue between the authorities is a bird in the status of a burnt-offering that is in fact invalid.

S. "The one who derives proof from the reference to 'lambs' then rules that the law applies to lambs but not to birds in the status of a burnt-offering.

T. "And the one who derives his proof from the reference to 'burnt-offering' will conclude that even a bird offering as a burnt-offering is covered by the law at hand."

U. Rather, said R. Ashi, "It is in accord with that which has been taught on Tannaite authority:

V. "Blood shall be imputed to that man he has shed blood" (Lev. 17:4).

W. "This serves to include the one who sprinkles [blood of a sacrifice outside of the Temple courts within the liability of extirpation," the words of R. Ishmael.

X. R. Aqiba says, "'...Or a sacrifice' (Lev. 17:4), serving to encompass the case of one who sprinkles [the blood, as above]."

Y. And what is it that both encompass with these distinct proof-texts? It is the matter of sprinkling. One authority derives proof from the words, "Blood shall be imputed," and the other from, "Or a sacrifice."

Z.   But has not R. Abbahu stated, "At issue between them is the one who both slaughtered and sprinkled the blood of the sacrifice outside of the Temple. [The person who did so acted unwittingly. He must bring a sin-offering in atonement. Does he bring one offering, covering both deeds, or two offering, one for each?]

AA.   "In the view of R. Ishmael, he is liable for only one sin-offering [since the same verse that covers the prohibition for sprinkling outside the court also prohibits slaughtering outside the court],

BB.   "R. Aqiba maintains that he is liable for two sin-offerings [on both counts, since the penalty for sprinkling and the penalty for slaughtering outside the Temple court come from different verses]."

CC.   But lo, it has been stated in this regard, Said Abayye, "Even in the view of R. Aqiba, he is liable for only a single sin-offering, for Scripture has said, 'There you shall offer your burnt offerings and there you shall do all that I command you' (Deut. 12:14). In this way the All-merciful has treated all acts [of the sacrificial rite in the same classification]. [Shachter, p. 217, n. 10: Hence there is only this one verse which commands that all acts of sacrifice, which includes slaughtering and sprk sprinkling, shall be done in the prescribed fashion. Therefore transgression of both involved only one sacrifice.]"

XIII.

A.   In property cases they try the case by day [and complete it by night. In capital cases they try the case by day and complete it the following day] [M. 4:1]:

B.   What is the scriptural basis for this rule?

C.   Said R. Hiyya bar Pappa, "It is because Scripture has said, 'And let them judge the people at all times' (Ex. 18:22) [even by night]."

D.   If that is the case, then why not begin the trial by night too?

E.   The answer accords with the statement of Raba.

F.   For Raba contrasted verses: "It is written, 'And let them judge the people at all times' (Ex. 18:22). And it is written, 'And in the day that he causes his sons to inherit' (Deut. 21:16). [In the latter vserse, we are told that a civil suit is taken up by day.

G.   "How do [we resolve the apparent discrepancy between the two verses]? The day is the time for the beginning of the trial, and the night may well serve for the end of the trial and the delivery of the verdict."

XIV.

A.   The Mishnah-passage before us does not accord with the view of R. Meir.

B.   For it has been taught on Tannaite authority:

C.   R. Meir would say, "What is the meaning of the verse of Scripture, 'According to their words shall every controversy and every leprosy be' (Deut. 21:5)? What have controversies [about civil matters] to do with [considerations of] leprosy? Scripture links civil suits to decisions on leprosy [to make the following points]. Just as decisions on the status of lepers are made by day, as it is written, 'And in the day on which the raw flesh appears in him' (Lev. 13:14), so decisions in civil suits are taken by day.

D. "And just as decisions on leprosy cannot be made by blind men, as it is written, 'Wherever the priest looks' (Lev. 13:12), so civil suits may not be decided by blind men.

E. "The text further links decisions on leprosy to decisions on civil suits [imposing on the former rules governing the latter], thus, just as civil suits may not be tried by relatives, so decisions on leprosy may not be made by relatives.

F. "Should you further propose that, just as civil suits must be decided by three judges, so decisions on matters of leprosy must be settled by three priests,

G. "and it is a matter of logic: if a person's property is disposed of by three, should not the status of his own body all the more so be settled by three?

H. "to forestall this conclusion, Scripture states, 'When he shall be brought to Aaron, the priest, to one of his sons, the priests' (Lev. 13:2), in which you learn that even a single priest may inspect leprosy-signs."

XV.

A. There was a blind man in the vicinity of R. Yohanan, who would judge cases, and R. Yohanan did not object in any way.

B. How could he have done so, for has not R. Yohanan stated, "The decided law is in accord with the Mishnah when it is stated anonymously [not in the name of a specific authority]"?

C. And we have learned in [an anonymous passage] of the Mishnah: Whoever is suitable to judge is suitable to give testimony, but there is one who is suitable to give testimony but is not suitable to judge [M. Nid. 6:4G].

D. And R. Yohanan stated, "That statement serves to encompass one who is blind in one eye [who can give testimony but not judge a case]."

E. R. Yohanan took note of a different passage of the Mishnah, one that is given anonymously, namely: In property cases they try the case by day and complete it by night [M. 4:1J].

F. What makes one anonymous Mishnaic rule more reliable than some other?

G. If you like, I shall say that an anonymous statement of the law that conforms to collective opinion is preferable [to one which, we know from other evidence, speaks only for an individual. Meir's view and the anonymous version of Meir's view therefore must take second place.]

H. And if you like, I shall propose that the framer of the Mishnah has cited the [anonymous version of the law in accord with the opposition to Meir] in the context of laws on the conduct of trials [and not merely incidentally].

I. And how does R. Meir deal with the verse, "And let them judge the people at all times" (Ex. 18:22)?

J. Said Raba, "It serves to include a cloudy day [in the proper time for holding civil cases or for examining leprosy-signs]."

K. For we have learned in the Mishnah:

L. They do not examine leprosy-signs at dawn or at sunset, or inside the house; or on a cloudy day, because the dim appears bright; or at noon, because the bright appears dim [M. Neg. 2:2A-D]. [But, in Meir's view, they would try a <u>civil</u> case on a cloudy day, and in that aspect he would distinguish the one sort of procedure from the other.]

M.   And how does R. Meir interpret the verse of, "And in the day that he causes his sons to inherit" (Deut. 21:16)? [Since Meir proves his point from the analogy of trials of civil cases to examination of leprosy-signs, how does he deal with the alternative proof for day-time trials, supplied here?]

N.   He requires that to serve as a proof-text for the following teaching on Tannaite authority given by Rabbah b. Hanina before R. Nahman:

O.   "'And in the day that he causes his sons to inherit' (Deut. 21:16):

P.   "By day you divide up an estate, and you do not divide up an estate by night."

Q.   He said to him, "But would you then say that one who dies in daytime may leave his estate to his children, while one who dies in the nighttime may not leave his estate to his children? Perhaps you refer to lawsuits concerning legacies [that these like any other civil suits must take place by day [Shachter, p. 219, n. 15)]?"

R.   For so it has been taught on Tannaite authority:

S.   "And it shall be for the children of Israel a statute of judgment" (Num. 27:11). [This sentence refers to inheritance-laws.] That statement imposes upon all of the laws of the chapter at hand the rules governing civil cases in general.

T.   That accords with what R. Judah said Rab said.

U.   For R. Judah said Rab said, "If three people came into visit the sick, [who wished to direct the disposition of his estate for them, if they wish, they write out [his instructions as a will], and if they wish, they serve as a court [and carry out the instruction directly]. But if two were there [not three], they write out [and witness] the will, but they can not serve as a court."

V.   And R. Hisda said, "That has been taught only if they came by day. But if they came by night, they write out a will and do not serve as a court, because they constitute witnesses, and a witness cannot serve as a judge."

W.   He said to him, "Yes indeed, that is just what I meant."

XVI.

A.   <u>In capital cases, they try the case by day [and complete it the following day] [M. 4:1]</u>:

B.   What is the scriptural basis for this rule?

C.   Said R. Shimi bar Hiyya, "Scripture has said, 'And hang them up unto the Lord in the face of the sun' (Num 25:4) [thus, by day, not by night]."

D.   Said R. Hisda, "How do we know that the word at hand means 'hanging'? As it is written, 'And we will hang them up to the Lord in Gibeah of Saul, the chosen of the Lord' (2 Sam. 21:6), and it is written [35A], 'And Rizpah, the daughter of Aiah, took sack-cloth and spread it for her upon the rock, from the beginning of harvest' (2 Sam. 21:6). [Shachter: So they must have been hanged on trees]."

XVII.

A.   It is written, "And the Lord said to Moses, take all the chiefs of the people" (Num. 25:4).

B.	While the people had sinned, how had the chiefs of the people sinned?

C.	Said R. Judah said Rab, "Said the Holy One, blessed be he, to Moses, 'Divide them up into courts' [to try sinners." [Shachter, p. 221, n. 3: The verse is accordingly translated: Take the chief chiefs of the people and appoint them as judges and hang up them whom they shall condemn].

D.	What is the reason [for this instruction]?

E.	If we say that it is because two are not to be judged on a single day [and condemned to death] [M. San. 6:4M], has not R. Hisda stated, "The rule applies only to two different forms of inflicting the death penalty, but if it is a single form of the death penalty, they do judge any number of cases in one day"?

F.	Rather it is so that "God's wrath may turn away from Israel" (Num. 25:4).

XVIII.

A.	In property cases they come to a final decision on the same day as the trial itself, [whether it is for acquittal or conviction. In capital cases they come to a final decision for acquittal on the same day but on the following day for conviction] [M. 4:1K]:

B.	What is the scriptural basis for this rule?

C.	Said R. Hanina, "It is in line with this verse of Scripture: 'She that was full of justice, righteousness lodged in her, but now murderers' (Is. 1:21) [Shachter, p. 221, nos. 8-9: Judgment was held over ['lodged over night'] lest points for acquittal might be found. But now they do not postpone the verdict until the next day and so are murderers.]"

D.	And Raba said, "Proof is from here: 'Relieve the oppressed' (Is. 1:17). [We have a play on words, that yields] [Shachter:] 'Bless the judge who reserves his verdict.'"

E.	And the other? "Relieve the oppressed [by attending to the plaintiff] and not the oppressor [the defendant]."

F.	And as to [Raba], how does he interpret the verse, "And she that was full of justice" (Is. 1:21)?

G.	He interprets that verse as does R. Eleazar in the name of R. Isaac.

H.	For R. Eleazar said R. Isaac said, "In the case of any fast day on which gifts to the poor are kept overnight, it is as if one sheds blood, as it is said, 'She that was full of justice, but now that charity [is made to lodge therein (and postponed overnight), they are as murderers]' [Shachter] (Is. 1:21)."

I.	And that rule pertains specifically to postponing distribution of bread and dates, but as to money, wheat, or barley, there is no objection [to postponing distribution by a day].

IX.

A.	Therefore they do not judge [capital cases either on the eve of the Sabbath or on the eve of a festival] [M. 4:1L]:

B.	What is the reason? Because it is impossible. How could someone do it? If someone were to try a case on Friday and complete the verdict on that day, perhaps they might find reason to convict the accused, in which case they would have to postpone the judgment overnight.

C.   But have the trial on Friday and complete the decision on the Sabbath, and if he is guilty put him to death on the Sabbath.

D.   Capital punishment does not override the restrictions of the Sabbath.

E.   Then why not put him to death in the evening?

F.   We require that the execution take place "in the face of the sun" (Num. 25:4) [in daytime].

G.   Then complete the trial on the Sabbath and put the convicted felon to death on Sunday.

H.   You will turn out to delay the course of justice [Shachter] [by postponing the execution].

I.   Then why not conduct the trial on Friday and complete the verdict on Sunday?

J.   The judges might forget their reasons [for taking the positions that they did].

K.   Even though two judges' clerks stand before them, one at the right and one at the left, and they write down the arguments of those who vote to acquit and of those who vote to convict [M. M. 4:3C-D]?

L.   Granted that they write down what they say, still, once the heart forgets, it is forgotten. Therefore it is not possible.

XX.

A.   Said R. Simeon b. Laqish to R. Yohanan, "The burial of a neglected corpse should override the restrictions of the Sabbath, on the basis of the following argument a fortiori:

B.   "Now if the performance of the Temple cult, which overrides the Sabbath is set aside on account of the burial of a neglected corpse, [the Sabbath, restrictions of which are abrogated for the Temple service, all the more so should be overridden for the burial of a neglected corpse].

C.   "[And how do we know that observance of the Sabbath is set aside on account of the requirement to bury a neglected corpse?]

D.   "It is learned from the teaching concerning "And on account of his sister" (Num. 6:7). [A Nazirite may not render himself unclean even should his father, mother, brother, or sister die.]"

E.   So it has been taught on Tannaite authority: "On account of his father, his mother, brother, and sister" [a Nazirite should not contract corpse-uncleanness, in connection with the necessity of burying them], (Num. 6:7).

F.   What is the purpose of this statement?

G.   Lo, if on a Nazirite was going to slaughter his Passover-sacrifice or to circumcize his son, [35B] and he heard that a relative had died, is it possible that to bury that person, the Nazirite should contract corpse-uncleanness?

H.   You say, "He shall not become unclean."

I.   Is it possible that, just as he may not contract corpse-uncleanness to bury his sister, so he may not contract corpse-uncleanness to bury a neglected corpse?

J.   Scripture states, "And on account of his sister" (Num. 6:7). For his sister he may not contract corpse uncleanness, but he must contract corpse-uncleanness on account of a neglected corpse.

K. [Simeon b. Laqish reverts to the original argument,] if the restrictions of the Sabbath are set aside on account of the conduct of the sacrificial cult, is it not logical that the burial of a neglected corpse should override the restrictions of the Sabbath [which overrides the cult]?"

L. He said to him, "Executing a condemned criminal should prove the contrary, for it will override the requirements of the sacrificial cult but it will not override the restrictions of the Sabbath."

M. [He replied,] But executing a convicted criminal should override the restrictions of the Sabbath, on the basis of an argument a fortiori:

N. "Now if the conduct of the Temple cult, which overrides the restrictions of the Sabbath, is itself overridden by the requirement to execute a murderer, as it is said, 'You shall take him from my altar that he may die' (Ex. 21:14), the Sabbath restrictions which are overridden by the Temple cult, surely should give way to the execution of the condemned criminal.

O. Said Raba, "The matter has already been settled by a Tannaite authority of the house of R. Ishmael."

P. For a Tannaite authority of the house of R. Ishmael [said], "You shall not kindle a fire [on the Sabbath]' (Ex. 35:3). What is the purpose of this statement?"

Q. What is the purpose of this statement?! [We all know the answer]. If we speak from the viewpoint of R. Yose, [that one should not kindle a flame]is singled out so as to indicate that [kindling a flame] is simply a negative commandment [violation of which is punished by flogging. Other violations of the Sabbath are punished by execution through stoning.]

R. If we speak from the viewpoint of R. Nathan, it is singled out in order to indicate that we treat a singular and punishable act each distinct violation of Sabbath-law [not grouping all of them and penalizing the whole].

S. For it has been taught on Tannaite authority:

T. "Specification of kindling a flame [as a prohibited act] serves to place such an act in the category of a negative commandment," the words of R. Yose.

U. R. Nathan says, "It serves to treat as a distinct act [punished by itself] that deed [or any other deed in violation of the Sabbath]."

V. Rather, said Raba, "What posed a problem to the Tannaite authority was the word 'habitations' [at Ex. 35:3, not to kindle a flame 'in all of Israel's habitations']. Why is that word included?

W. "[Here is what troubled the Tannaite authority at hand:] Since the Sabbath is an obligation that pertains to the person, and since an obligation pertaining to the person applies both in the Land and outside of the Land, why did the All-Merciful include the word 'habitations' [which speaks of the Land of Israel in particular]?"

X. In the name of R. Ishmael a disciple said, "It is because it is written, 'And if a man has committed a sin worthy of death and he be put to death' (Deut. 21:22). I might then take the view that that may be done whether on a weekday or on the Sabbath. In that case how shall I carry out the verse, 'Those who profane [the Sabbath] shall certainly be put to death' (Ev. 31:14)? It would refer to other forms of labor prohibited on the Sabbath, but not carrying out the death penalty imposed by a court.

Y. "Or perhaps that statement encompasses also the execution of criminals convicted by a court.

Z. "In that case how shall I interpret 'And he shall be put to death' (Deut. 21:22)?

AA. "It would speak of weekdays, and not the Sabbath.

BB. "Or perhaps it means that the execution is carried out even on the Sabbath?

CC. "Scripture states, 'You shall not kindle a fire throughout your habitations' (Ex. 35:3), and elsewhere it is written, "And these things shall be for a statute of judgment for you throughout your generations in all your habitations' (Num. 35:29).

DD. "Just as 'habitations' in that context speaks of matters pertaining to courts, so 'habitations' here speaks of matters pertaining to courts.

EE. "Now when the All-Merciful has said, 'You shall not kindle a fire in all your habitations' (Ex. 35:3) [that must encompass not imposing the death penalty for the Sabbath, since one form of the death penalty is through 'burning.' So one cannot inflict the death penalty on the Sabbath, despite the argument a fortiori given above. And it further follows that one may not bury a neglected corpse on the Sabbath either.]"

FF. Said Abayye, "Now that you have shown that the death penalty does not override the restrictions of the Sabbath, it should follow that the death penalty does not override the requirements of the Temple cult. This would be based on an argument a fortiori.

GG. "Now, if the Sabbath, which is set aside in favor of the requirements of the Temple cult, does not give way to the need to inflict the death penalty, the Temple cult, itself, which does override the restrictions of the Sabbath, surely should not give way before the requirement to inflict the death penalty.

HH. "And as to the verse of Scripture, 'You shall take him from my altar that he may die' (Ex. 21:14) [which contradicts the foregoing proposition], that speaks of an offering made in behalf of an individual, which also would not override the restrictions of the Sabbath. [On the Sabbath offerings in behalf of individuals, as distinct from the community as a whole, are not prepared.]"

II. Said Raba, "Inflicting the death penalty should not override the offering of a sacrifice in behalf of an individual, on the basis of an argument a fortiori:

JJ. "[36A] Now if a festival, prohibitions of which are set aside on account of the requirement of an individual to bring an offering [e.g., the Passover, the appearance-offering, and the like], does not give way before the requirement to inflict the death penalty on a convicted felon, the offering of an individual, which does override the restrictions of the festival day, surely should not give way before the requirement to inflict the death penalty."

KK. [The contrary view, that inflicting the death penalty does override the offering of a sacrifice in behalf of an individual] poses no problems to the position of him who has said, "Offerings brought in fulfillment of vows and freewill offerings are not offered on a festival day."

LL. But from the viewpoint of him who has said, "Offerings brought in fulfillment of vows and freewill offerings <u>are</u> offered on the festival day," what is there to say [to the argument just now presented?] [Shachter, p. 226, n. 6: The premise being correct, the deduction is likewise correct, <u>viz.</u>, that an execution cannot supersede a private offering. How then can the verse, "You shall take from my altar," be reconciled with this conclusion?]

MM. Rather, said Raba, "[The position of Abayye is not acceptable] from the viewpoint of him who has said that offerings brought in fulfillment of vows and freewill offerings are offered on the festival day, for in such a case, the cited verse, 'From my altar' simply does not apply [Shachter, p. 226, n. 7: for as shown above, if Abayye's reasoning is accepted, execution does not suspend even private offerings. To what then can 'From my altar' refer?]

NN. "But even from the viewpoint of him who has said, 'Offerings brought in fulfillment of vows and freewill offerings are not offered on the festival day, [in which case the cited verse may refer to private offerings, nonetheless, Abayye's view is not acceptable].

OO. "For is it not written, 'From my altar' with the sense of 'my altar in particular. What is <u>that</u> altar? It is the altar on which the daily whole offering is made.

PP. "And in that connection, the All-Merciful has stated, 'You shall take him from my altar that he may die' (Ex. 21:14). [Shachter, p. 226, n. 11: Thus Scripture expressly stands in the way of the argument a fortiori proposed by Abayye (Shachter, p. 226, n. 11)]."

<u>XXI.</u>

A. <u>In cases involing questions of property, uncleanness and cleanness, [they begin voting from the eldest, In capital cases they begin from the side (with the youngest)] [M. 4:2A]</u>:

B. Said Rab, "I was among those who voted in the house of Rabbi, and it was from me that they began to count."

C. But have we not learned in the Mishnah: <u>They begin voting from the eldest [Rabbi should count first]</u>?

D. Said Rabbah, son of Raba, and some say, R. Hillel, son of R. Vallas, "The voting in the house of Rabbi was different, For there all votes began from the side [as an act of humility on the part of Rabbi]."

<u>XXII.</u>

A. And said Rabbah, son of Rabba, and some say, R. Hillel, son of R. Vallas, "From the time of Moses to Rabbi, we do not find the combination of foremost status in learning in Torah and preeminence in worldly greatness joined in a single person."

B. And is that not so? And there was the case of Joshua?

C. With him was Eleazar [equal in learning].

D. There was Phineas? With him were the elders.

E. There was Saul? With him was Samuel.

F. But lo, [Samuel] died before him? We refer to the entire lifetime [of such a unique figure].

G. There was David? With him was Ira the Jairite [2 Sam. 20:26].

H. But lo, [Ira] died before him? We refer to the entire lifetime [of such a unique figure].

I. There was Solomon? With him was Shimei, son of Gera [2 Sam. 19:18].

J. But lo, [Solomon] killed [Shimei]? We refer to the entire lifetime.

K. There was Hezekiah? With him was Shebnah.

L. But he was killed [during Hezekiah's lifetime]? We refer to the entire lifetime.

M. There was Ezra? No, with him was Nehemiah, son of Hachaliah.

N. Said R. Ada bar Ahbah, "I too say, 'From the time of Rabbi to R. Ashi, we do not find the combination of learning in Torah and worldly greatness joined in a single person."

O. Do we not? And lo, there was Huna bar Nathan.

P. Huna bar Nathan was subordinate to R. Ashi.

XXIII.

A. In capital cases they begin from the side [M. 4:2A]:

B. What is the scriptural basis for this rule?

C. Said R. Aha bar Pappa, "Said Scripture, 'You shall not speak in a case (ryb)' (Ex. 23:2), meaning "do not speak against the chief judge (rb)' [a shift in meaning attained by supplying the consonants of "in a case' with different vowels]."

D. Rabbah b. b. Hannah said R. Yohanan [said], "Proof derives from here, 'And David said to his men, gird you on every man his sword, and they girded on every man his sword; then David also girded on his sword' (1 Sam. 25:13). [Shachter, p. 228, n. 3: The question whether Nabal the Carmelite's act was to be treated as rebelliousness against the king was here discussed and a vote taken in the form of girding on the sword. David was the last to express his opinion.]"

XXIV.

A. Said Rab, "A person may teach his disciple [the rule on capital offenses] and then vote right along side of him in capital cases [with master and disciple each having a separate vote]."

B. An objection was raised on the basis of the following passage:

C. **And in matters pertaining to questions of uncleanness or of cleanness, as to the father and his son, the master and his disciple, both of them are counted as two votes.**

D. **In property and capital cases and cases involving flogging, the sanctification of the new month, or the intercalation of the year, they count as only one [T. San. 7:2 O-R].**

E. [36B] When Rab made that statement, he referred to such disciples as R. Kahana and R. Assi, who required Rab's mastery of traditions but did not need help in reasoning about them."

XXV.

A. Said R. Abbahu [speaking of M. 4:1-2], "There are ten points of difference in the rules governing trials for property cases from those for capital cases.

B.   "And none of those differences pertains to the trial of an ox that is to be stoned, except for the requirement of a court of twenty-three judges, that alone."

C.   What is the scriptural source for that rule [B]?

D.   Said R. Aha bar Pappa, "It is because Scripture has said, 'You shall not bend the judgment of your poor in his cause' (Ex. 23:6) [Shachter, p. 228, n. 13: This is interpreted to mean that judgment must not be inclined in favor of conviction by a majority of only one].

E.   "The judgment of your poor you may not bend, but you may bend the judgment in the case of an ox that is to be stoned. [Shachter, p. 229, n. 2: From this it may be inferred that the procedure in the trial of an ox to be stoned is other than that of capital cases, except in the number of judges, and that difference is extended to all the other peculiarities of capital procedure, since the object of particularly applying that procedure in capital cases was to achieve the acquittal of the accused -- not so with an ox]."

F.   Do you say there are ten? But they are only nine. But ten are listed.

G.   It is [nine] because the rule that not everyone is valid to serve and the requirement that there be twenty-three judges constitute a single rule.

H.   And lo, there is another.

I.   For it has been taught on Tannaite authority:

J.   The eunuch and one who has never had children are [T.: suitable for judging property cases but are not suitable for judging capital cases] not to be seated on a Sanhedrin.

K.   R. Judah adds [to the list] also the one who is too harsh or too forgiving [M. 4:2B-C] [T. San. 7:5A-B].

L.   And the opposite to these rules apply in the case of one who incites [Israel to commit idolatry], for the All-Merciful has said, "Neither shall you spare, nor shall you conceal him" (Deut. 13:9).

XXVI.

A.   All are valid to engage in the judgment of property cases, [but all are not valid to engage in the judgment of capital cases] [M. 4:2B].

B.   What classification of persons does the specification of "all" serve to include?

C.   Said R. Judah, "It includes children of prohibited marriages."

D.   Lo, we have learned that in the Mishnah in a different context:

E.   Whoever is worthy to judge capital cases is worthy to judge property cases, and there is one who is worthy to judge property cases and is not worthy to judge capital cases [M. Nid. 6:4F].

F.   And in reflection on that passage, it was asked, "...to include what classification of persons?"

G.   And [in that connection], said R. Judah, "It includes children of prohibited marriages."

H.   In point of fact, one such reference includes a proselyte, the other, the child of a forbidden union.

I.   And it was necessary to make both points explicit. For had we the rule concerning the proselyte, I might have supposed that [he may judge property because] he can enter the congregation [marrying Israelite], but the child of an illegal union [who may not enter the congregation and marry an Isrealite] may not judge [property cases].

J.   And had we learned the rule governing the child of an illegal union, I might have supposed that that is because he derives from valid seed, but a proselyte, who does not derive from a valid seed, would not be suitable [for judging property cases].

K.   So it was necessary to specify both facts.

XXVII.

A.   But all are not valid to engage in the judgment of capital cases [M. 4:2B]:

B.   What is the reason for this rule?

C.   It accords with what R. Joseph repeated on Tannaite authority, "Just as a court must be clear in righteousness, so it must be clear of all blemishes."

D.   Said Smemar, "What is the verse of Scripture that says so? 'You are fair, my love, and there is no blemish in you/ (Song 4:7)."

E.   But perhaps this refers to the absence of physical blemishes [on the persons of the judges]?

F.   Said R. Aha bar Jacob, "Scripture has said, 'That they may stand there with you' (Num. 11:16). 'With you' means those who are equivalent to you."

G.   But then perhaps the rule in that case is [in particular] on account of the Presence of God [with Moses] [and the rule would not apply now]?

H.   Rather, said R. Nahman bar Isaac, "Scripture has said, 'And they shall bear with you' (Ex. 18:22), meaning, they must be like you."

Units I-II addresses M. 4:1A, and unit III carries forward that same discussion. Unit IV was joined to unit III prior to the insertion of the whole in the present setting. Unit V moves on to M. 4:1E, unit VI, to M. 4:1D-G. Unit VII complements the foregoing. Unit VIII proceeds with a further analysis of M. 4:1G. Unit IX deals with M. 4:1G, unit X, M. 4:1H, unit XI, M. 4:1I, unit XII complements the foregoing unit. Unit XIII carries us to M. 4:1J and is continued at unit XIV. Unit XV intersects with M. 4:1J. Unit XVI then takes up M. 4:1J. Unit XVII deals with a proof-test adduced in the foregoing. Units XVIII, XIX, turn to M. 4:1K, L, and unit XX provides a very long supplement, focused on its own interests, for unit XIX. Unit XXI proceeds to M. 4:2A, and XXII carries forward materials of the tradents of XXI. Unit XXIII deals with M. 4:2A, and so does unit XXIV, the latter taking up a problem of Tosefta's supplement to the Mishnah's rule. Unit XXV proposes to sum up the entire lot, that is, counting up the number of rules actually given by the Mishnah-paragraph, and then units XXVI and XXVII take up M. 4:2B. It would have been somewhat more logical for unit XXV to come at the end, but in the aggregate we must conclude that the organizer of the Talmud has simply arranged his materials to serve as line by line expansions of the Mishnah's rules.

4:3-4

A.   The sanhedrin was [arranged in the shape of a half of a round thresh-ing-floor [that is, as an amphitheatre],

B.   so that [the judges] should see one another,

C.   And two judges' clearks stand before them, one at the right and one at the left.

D.   And they write down the arguments of those who vote to acquit and of those who vote to convict.

E.   R. Judah says, "Three: One writes the opinion of those who vote to acquit, one writes the opinion of those who vote to convict, and the third writes the opinions both of those who vote to acquit and of those who vote to convict."

M. 4:3

A.   [37A] And three rows of disciples of sages sit before them.

B.   Each and every one knows his place.

C.   [If] they found need to ordain [a disciple to serve on the court],

D.   they ordained one who was sitting in the first row.

E.   [Then] one who was sitting in the second row joins the first row, and one who was sitting in the third row moves up to the second row.

F.   And they select for themselves someone else from the crowd and set him in the third row.

G.   [The new disciple] did not take a seat in the place of the first party [who had now joined in the court] but in the place that was appropriate for him [at the end of the third row].

M. 4:4

I.

A.   What is the scriptural source for the rule [at M. 4:3A]?

B.   Said R. Aha bar Hanina, "It is because Scripture has said, 'Your navel is like a round goblet, wherein no mingled wine is wanting' (Song 7:3).

C.   "'Thy navel' refers to the sanhedrin.

D.   "Why is it called 'navel'?

E.   "Because it is in session [on the Temple mount] at the navel of the world.

F.   "Why is it called 'round'?

G.   "Because [like a round shield] it protects the entire world.

H.   "Why is it called 'goblet'? Because it is shaped like the moon [as is the goblet]. [Shachter, p. 231, n. 11: They were seated in circular form like a moon.]

II.

A.   "Wherein no mingled wine is wanting:"

B.   [If] one of them had to go out, he looks around to see whether there would be twenty-three left [after he departs]. If there would be twenty-three left, enough for a small Sanhedrin, he goes out, and if not, he does not go out.

C.   [T.: unless there would be twenty-three left] [T. San. 7:1J-K].

III.

A.   "Your belly is like a heap of wheat" (Song 7:3): just as in the case of a heap of wheat, everyone derives benefit,

B.   so with the sanhedrin everyone benefits from their deliberations.

IV.

A.   "Set about with lilies" (Song 7:3): For even through a fence made up only of lilies [the members of the sanhedrin] will make no breaches.

B.   That is in line with what a <u>man</u> said to R. Kahana, "You say that a menstruating woman may be alone with her husband. Is it possible that there can be fire near two without singeing it?"

C.   He said to him, "The Torah has given testimony in our regard:

D.   "'Set about with lilies:' For even through a fence made up only of lilies [Israelites] will make no breaches."

E.   R. Simeon b. Laqish said, "Proof derives from here: 'Your temples are like a pomegranate split open' (Song 6:7): Even the empty-heads among you [play on the consonants that serve for both 'temple' and 'empty'] are as full of the accomplishment of religious duties as a pomegranate."

F.   R. Zira said, "Proof derives from here: 'And he smelled the scent of his raiment' (Gen. 27:27). Do not read it as 'remaint' but as 'his traitors.' [Shachter, p. 232, n. 10: Even those who are traitors to Judaism diffuse the fragrance of good deeds]."

V.

A.   There were some transgressors who lived in the neighborhood of R. Zira, who tried to draw them near so that they would return in penitence. Rabbis criticized him [for this relationship]. When R. Zira died, [the wicked men] said, "Up to now, the burned man with dwarfed legs would pray for mercy for us. Now who will pray for mercy for us?"

B.   They reflected on the matter in their hearts, and they carried out an act of repentence.

VI.

A.   Said Abayye, "We may infer from this rule that, when they move, all of them move."

B.   But cannot [the one who moves up a row] now say to them, "Up to now I was sitting at the head [of my row], and now you have seated me at the tail]"?

C.   Said Abayye, "They may say this to him: '<u>Be a tail to lions and not a head to foxes</u>' [M. Abot 4:15]."

Once the proof-text, Song 7:3, is introduced in unit I, the remainder of the passage at hand carries forward the exegesis of that verse, mostly in the context of the present theme.

4:5

A. How do they admonish witnesses in capital cases?

B. They would bring them in and admonish them [as follows]: "Perhaps it is your intention to give testimony on the basis of suppostion, hearsay, or of what one witness has told another;

C. "[or you may be thinking], 'We heard it from a reliable person'"

D. "Or, you may not know that in the end we are going to interrogate you with appropriate tests of interrogation and examination.

E. "You should know that the laws governing a trial for property cases are different from the laws governing a trial for capital cases.

F. "In the case of a trial for property-cases, a person pays money and achieves atonement for himself. In capital cases [the accused's] blood and the blood of all those who were destined to be born from him [who was wrongfully convicted] are held against him [who testifies falsely] to the end of time.

G. "For so we find in the case of Cain who slew his brother, as it is said, 'The bloods of your brother cry' (Gen. 4:10).

H. "It does not say, 'The blood of your brother,' but, 'The bloods of your brother' -- his blood and the blood of all those who were destined to be born from him."

I. Another matter: 'The bloods of your brother' -- for his blood was spattered on trees and stones.

J. Therefore man was created alone, to teach you that whoever destroys a single Israelite soul is deemed by Scripture as if he had destroyed a whole world.

K. And whoever saves a single Israelite sould is deemed by Scripture as if he had saved a whole world.

L. And it was also for the sake of peace among people, so that someone should not say to his fellow, "My father is greater than your father."

M. And it was also on account of the minim, so that the minim should not say, "There are many domains in Heaven."

N. And to portray the grandeau of the Holy One, blessed be He. For a person mints many coins with a single seal, and they are all alike one another, But the King of kings of kings, the Holy One, blessed be He, minted all human beings with that seal of his with which he made the first person, yet not one of them is like anyone else. Therefore everyone is obligated to maintain, "On my account the world was created."

O. Now perhaps you [witnesses] would like now to say, [37B] "What business have we got with this trouble?"

P. But it already has been written, "He being a witness, whether he has seen or known, if he does not speak it, then he shall bear his iniquity" (Lev. 5:1).

Q.   And perhaps you might want to claim, "What business is it of ours ot convict this man of a capital crime?"

R.   But has it not already been said, "When the wicked perish there is rejoicing" (Prov. 11:10).

M. 4:5

I.

A.   Our rabbis have taught on Tannaite authority: What is the sense of "conjecture'?

B.   He says to them, "Perhaps this is what you saw: he was running after his fellow into a ruin [with a sword in his hand]. [The victim ran in front of him into a ruin, and then the other went after him into the ruin]. You went in after them and found [the victim slain on the floor], with a knife in the hand of the murderer, dripping blood."

C.   "If this is what you have seen, you have seen nothing [you must be admonished that this is not valid evidence]."

D.   It has been taught on Tannaite authority: Said Simeon b. Shatah, "May I [not] see consolation, if I did not see someone run after his fellow into a ruin, [with a sword in his hand, and the pursued man went before him into a ruin, and the pursuer ran in after him,] and then I came in right after him, and saw [the victim] slain, with a knife in the hand of the murderer, dripping blood, and I said to him, 'You evil person! Who killed this one? [May I [not] see consolation if I did not see him [run in here].] Either you killed him or I did! But what can I do to you? For your blood is not handed over to me, For lo, the Torah has said, 'At the testimony of two witnesses or at the testimony of three witnesses shall he who is on trial for his life be put to death' (Deut. 17:6).

E.   "'But He who knows the thoughts of man will exact punishment from that man.'

F.   He did not move from the spot before a snake bit him, and he died" [T. San. 8:3]. But is this one subject to death by snake bite?

G.   For has not R. Joseph said, and so too did the house of Hezekiah teach: "From the day on which the house of the sanctuary was destroyed, even though the sanhedrin ceased to be, the four forms of inflicting the death penalty did not cease to be."

H.   Lo, they surely have ceased!

I.   Rather, "the law governing the four forms of the death penalty has not ceased to be.

J.   "He who became liable to the death penalty through stoning either falls from the roof or is trampled by a wild beast.

K.   "He who became liable to the death penalty through burning either falls into a fire or is bitten by a snake.

L.   "He who became liable to the death penalty through decapitation either is handed over for execution by the government, or thugs attack him [and cut off his head].

M.   "He who becomes liable to the death penalty through strangulation either drowns in a river or dies by a quinsy."

N.   One may replay that that man was already guilty on account of a different sin as well.

O.   For a master has said, "Someone who is liable to the death penalty on two different counts is subjected to the more severe of the two."

II.

A.   On the basis of supposition [M. 4:5B]:

B.   It is in capital cases that we do not accept testimony based on supposition [or conjecture]. Lo, in the case of property cases, we do so.

C.   In accord with whose view is that statement made?

D.   It accords with R. Aha, for it has been taught on Tannaite authority:

E.   R. Aha says, "A camel which was covering females among the camels, and one of the camels was found dead —

F.   "[the owner of the one in heat] is liable, in the certainty that this one killed it" [T. B.Q. 3:6Q-R].

G.   And in accord with the reasoning just now proposed [B], it is in particular in capital cases that we reject hearsay evidence. Lo, in property cases we accept it.

H.   And yet, have we not learned in the Mishnah.

I.   If he said, "He told me, 'I owe him,' 'So-and-so told me that he owed him,'" he has said nothing whatsoever, unless he says, "In our presence he admitted to him that he owes him two hundred zuz? [M. 3:6E-F].

J.   Therefore, even though that form of evidence is also invalid in property cases, we state the rule in particular for capital cases. Here too even though that form of evidence is also invalid in property cases, we state the rule in particular for capital cases.

III.

A.   Know that ... [M. 4:5]:

B.   Said R. Judah, son of R. Hiyya, "[Gen. 4:10, 'The bloods of your brother cry...'] teaches that Cain made on Abel, his brother, wound after wound, blow after blow, for he did not know from which one the soul would go forth, until he came to his neck."

C.   And said R. Judah, son of R. Hi Hiyya, "From the day on which the earth opened its mouth to receive the blood of Abel, it has never again opened up, for it is said, 'From the edge of the earth have we heard songs, glory to the righteous' (Is. 24:16).

D.   "'From the edge of the earth' and not from the mouth of the earth.'"

E.   Hezekiah, his brother, objected, "'And the earth opened her mouth' (Num. 16:32)."

F.   He said to him, "For evil the earth opened, but not for good [and it was only to swallow Korah]. [Shachter, p. 237, n. 5: The opening to receive Abel's blood is accounted for good, to hide Cain's guilt.]"

G.   And said R. Judah, son of R. Hiyya, "Exile atones for half of one's transgressions. To begin with, it is written [about Cain], 'And I shall be a fugitive and a wanderer' (Gen. 4:14).

H.   "And afterward: 'And he dwelt in the land of wandering' (Gen. 4:14). [Shachter, p. 237, n. 7: The other half of the course, 'to be a fugitive' was remitted because of his exile.]"

IV.

A.   Said R. Judah [said Rab,] "Exile atones for three things.

B.   "For it is said, 'Thus says the Lord, He who abides in this city shall die by the sword, famine, and pestilence, but he who goes out and falls away to the Chaldeans who besiege you shall live, and his life shall be unto him for a prey' (Jer. 21:8-9). [Shachter, p. 237, n. 8: He who remained at home was subject to these three evils, but wandering and its consequent hardships outweighed them all.]"

C.   Said R. Yohanan, "Exile atones for everything, for it is said, 'Thus says the Lord, Write this man childless, a man that shall not prosper in his days, for no man of his seed shall prosper sitting upon the throne of David and ruling any more in Judah' (Jer. 22:30).

D.   "After [the king] was exiled, it is written, 'And the sons of Jechoniah, the same is Assir, Shealtiel, his son ... ' (1 Chr. 3:17). [So he was not childless, and through exile he had atoned for his sins.]"

E.   "Assir" because his mother conceived in prison [a word using the same consonants].

F.   "Shealtiel" because God planted him in a way different from the way in which people usually are planted. We know that a woman cannot become pregnant through intercourse done standing up, [38A] but she became pregnant through intercourse done standing up.

G.   Another explanation: "Shealtiel" because God consulted [using the same root] [sages] concerning his oat!.. [So as to have it remitted].

H.   "Zerubbabel" because he was conceived in Babylonia.

I.   And what was his name? It was Nehemiah, son of Hachaliah.

V.

A.   Judah and Hezekiah, sons of R. Hiyya, were seated at a meal before Rabbi and they were not saying anything. He said to the [waiter], "Give more strong wine to the young men so that they will say something."

B.   When the wine had [Shachter] taken effect, they commenced by saying, David will not come until the two houses of patriarchal authority come to an end, specifically, the head of the exile in Babylonia and the patriarch in the Land of Israel.

C.   "For it is said, 'And he shall be for a sanctuary, for a stumbling block and for a rock of offense to both houses of Israel' (Is. 8:14)."

D.   He said to them, "You toss thorns into my eyes, my sons."

E.   Said R. Hiyya to Rabbi, "Do not take offense. The numerical value of the letters composing the word, 'wine,' is seventy, and the same is so for the word, 'secret.' When wine goes in, secrets come out."

VI.

A.   Said R. Hisda said Mar Uqba, and some say, said R. Hisda, Mari bar Mar expounded, "What is the meaning of the verse of Scripture, 'And so the Lord has hastened the evil and brought it upon us, for the Lord our God is righteous' (Dan. 9:14)?

B.   "Because 'the Lord is righteous' 'does he hasten the evil and bring it upon us'"

C.   "Indeed so. The Holy One, blessed be he, acted in a righteous way with Israel by bringing the exile of Zedekiah while the exile of Jechoniah was still alive.

D.   "It is written with reference to the exile of Jechoniah, 'And the craftsmen and smiths, a thousand' (2 Kgs. 24:16).

E.   "[Since the word for craftsman may be read as 'deaf,' we may say,] as soon as they opened discourse, everyone became as deaf.

F.   "[Since the word for smith may be read to mean, 'close,'] as soon as they completed the discussion of a law, it was not again taken up.

G.   "How many were they? A thousand."

H.   Ulla said, "He put the exile up by two years [Shachter:] as compared with the period indicated by venoshantem. [Shachter, p. 239, n. 6: And ye shall have been long (lit., 'grown old'), Deut. IV, 25. The numerical value of   (6+50+6+300+50+400+40) is eight hundred and fifty-two. Subtracting two years according to this Haggadah, there are eight hundred and fifty-two. Subtracting two years according to this Haggadah, there are eight hundred and fifty years left, which is the length of time between Israel's entry into Palestine and the destruction of the Temple. The Temple was erected in the four hundred and eightieth year from the Exodus out of Egypt, and it stood for four hundred and ten year. Subtracting forty years for the period of their wanderings in he desert, we reach a total of eight hundred and fifty years. That acceleration by two years is here regarded as a 'righteous' (i.e., charitable) act, since it averted the complete destruction threatened in Deut. IV, 26.]

I.   Said R. Aha bar Jacob, "That calculation indicates that 'promptness' for the Lord of the world means eight hundred and fifty two years [Shachter, p. 239, n. 7: (7) For the following verse states, Ye shall speedily perish completely from off the land. Thus by 'speedily' God meant 852 years, alluded to by we-noshantem].

VII.

A.   Therefore [man was created alone] [M. 4:5J]:

B.   Our rabbis have taught on Tannaite authority:

C.   On what account was man created alone?

D.   So that the minim should not say, "There are many domains in heaven" [M. 4:5].

E.   Another matter:

F.   [T.:] Man was created one and alone.

G.   And why was he created one and alone in the world? Because of the righteous and the wicked

H.   So that the righteous should not say, "We are the sons of the righteous one," and so that the evil ones should not say, "We are the sons of the evil one."

I.   Another matter: Why was he created one and alone? So that families should not quarrel with one another. For if now, that man was created one and alone, they quarrel with one another, had there been two created at the outset, how much the more so! [cf. M. 4:5L].

J.   Another matter: Why was he created one and alone? Because of the thieves and robbers. And if now, that he was created one and alone, people steal and rob, had there been two, how much the more so! [T. San. 8:4A-E].

VIII.

A.   To portray the grandeus ... [M. 4:5N]:

B.   Our rabbis have taught on Tannaite authority:

C.   [T:] Another matter: Why was he created one and alone?

D.   To show the grandeur of the king of the kings of kings, blessed be he.

E.   For if a man mints many coins with one mold, all are alike.

F.   But the Holy One, blessed be he, mints every man with the mold of the first man [T: for with a single seal, he created the entire world], and not one of them is like another [T. from a single seal all those many diverse seals have come forth],

G.   as it is said, "It is changed as clay under the seal, and all this things stand forth as in a garment" (Job 38:14) [M. 4:5N] [T. San. 8:5A-D].

H.   And on what accounts are faces not like one another?

I.   On account of imposters,

J.   so no one should see a lovely house or woman and say "It is mine" [T.S: jump into his neighbor's field or jump in bed with his neighbor's wife],

K.   as it is said, "And from the wicked their light is withheld and the strong arm is broken" (Job. 38:15).

L.   It has been taught on Tannaite authority: R. Meir says, "The omnipresent has varied a man in three ways: appearance, intelligence, and voice

M.   intelligence, because of robbers and thieves, and appearance and voice, because of the possibilities of licentiousness" [T. San. 8:6A-F].

N.   Our rabbis have taught on Tannaite authority:

O.   man was created on Friday [T.: last in order of creation.

P.   And why was man created last?

Q.   Sop that the minim should not be able to say, "There was a partner with him in his work [of creation]" [cf. M. 4:5M], [T. San. 8:7] Z

R.   Another matter: [Why was he created last]?

S.   So that he should not grow proud.

T.   For they can say to him, "The mosquito came before you in the [order of the] works of creation."

U.   Another matter: So that he might immediately take up the doing of a religious duty. [T. San. 8:8].

V.   Another matter: So that he might enter the banquet at once [with everything ready for him].

W.   They have made a parable: To what is the matter is comparable?

X.   To a king who built a palace and dedicated it and prepared a meal and [only] afterward invited the guests.

Y.   And so Scripture says, "The wisest of women has built her house" (Prov. 9:1).

Z.   This refers to the King of the kings of kings, blessed be He, who built his world in seven [days] by wisdom.

AA. "She has hewn out her seven pillars" (Prov. 9:1) -- these are the seven days of creation.

BB. **"She has killed her beasts and mixed her wine"** (Prov. 9:2) -- these are the oceans, rivers, wastes, and all the other things which the world needs.

CC. And afterwards: <u>She has sent forth her maidens, she criest on the high places of the city, Who is simple -- let him turn in hither, and he who is void of understanding</u> (Prov. 3:4) -- these refer to Adam and Even [T.: mankind and the wild beasts [T. San. 8:9A-H].

DD. "Upon the highest places of the city" (Prov. 9:14):

EE. Rabbah b. b. Hanna contrasted these verses: "It is written, 'Upon he top of the highest places' (prov. 9:3) and it is written, 'On a seat on the high places' (Prov. 9:14).

FF. "At first 'on top,' and then, 'upon a seat.'"

GG. "Who is thoughtless, let him turn in hither, as for him who lacks understanding, she says to him" (Prov. 9:4):

HH. Said the Holy One, blessed be he, "Who enticed this one?

II. "It is a woman who spoke to him, for it is written, 'He who commits adultery with a woman lacks understanding' (Prov. 6:32)."

VIII.

A. It has been taught on Tannaite authority:

B. R. Meir would say, "The first man was [formed out] of dust gathered from every part of the world,

C. "for it is said, 'Your eyes saw my unformed substance' (Ps. 139:16), and it is written, 'The eyes of the Lord run to and fro through every part of the earth' (Zech. 4:10)."

D. Said R. Oshaiah in the name of Rab, "As to the first man, [38B], his body came from Babylonia, his head from the Land of Israel, and his limbs from other lands."

E. As to his private parts? Said R. Aha, "They come from Aqra deAgma."

IX.

A. Said R. Yohanan bar Hanina, "The day [on which Adam was made] was twelve hours.

B. "At the first hour the dust for making him was gathered together. At the second hour he was made kneaded into an unformed mass. At the third hour his limbs were shaped. At the fourth hour breath was poured into him. At the fifth hour he stood on his feet. At the sixth hour he named [the beasts]. At the seventh hour Eve as mated with him. At the eighth hour they went to bed two and came away from bed four. At the ninth hour he was commanded not to eat from the tree. At the tenth hour he went rotten. At the eleventh hour he was judged. At the twelfth hour he was sent off and went his way.

C. "For it is written, 'Adam tarries not in honor' (Ps. 49:13)."

D. Said Rami bar Hama, "A vicious wild beast can rule over man only if [man] appears to him as a domesticated beast.

E. "For it is said, 'Men are overruled when they appear as beasts' [So Shachter] (Ps. 49:13)."

X.

A. Said R. Judah said Rab, "When the Holy One, blessed be he, proposed to create man, he created a group of ministering angels. He said to them, 'Shall we make man in our image?'

B. "They said to him, 'Lord of the ages, what sort of things will he do?'

C. "He said to them, 'These are the sorts of the things he will do.'"

D. "They said before him, 'Lord of the ages, 'What is man that you are mindful of him, and the son of man that you think of him' (Ps. 8:5)?

E. "He poked his little finger among them and burned them up, and so with the second group of ministering angels.

F. "The third group said to him, 'Lord of the ages, As to the first two groups that spoke to you, what good did they do? The whole world is yours. Whatever you want to do in your world, go and do it.'

G. "When he reached the time of the men of the generation of the flood and the men of the generation of the division of languages, whose deeds were corrupt, they said to him, 'Lord of the worlds, did not the first groups of ministering angles speak well to you?'

H. "He said to them, 'Even to old age, I am the same, and even to hoary hairs will I carry (Is. 46:4)."

XI.

A. Said R. Judah said Rab, "The first man stretched from one end of the world to the other, as it is said, 'Since the day that God created man upon the earth, even the one end of heaven to the other' (Deut. 4:32).

B. "When he turned rotten, the Holy One, blessed be he, put his hand on him and cut him down to size,

C. "for it is said, 'You have hemmed me in behind and before and laid your hands upon me' (Ps. 139:5)."

D. Said R. Eleazar, "The first man stretch from the earth to/ the firmament, as it is said, 'Since the day that God created man upon the earth, and from one end of the heaven to the other' (Deut. 4:32).

E. "When he turned rotten, the Holy One, blessed be he, put his hand on him and cut him down to size,

F. "for it is said, 'You have hemmed me in behind and before' (Ps. 139:5)."

G. But the two verses are contradictory.

H. This and that refer to a single standard.

XII.

A. And said R. Judah said Rab, "The first man spoke Aramaic.

B. "For it is written, 'How weighty are your thoughts to me O God' (Ps. 139:17). [Shachter: 'Weighty' and 'thoughts' are Aramaisms.]"

C. That is in line with what R. Simeon b. Laqish said, "What is the meaning of that which is written, 'This is the book of the generations of Adam' (Gen. 5:1)?

D. "This teaches that the Holy One, blessed be he, showed [Adam] each generation and those who expounded for it, each generation and those who served as its sages.

E. "When he came to the generation of R. Aqiba, he took pleasure in his mastery of Torah and was saddened by the form of his death.

F.   "He said, 'How much a source of grief are your friends to me, O God' (Ps. 139:17). ['Weighty' may take on the meaning of a source of heaviness and grief, and the word for 'thoughts' in Aramaic bears the meaning in Hebrew of 'friends' (Shachter)]."

XIII.

A.   And R. Judah said Rab said, "The first Man was a <u>min</u>.

B.   "For it is said, 'And the Lord God called to Adam and said to him, where are you' (Gen. 3:9), meaning, 'Where has your heart gone?'"

C.   Said R. Isaac, "He drew out his foreskin [to obliterate the mark of circumcision.

D.   "Here it is written, 'But like Adam, they have transgressed the covenant' (Hos. 6:7), and it is written further, 'He has broken my covenant' (Gen. 17:14)."

E.   R. Nahman said, 'He denied the very principle [that God ruled]. Here it is written, 'They have transgressed the covenant' (Hos. 6:7), and elsewhere it is written, 'Because they forsook the covenant of the Lord their God' (Jer. 22:9) [speaking of belief in God's rule]."

XIV.

A.   There we have learned in the Mishnah:

B.   <u>R. Eliezer says, "Be diligent to study the Torah and know what to say to an unbeliever" [M. Abot 2:14].</u>

C.   Said R. Yohanan, "That rule applies to a gentile unbeliever. But as to an Israelite unbeliever, all the more is he beyond the rule."

XV.

A.   Said R. Yohanan, "In every passage in which the <u>minim</u> have found evidence for their heresy, [in which God is spoken of in the plural], a refutation for their position is provided right at hand.

B.   "'Let us make man in our image' (Gen. 1:26) -- And God created [in the singular] man in his own image' (Gen. 1:27).

C.   "'Come, let us go down and there confound their language' (Gen. 11:7) -- 'And the Lord came down [in the singular] to see the city and the tower' (gen. 11:5).

D.   "'Because there were revealed to him God' (Gen. 35:7) -- 'Unto God who answers me in the day of my distress' (Gen. 35:3).

E.   "'And what great nation is there that has Gad so night [in the plural] into it, as the Lord our God is unto us whenever we call upon him [singular]' (Deut. 4:7).

F.   "'And what one nation in the earth is like your people, Israel, whom God have gone [plural] to redeem for a people unto himself [singular]' (2 Sam. 7:23).

G.   "'Till thrones were placed and one that was ancient did sit' (Dan. 7:9)."

H.   And what need was there for all of these passages?

I.   The answer accords with what R. Yohanan said.

J.   For R. Yohanan said, "The Holy One, blessed be he, does nothing unless he consults with the heavenly family.

K.   "For it is said, 'The matter is by the decree of the watchers and the sentence by the word of the Holy Ones' (Dan. 4:14)."

L.   Now all of the others are suitably [explained], but how shall we explain "Till thrones were placed" (Dan. 7:9)?

M.   One is for him, the other for David.

N.   As it has been taught on Tannaite authority:

O.   "One is for him, the other for David," the words of R. Aqiba.

O.   Said to him R. Yose, "Aqiba, how long are you going to treat in a profane way the Presence of God?

Q.   "Rather, one is for bestowing judgment, the other for bestowing righteousness."

R.   Did he accept this answer or not?

S.   Come and take note, for it has been taught on Tannaite authority:

T.   "One is for bestowing judgment and the other for bestowing righteousness," the words of R. Aqiba.

U.   Said to him R. Eleazar b. Azariah, "Aqiba, what business have you in matters of lore? Go over to rules governing the skin disease [of Lev. 13] and uncleanness imparted through overshadowing of the corpse [in Ohalot M. Num. 19:1ff.].

V.   "Rather, one is a throne for a seat, the other for a footstool for his feet."

XVI.

A.   Said R. Nahman, "If someone knows how to refute the position of the minim as well as does R. Idit, let him undertake to refute them, and if not, he should not reply to them."

B.   Said a min to R. Idit, "It is written, 'And to Moses he said, Come up to the Lord' (Ex. 24:1). Ought it not have said, 'Come up to me'?

C.   He said to him, "This refers to Metatron, who is called by the name of his master, for it is written, 'For my name is in him' (Ex. 23:21)."

D.   "If so, let us worship him."

E.   "It is written, 'Be not rebellious against him' (Ex. 23:21). 'Do not exchange me for him.'"

F.   "If so, what need do I have for the statement, 'He will not pardon your transgression' [since Metatron has no right to do so anyhow]?"

G.   He said to him, "By the faith that we hold ! We should not accept him even as a messenger, for it is written, 'And he said to him, if you personally do not go out with us' (Ex. 33:15)."

XVII.

A.   A min said to R. Ishmael b. R. Yose, "It is written, 'Then the Lord caused to rain upon Sodom and Gomorrah brimstone and fire from the Lord' (Gen. 19:24). It should have said, 'From him.'"

B.   A certain laundryman said to him, "Let me answer him. It is written, 'And Lamech said to his wives, Ada and Zillah, Hear my voice, you wives of Lamech' (gen. 4:23). It should have said, 'my wives.'

C.   "But that just is how Scripture says things, and here too, that just is how Scripture says things."

D.   [Ishmael] said to him, "How do you know that?"

E.   "I heard if from the public lesson of R. Meir."

F.   For said R. Yohanan, "When R. Meir would give a public lecture, he would speak one third of the time on traditions [of law], a third on lore, and a third on parables."

G. And said R. Yohanan, "R. Meir had three hundred parables of foxes, and of them all we have only three.

H. [39A] "'The fathers have eaten sour grapes and the children's teeth are set on edge' (Ex. 18:2).

I. "'Just balances, just weights' (Lev. 19:36).

J. "'The righteous is delivered out of trouble and the wicked comes in in his stead' (Prov. 11:8)." [Shachter, p. 246-7, n. 14: Rashi gives the parables in question, as follows, combined in a single story. [Cf., however, Ms. M.: 'We have only one.'] A fox once craftily induced a wolf to go and join the Jews in their Sabbath preparations and share in their festivities. On his appearing in their midst the Jews fell upon him with sticks and beat him. He therefore came back determined to kill the fox. But the latter pleaded: 'It is no fault of mine that you were beaten, but they have a grudge against your father who once helped them in preparing their banquet and then consumed all the choice bits.' 'And was I beaten for the wrong done by my father?' cried the indignant wolf. 'Yes,' replied the fox, 'the fathers have eaten sour grapes and the children's teeth are set on edge. However,' he continued, 'come with me and I will supply you with abundant food.' He led him to a well which had a beam across it from either end of which hung a rope with a bucket attached. The fox entered the upper bucket and descended into the well whilst the lower one was drawn up. 'Where are you going?' asked the wolf. The fox, pointing to the cheese-like reflection of the moon, replied: 'Here is plenty of meat and cheese; get into the other bucket and come down at once.' The wolf did so, and as he descended, the fox was drawn up. 'And how am I to get out?' demanded the wolf. 'Ah' said the fox, 'the righteous is delivered out of trouble and the wicked cometh in in his stead. Is it not written, Just balances, just weights'?]

XVIII.

A. Said the emperor [printed ed.: infidel] to Rabban Gamaliel, "Your God is a thief, for it is written, 'And the Lord God caused a deep sleep to fall upon Adam, and he slept, and he took one of his ribs' (Gen. 2:21)."

B. [The emperor's] daughter said to him, "Let me answer him." She said to [the emperor], "Give me a commander [and troops]."

C. He said to her, "What do you need him for?"

D. He said to him, "Thieves invaded us last night and stole a silver goblet and left a gold one."

E. He said to her, "Would that they should come invade us every day!"

F. "And was it not good for the first Man, that one rib should be taken for him, and a serving maid should be given to him to serve him?"

G. He said to her, "What I meant to say only was that he should have taken [the rib] from him in public."

H. She said to him, "Bring me a piece of meat." They brought it to her. She put it in her armpit and then took it out and said to him, "Eat a piece of this."

I. He said to her, "It disgusts me."

J.   She said to him, "And with the first man too, if she had been taken from him in full light of day, she would have been disgusting to him."

XIX.

A.   The emperor said to Rabban Gamaliel, "I know what your God is doing."

B.   [Gamaliel] was overcome and sighed.

C.   He said to him, "Why so?"

D.   He said to him, "I have a son overseas, and I miss him and I ask you to tell me about him."

E.   He said, "Do I know where he is?"

F.   He said to him, "What is going on on earth you do not know, what is going on in heaven are you going to know?"

XX.

A.   The emperor said to Rabban Gamaliel, "It is written, 'He counts the number of the stars' (Ps. 147:4). What's the big deal? I can count the stars."

B.   [Gamaliel] took some quinces and put them into a sieve. He twisted them about. He said to him, "Count them."

C.   He said to him, "Keep them still."

D.   He said to him, "The firmament goes around this way too."

E.   There are those who say that this is what he said to him, "I can count the stars."

F.   He said to him, "Tell me how many are your molars and other teeth."

G.   He put his hand into his mouth and counted them.

H.   He said to him, [What is in your mouth you don't know, what is in the firmament are you going to know?"

XXI.

A.   The emperor said to Rabban Gamaliel, "He who created the mountains did not create the wind, as it is said, 'For lo, there is one who forms mountains and one who creates wind' (Amos 4:13)."

B.   "But how about this verse having to do with Adam: 'And he created...' (Gen. 1:27) 'and he formed...' (Gen. 2:7)? Here too, will you claim that the one who created this did not create that one?

C.   "There is an area of a handbreadth square in man, with two apertures [the eye and the ear], and since it is written, 'He who plants the ear, shall he not hear, he who forms the eye, shall he not see' (Ps. 94:9), here too, will you say that the one who created this did not create that?"

D.   He said to him, "Yes."

E.   He said to him, "When someone dies, the two [creators] have to be brought to a common opinion."

XXII.

A.   Said a _magus_ to Amemar, "The part of you from the middle and above belongs to Hormiz, and the part of you from the middle and downward belongs to Ahormiz."

B.   He said to him, "If so, how can Ahormiz let Hormiz pass water to the ground."

XXIII.

A. Caesar said to R. Tanhum, "Come, we shall all be one people."

B. He said, "Well and good. But we who are circumcized cannot become like you, so you circumcize and become like us."

C. He said to him, "You have said a good word. But whoever wins an argument with the king has to be thrown to the beasts."

D. They threw him to the beasts, who did not eat him.

E. A min said to him, "The reason that they did not eat him is that they were not hungry."

F. They threw him in, and the animals ate him.

XXIV.

A. An emperor said to Rabban Gamaliel, "You say that wherever there are ten, the Presence of God comes to rest. How many Presences of God are there?"

B. He called [Caesar's] servant and struck him with his ladle, saying to him, "Why is there sun in Caesar's house [and you let it in]?"

C. He said to him, "The sun fills the whole world."

D. "Now if the sun, which is only one of the thousand thousands of myriads of servants of the Holy One, blessed be he, fills the whole world, the Presence of the Holy One, blessed be he, himself, how much the more so!"

XXV.

A. Said a min to R. Abbahu, "Your God is a joker [ridiculing the prophets].

B. "For he said to Ezekiel, 'Lie down on your left side' (Ez. 4:4) and it is written, 'Lie on your right side' (Ez. 4:6)."

C. A disciple came along and said to him, "What is the reason for the Sabbatical Year?"

D. He said to him, "Now I shall say something to you both which will be appropriate to the question of each of you. Said the Holy One, blessed be he, to Israel, 'sow seed for six years, and let the land rest in the Seventh Year, so that you shall know that the land belongs to me.'

E. "Now they did not do so, and they sinned and went into exile.

F. "The custom of the world is that when a province rebels against a mortal king, if he is cruel, he kills all of them, if he is merciful, he kills half of them, if he is unusually forgiving, he punishes the greatest ones among them with torture.

G. "For the Holy One, blessed be he, inflicted pain on Ezekiel so as to wipe away the sins of Israel."

XXVI.

A. Said a min to R. Abbahu, "Your God is a priest. For it is written, 'That they take heave-offering for me' (Ex. 25:2) [and that sort of offering is assigned to priests, so God is a priest].

B. "Now when he buried Moses, in what did he immerse [to remove the corpse-un-cleanness he contracted through the burial]?

C. "Should you say it was in water, is it not written, 'Who has measured the waters in the hollow of his hand' (Is. 40:12)? [The water would not suffice]"

D.   He said to him, "He immersed in fire, for it is written, 'For lo, the Lord will come in fire' (Is. 66:15)."

E.   "And is immersion in fire effective?"

F.   He said to him, "Quite to the contrary, the main point of immersion [for purification] is in fire, for it is written, 'And all that cannot stand fire you shall pass through water' (Num. 31:23)."

XXVII.

A.   Said a <u>min</u> to R. Abina, "It is written, 'Who is like your people, Israel, a unique people on earth' (2 Sam. 7:23)?

B.   "What is so good about you? You are joined [in the same category] with us, for it is written, 'All the nations are as nothing before him' (Is. 40:17)."

C.   He said to him, "One of you [Balaam] has testified in our behalf.

D.   "For it is written, [39B] 'And [Israel] shall not be counted among the nations' (Num. 23:9)."

XXVIII.

A.   R. Eleazar contrasted verses, "It is written, 'The Lord is good to all' (Ps. 145:9), and it is written, 'The Lord is good to those who wait for him' (Lam. 3:25).

B.   "The mater may be compared to the case of a man who has an orchard. When he waters it, he waters the whole thing.

C.   "When he prunes it, he prunes only the good trees."

XXIX.

A.   <u>Therefore man was created alone [4:5]</u>:

B.   "And there went out a song throughout the host" (1 Kgs. 22:36) [at Ahab's death at Ramoth in Gilead].

C.   Said R. Aha b. Hanina, "'When the wicked perish, there is song' (Prov. 11:10).

D.   "When Ahab, b. Omri, perished, there was song."

E.   But does the Holy One, blessed be he, rejoice at the downfall of the wicked?

F.   Is it not written, "That they should praise as they went out before the army and say, 'Give thanks to the Lord, for his mercy endures forever' (2 Chr. 20:21),

G.   and said R. Jonathan, "On what account are the words in this psalm of praise omitted, 'Because he is good'? Because the Holy One, blessed be he, does not rejoice at the downfall of the wicked."

H.   For R. Samuel bar Nahman said R. Jonathan said, "What is the meaning of the verse of Scripture, 'And one did not come near the other all night' (Ex. 14:20)?

I.   "At that time, the ministering angels want to recite a song [of rejoicing] before the Holy One, blessed be he.

J.   "Said to them the Holy One, blessed be he, 'The works of my hands are perishing in the sea, and do you want to sing a song before me?'"

K.   Said R. Yose bar Hanina, "He does not rejoice, but others do rejoice. Note that it is written, '[And it shall come to pass, as the Lord rejoiced over you to do good, so the Lord] will <u>cause</u> rejoicing over you by destroying you' (Deut. 28:63) -- and not 'so will the Lord [himself] rejoice'"

L.   That proves the case.

XXX.

A.   "And dogs licked his blood] and harlots washed themselves, [according to the word of the Lord which he spoke]" (1 Kgs. 22:38):

B.   Said R. Eleazar, "This was to carry out two visions, one of Micaiah, the other of Elijah.

C.   "In regard to Micaiah it is written, 'If you indeed return whole, the Lord has not spoken by me' (1 Kgs. 22:28).

D.   "As to Elijah, it is written, 'In the place where dogs licked blood of Naboth' (1 Kgs. 21:19)."

E.   Raba said, "The reference is to actual harlots. Ahab was a cold man, and Jezebel made two pictures of harlots on his chariot, so that he would see them and heat up."

F.   "And a certain man drew his bow innocently and smote the king of Israel' (1 Kgs. 22:34):

G.   R. Eleazar said, "It was in all innocence."

H.   Raba said, "It was to perfect two visions, the one of Micaiah, the other of Elijah. ['Perfect' uses the same root as 'innocence.']"

XXXI.

A.   It is written, "And Ahab called Obadiah, who was in charge of the household. Now Obadiah fear the Lord very much" (1 Kgs. 18:3):

B.   What did he say?

C.   Said R. Isaac, "He said to him, 'In the case of Jacob it is written, 'I have observed the signs, and the Lord has blessed me [Laban] on your account' (Gen. 30:27). In the case of Joseph, it is written, 'The Lord blessed the Egyptian's house for Joseph's sake' (Gen. 39:5). The house of 'that man' [me] has not been blessed. Is it possible that you do not fear God?'

D.   "An echo came forth and said, 'Now Obadiah feared the Lord very much' (1 Kgs. 18:3). But the house of Obadiah is not designated to receive a blessing."

E.   Said R. Abba, "What is said with regard to Obadiah is greater than what is said with regard to Abraham.

F.   "For with respect to Abraham, the word 'very much' is not written, while with regard to Obadiah, the word 'very much' is written."

XXXII.

A.   Said R. Isaac, "On what account did Obadiah have the merit of receiving prophecy? Because he hid a hundred prophets in a cave.

B.   "For it is said, 'For it was so when Jezebel cut off the prophets of the Lord that Obadiah took a hundred prophets and hid them, fifty to a cave' (1 Kgs. 18:4)."

C.   Why fifty?

D.   Said R. Eleazar, "He took to heart the lesson of Jacob, for it is said, 'Then the camp that is left shall escape' (Gen. 32:9)."

E.   R. Abbahu said, "Because a cave cannot hold more than fifty."

XXXIII.

A. "The vision of Obadiah. Thus said the Lord God concerning Edom" (Obad. 1:1):

B. What made Obadiah in particular [the appropriate choice of a prophet to] speak against Edom?

C. Said R. Isaac, "Said the Holy One, blessed be he, 'Let Obadiah come, who dwelled among two wicked people [Ahab and Jezebel] but did not learn from their deeds, and prophesy against the wicked Esau, who dwelled among two righteous people [Isaac and Rebecca] and did not learn from their deeds.'"

D. Ephraim the Contentious, disciple of R. Meir, in the name of R. Meir, said, "Obadiah was an Edomite proselyte. That is in line with what people say, '[Shachter:] From the very forest itself comes the handle of the axe that fells it.'"

E. "And [David] smote Moab and measured them with a line, casting them down to the ground" (2 Sam. 8:2):

F. Said R. Yohanan in the name of R. Simeon b. Yohai, "That is in line with what people say, 'From the very forest itself comes the handle of the axe that fells it.'"

G. When R. Dimi came, he said, "'[Shachter:] The joint putrefies from within.'"

XXXIV.

A. "Then he took his first-born son, who should have reigned in his place, and offered him for a burnt offering upon the wall" (2 Kgs. 3:27):

B. Rab and Samuel:

C. One said, "It was an offering for the sake of heaven."

D. The other said, "It was an offering to idolatry."

E. Now in line with the view of the one who said, "It was an offering for the sake of Heaven," that is in line with the following verse of Scripture: "And there came great wrath on Israel" (2 Kgs. 3:27) [Shachter, p. 254, n. 2: because of their failure to show loyalty to God in comparison with the devotion shown by the Moabite king].

F. But in line with the view of the one who said, "It was an offering for idolatry," why did "great wrath come on Israel"?

G. It is in accord with what R. Joshua b. Levi said.

H. For R. Joshua b. Levi contrasted verses of Scripture: "It is written, 'Neither have you done according to the ordinances of the nations that were round about you' (Ez. 5:7), but is also is written, 'But you have done according to the ordinances of the nations that were round about you' (Ez. 11:12).

I. "You did not do as did the upright among them, but you did in accord with the deeds of the disreputable ones among them" [as at XXXII C].

XXXV.

A. "And they departed from him and returned to the earth" (2 Kgs. 3:27):

B. Said R. Hanina bar Pappa, "At that moment the wicked ones of Israel descended to the lowest rung [of depravity]."

C. "And the damsel was fair, up to being exceedingly so" (1 Kgs. 1:4):

D. Said R. Hanina b. Pappa, "She did not yet reach even half of the beauty of Sarah, for it is written, 'up to being... exceedingly so,' but not attaining 'exceedingly.'"

The Talmud follows the program of the Mishnah-paragraph, augmenting the theological themes with mostly-relevant illustrative materials, including a large portion of Tosefta's topical complement. Unit I clarifies an item of the Mishnah's statement, so too units II, III. I assume that unit IV is tacked on to unit III because of the reference to Cain's exile. My best guess on the reason for inserting unit V is that it complements the reference to the Davidic household in Babylonia, represented (in its imputed genealogy) by the exilarch. Unit VI pursues the same theme, that is, Israel in exile. So everything not relevant to the Mishnah is part of a large, autonomous construction on the Exile (Babylonia) and exile. Unit VII reverts to the amplification or repetition of the points of the Mishnah, drawn from Tosefta, as we note. Units VIII-XIII deal with the theme of the first man, Adam, which the Mishnah has introduced. Since unit XIII brings us to M. 4:5M when it refers to the first man as a min, or heretic, we have another sizable composite of disputes-with-min-materials, units XIV-XXVIII. While unit XXIX begins with an allusion to M. 4:5J, its focus is on Ahab, by way of treating Prov. 11:10, M. 4:5R. The rest of the Talmud flows from the theme of Ahab. So while the units on biblical lore appear to be prolix, in fact they serve the themes of the Mishnah -- and in a rather disciplined way at that.

A.   They interrogated [the witness] with seven points of interrogation:

B.   (1) In what septennate? (2) In what year? (3) In what month? (4) On what day of the month? (5) On what day [of the week]? (6) At what time? (7) In what place?

C.   R. Yose says, "(1) On what day? (2) At what time? (3) In what place? (4) Do you know him? (5) Did you warn him [of the consequences of his deed]?"

D.   [In case of] one who worships an idol: Whom did he worship, and with what did he worship [the idol]?

M. 5:1

A.   The more they expand the interrogation, the more is one to be praised.

B.   The precedent is as follows: Ben Zakkai examined a witness as to the character of the stalks of figs [under which the incident took place].

C.   What is the difference between interrogation [about the date, time, and place] and examination [about the circumstances]?

D.   In the case of interrogation, [if] one witness says, "I don't know the answer," the testimony of the witness is null.

E.   [In the case of] examination, [if] one of the witnesses says, "I don't know," or even if both of them say, "We don't know," their testimony nonetheless stands.

F.   All the same are interrogation and examination: When [the witnesses] contradict one another, their testimony is null.

M. 5:2

A.   [If] one [of the witnesses] says, "It was on the second of the month," and one of the witnesses says, "It was on the third of the month," their testimony stands,

B.   for one of them may know about the intercalation of the month, and the other one may not know about the intercalation of the month.

C.   [if] one of them says, "On the third," and one of them says, "On the fifth," their testimony is null.

D.   [If] one of them says, "At two," and one of them says, "At three," their
      testimony stands.

E.   [If] one of them says, "At three," and one of them says, "At five," their
      testimony is null.

F.   R. Judah says, "It stands."

G.   [If] one of them says, "At five," and one of them says, "At seven," their
      testimony is null.

H.   For at five the sun is at the east, and at seven the sun is at the west.

                              M. 5:3

A.   And afterward they bring in the second witness and examine him.

B.   If their statements check out, they begin the argument in favor of
      acquittal.

C.   [If] one of the witnesses said, "I have something to say in favor of
      acquittal,"

D.   or [if] one of the disciples said, "I have something to say in favor of
      conviction,"

E.   they shut him up.

F.   [If] one of the disciples said, "I have something to say in favor of
      acquittal," they promote him and seat him among the [judges], and he did
      not go down from that position that entire day.

G.   If there is substance in what he says, they pay attention to him.

H.   And even if [the accused] said, "I have something to say in my own
      behalf," they pay attention to him,

I.   so long as there is substance in what he has to say.

                              M. 5:4

A.   If they found him innocent, they sent him away. If not, they postpone
      judging him till the next day.

B.   They would go off in pairs and would not eat very much or drink wine
      that entire day, and they would discuss the matter all that night.

C.   And the next day they would get up and come to court.

D.   The one who favors acquittal says, "I declared him innocent [yesterday],
      and I stand my ground and declare him innocent today."

E.   And the one who declares him guilty says, "I declared him guilty
      [yesterday] and I stand my ground and declare him guilty today."

F.   The one who argues in favor of guilt may [now] argue in favor of
      acquittal, but the one who argues in favor of innocence may not now go
      and argue in favor of guilt.

G.   [If] they made an error in some matter, the two judges' clerks remind them [of what had been said].

H.   If they now found him innocent, they sent him off.

I.   And if not, they arise for a vote.

J.   [If] twelve vote for acquittal and eleven vote for conviction, he is acquitted.

K.   [If] twelve vote for conviction and eleven vote for acquittal,

L.   and even if eleven vote for acquittal and eleven vote for conviction,

M.   but one says, "I have no opinion,"

N.   and even if twenty-two vote for acquittal or vote for conviction,

O.   but one says, "I have no opinion,

P.   they add to the number of the judges.

Q.   How many do they add? Two by two, until there are seventy-one.

R.   [If] thirty-six vote for acquittal and thirty-five vote for conviction, he is acquitted.

S.   [If] thirty six vote for conviction and thirty-five vote for acquittal, they debate the matter, until one of those who votes for conviction accepts the arguments of those who vote for acquittal.

M. 5:5

I.

A.   What is the source of this rule [concerning seven points of interrogation]?

B.   Said R. Judah, "It is because Scripture has said, 'Then you shall inquire and search and ask diligently' (Deut. 13:15), and it is said, 'And if it be told you and you shall hear it, then you shall inquire diligently' (Deut. 17:4), and it says, 'And the judges shall inquire diligently' (Deut. 19:18). [Thus seven questions are specified.]"

C.   [40B] But might I say that the rule for each is as specified [and since the three cited verses refer, respectively, to trials concerning the apostate city, the trial of an idolator, and witnesses proved conspiring to commit perjury], then there should be three questions for the case of the apostate city, two for idolatry, and two for the trial for perjury? For if it were the case [that on any charge, we have to pose seven questions to the witnesses,] the All-Merciful should have written all entries in a single setting [e.g., seven references to searching and asking diligently in the matter of the apostate city].

D.   [Shachter:] Since all seven are severally prescribed, the requirements of each are inferred from the other [Shachter, p. 258, n. 11: since close examination is stated in the case of each, the three charges are assimilated to each other, and therefore the questions that are to be put in one case are to be put in the others too], and since that is the case, it is as if the seven items were stated with reference to each type of trial.

E.   But the three types of trials really are not equivalent to one another.

F.   [Why not?] The apostate city does not fall into the category of the others [idola-tors'and perjurers' trials], because the property [of the others] is spared [while the property of an apostate city is condemned too].

G.   A trial for idolatry is not parallel to the other two, for the idolator is put to death by the sword.

H.   The trial of the conspiratorial witnesses does not fall into the category of the other two, because others [but not the conspiratorial witnesses] are subject to admonition in advance. [So the proposed argument does not work.]

I.   [We shall now propose an exegetical argument:] Let us derive the commonality of the cases from the use of the word "diligently" [in all three verses cited above], and the use of that word constitutes the establishment of an analogy among the three passages serving no other purpose. Were it to serve some other purpose, one could refute the proposed analogy.

J.   But in point of fact it serves no other purpose, for Scripture could as well have written, "And they shall inquire and they shall search" without using the word "diligently." But Scripture in using that word made a variation in its formulation by stating, "diligently," so that the use of the word is with no other purpose [but to establish an analogy as proposed just now].

L.   Now as to the two uses, it indeed serves no other purpose, for the Scripture could have stated matters in some other way. But as to the apostate city, how should matters have been said in some way other than they are phrased? All usages in that instant are required.

M.   No, there too the reference serves no other purpose and is available for establishing the analogy. For Scripture could have stated, "Asking, you shall ask," or "Searching, you shall search" [which would have conveyed the same meaning].

N.   But the framer of Scripture has made use of a variant mode of expression when he used the word "diligently," which indicates that it was to leave the phrase available for the purpose proposed here.

II.

A.   [Since trials covering idolatry, punished by stoning, and perjury, punished by decapitation in the case of perjury in a murder trial, now have been shown to require cross-examination through seven questions, we proceed to deal with other cases, in which the two further modes of inflicting the death penalty are invoked]. We may infer the requirement to cross-examine witnesses in cases in which the death penalty is through strangulation, on the basis of an argument a fortiori from the requirement of the same in cases ending in the death penalty through stoning or decapitation. [The former are regarded as milder modes of execution than strangulation.]

B.   And we infer by an argument a fortiori that the same mode of careful cross examination is required for cases involving the death penalty of burning, on the basis of the fact the same is required in cases ending in stoning. [Here, stoning is regarded as more severe mode of execution than burning; decapitation is less severe.] [If we require cross examination for the one, we surely should do so in the other.]

C.   That poses no problems to the view of rabbis, who maintain that stoning is a more severe mode of execution.

D.   But in the view of R Simeon, who holds that burning is the more severe mode of execution, what is there to be said?

E.   Rather, said R. Judah, "'Behold, if it be truth and the thing certain' (Deut. 13:15) [concerning the apostate city], and 'Behold, if it be truth and the thing certain' (Deut. 17:4) [concerning the idolator] provides eleven [instances of inquiry]. [Shachter, p. 260, n. 16: 'If it be truth' implies that a question is put to ascertain it, likewise, 'And if the thing be certain' implies another question, hence the two sentences imply another four questions in addition to the seven]. Seven cover the seven questions, and taking away three required for the argument from analogy [diligently in inquiries for idolatry, conspiratorial perjury, and the apostate city], leaves one.

F.   "That [extra entry], from R. Simeon's viewpoint, is to encompass trials in which the death penalty is burning, and, from the viewpoint of rabbis, [who prove that fact from an argument a fortiori from stoning], it may be explained that, as to a matter that can be proved from an argument a fortiori, Scripture may at times take the bother to write it out on the basis of a specific allegation of a verse of Scripture.

G.   R. Abbahu made fun of this explanation, "Might I say that the usage serves to add an eighth question for interrogation?'

H.   But is it possible that there are to be eight questions for interrogation?

I.   Why not? For lo, there is the possibility of adding the question concerning what time within the hour [the event took place].

J.   And so too it has been taught on Tannaite authority:

K.   They interrogated him with eight questions.

L.   Now that view [that there are eight inquiries] poses no problems to the position of Abayye vis a vis R. Meir, who has said, "Someone will error in no way at all." In the formulation that says, "Someone may make a minor error," there is no problem either. [As to Abayye on Meir, we assume that witnesses will not err by half an hour, and if they say that the murder they witnessed took place at 4:30, and they are proved to have been elsewhere at that hour, we do not assume the murder they saw took place at 4 or 5 (Shachter). So too, one may ask at what part of the hour the event took place.]

M.   But as to the position of Abayye vis a via R. Judah, who said, "Someone may make an error by as much as half an hour,"

N.   and from the viewpoint of Raba, who has said, "People may make an error of still greater a magnitude than that," what is there to say? [How shall we reach eight points of interrogation], that is to say, to utilize the eleventh proof-text]?

O.   One may encompass questions on which year in the Jubilee.

P.   But that is covered by the question, In what septennate [M. 5:1B]?

Q.   Rather, the question will be, In which Jubilee.

R.   And the other party?

S.   Since the witness has stated in which year of the septennate, it is not necessary to ask in which Jubilee.

III.

A.   R. Yose says, ["On what day? At what time? In what place? Do you know him? Did you warn him of the consequences of his deed?"] [M. 5:1C]:

B.   It has been taught on Tannaite authority:

C.   Said R. Yose to sages, "In accord with your view, if someone came and said, 'Last night he killed him,' one says to him, 'In what septennate? In what year? In what month? On what day of the month?'"

D.   They said to him, "But in accord with your position, if someone came and said, 'He killed him just now,' one still has to say to him, 'On what day? At what time? In what place?'

E.   "But even though it is not necessary [in this particular case to ask such questions], we pose those questions.

F.   "That accords with the view of R. Simeon b. Eleazar [that they move the witness from place to place to confuse him (T. San. 9:1A)]. Here too, even though it is not necessary, we impose these tests upon the witness, in accord with the view of R. Simeon b. Eleazar."

G.   And R. Yose? The case of testimony, "Last night he killed him," is commonplace in most matters of testimony. But, "Just now he killed him" is not common in most cases of testimony.

IV.

A.   Do you know him [M. 5:1C]:

B.   Our rabbis have taught on Tannaite authority:

C.   "Do you know him? Did he kill a gentile? Did he kill an Israelite? Did you admonish him? Did he accept the admonishment? Did he [Shachter:] admit his liability to the death penalty? Did he commit murder within the span of the utterance [that he made, admitting his liability]?

D.   In the case of idolatry: "What idol did he worship? Did he worship Peor? Did he worship Merqolis? With what did he conduct the rite? Was it by a sacrifice? Incense? Libation? Prostration?"

V.

A.   Said Ulla, "How on the basis of the Torah do we know that it is necessary to admonish [the felon prior to his act, so that we may know that what he did was with full knowledge of the consequences]?

B.   "As it is said, 'And if a man shall take his sister, his father's daughter, or his mother's daughter, and see her nakedness' (Lev. 20:17).

C.   "Now does the matter depend upon what he sees? [Surely it depends upon what it is done.]

D.   "But unless he is shown the reason for the prohibition [of what he proposes to do, he is not culpable.]

E. "Since this matter does not pertain the extirpation [41A], apply it to the penalty of flogging."

F. A Tannaite authority of the house of Hezekiah [taught], "'And if a man come presumptuously upon his neighbor to slay him with guile' (Ex. 21:14) -- for witnesses admonished him, and he still acted intentionally."

G. A Tannaite authority of the house of R. Ishmael [taught], "'And they who found him gathering wood' (Num. 15:33) -- for they had warned him and he continued to collect the wood."

H. A Tannaite authority of the house of Rabbi [taught], "'On account of the word that he humbled his neighbor's wife' (Deut. 22:34) -- it was on account of matters pertaining to words."

I. And it is necessary [that we have all three proofs].

J. For had the All-Merciful written the rule only in respect to the prohibition of sexual relations with one's sister, I might have supposed that those who are liable to flogging must be admonished, but those who are liable to the death penalty may be punished even though they were not warned in advance. So Scripture stated, "If a man come presumptuously [in a case in which the death penalty pertains].

K. And if the All-Merciful had stated that the rule requiring admonition applies in the case, "If a man come presumptuously," I might have concluded that that rule pertains to a crime punishable by the sword, which is a lighter form of execution, but as to a case in which the penalty is stoning, which is a more severe form of execution, I might have had that that is not the rule.

L. So it was necessary to make that point.

M. And why was it necessary to make the same point twice with respect to crimes punishable by stoning [both for the one who gathered wood on the Sabbath, the other in respect to the betrothed maiden]?

N. In the perspective of R. Simeon, it serves to encompass crimes punishable by burning.

O. In the view of rabbis, even though one may prove a matter through an argument a fortiori, Scripture will take the trouble and write the matter out [expressly].

P. And why should Scripture not have stated the rule [requiring admonition] in the case of those who are stoned on account of their crimes, and the other classifications of crimes would have been derived from that fact [by an argument a fortiori]?

Q. Here too, a matter which can be shown to be the case by an argument a fortiori Scripture may well take the trouble to write out explicitly.

VI.

A. "Did he admit his liability to the death penalty"?

B. How do we know that this is a requirement?

C. Said Raba, and some say Hezekiah, "Scripture has stated, 'He who is to die shall be put to death' (Deut. 17:6).

D. "[He is put to death only] if he admits his liability to the death penalty."

VII.

A. Said R. Hanan, "Witnesses who have testified against a betrothed maiden [that she has been unfaithful], who then were proved to have been formed conspiracy for perjury, are not to put to death. [Though had the woman been found guilty, she would have been put to death, in this case the perjurers do not suffer retaliation].

B. "[Why not?] Because they can plead, "Our intent was to prohibit her from consummating the marriage to her betrothed husband [but not to have her put to death]."

C. But lo, they had admonished her [if their evidence had been valid. What sort of a defense is this?]

D. It was a case in which they had not admonished her [or claimed to have done so].

E. If they had not admonished her, on what basis could she have been subject to the death penalty?

F. We deal with a wife in the status of an associate [who is presumed to know the law], and that accords with the position of R. Yose b. R. Judah.

G. For it has been taught on Tannaite authority:

H. R. Yose b. R. Judah says, "It is not necessary to admonish an associate [who is presumed to know the law and the consequences of violating it], for the purpose of admonition is only to allow for the distinction between inadvertent and deliberate action [but the associate knows the law and therefore could not act out of ignorance of the consequences]."

I. Then if [the witnesses] cannot be put to death, how could the woman be subject to the death penalty? For you have at hand testimony which is not subject to a test as to conspiratorial perjurers, and any testimony that is not subject to the test for conspiratorial perjury does not fall into the category of testimony at all.

J. That is exactly the sense [of R. Hanan], "Since the perjurers cannot be executed, because they can claim, 'We intended to prohibit her from marrying her betrothed husband,' she too is not subject to the death penalty. The reason is that this is testimony which is not subject to a test [as to conspiratorial perjury, and any testimony that is not subject to the test for conspiratorial perjury does not fall into the category of testimony at all]."

K. And as to a woman in the status of an associate, who, we have determined, is subject to the death penalty in accord with the theory of R. Yose b. R. Judah, how do you find an appropriate case [in which she would be subject to execution, since for their part the witnesses would not be subject to the death penalty if they are proved perjurers]?

L. It would be a case in which the woman committed adultery and went and did so a second time.

M. The witnesses can claim, "We came to prohibit her from marrying her second lover." [So that would not exemplify matters.]

N. We deal with a case in which she committed adultery against her first husband [Shachter, p. 265, n. 7: to whom she is already prohibited in consequence of their earlier relations] or with a relative [Shachter, p. 265, n. 8: whom she is absolutely forbidden to marry at all].

O.   Why single out a betrothed woman for the present case? The same would apply even to a married one.

P.   That is indeed so, but the distinctive point is that even in the case of this woman, who has not yet lived with the man, the witnesses may make the claim, "We came to prohibit her from marrying her betrothed husband."

VIII.

A.   Said R. Hisda, "If one said, 'He killed him with a sword,' and the other said, 'He killed him with a dagger,' this is 'not certain' testimony [in line with Deut. 13:15, 17:4: 'Behold, if it be truth and the thing certain' (Shachter, p. 265, n. 9)].

B.   "If one says, 'His clothing was black,' and the other says, 'His clothing was white,' lo, this is 'certain.' [These statements do not refer to the act, but only to the circumstances]."

C.   An objection was raised from the following:

D.   "Certain" means that [all elements of the testimony must stand] firm. If one says, "He killed him with a sword," and the other says, "It was with a dagger that he killed him,"

E.   if one says, "His clothing was black," and the other says, "His clothing was white," this is not certain.

F.   R. Hisda explained the passage [vis a vis clothing] to refer to a scarf with which the murderer had strangled the other [so we speak not of clothing but of the murder weapon in particular, in which case the clothing] falls into the category of a sword or dagger.

G.   Come and take note: If one says, "His sandals were black," and the other says, "His sandals were white," this is not certain [testimony, and is null, contrary to Hisda's claim as to what constitutes valid evidence].

H.   Here too, it would be a case in which the murderer kicked the victim with his sandal and so killed him.

I.   Come and take note of the following: The precedent is as follows: Ben Zakkai examined a witness as to the character of the stems of figs [M. 5:2B].

J.   Said Rami b. Hama, "It would be a case in which [the witnesses testified that] he had cut off a fig on the Sabbath, on account of which he would be subject to the death penalty. [In this case what sort of fig is at hand matters as to the actual crime]."

K.   But has it not been taught on Tannaite authority:

L.   They said to him, "He killed him under a fig tree" [and that is the context for the testimony at hand, contrary to Rami's thesis at J].

M.   Rather, said Rami bar Hama, "It would be a case in which the murderer was accused of piercing the deceased with the sharp end of a fig branch."

N.   Come and take note:

O.   He said to them, "As to this fig tree, were its stalks thin or thick?"

P.   "Were the figs black or white?" [!] [Shachter, p. 266, n. 7: Now surely he could not have killed anyone with the figs. This proves that the meaning is that the witnesses deposed that the accused had killed his victim under or near a fig-tree, and thus this again refutes Hisda.]

Q.   Rather, said R. Joseph, "Can anyone object on the basis of the position of Ben Zakkai? Surely he is in his own category, for he treats as equivalent to one another both interrogation and examination [and maintains (Shachter, p. 266, n. 8:) just as contradictions on the latter invalidated the evidence, so on the former. The general view disagrees with this, and Hisda's dictum was likewise in accordance with the general view.]

IX.

A.   Who is this "Ben Zakkai"?

B.   If we should proposed that it is R. Yohanan ben Zakkai, did he ever sit in a sanhedrin [that tried a murder case]?

C.   And has it not been taught on Tannaite authority:

D.   The lifetime of R. Yohanan ben Zakkai was a hundred and twenty years. For forty years he engaged in trade, for forty years he studied [Torah], and for forty years he taught.

E.   And it has been taught on Tannaite authority: Forty years before the destruction of the Temple the sanhedrin went into exile and conducted its sessions in Hanut.

F.   And said R. Isaac bar Abodimi, "That is to say that the sanhedrin did not judge cases involving penalties."

G.   Do you think it was cases involving penalties? [Such cases were not limited to the sanhedrin but could be tried anywhere in the Land of Israel.]

H.   Rather, the sanhedrin did not try capital cases.

I.   And we have learned in the Mishnah:

J.   <u>After the destruction of the house of the sanctuary, Rabban Yohanan b. Zakkai ordained ... [M. R.H. 4:1]</u>. [So the final forty years encompassed the period after the destruction of the Temple, and Yohanan could not, therefore, have served on a sanhedrin that tried capital cases.]

K.   Accordingly, at hand is some other Ben Zakkai [than Yohanan b. Zakkai].

L.   That conclusion, moreover, is reasonable, for if you think that it is Rabban Yohanan ben Zakkai, would Rabbi [in the Mishnah-passage] have called him merely, "Ben Zakkai"? [Not very likely.]

M.   And lo, it has been taught on Tannaite authority:

N.   There is the precedent that Rabban Yohanan ben Zakkai conducted an interrogation about the stalks on the figs [so surely this is the same figure as at M. 5:2B].

O.   But [at the time at which the incident took place, capital cases were tried by the sanhedrin and] he was a disciple in session before his master. He said something, and the others found his reasoning persuasive, [41B] so they adopted [the ruling] in his name.

P.   When he was studying Torah, therefore, he was called Ben Zakkai, as a disciple in session before his master, but when he [later on] taught, he was called Rabban Yohanan ben Zakkai.

Q.   When, therefore, he is referred to as Ben Zakkai, it is on account of his being a beginning [student] and when he is called Rabban Yohanan b. Zakkai, it is on account of his status later on.

X.

A.   The precedent is ... What is the difference between interrogation [about the date, time and place] and examination [about the circumstances]? [M. 5:2B-C]:

B.   [In the case of examination, if one of the witnesses says, "I don't know," or even if both of them say, "We don't know," their testimony nonetheless stands (M. 5:2E)]. What is the meaning of, "even if both of them say ..."?

C.   Surely it is obvious that, if one of them says, "I don't know," the testimony is validated, so if both of them say so, the testimony obviously will be valid? [Shachter, p. 268, n. 5: For if one is ignorant on a certain point, the other's knowledge therefore is valueless. Hence whatever evidence is valid when one is ignorant is also valid when both are ignorant.]

D.   Said R. Sheshet, "The reference is to the opening clause, [dealing with interrogation]. And this is the sense of the passage: 'In the interrogation, even if both of them say, "We know," but one of them [the third of three witnesses to the same crime] says, "I don't know," the testimony is null.'

E.   "In accord with whose view is this interpretation? It accords with the position of R. Aqiba, who treats as analogous [the testimony of] three witnesses and [the testimony of] two [imposing upon both the same rules of evidence]."

F.   Said Raba, "But lo, [the language of the passage at hand] explicitly says, Their testimony nonetheless stands [M. 5:2E]!"

G.   Rather, said Raba, "This is the sense of the passage: 'Even in the case of interrogation, if two witnesses say, "We know," but one of the witnesses [of a group of three] says, "I don't know," their testimony nonetheless stands.'

H.   "In accord with which authority is the passage framed? It is not in accord with the view of R. Aqiba."

XI.

A.   R. Kahana and R. Safra were repeating [rules of] the sanhedrin in the house of Rabbah. Rami bar Hama met them. He said to them, "What is it that you people say about [the laws of] the sanhedrin at the house of Rabbah?"

B.   They said to him, "And what should we say about the rules of sanhedrin by themselves [without respect to what Rabbah has to teach us]? What's your problem?"

C.   He said to them, "On the basis of this passage: What is the difference between interrogation [about the date, time and place] and examination [about the circumstances], in the case of interrogation, if one witness says, 'I don't know the answer,' the testimony of the witness is null. In the case of examination, if one of the witnesses says, 'I don't know,' or even if both of them say, 'We don't know,' their testimony nonetheless stands [M. 5:2C-E], [I have the following problem:]

D.   "since the requirement to conduct both procedures rests on the authority of the Torah, what validates the distinction between interrogation and examination?"

E.   They said to him, "Now wait a minute. In the case of interrogation, if one of them said, 'I don't know,' their testimony is null, because in this case you have testimony which is not subject to the test of conspiratorial perjury.

F.   "In the case of examination, if one of them said, 'I don't know,' their testimony nonetheless stands, because you do have testimony which you can subject to the test of conspiratorial perjury."

G.   He said to them, "If this is what you have to say about the rules, then you have a great deal to say about them."

H.   They said to him, "It was because of the patience of the master that we spoke about the matter a great deal. If it had been on account of his contentiousness, we should have said not a thing about it."

XII.

A.   If one of the witnesses says, ["It was on the second of the month," and one of the witnesses says, "It was one the third of the month, their testimony stands, for one of them may know about the intercalation of the money and the other one may not know about the intercalation of the month] [M. 5:3A-B]:

B.   Until what day [of the month do we assume that people may not know whether it is a full month of thirty days or a defective one of twenty-nine days]?

C.   Said R. Aha bar Hanina said R. Assi said R. Yohanan, "Until the greater part of the month [has gone by]."

D.   Said Rabba, "Also we have learned that view in the Mishnah itself:

E.   "If one of them says, 'On the third,' and one of them says, "on the fifth,' their testimony is null [M. 5:3C].

F.   "Now why should that be the case? Might I not say that one party knows about the intercalation of two months and the other party does not know about the intercalation of two months?

G.   "Rather, is it not because once the greater part of a month has passed people know [the calendar]?"

H.   To the contrary, I may say to you, indeed people do not know when the greater part of the month has gone by [that a month has been intercalated], [so the Mishnah-passage proves nothing].

I.   But people do know about the sounding of the ram's horn [to signal the advent of the new month]. Our basic claim, then, is that someone may err in the case of the sounding of the ram's horn one time, but he is not likely to err about the sounding of the ram's horn two times. [Shachter, p. 270, n. 3, 4: Though knowing that the ram's horn had been sounded, he may have erred once as to the day on which it was sounded] [but one would not make two mistakes in that connection].

XIII.

A.   And said R. Aha bar Hanina said R. Assi said R. Yohanan, "Up to what point in the month do people say the blessing over the new month?

B.   "Until its [Shachter:] concavity is filled up."

C.   And how long does that take?

D.   Said R. Jacob Idi said R. Judah, "Up to seven [days]."

E.   The Nehardeans say, "Up to sixteen [days]."

F.   [42A] And both parties concur with the view of R. Yohanan, but one holds that it is [Shachter] until it is like a strung bow, and the other, until it is like a sieve.

G.   Said R. Aha of Difti to Rabina, "[After a week has passed, in line with Judah's view at D, one may nonetheless] say the blessing, ' ... who is good and does good.' [Even though it is no longer a new moon, still the moon continues to grow, so the cited blessing is called for.]"

H.   He said to him, "But when the moon is waning [in the given lunar month], should we then say the blessing, '... true judge' [which is said on the occasion of bad news], that [in the earlier part of the lunar month] we should say the blessing, 'Who is good and does good'?"

I.   Then why not say both [one for the earlier part, the other for the later part, of the lunar month]?

J.   Since this is the usual course of events, it is not necessary for us to say any blessing at all.

XIV.

A.   And said R. Aha bar Hanina said R. Assi said R. Yohanan, "Whoever says a blessing for the new moon at the proper time is as if he receives the Presence of God.

B.   "here it is written, 'This month ...' (Ex. 12:1), and elsewhere, 'This is my God, and I shall glorify him' (Ex. 15:2)."

XV.

A.   Tannaite authority of the house of R. Ishmael [stated], "If Israel had had the sole merit of receiving the presence of their father in heaven month by month, it would have been enough for them."

B.   Said Abayye, "Therefore we should say the blessing standing."

C.   Maremar and Mar Zutra would be helped up on the shoulders [of others] so as to say the blessing.

XVI.

A.   Said R. Aha to R. Ashi, "In the West, they say the blessing, 'Blessed ... is he who renews the months.'"

B.   He said to him, "A blessing such as that our women recite. Rather, it accords with the view of R. Judah.

C.   "For R. Judah said, '[We say,] "Blessed ... who with his word created the heavens, and with the breath of his mouth all of their hosts. He assigned to them a rule and a time, so that they should not vary from their assignment. They rejoice and take pleasure in doing the will of their creator, working in truth, for their task is truth. And he instructed the moon to come anew as a crown of beauty for those who are sustained for from the womb. For they are destined to be renewed as is she, so as to glorify their creator on account of the glory of his dominion. Blessed are you, Lord, who renews each month."'"

XVII.

A.   "For with wise advice you shall make your war" (Prov. 24:6):

B.   Said R. Aha bar Hanina said R. Assi said R. Yohanan, "In whom do you find [ability
        to conduct] the 'war of the Torah' [of rigorous reasoning]? He who possesses 'the
        wise advice' of Mishnah-learning."

C.   R. Joseph recited in his own regard, "Much increase of grain is by the strength of
        the ox" (Prov. 14:4).

XVIII.

A.   If one of them says, "At two," [and one of them says, "At three," their testimony
        stands] [M. 5:3D]:

B.   Said R. Shimi bar Ashi, "The rule applies only to differences in hours [of the day for
        there is a margin of error]. But if one of them says, 'It was before dawn,' and the
        other says, 'It was after dawn,' their testimony is null."

C.   That is self-evident.

D.   Rather: If one of them says, "It was before dawn,' and the other says, "It was just
        during sunrise, ..."

E.   That too is self-evident.

F.   [No, it requires explicit statement, for] what might you have thought?

G.   The witness was referring to the glow [before sunrise] and he saw only a gleam [but
        thought it was sunrise].

H.   So we are informed that we do not [treat that as a routine margin of error].

XIX.

A.   And afterward they bring in [the second witness and examine him ... and he did not
        go down from that position that entire day] [M. 5:4A-F]:

B.   That day and no more?

C.   And has it not been taught on Tannaite authority:

D.   **If there is substance in what he says [the disciple] did not go down from that position
        ever.**

E.   **And if not, he did not go down from that position that entire day [M. 5:4D],**

F.   **so that people should not say, "His going up was his downfall [T. San. 9:3D-F].**

G.   Said Abayye, "Refer [the allusion to that entire day] to a case in which there was no
        substance in what he says."

XX.

A.   If they found him innocent ... or drink wine that entire day] [M. 5:5A-B]:

B.   What is the reason for not [drinking] wine?

C.   Said R. Aha bar Hanina, "Scripture has said, "[It is not] for princes [RWZN] [to say],
        Where is strong drink' (Prov. 31:4).

D.   "Those who are dealing with the secrets [RZW, letters appearing in the word for
        princes] of the world should not get drunk."

XXI.

A.   They debate the matter [until one of those who votes for conviction accepts the
        arguments of those who vote for acquittal] [M. 5:5S]:

B.   And if they do not accept [the arguments]?

C.   Said R. Aha, "They dismiss [the accused]."

D. And so said R. Yohanan, "They dismiss [the accused]."

E. Said R. Pappa to Abayye, "Then let him go free to begin with [if the court of seventy-one produces no clear majority? Why debate, when the entire court is not likely to convict?]"

F. He said to him, "This is what R. Yohanan said, 'It is so that they should not leave the court while in a state of confusion.'"

G. There are those who say, Said R. Pappa to Abayye, "And why add to the court? Why not just dismiss him from the original court [of twenty-three judges]? [Shachter, p. 273, n. 7: If there was then no clear majority, both sides should have endeavored to win one more vote over to their opinion, and in the case of failure, he should have been set free there and then.]"

H. He said to him, "R. Yose takes your view."

I. For it has been taught on Tannaite authority:

J. R. Yose says, "Just as they do not add to a court of seventy-one judges, so they do not add to a court of twenty-three judges."

XXII.

A. Our rabbis have taught on Tannaite authority:

B. In property cases [the court may] rule, "The case is stale."

C. In capital cases [the court may] not rule, "The case is stale [T. San. 7:7A-B]."

D. What is the sense of, "The case is stale"?

E. Should I say, "The case is a difficult one [requiring protracted debate]? Then one should reverse the formulation of this rule just now cited [and dismiss a case capital case on the grounds that the debate is too prolonged. One should in point of fact dismiss the accused under such circumstances.]

F. Said R. Huna bar Manoah in the name of R. Aha son of R. Iqa, "Reverse matters."

G. R. Ashi said, "Under no circumstances should you reverse matters. What is the sense of 'The case is stale'? The case has been subjected to most learned [debate]."

H. An objection was raised on the basis of the following:

I. The chief judge alone has the right to say, "The case is stale" [T. San. 7:7C].

J. Now if you maintain that the sense of the statement is, "The case has been subjected to most learned [debate]," then there is no problem in having the chief judge make such a pronouncement.

K. But if you hold that the sense of the phrase is, "The case is a difficult one," it surely would not be appropriate for the chief judge to make such a statement, since he thereby disgraces himself.

L. Indeed so, for the one who pronounces his own disgrace himself is not the same as one who is pronounced a disgrace by others [so it is better for the chief judge, than for a lesser one, to make the statement].

M. There are those who state this as follows:

N. Now if you maintain that the sense of the statement is, "The case is a difficult one," then that is in line with the principle: The one who pronounces his own disgrace is not the same as the one who is pronounced a disgrace by others.

O.   But if you hold that the sense of the statement is, "The case has been subjected to
     most learned [debate], "should the chief judge praise himself in such a manner? And
     has it not been written, "Let another praise you, and not your own mouth" (Prov.
     27:2)?

P.   A rule governing court procedure is in its own category, for it is the duty of the
     head of the court to pronounce [the verdict].

Q.   For so we have learned in the Mishnah:

R.   When they have completed the matter, they bring him back in. The chief judge says,
     "Mr. So-and-so, you are innocent," "Mr. So-and-so, you are guilty" [M. 3:7A-B].

Most of the Talmud focuses upon the exposition of the Mishnah-chapter at hand.
Only an extended collection of materials forming a tradental aggregate (Aha-Assi-Yo-
hanan) carries us far from the topic at hand. Unit I begins with the expected inquiry into
the scriptural basis for the rule. Unit II then carries forward the discussion of unit I. Unit
III turns to M. 5:1C; unit IV deals with the same clause. Unit V asks about the scriptural
basis for the requirement to admonish a person prior to commission of a felony. Units VI,
VII carry forward the discussion inaugurated in unit V. Unit VIII brings us back to the
substance of the matter, the interrogation of witnesses. Unit IX completes the fore-
going. Unit X takes up M. 5:2B-C, unit XI treats the same matter. Unit XII moves on to
M. 5:3. As noted, because of XII C, units XIII-XVII are inserted whole. Units XVIII, and
XIX, move on to M. 5:3, M. 5:4, respectively. Unit XX deals with M. 5:5A-B, and unit
XXI, M. 5:5S. The reason for the inclusion of unit XXII is that it neatly complements the
basic thesis of M. 5:5 about protracted debate, providing us with Tosefta's complement.
So the composition of the chapter as a whole follows 5:5A-B, and unit XXI, M. 5:5S,
following entirely familiar rules.

6:1 A-G

A. [When] the trial is over, [and the felon is convicted], they take him out to stone him.

B. The place of stoning was well outside the court, as it is said, "Bring forth him who cursed [to a place outside the camp]" (Lev. 24:14).

C. One person stands at the door of the courthouse, with flags in his hand, and a horseman is some distance from him, so that he is able to see him.

D. [If] one [of the judges] said, "I have something to say in favor of acquittal," the one [at the door] waves the flags, and the horseman races off and stops [the execution].

E. And even if [the convicted party] says, "I have something to say in favor of my own acquittal," they bring him back,

F. even four or five times,

G. so long as there is substance in what he has to say.

I.

A. Now was the place of stoning merely outside the court?

B. And has it not been taught on Tannaite authority,

C. The place of stoning was outside the three camps?

D. Yes, it is as you say. But the reason that the author of the passage has stated matters this way is to indicate that if the court should go into session outside of the three camps, they establish a place of stoning outside the court, so that it will not appear as if the court is committing murder,

E. or so that there may be the possibility of saving the man [by establishing some distance between the place at which the verdict is handed down and the place of stoning].

II.

A. What is the scriptural basis [for the rule that the place of stoning must be outside the three camps]?

B. It is as our rabbis have taught on Tannaite authority:

C. "Bring forth him who cursed [to a place] outside the camp" (Lev. 24:14).

D. That is, outside the three camps.

E. You say that it is outside the three camps. But perhaps it means only outside a single camp?

F. Here the phrase, "outside the camp" is used (Lev. 24:14) and elsewhere, with regard to bulls that were burned up [as whole offerings], it is said, "Outside the camp" (Lev. 12:21).

G. Just as in that context, it means outside the three Israelite camps, so the same rule applies here.

H. And how do we know that is the case in that context?

I. It is as our rabbis have taught on Tannaite authority:

J. "The whole bullock he shall carry away outside the camp" (Lev. 12:12).

K. That means, outside the three camps.

L. You say that it is outside the three camps.

M. But may it not mean outside one camp?

N. When, with respect to the bull offered for the community [in case of an unwitting public transgression], Scripture says, "Outside the camp," there is no need for Scripture to say so explicitly, for lo, it already has been stated, "And he shall burn it as he has burned the first bullock" (Lev. 12:12). Accordingly, the statement requires carrying it beyond the second camp.

O. And when it says, with respect to the ashes [Shachter, p. 276, n. 12: beyond which the burning is to take place], "Outside the camp," which Scripture also need not make explicit, since it already has been stated, "Where the ashes are poured out shall it be burned" (Lev. 4:12), the statement further requires carrying it beyond the third camp.

P. But why not interpret [the phrase, "without the camp" (Lev. 24:14), in the sense imputed to that phrase] in the context of sacrifices slaughtered outside [of the proper location, the Temple]? Just as, in that context, the meaning is "outside the one camp," so there the meaning would be, "outside the one camp"? [Hence the requirement is outside one camp, not all three].

Q. It is more logical [to derive the meaning of the phrase] from [its sense in the context of] the bullocks that are to be burned, for [Shachter:] they have the following points in common: [1] "Bring forth ... without the camp" (Lev. 12:12), [2] the bringing forth is a prerequisite to the act, and [3] atonement. [Shachter, p. 277, n. 3: In both cases there is a positive command, "Bring forth." Further, bringing forth without the camp is a prerequisite for the fitting performance of the act, whereas in the case of sacrifices slaughtered outside the Temple court it is a transgression. Moreover, the burning of the bullock is an atonement for the high priest and the whole congregation, and stoning likewise is an atonement for the malefactor; but that feature is absent in the case of sacrifices slaughtered without.]

R. Quite to the contrary, [he should have derived the meaning of the phrase] from [its sense in the context of] sacrifices slaughtered outside the Temple, [Shachter:] since they have the following in common: [1] human being, [2] sinners, [3] life is taken and [4] the application of the rule that the sacrifice is rendered refuse by an improper attitude of the officiating priest. [Shachter, p. 277, n. 4: "Without the camp" in both places refers to a human being, the blasphemer was to be taken without the camp, and a human being slaughtered without the camp, while in connection with the bullocks that are burned, the phrase speaks of animals. The blasphemer and the one who slaughters outside the camp both commit sins, while the bullock is not a sinner. In both cases the leading "outside the camp" occurs in order to take life, that of the blasphemer and the sacrifice yet to be slaughtered, while the bullocks already have been slaughtered, while "without the camp" with respect to the bullocks speaks only of the case after they have been slaughtered. Finally, the law of unfitness caused by the improper intention of the officiating priest has no application to the two items at hand, neither to stoning -- by definition -- nor to sacrifices slaughtered outside of the Temple.]

S.   It is better [to derive the meaning of the word as it occurs in one context relating to a prerequisite to proper performance from its meaning in another such setting [as above Shachter, p. 277, n. 3].

III.

A.   [Dealing with the same issue], R. Pappa said, "Where did Moses dwell? It was in the camp of the Levites. And the All-Merciful said to him, 'Bring forth him that has cursed outside the camp' (Lev. 24:14), meaning outside the camp of the Levites.

B.   "'And they brought him who had cursed outside the camp' (Lev. 24:14), means outside the camp of the Israelites [since specifying, once more, 'outside the camp' must have been intended to supply another meaning.]"

C.   [No,] it was necessary to indicate the carrying out [of what God had commanded].

D.   [No,] the carrying out is stated explicitly: "[43A] And the Children of Israel did as the Lord had commanded Moses" (Lev. 24:23).

E.   Then how do you deal with the following verse: "And they stoned him with a stone" (Lev. 24:23). [Shachter, p. 278, n. 7: It was not needed to show how the execution was carried out, as that was already stated in the words quoted above; hence by analogy this too needs a distinctive interpretation.]

F.   It was required to serve the purpose of the following teaching on Tannaite authority:

G.   "And they stoned him with a stone" (Lev. 24:23) --

H.   "Him," -- and not his clothing, [so the man is naked].

I.   "A stone," for if he died after being struck by a single stone, [the rite] has been properly carried out.

J.   And it was necessary to write both "stone" and "stones" [at Num. 15:36, the gatherer of woods is stoned with <u>stones</u>].

K.   For had the All-Merciful written only, "stone," I might have supposed that when the guilty party did not die from a blow by a single stone, we should not bring other stones with which to kill him.

L.   The All-Merciful had to write, "stones."

M.   And if the All-Merciful had written only, "stones," I might have supposed that in the first place, one has to bring two stones. So the All-Merciful wrote, "stone."

N.   Now [why does] the Tannaite authority at hand invoke the notion that "it is written" [that is, referring to the argument from analogy worked out in unit II] [while Pappa deduces the matter in a different way]?

O.   This is what he meant to say, "If it had not been written, that is, even if the verse [cited by Pappa] were not available, I should have been able to derive the rule by analogy. Now that we are able to derive the rule from a verse of Scripture, of course there is no need to invoke an argument by analogy.

IV.

A.   R. Ashi said, "Where did Moses dwell? It was in the camp of the Levites. And the All-Merciful said to him, 'Bring forth him that has cursed outside the camp' (Lev. 24:14), meaning outside the camp of the Levites.

B.   "'Outside the camp' -- outside the camp of the Israelites.

C.   "'And they brought him who had cursed outside the camp' (Lev. 24:14) this serves to indicate the carrying out [of what God had commanded]."

D.   But the carrying out is stated explicitly: "And the children of Israel did as the Lord had commanded Moses" (Lev. 24:23).

E.   That was necessary for two purposes, first to indicate [that the participants in the rite] lay hands [on the guilty party], and second to indicate [that the execution is carried out by pushing the man [off a high place].

F.   The rabbis said to R. Ashi, "In your view, then, concerning all these references to 'he shall take out,' that are noted in the context of the bullocks that are to be burned, how do you interpret them?"

G.   This is a problem.

V.

A.   <u>One person stands ... [M. 6:1C]:</u>

B.   Said R. Huna, "It is obvious to me that the same rule applies to the stone which is used for the stoning, the tree on which the corpse is hung, the sword with which the criminal is put to death, and the scarf with which he is strangled. All of them are [paid for by the funds] of the community.

C.   What is the reason? Because we cannot say to a man to go and supply his own property so that he may be put to death."

D.   But, R. Huna asked, "As to the flag with which they wave and the horse that runs and holds up the execution [M. 6:1C], to whom to they belong?

E.   "Since they serve to save the man himself, should they come from his own property? Or perhaps since the court is obligated to provide for saving the man, should these things come from public funds?"

F.   And further, with regard to what R. Hiyya bar R. Ashi said R. Hisda said, "As to him who goes forth to be put to death, they give him a glass of wine containing a grain of frankincense, so as to distract him, as it is said, 'Give strong drink to him who is ready to perish and wine to the bitter in soul' (Prov. 31:6),

G.   And it has also been taught on Tannaite authority,

H.   The aristocratic women in Jerusalem would voluntarily provide it.

I.   But if the aristocratic women had not voluntarily provided it, who would have done so?

J.   Surely it comes from public funds, since it is written, "Give" -- of what is theirs.

VI.

A. [With regard to M. 6:1D], R. Aha bar Huna asked R. Sheshet," If one of the disciples said, 'I have an argument to make in behalf of a verdict of innocence,' and then the disciple was struck dumb, what is the law?"

B. R. Sheshet blew into his hands, "If someone was struck dumb? Even on the other side of the world [there may be someone who has an argument to give]. [Obviously, we deal with realities.]"

C. But in that case, no such statement has been made, while here, such a statement has been made.

D. What is the rule?

E. Come and take note of what R. Yose bar Hanina said, "If one of the disciples who voted for acquittal died, they regard him as if he were living and taking a position on the case."

F. If he voted to acquit, that is so, but if he did not vote to acquit, that is not so.

G. That is obvious to me. Where there is a question for you is if he had said [that he would do so]. [Shachter, p. 280, n. 7: When R. Yose states, "argued for acquittal," did he mean that he must have given reasons for his statement, or that he merely said he could do so, even if he was subsequently prevented from giving his reasons?]

VII.

A. <u>And even if the convicted party says [M. 6:1E]</u>:

B. [Must there be substance in what he has to say] even the first and the second time?

C. Has it not been taught on Tannaite authority:

D. [And even if the convicted party says, "I have something to say in favor of my own acquittal," they bring him back (M. 6:1E)], one time, two times, [T: Even three times],

E. whether or not there is substance in what he has to say, they bring him back [T: pay attention to him].

F. From that point on, if there is substance in what he has to say, they bring him back [pay attention to him], and if not, they do not [pay attention to him] [T. San. 9:4H-J].

G. Said R. Pappa, "Explain the passage, "From the second time onwards, [that is, the third time and beyond]."

VIII.

A. How do [the judges] know [whether or not there is substance]?

B. Said Abayye, "They send along a pair of rabbis. If there is substance in what he says, they affirm it, if not, they do not."

C. And let them send [a pair of rabbis] along with him to begin with?

D. Because he is frightened, he may not be able to say everything that he wants [so twice he is allowed to speak in his own behalf without preliminaries].

Units I-IV deal with the location of the place of execution. Unit V turns to a somewhat subsidiary question pertinent to M. 6:1C, unit VI to M. 6:1C, and units VII-VIII to M. 6:1E.

6:1H-J

H.   [If] they then found him innocent, they dismiss him,

I.   And if not, he goes out to be stoned.

J.   And a herald goes before him, crying out, "Mr. So-and-so, son of Mr. So-and-so, is going out to be stoned because he committed such-and-such a transgression, and Mr. So-and-so and Mr. So-and-so are the witnesses against him. Now anyone who knows grounds for acquittal -- let him come and speak in his behalf!"

I.

A.   Said Abayye, "And it is necessary to say [at M. 6:1J], 'On such and such a day, at such and such an hour, in such and such a place.'

B.   "Perhaps there are people who have knowledge of the matter and they will come and prove the witnesses against the man to be perjurers."

II.

A.   A herald goes before him [M. 6:1J]:

B.   Just before [the execution], but not prior to that time. [Schachter, p. 281-2, supplies a full translation of the following, which is omitted in censored editions of the Talmud and is not found in the standard printed text, translated here. What follows is entirely Schachter's translation.]

This implies, only immediately before [the execution], but not previous thereto. [In contradiction to this] it was taught: On the eve of the Passover Yeshu was hanged. For forty days before the execution took place, a herald went forth and cried, 'He is going forth to be stoned because he has practiced sorcery and enticed Israel to apostasy. Any one who can say anything in his favor, let him come forward and plead on his behalf.' But since nothing was brought forward in his favor he was hanged on the eve of the Passover!

'Ulla retorted: Do you suppose that he was one for whom a defense could be made? Was he not a Mesith [enticer], concerning whom Scripture says, Neither shalt thou spare, neither shalt thou conceal him (Deut. 13:9)? With Yeshu however it was different, for he was connected with the government [or royalty, i.e., influential].

C.   Our Rabbis taught: Yeshu had five disciples, Matthai, Nakai, Nezer, Buni and Todah. When Matthai was brought [before the court] he said to them [the judges], Shall Matthai be executed? Is it not written, Matthai [when] shall I come and appear before God? (Ps. 42:3). Thereupon they retorted: Yes, Matthai shall be executed, since it is written, Matthai [when] shall [he] die and his name perish (Ps. 41:6). When Nakai was brought in he said to them: Shall Nakai be executed? It is not written, Naki [the innocent] and the righteous slay thou not (Ex. 23:7)? Yes, was the answer, Nakai shall be executed, since it is written, In secret places does Naki [the innocent] slay (Ps. 10:8). When Nezer was brought in, he said: Shall Nezer be executed? Is it not written, And Nezer [a twig] shall grow forth out of his roots (Is. 11:1). Yes, they said, Nezer shall be executed, since it is written, But thou art cast

forth away from the grave like Nezer [an abhorred offshoot] (Is. 14:19). When Buni
was brought in, he said: Shall Buni be executed? Is it not written, Beni [my son], my
first born (Ex. 4:220. Yes, they said, Buni shall be executed, since it is written,
Behold I will slay Bine-ka [thy son] thy first born (Ex. 4:23). And when Todah was
brought in, he said to them: Shall Todah be executed? Is it not written, A psalm for
Todah [thanksgiving] (Ps. 100:1)? Yes, they answered, Todah shall be executed,
since it is written, Whoso offereth the sacrifice of Todah [thanksgiving] honoreth
me. (Ps. 50:23)

III.

A. [43B] Said R. Joshua b. Levi, "Whoever sacrifices his impulse to do evil and
    confesses on that account is regarded by Scripture as though he had honored the
    Holy One, blessed be he, in the two worlds, this world and the world to come, for it
    is written, 'Who offers the sacrifice of confession honors me' (Ps. 50:23)."

B. R. Joshua b. Levi said, "When the Temple stood, a person would offer a burnt
    offering, and the reward of a burnt offering would go to his credit, or he would do
    the same with a meal offering, and the reward of a meal-offering would go to his
    credit.

C. "But he who is humble is regarded by Scripture as though he had offered up all
    sacrifices.

D. "For it is said, 'The sacrifices of God are a broken spirit' (Ps. 51:19).

E. "And his prayers are not rejected, for it is written, 'A broken and contrite heart, O
    God, you will not despise' (Ps. 51:19)."

Unit I complements M. 6:2J, and unit II (in Schachter's translation of the Munich
manuscript) illustrates the law. Unit II is attached because of the exegesis of Ps. 50:23.

6:2

A. [When] he was ten cubits from the place of stoning, they say to him,
    "Confess," for it is usual for those about to be put to death to confess.

B. For whoever confesses has a share in the world to come.

C. For so we find concerning Achan, to whom Joshua said, "My son, I pray
    you, give glory to the Lord, the God of Israel, and confess to him, [and
    tell me now what you have done; hide it not from me.] And Achan
    answered Joshua and said, Truly have I sinned against the Lord, the God
    of Israel, and thus and thus I have done" (Josh. 7:19). And how do we
    know that his confession achieved atonement for him? For it is said,
    "And Joshua said, Why have you troubled us? The Lord will trouble you
    this day" (Josh. 7:25) -- This day you will be troubled, but you will not be
    troubled in the world to come.

D. And if he does not know how to confess, they say to him, "Say as
    follows: 'Let my death be atonement for all of my transgressions.'"

E. R. Judah says, "If he knew that he had been subjected to perjury, he says, 'Let my death by atonement for all my sins, except for this particular sin [of which I have been convicted by false testimony]'"

F. They said to him, "If so, then everyone is going to say that, so as to clear himself."

I.

A. Our rabbis have taught on Tannaite authority:

B. The word, "I pray you," [at Josh. 7:19] means only supplication.

C. When the Holy One, blessed be he, said to Joshua, "Israel has sinned" (Josh. 7:11), he said to him, "Lord of the world, Who sinned?"

D. He said to him, "Am I a squealer? Go and cast lots."

E. He went and cast lots, and the lot fell on Achan. He said to him, "Joshua, by lot are you going to accuse me? You and Eleazar the priest are the two great figures of the generation. If I were to cast lots concerning you, the lot would come up on one of you."

F. He said to him, "I ask you not to cast doubt on the lots, for the Land of Israel is destined to be divided up by lot, as it is said, 'The land shall be divided by lot' (Num. 26:55). So make confession."

G. Said Rabina, "He enticed him in words: 'We are not we going to ask anything more from you than a mere confession. Confess to him and be exempt [from further penalty].'"

H. Forthwith: "Achan answered Joshua and said, Of a truth, I have sinned against the Lord, the God of Israel, and thus have I done" (Josh. 7:20).

I. Said R. Assi said R. Hanina, "This teaches that Achan committed sacrilege on the occasion of three herems, twice in the time of Moses, and once in the time of Joshua, for it is written, 'I have sinned, and thus and thus have I done' (Josh. 7:20)."

J. R. Yohanan said in the name of R. Eleazar b. R. Simeon, "It was five times, four in the days of Moses, and once in the days of Joshua, as it is said, 'I have sinned and thus and thus have I done' (Josh. 7:20) [a sentence containing five words in Hebrew (Shachter)]."

K. What is the reason that he was not punished until that time?

L. Said R. Yohanan in the name of R. Eleazar b. R. Simeon, "Because concealed transgressions were not punished until the Israelites had crossed the Jordan."

II.

A. This matter is subject to dispute among Tannaite authorities:

B. "The hidden things belong to the Lord our God, but the things that are revealed belong to us and our children for ever" (Deut. 29:28):

C. Why [in the Hebrew version] are the words "to us and to our children" as well as the first letter of the word "for ever" dotted on the top?

D. "This teaches that punishment was not inflicted on account of hidden sins until Israel had crossed the Jordan," the words of R. Judah.

E. Said to him R. Nehemiah, "And is punishment ever [even afterward] inflicted on account of hidden sins? And has it not been stated, 'Until eternity' [but not before]?

F. "But just as punishment was not inflicted for hidden sins, so punishment was not inflicted for infractions committed in public, until the Israelites had crossed the Jordan."

G. Then [44A] why was Achan punished [prior to that time]?

H. It was because his wife and children knew about it.

I. "Israel has sinned" (Josh. 7:11):

J. Said R. Abba bar Zabeda, "Even though it has sinned, it remains Israel."

K. Said R. Abba, "This is in line with what people say: 'A myrtle standing among reeds is still a myrtle and still called a myrtle.'"

III.

A. "Yes, they have even transgressed my covenant which I have commanded them, yes, they have even taken of the devoted thing and have also stolen it, and dissembled also, and they have even put it among their own property" (Josh. 7:11):

B. Said R. Ilaa in the name of R. Judah bar Misparta, "This teaches that Achan violated all five books of the Torah, for the word 'yes' ['even'] is used five times."

C. And said R. Ilaa in the name of R. Judah bar Misparta, "Achan had covered up the sign of his circumcision. Here it is written, 'They have even transgressed my covenant' (Josh. 7:11), and elsewhere it is stated, 'He has broken my covenant' (Gen. 17:14). [So 'covenant' refers to the mark of circumcision.]"

D. That is perfectly obvious.

E. What might have you maintained? [Achan] would not have violated a religious duty that fell upon his own body. So we are informed [that that was not the case and he violated even that requirement].

IV.

A. "And because he has wrought a wanton deed in Israel" (Josh. 7:19):

B. Said R. Abba bar Zabeda, "This teaches that Achan had sexual relations with a betrothed girl. It is written here, 'Because he has wrought a wanton deed,'' and it is written elsewhere, 'For she has wrought a wanton deed in Israel' (Deut. 22:21)."

C. That is perfectly obvious.

D. What might you have maintained? [Achan] would not have permitted himself to violate the law to such an extent. So we are informed [that that was not the case, and he did violate that rule as well].

E. Rabina said, "His punishment is like that of a betrothed girl [who had committed adultery], that is, execution by stoning. [Shachter, p. 287, n. 1: He should legally have been burned for taking of the things under the ban, cf. Josh. 7:15.]

V.

A. Said the exilarch to R. Huna, "It is written, 'And Joshua took Achan the son of Zerah and the silver and the mantle and the wedge of gold and his sons and his daughters and his oxen and his asses and his sheep and his tent and all that he had' (Josh. 7:24). While he had sinned, how had his sons and daughters sinned?"

B.   He said to him, "And by the same reasoning, we must ask, If he had sinned, how had all Israel sinned?

C.   "It is written, 'And all Israel with him' (Josh. 7:24).

D.   "But [Joshua took all Israel to the execution] in order to impose his rule on them, and here too it was for the same purpose. [But they were not in fact executed.]"

VI.

A.   "And they burned them with fire and stoned them with stones" (Josh. 7:25):

B.   By two modes [of inflicting the death penalty]?

C.   Said Rabina, "What was suitable for burning was burned, what was suitable for stoning was stoned."

VII.

A.   "And I saw among the spoil a goodly mantle of Shinar and two hundred shekels of silver" (Josh. 7:21):

B.   Rab said, "It was [Shachter:] a silk mantle."

C.   Samuel said, "It was a cloak dyed with alum."

VIII.

A.   "And they laid them down before the Lord" (Josh. 7:23):

B.   Said R. Nahman, "He came and threw them down before the Lord. He said, 'Lord of the world, on account of these will [as many people as constitute] a majority of the great sanhedrin [thirty-six of seventy-one] be put to death?

C.   "For it is written, 'And the men of Ai smote of them about thirty six' (Josh. 7:5)."

D.   And it has been taught on Tannaite authority,

E.   "It was actually thirty-six," the words of R. Judah.

F.   Said to him R. Nehemiah, "Were they thirty six? And is it not stated, 'about thirty six'? But this refers to Jair, son of Manasseh, who was reckoned as equivalent in value to the majority of a sanhedrin."

IX.

A.   Said R. Nahman said Rab, "What is the sense of the verse of Scripture, 'The poor uses entreaties, but the rich answers insolently' (Prov. 18:23)?

B.   "'The poor uses entreaties' refers to Moses.

C.   "'The rich answers insolently' refers to Joshua."

D.   What is the scriptural basis for that view?

E.   Should we say that it is because it is written, "And they laid them down before the Lord" (Josh. 7:23), R. Nahman said "He came and threw them down before the Lord"?

F.   Phineas did it that way, for it is written, "Then Phineas stood up and laid out prayer, and so the plague was stayed" (Ps. 106:30), and R. Eleazar said, "It is not said, 'And he prayed,' but 'And he laid out prayer,' teaching that he behaved contentiously with his creator.

G.   "He came and cast [Zimri and Cozbi, Num. 25:7ff.] before the omnipresent, and said before him, 'Lord of the world, on account of these should twenty-four thousand Israelites fall?'

H.   "For it is written, 'And those that died by the plague were twenty-four thousand' (Num. 25:9)."

I.   But [it derives] from the following [that Joshua spoke in an insolent way,] "[And Joshua said, Alas, O Lord,] why have you brought this people over the Jordan" (Josh. 7:7).

J.   Moses also spoke in that way, "Why have you dealt ill with this people?" (Ex. 5:22).

K.   Rather, [proof derives] from here: "Would that we had been content to dwell beyond the Jordan" (Josh. 7:7)!

X.

A.   "And the Lord said to Joshua, Get you up" (Josh. 7:10):

B.   R. Shila expounded this verse, "Said the Holy one blessed be he to him, 'Your [sin] is more weighty than theirs. For I commanded, "And it shall be when you have passed over the Jordan you shall set up [these stones]" (Deut. 27:4), but you went a distance of sixty miles [to Gerizim and Ebal after crossing the Jordan before setting them up].'"

C.   After he had gone out, Rab appointed an Amora [to deliver his message to those assembled], and interpreted [matters in this way]: "'As the Lord commanded Moses his servant, so did Moses command Joshua, and so did Joshua; he left nothing undone of all that the Lord had commanded Moses' (Josh. 11:15).

D.   "What then do the words, 'Get you up' (Josh. 7:10) mean?

E.   "He said to him, 'You were the one who caused them [to sin]' [Shachter: p. 289, n. 3: by forbidding them the spoil of Jericho].

F.   "So [God] said to him in regard to Ai, 'And you shall do to Ai and her king as you did to Jericho and her king, [only the spoil thereof and the cattle thereof shall you take as a prey].' (Josh. 8:2) [But Joshua was not to proclaim a ban of herem on Ai, as he had done on Jericho]."

XI.

A.   "And it came to pass when Joshua was by Jericho that he lifted up his eyes and looked ... And he said, No, but I am captain of the host of the Lord, I am now come. And Joshua fell on his face to the earth and bowed down" (Josh. 5:13-14):

B.   How did he do this? And has not R. Yohanan said, "It is forbidden for someone to greet his fellow by night, for we take account of the possibility that it might be a shade"? [So how did Joshua greet the man and talk with him?]

C.   That case is different, for [the man] had said to him, "I am captain of the host of the Lord, I am now come ..." [thus identifying himself].

D.   But maybe he was lying?

E.   We have a tradition that [a being such as this] will not express the Name of heaven in vain.

F.   [44B] [The stranger] said to him, "Last night you neglected the daily whole offering of the evening and now you have neglected the study of Torah. [Shachter, p. 289, n. 10: The conversation took place during the night when fighting was at a standstill, and they should have been studying the law.]

G.   "On which account have you come?" [said Joshua.]

H.   He said to him, "I have now come [on account of your failure to study Torah]."

I.   Forthwith: "And Joshua lodged that night in the midst of the vale (EMEQ)" (Josh. 5:13).

J.   And R. Yohanan said "This teaches that he spent the night in the depths (OMEQ) of the law."

K.   Said Samuel bar Onia in the name of Rab, "Study of the Torah is more important than offering the daily whole-offerings.

L.   "For it is said, 'I have now come ...' (Josh. 5:13)."

XII.

A.   Said Abayye to R. Dimi, "How in the West do you apply this verse: 'Go not forth hastily to strife, for what will you do in the end of it, when your neighbor has put you to shame. Debate your cause with your neighbor, but do not reveal the secrets of another' (Prov. 25:8-9)?"

B.   [He said to him,] "When the Holy One, blessed be he, said to him, 'Go and tell Israel, An Amorite was your father, and a Hittite was your mother' (Ez. 16:3), the [Shachter:] intercessory spirit [Gabriel] said before the Holy One, blessed be he, 'Lord of the world, if Abraham and Sarah come and stand before them, will you speak this way to them and humiliate them?

C.   """Debate your cause with your neighbor, but do not reveal the secret of another!"""

D.   And does [Gabriel] have so much freedom [to speak to God in this way]?

E.   Indeed so, for said R. Yose b. R. Hanina, "He bears three names: intercessor, sealer, and locker -- intercessor, because he intercedes and argues against the Most High, sealer, because he seals off the sins of Israel, locker, because once he has closed [discourse on those sins], no one again can reopen discourse about them."

F.   "Had you prepared your prayer before your trouble came" (Job 36:19):

G.   Said R. Eleazar, "A person should always get his prayer ready for trouble, for had Abraham not gotten his prayer for trouble ready between Beth El and Ai [Gen. 12:8] not a single one of (the wicked of) Israel should have been left as a remnant and survivor [in the time of Joshua, when the battle of Ai was fought]."

H.   R. Simeon b. Laqish said, "Whoever puts forth great effort in prayer down below will have none to oppose him up above."

I.   R. Yohanan said, "A person should always seek mercy that all [the heavenly beings] may strengthen his power, so that he will not have opposition up above."

XIII.

A.   And how do we know that his confession achieved atonement for him [M. 6:2C]?

B.   Our rabbis have taught on Tannaite authority:

C.   And how do we know that his confession achieved atonement for him?

D.   For it is said, "And Joshua said, Why have you troubled us? The Lord will trouble you this day"] (Josh. 7:25).

XIV.

A.   "This day you are troubled, but you will not be troubled in the world to come" [M. 6:2C].

B.   And it is written, "And the sons of Zerah are Zimri, Ethan, Heman, Calcol, Darda, five in all" (1 Chr. 2:6).

C.   What is the sense of "five in all"?

D.   They are five in all destined for the world to come [cf. T. San. 9:5D-F].

E.   Here it is Zimri, but elsewhere Achan [Josh. 7:24].

F.   Rab and Samuel:

G.   One said, "His name was Achan, and why was he called Zimri? Because he acted like Zimri."

H.   The other said, 'His name was Zimri, and why was he called Achan? Because he [Shachter:] wound the sins of Israel about them like a serpent [Achan = snake in Greek, _echidna_]."

XV.

A.   And if he does not know how to confess ... R. Judah says ... so as to clear themselves [M. 6:2D-F]:

B.   And why not let them clear themselves?

C.   It is so as not to discredit the court and the witnesses.

XVI.

A.   Our rabbis have taught on Tannaite authority:

B.   There was the case of a man who went out to be executed. He said, "If I have committed this sin, then let my death not be atonement for all my sins. But if I did not commit this sin, let my death be atonement for all my sins, and the court and all Israel are guiltless, but let the witnesses against me not enjoy forgiveness forever."

C.   Now when sages heard this statement, they said, "It is not possible to bring him back, because the verdict had already been decreed. But let him be put to death, and let [Shachter] the chain [of responsibility] ever hang on the neck of the witnesses" [T. San. 9:5C].

D.   It is self-evident [that he cannot by his confession retract the court's decree], for he surely has not got the power to do so.

E.   It is indeed necessary to indicate that fact, to deal with a case in which the witnesses retract.

F.   But if the witnesses retract, what difference does it make?

G.   Once a witness has made his statement, he cannot then go and retract and make some other statement.

H.   It is necessary to deal with a case in which [the witnesses give a reason for what they have said, as in the case of Baya the tax collector]. [Shachter, pp. 292-3, n. 6: In the case in question he had denounced the tax defaulters to the Government, an act which, of course, aroused the enmity of the people. According to Rashi, the subject matter of the text is connected with this name as follows: The funeral of the said collector coincided with that of a very pious man, but accidentally the coffins were exchanged, so that the honor intended for the Rabbi was paid to the other, and vice versa. An explanation of the happening was given by the Rabbi in a dream to one of his pupils who was disturbed at the occurrence, and he also informed him that severe punishment lay in store for Simeon b. Shetah in the world to come for the neglect of his duty in tolerating eighty women in Ashkelon guilty of sorcery. Simeon, on being informed about it, took a serious view of the matter and had them executed. The relatives of these women, however, inflamed with a passion for revenge, plotted against his son, charging him with a capital crime, as a result of which he was sentenced to death. On his way to the place of execution the condemned man protested his innocence so vehemently that even the witnesses were moved to admit the falsity of their evidence, giving as ground for their former act their feelings of enmity against Simeon b. Shetah. Yet their latter statement was not accepted, according to the law expounded in the text, that a witness is not to be believed when he withdraws a former statement.]

The Mishnah's reference to Achan explains why the former of the Talmud has developed a sizable conglomerate of materials on that subject.

6:3

A. [When] he was four cubits from the place of stoning, they remove his clothes.

B. "In the case of a man, they cover him up in front, and in the case of a woman, they cover her up in front and behind," the words of R. Judah.

C. And sages say, "A man is stoned naked, but a woman is not stoned naked."

I.

A. [45A] Our rabbis have taught on Tannaite authority:

B. ["When he was four cubits from the place of stoning, they remove his clothes.]

C. "In the case of a man, they cover him up in front [M. 7:3A-B] in part, and in the case of a woman, in front and in back in part.

D. "For a woman is wholly subject to licentious thoughts," the words of R. Judah [T. adds: which he said in the name of R. Eliezer].

E. And sages say, "A man is stoned naked, but a woman is not stoned naked" [M. 7:3C] [T. San. 9:6B-D].

F. What is the scriptural basis for the view of rabbis?

G. Scripture says, "And stone him" (Lev. 24:14).

H. What is the sense of "him"?

I. If I maintain, "him" but not "her," is it not written, "You shall bring forth that man or that woman" (Deut. 17:5)?

J. But the sense must be him without clothing, but her with clothing.

K. R. Judah says, "'... him' -- without his clothing, and there is no difference between a man and a woman [in this regard]. [Shachter, p. 294, n. 1: Since the emphatic word, 'him,' serves for one exclusion, that of clothes, it cannot serve as excluding women from that requirement.]"

II.

A. Does this then imply that rabbis take account of licentious thoughts, while R. Judah does not?

B. Lo, we have heard the traditions in exact reverse, for so we have learned in the Mishnah:

C. And a priest grabs her clothes. If they tear, they tear, and if they are ripped up, they are ripped up. He does so until he bares her breast. And he tears her hair apart [Num. 5:18]. R. Judah says, "If she had pretty breasts, he did not let them show, and if she had pretty hair, he did not pull it apart" [M. Sot. 1:4E-G].

D. Said Rabbah, "The reason for the other rule is this: the woman may go forth vindicated in court, and [if beforehand they saw her nude] the junior priests will lust after her. In the present case, lo, the woman is stoned. [No one takes account of necrophilia.]"

E. And should you maintain that by looking at her nude, the men will think lustful thoughts about some other woman [which we should want to forestall], has not Rabbah stated, "We have learned that the sexual desire is aroused only by what the eyes actually see."

F. Said Raba, "[Shall we then say that] the statement by R. Judah contradicts another statement of R. Judah, while the statement of rabbis at hand does not contradict another statement of rabbis? [Surely not!]"

G. Rather, said Raba, "The statement of R. Judah does not contradict another statement of R. Judah, as we have just explained, and the statement of rabbis likewise does not contradict another statement of rabbis.

H. "Here what is the scriptural basis [for rabbis' view that one must humiliate the woman, even if she is not unclean]? 'So that all women may be taught not to do after your lewdness' (Ez. 23:48). [Accordingly, there is no consideration shown to the accused woman.] But in that other instance, [namely, stoning the woman to death], you have no greater warning than that."

L. Now should you wish to propose that both be done to her [namely, humiliation as well as stoning],

J. said R. Nahman said Rabbah bar Abbuha, "Said Scripture, 'You shall love your neighbor as yourself' (Lev. 19:18). Select for him a praiseworthy form of death [and do not needlessly humiliate him in the process]."

K. May I propose that Tannaite authorities differ with regard to the view of R. Nahman?

L. No, all parties concur with the view of R. Nahman. But here the dispute at hand is that one authority [rabbis] holds the position that humiliation is worse than the pain of death, and the other party [Judah] holds that the pain of death is worse than humiliation.

Unit I provides a scriptural basis for the Mishnah-paragraph's rule, and unit II then compares the present rulings of the named authorities with positions taken by them in a parallel case.

6:4A-G

A. The place of stoning was twice the height of a man.

B. One of the witnesses would push him over from the hips, so [hard] that he turned upward [in his fall].

C. He turned him over on his hips again [to see whether he had died].

D. [If] he had died thereby, that sufficed.

E. If not, the second [witness] would take a stone and put it on his heart.

F. [If] he died thereby, it sufficed.

G. And if not, stoning him is [the duty] of all Israelites, as it is said, "The hand of the witnesses shall be first upon him to put him to death, and afterward the hand of all the people" (Deut. 17:7).

I.

A. It has been taught on Tannaite authority:

B. **And with his own height, lo, the place of stoning was three heights of a man [T. San. 9:6F].**

C. Do we require such a height? And an objection was raised on the basis of the following:

D. [It is all the same whether one digs a pit, a trench, cavern, ditches, or channels: he is liable. Why then is it written, A pit (Ex. 21:33)]?

E. Just as a pit [under discussion] is one which is [sufficiently deep] to cause death, namely, ten handbreadths in depth, so anything which is [sufficiently deep] to cause death will be at least ten handbreadths in depth [M. B.Q. 5:5F-H].

F. "[The reason that three times a human being's height is required here], "said R. Nahman said Rabbah bar Abbuha, "is that Scripture has said, 'You will love your neighbor as yourself' (Lev. 19:18), [meaning,] select for him a pleasant form of death [and do not inflict needless suffering]."

G. If so, let it be even higher?

H. That would cause disfigurement [of the corpse].

II.

A. One of the witnesses would push him over [from the hips] [M. 6:4B]:

B. Our rabbis have taught:

C. How do we know that [the death penalty is executed] by throwing someone down?

D. Scripture says, "And he shall be cast down" (Ex. 19:13).

E. And how do we know [that the death penalty is executed] by stoning?

F. Scripture says, "He shall be stoned" (Ex. 19:13) [Cf. Deut. 22:24].

G. And how do we know that [it is executed] both by stoning and by throwing down?

H. Scripture says, "Stoning, he shall be stoned or thrown down" (Ex. 19:13).

I. And how do we know that if he died after being thrown down, the matter is accomplished?

J. Scripture says, "...or cast down" (Ex. 19:13).

K. And how do we know that that is to be done in the generations to come?

L.   [45B] Scripture says, "And stoning, he shall be stoned" (Ex. 19:13).

III.

A.   <u>And if not, the second witness would take a stone [and puts it on his heart] [M. 6:4E]</u>:

B.   Takes it? [All by himself?!] And has it not been taught on Tannaite authority:

C.   R. Simeon b. Eleazar says, "There was a stone there, [a load so heavy that] it was a burden for two to carry. One would take it and put it on his heart. If he died thereby, it sufficed" [T. San. 9:6G-H].

D.   But from your viewpoint, the cited passage poses a problem, for it states that while [it was a load so heavy that] it was a burden for two to carry,

E.   nonetheless, one takes it and puts it on his heart.

F.   But the point is that he lifts it up with his friend's help and he himself throws it, so that it may drop with force.

IV.

A.   <u>And if not, stoning him is the duty of all Israelites [M. 6:4G]</u>:

B.   But has it not been taught on Tannaite authority:

C.   It was never necessary for someone to do it a second time.

D.   Did I say that anyone did it? I said that if necessary, [that is how it would be done].

E.   Said a Master, "A stone was there...! But has it not been taught on Tannaite authority:

F.   All the same are the stone with which [a person] is stoned, the tree on which he is hung, the sword with which he is killed, and the scarf with which he is strangled -- all of them are buried with him [T. San. 9:8A II]. [So how can we say that a particular stone was used regularly for this purpose?]

G.   The sense is that they make ready and bring others to take their place.

H.   They are buried with him?

I.   But has it not been taught on Tannaite authority:

J.   They are not buried with him [cf. T. San. 9:8A]?

K.   Said R. Pappa, "What is the sense of 'with him?' In the area affected by his [corpse]."

V.

A.   Said Samuel, "If [after they have testified], the hand of the witnesses should be cut off, the condemned is exempt from the penalty of stoning.

B.   "What is the scriptural basis for this rule? We require that 'the hand of the witness shall be first upon him to put him to death' (Deut. 17:7), and [that condition] would not be [fulfilled in the present case]."

C.   In that case, how would you deal with the testimony of witnesses who are without hands to begin with? In such a case would they be ineligible to testify?

D.   That case is different, for Scripture has said, "The hand of the witnesses" (Deut. 17:7), with the sense of the "hand that they had already possess." [Shachter, p. 1 297, n. 12: But if they lack hands at the outset they are eligible to testify.]

E.   An objection was raised [based on the following passage]:

F.   [He whose trial ended and who fled and was brought back before the same court --
      they do not reverse the judgment concerning him and retry him].

G.   In any situation in which two get up and say, "We testify concerning Mr. So-and-so
      that his trial ended in the court of such-and-such, with Mr. So-and-so and Mr.
      So-and-so as the witnesses against him,"

H.   lo, this one is put to death [M. Mak. 1:10A-D]. [Shachter, p. 297, n. 14: He is
      executed even in the absence of the original witnesses. This proves that the
      injunction in Deut. 17:7 is not indispensable but only desirable when possible.]

I.   Samuel interpreted the case to speak of a situation in which the witnesses were the
      ones who had originally testified.

J.   But do we require that every verse be carried out just as it is written?

K.   And has it not been taught on Tannaite authority:

L.   "He who killed him shall surely be put to death, he is a murderer" (Num. 35:21).

M.   I know only that he is to be put to death with the mode of execution that is stated in
      Scripture in that regard.

N.   How do we know that, if you cannot put him to death in the mode of execution
      prescribed by Scripture, you may put him to death in any other means by which you
      can do so?

O.   Scripture says, "He who killed him shall surely be put to death" -- by any means.

P.   But that case is different because Scripture has made it explicit, "He shall surely be
      put to death...."

Q.   Then let us construct an argument from that case [Shachter, p. 298, n. 6: that just
      as there, where he should be decapitated, he is nevertheless executed by any means
      possible, so here too, where he should be hurled down by the hands of the witnesses,
      he is still to be executed even if their hands have been cut off].

R.   It is because you have references to "murderer" and "avenger of blood," that is, two
      verses of Scripture that serve to make the same point, and in any case where two
      verses of Scripture serve to make the same point, one cannot derive [any further
      arguments from them].

S.   As to the murderer, it is just as we said now.

T.   As to the avenger of the blood, what is [the source of the same lesson]?

U.   It is as it has been taught on Tannaite authority:

V.   "The avenger of blood shall himself put the murderer to death" (Num. 35:19).

W.   It is the religious duty that the avenger of the blood do it.

X.   But how do we know that if there is no avenger of the blood, the court appoints an
      avenger of the blood for [the deceased]?

Y.   As it is said, "When he meets him" (Num. 35:19) -- under all circumstances.
      [Shachter, p. 298, n. 12: This shows that the provisions of an avenging kinsman are
      not limited to the precise statement of the Bible.]

Z.   Said Mar Kashisha, son of R. Hisda, to R. Ashi, "And do we not require that the
      verse of Scripture be carried out in exactly the manner in which it is written?

AA.   "And have we not learned in the Mishnah:

BB. [If] one of them was maimed in the hand, lame, dumb, blind, or deaf,

CC. he is not declared a rebellious and incorrigible son,

DD. since it is said, "Then his father and his mother will lay hold of him" (Deut. 21:20) -- so they are not maimed in their hands;

EE. "and bring him out" -- so they are not lame;

FF. "and they shall say" -- so they are not dumb;

GG. "This is our son" -- so they are not blind;

HH. "He will not obey our voice" -- so they are not deaf [M. San. 8:4 F-L].

II. "What is the reason for this rule?

JJ. "It is not because we have to carry out the verse exactly as it is written?"

KK. No, that case is different, because the entire verse of Scripture is superfluous [and so has to be carried out literally, but in other cases that would not be the rule].

LL. Come and take note:

MM. If the apostate city does not have a street [to which to carry out the goods of the people], it cannot be condemned as an apostate city," the words of R. Ishmael.

NN. R. Aqiba says, "If it has no street, they make a street for it [for that purpose]."

OO. The dispute up to this point is only that one authority maintains that we require the street to be there to begin with, and the other authority takes the view that a street made just now falls into the category of one that has been there from the beginning. But all parties surely concur that we require that the verse be carried out just as it is written.

PP. It is a [principle subject to] Tannaite dispute.

QQ. For we have learned in the Mishnah:

RR. [With respect to Lev. 14:14, which has the priest daub blood on the thumb, big toe, or right ear of the leper as part of the rite of purification,] if the leper did not have a thumb, big toe, or right ear, he can never have purification.

SS. R. Eliezer says, "One puts the blood on their place, and has carried out his obligation."

TT. R. Simeon says, "If he put it on the left side [instead of on the right], he has carried out his obligation" [M. Neg. 14:9E-G].

The Talmud works its way through the Mishnah-paragraph's statements, unit I takes up M. 6:4A, unit II, M. 6:4B, unit III, M. 6:4E. unit IV, M. 6:4G. Then unit V introduces a speculative question, invited by the topic of the Mishnah-paragraph but hardly demanded by it.

6:4H-M

H. "All those who are stoned are hung on a tree [afterward]," the words of R. Eliezer.

I. And sages say, "Only the blasphemer and the one who worships an idol are hung."

J.   "As to a man, they hang him facing the people, and as to a woman, her face is toward the tree," the words of R. Eliezer.

K.   And sages say, "The man is hung, but the woman is not hung."

L.   Said to them R. Eliezer, "And did not Simeon b. Shetah hang women in Ashkelon?"

M.   They said to him, "He hung eighty women, and they do not judge even two on a single day."

I.

A.   Our rabbis have taught on Tannaite authority:

B.   "And if he be put to death, then you shall hang him on a tree" (Deut. 21:22).

C.   Might one not think that all those who are put to death are hung?

D.   Scripture states, "For he is hanged because of a curse against God" (Deut. 21:23).

E.   "Just as the one who blasphemes [is executed] by stoning, so all who are subject to execution by stoning [are hung]," the words of R. Eliezer [=M.6:4H].

F.   Sages say, "Just as the blasphemer is one who has denied God's rule, so all who have denied God's rule [are hung]," [=M.6:4I].

G.   What is at issue?

H.   Rabbis interpret scripture in accord with the rule of the general and the particular, and R. Eliezer interprets it in accord with the rule of extension and limitation.

I.   Rabbis interpret scripture in accord with the rule of the general and the particular, thus:

J.   "And if he be put to death, then you shall hang him" (Deut. 21:22) constitutes a general rule.

K.   "Because of a curse against God" (Deut. 21:23) constitutes a particularization [of that general rule].

L.   Now if the two clauses had been stated side by side, we should have reached the conclusion that the general rule is limited to what is made explicit in the particularization [of the rule].

M.   So only this one [who has cursed God] but no one else [would have been encompassed]. [46A] But seeing that they are given separately from one another, the formulation serves to encompass one who commits idolatry, for such a one is parallel to [the blasphemer] in every aspect.

N.   And R. Eliezer interprets the passage in accord with the rule of extension and limitation, thus:

O.   "And if he be put to death, then you shall hang him" (Deut. 21:22) constitutes an extension.

P.   "Because of a curse against God" (Deut. 21:23) then constitutes a limitation on the foregoing extension.

Q.   If the two phrases had been stated side by side, they would together have served to encompass only the one who is guilty of idolatry, who falls into the same category in every aspect.

R.   But seeing that the two are given separately from one another, the construction serves to encompass all others who are put to death by stoning.

II.

A.   As to a man, they hang him ... [M. 6:4J].

B.   What is the scriptural basis for the position of rabbis?

C.   Scripture states, "And you shall hang him" (Deut. 21:22) -- him but not her.

D.   And R. Eliezer? "Him" -- without his clothing.

E.   And rabbis? That is indeed the case. But Scripture has said, "And if a man has committed a sin" (Deut. 21:22 -- a man but not a woman.

F.   And how does R. Eliezer interpret the phrase "And if a man has committed a sin"?

G.   Said R. Simeon b. Laqish, "In his view that serves to exclude the stubborn and rebellious son [meaning that a man may be dealt with in this way, but not a son who has not reached manhood. Furthermore, a son cannot be declared rebellious once he has reached manhood at thirteen].

H.   But has it not been taught on Tannaite authority:

I.   "A stubborn and rebellious son first is stoned and then hanged," the words of R. Eliezer. [This excludes Simeon's thesis on Eliezer's reading of the cited verse.]

J.   Rather, said R. Nahman bar Isaac, "It serves [in Eliezer's view] to encompass a stubborn and rebellious son.

K.   "What is the scriptural basis for this view? Scripture has said, 'And if a man has committed a sin' -- a man and not a son.

L.   "Sin -- referring to one who is put to death on account of his [already committed] sin -- excluding a stubborn and rebellious son, who is put to death on account of what he will become [not what he now has done].

M.   "Accordingly, you have one exclusionary phrase after another such phrase, and when there is one exclusionary phrase after another such phrase, it serves only to encompass [what the two phrases on their face would exclude. Hence the stubborn and rebellious son is subject to the stated law, just as Eliezer maintains in the Tannaite teaching.]"

III.

A.   Said to them R. Eliezer, "And did not Simeon b. Shetah hang women in Ashkelon?" [M. 6:4L]

B.   Said R. Hisda, "That teaching applies only when there are two different modes of inflicting the death penalty, but if it is a single mode of inflicting the death penalty, they do judge [any number of capital cases in a single day].

C.   But lo, the case of Simeon b. Shetah involved a single mode of inflicting the death penalty, and lo, they have said to him, that they judge only [one capital case a day].

D.   Rather, if the matter was stated, this is how it was stated:

E.   [Said R. Hisda.] "that teaching applies only in the case of a single form of the death penalty that looks like two different forms of the death penalty.

F.   "What would such a case be? For example, if there were two transgressions [punishable by death].

G.   "But if it is a single form of the death penalty and a single transgression, they do judge [any number of capital cases on one day]."

H.   R. Adda b. Ahbah objected, **"They do not judge two [capital] cases in one day, even an adulterer and an adulteress [T. San. 7:2A]."**

I.   R. Hisda interpreted this passage [H] to speak of the daughter of a priest and her lover [executed by different means], or of the daughter of a priest and the witnesses who come to prove that the witnesses against her are conspiratorial perjurers [in which, again the witnesses and the girl are punished in different ways].

IV.

A.   It has been taught on Tannaite authority:

B.   R. Eliezer b. Jacob says, "I heard that a court may inflict floggings and penalties not in accord with the law of the Torah.

C.   "But this is not so as to violate the teachings of the Torah, but so as to establish a fence around the Torah.

D.   "And there is the precedent concerning one who rode a horse on the Sabbath in the time of the Greeks, and they brought him to court and stoned him, not because it was appropriate, but because the times required it.

E.   "And there was another precedent concerning a man who had sexual relations with his wife under a date tree, and they brought him to court and flogged him, not because it was appropriate, but because the times required it.

Unit I takes M. up M. 5:3H-I, providing the expected scriptural basis for the Mishnah's rulings. Unit II moves on to M. 6:4J and does the same. Units III and IV deal with the extra-legal penalties imposed by Simeon b. Shetah, M. 6:4M. So the entire composition is constructed around the Mishnah's statements.

6:4N-S, 6:5-6

N.   How do they hang him?

O.   They drive a post into the ground, and a beam juts out from it, and they tie together his two hands, and thus do they hang him.

P.   R. Yose says, "The post leans against a wall, and then one suspends him the way butchers do it."

Q.   And they untie him forthwith.

R.   And if he is left overnight, one transgresses a negative commandment on his account, as it is said, "His body shall not remain all night on the tree, but you will surely bury him on the same day, for he who is hanged is a curse against God" (Deut. 21:23).

S.   that is to say, On what account has this one been hung? Because he cursed the Name, so the Name of Heaven turned out to be profaned.

M.6:4N-S

A. Said R. Meir, "When a person is distressed, what words does the Presence of God say? As it were: 'My head is in pain, my arm is in pain'.

B. "If thus is the Omnipresent distressed on account of the blood of the wicked when it is shed, how much the more so on account of the blood of the righteous!'"

C. And not this only, have [sages] said, but whoever allows his deceased to stay unburied overnight transgresses a negative commandment.

D. But [if] one kept [a corpse] overnight for its own honor, [e.g.,] to bring a bier for it and shrouds, he does not transgress on its account.

E. And they did not bury [the felon] in the burial grounds of his ancestors.

F. But there were two graveyards made ready for the use of the court, one for those who were beheaded or strangled, and one for those who were stoned or burned.

M. 6:5

A. When the flesh had rotted, they [they do] collect the bones and bury them in their appropriate place.

B. And the relatives [of the felon] come and inquire after the welfare of the judges and of the witness.

C. As if to say, "We have nothing against you, for you judged honestly."

D. [46B] And they did not go into mourning.

E. But they observe a private grief, for grief is only in the heart.

I.

A. Our rabbis have taught on Tannaite authority:

B. Had Scripture stated, "If he has sinned, then you shall hang him," I might have maintained that first the felon is hung, and then he is put to death, just as the government does it.

C. Scripture accordingly says, "And he be put to death, then you shall hang him" (Deut. 21:22).

D. The felon is put to death and afterward hung.

E. How so?

F. They delay matters until close to sunset, then they complete the court process and put him to death, then they hang his body.

G. One person ties him up and then another unties him, so as to carry out the religious duty of hanging [the body].

II.

A. Our rabbis have taught on Tannaite authority:

B. "[Then you shall hang him on] a tree" (Deut. 21:22).

C. May I suppose that that would apply whether the tree is cut down [from the ground] or whether it is attached to the ground?

D. Scripture says, "You shall surely bury him" (Deut. 21:22).

E.   That applies to [a tree] that now lacks only burial, excluding use of one that lacks both felling and burial. [So the tree has to have been cut down before it is used.]

F.   R. Yose says, "It refers to one that lacks only burial, excluding this one, which lacks both uprooting and burial. [Thus the post should not be driven into the ground.]"

G.   And rabbis? They treat uprooting as of no consequence.

III.

A.   That is to say, On what account has this one been hung? Because he cursed the Name [M. 6:4S]:

B.   It has been taught on Tannaite authority:

C.   R. Meir says, ["T.: Why does Scripture say, 'For one who is hanged is cursed by God' (Deut. 21:23)?]

D.   "The matter is comparable to two brothers, who were identical twins in one town. One was made king [over the whole world], and the other joined a gang of thieves.

E.   "[T.: After a while this one who had gone out to join the thieves was caught, and] the king commanded to crucify him on a cross.

F.   "And everyone who saw him said, 'It looks as though the king is being crucified.' The king commanded them to cut him down.

G.   "[T.: Therefore it is said, 'For one who is hanged is a curse of God]." [T. San. 9:7A-E].

IV.

A.   R. Meir said, "[When a person is distressed...]" [M. 6:5A]:

B.   What is the basis [of Meir's interpretation of the word 'a curse of ...' (QLLT)]?

C.   Said Abayye, "It is as if he said, 'It is not light' (QL LYT)."

D.   Said Raba to him, "If so, what he should have said, is, 'My head is <u>heavy</u> for me, my arm is <u>heavy</u> for me.'"

E.   Rather, said Raba, "It is like one who said, 'Everything is light for me (QYL LY).'" [Shachter, p. 306, n. 11: Euphemistically for 'heavy,' as no one is inclined to speak evil in connection with his own person.]"

F.   But the word under discussion [a curse of ...] is needed to make its own point [and is not available for exegetical purposes].

G.   If so, Scriptural should have said, "One who curses." Why state matters as "a curse of ..."?

H.   And might I say that the whole verse serves for that one purpose?

I.   If so, [in line with Raba's view] the passage should have said "lightness of" (QLT). Why [write the word with two L's] (QLLT)? It is to indicate that two [meanings are to be derived from the word].

V.

A.   And not this only have sages said, [but whoever allows his deceased to stay unburied overnight transgresses a negative commandment] [M. 6:5C]:

B.   Said R. Yohanan in the name of R. Simeon b. Yohai, "How on the basis of Scripture do we know that one who keeps his deceased overnight violates a negative commandment? Because Scripture says, 'You shall surely bury him' (Deut. 21:23).

C. "On the basis of the cited verse [we learn that] one who keeps his deceased overnight violates a negative commandment."

D. There are those who say:

E. Said R. Yohanan in the name of R. Simeon b. Yohai, "Where in the Torah do we find an allusion to burial [as the required way of dealing with the deceased]?

F. "Scripture says, 'You shall surely bury him' (Deut. 21:23).

G. "On the basis of the cited verse we derive an indication in the Torah concerning the requirement of burial."

VI.

A. Said King Shapur to R. Hama, "When in the Torah is there proof that one has to bury the deceased?"

B. He remained silent and said nothing.

C. Said R. Aha bar Jacob, "The world is handed over to idiots. He should have said to him, 'For you shall surely bury' (Deut. 21:23) [which surely indicates burial is required]."

D. [But that passage may merely indicate] that one should make a casket [for the deceased].

E. [But it is stated] "You shall surely bury him" (Deut. 21:23).

F. [To King Shapur] that would not have carried [a general] meaning.

G. Then he should have said to him that [Scripture reports that] the righteous are buried.

H. [Shapur] could have said that that was the custom in general.

I. Since the Holy One blessed be he buried Moses [it should have indicated to Shapur that Scripture requires burial].

J. That too was so as not to diverge from accepted practice.

K. Come and take note: "And all Israel shall make lamentation for him and bury him" (1 Kgs. 14:33).

L. That too was so as not to diverge from accepted practice.

M. "They shall not be lamented, nor shall they be buried; they shall be as dung upon the face of the ground" (Jer. 16:4).

N. That too was so as to diverge from accepted practice.

VII.

A. The question was raised: Is burial [performed] for [the purpose of avoiding] disgrace or for [the sake of] atonement?

B. What difference does it make?

C. It would matter in a case in which one said, "I do not wish to be buried."

D. If you say it is to avoid disgrace, he would not have the power [to inflict such a disgrace on his relatives].

E. But if you say it is for the sake of atonement, then he means that he does not want atonement [so even if he is buried, he does not attain forgiveness (Shachter, p. 308, n. 9)].

F. What [then is the purpose]?

G.   Come and take note [of the fact] that the righteous are buried [so the biblical narrative indicates].

H.   Now if you say [that the reason is] to afford atonement, do the righteous need atonement?

I.   Indeed they do, for it is written, "For there is not a righteous man upon earth who does good and sins not" (Qoh. 7:20).

J.   Come and take note:

K.   "And all Israel shall make lamentation for him, and they shall bury him, [for only he of Jeroboam shall come to the grave]" (1 Kgs. 14:13).

L.   Now if you should maintain that it was so that he should have atonement, this proves that the others also should be buried so that they should have atonement.

M.   This one, who was a righteous man, is the one who should have atonement. But this proves that those should not have atonement.

N.   Come and take note: "They shall not be lamented, neither shall they be buried" (Jer. 16:4). [Shachter, p. 309, n. 1: If burial is a means of expiation, why should they too not attain it?]

O.   It is so that they should not have atonement [for their sins].

VIII.

A.   The question was raised: Is the eulogy for the sake of the living or for the sake of the dead?

B.   What difference does it make?

C.   It helps us to deal with a case in which someone said before dying, "Do not pronounce a eulogy for me."

D.   Or it may serve to require the fee for the eulogy to be paid by the heirs, [for they will have to do so if it is for the deceased, but they may dispense with it if it is for their sake].

E.   Come and take note: "And Abraham came [from afar] to mourn for Sarah and to weep for her" (Gen. 23:2).

F.   If you say it is for the honor of the living, then for the honor of Abraham did they hold up Sarah's burial?

G.   Sarah herself wanted it that way so as to honor Abraham on her account.

H.   Come and take note: "And all Israel shall make lamentation for him and they shall bury him" (1 Kgs. 14:13).

I.   If you say it is for the sake of the living, is his family worthy for such honor to be paid on their account?

J.   The righteous want people to be honored on their account.

K.   Come and take note: "They shall not be lamented, nor shall they be buried" (Jer. 16:14).

L.   The righteous do not want evil-doers to be honored on their account.

M.   Come and take note: "You [Zedekiah] shall die in peace and with the burnings of your fathers, the former kings who were before you, so shall they make a burning for you, and they shall lament you, saying, Ah! Lord" (Jer. 34:5).

N. Now if you say that it is for the honor of the living, what difference did they make to him [since Zedekiah would be the last king of Judah]?

O. This is the sense of what he said to him: "Through you will Israel be honored, as they were honored through your fathers."

P. [47A] Come and take note: "In whose eyes a vile person is despised" (Ps. 15:4).

Q. This speaks of Hezekiah, King of Judah, who dragged the bones of his father on a bier of ropes.

R. Now if it is for the sake of the living, why [did he do it]? [Shachter, p. 310, n. 4: Surely he had no right to deprive the living of their due.]

S. It was so that his father might be have atonement.

T. And on account of atonement for his father, did he deprive Israel of honor?

U. The Israelites themselves were pleased to give up honor for the sake of [his atonement].

V. Come and take note: [Judah the Patriarch] said to [his testators], "Do not hold eulogies for me in the various towns [but only before large audiences in cities]."

W. Now if you say that is for the sake of the living, what difference did it make [to Judah the Patriarch]?

X. It was so as to give greater honor to the Israelites [by having large audiences gathered for his sake."]

Y. Come and take note of the following: But if one kept the corpse overnight for its own honor, for example, to bring a bier for it and shrouds, he does not transgress on its account [M. 6:5D].

Z. Is not the sense of "for its honor," "for the honor of the deceased]?

AA. No, it is for the honor of the living.

BB. And for the honor of the living do people keep the deceased overnight?

CC. Indeed so. When the All-Merciful said, "His body shall not remain all night upon the tree" (Deut. 21:22), that rule applies to a case in which it would be humiliating.

DD. But here, where there is no intent to humiliate the corpse, it is not objectionable.

EE. Come and take note: If [a mourner] kept the body overnight for the deceased's honor, to let word get out to the small towns, to bring professional mourners, to bring a casket and shrouds, then he does not violate the rule, for whatever he does is only for the honor of the deceased. [Hence the oration is for the sake of the deceased.]

FF. This is the sense of the passage: Whatever one does for the honor of the living does not constitute a disgrace for the ceased.

GG. Come and take note: R. Meir says, "This is a good sign for the deceased, indicating that penalty is exacted from him in this world when he dies [and not afterward]: that he is not given a eulogy; that he is not buried; that a wild beast drags his carcass; or that it rains on his bier. This would be a good omen for the deceased."

HH. This proves that it is for the sake of the deceased [that the eulogy is spoken].

II. It does indeed prove it.

IV.

A. <u>They did not bury [the felon in the burial grounds of his ancestors]</u> [M. 6:5E-F]:

B. Why such arrangements [as having two burial grounds, M. 6:5F]:

C. It is because people do not bury a wicked person next to a righteous person.

D. For R. Aha bar Hanina said, "How [on the basis of Scripture] do we know that people do not bury a wicked person next to a righteous person? As it is said, 'And it came to pass as they were burying a man that behold, they spied a band and they cast the man into the sepulchre of Elisha, and as soon as the man touched the bones of Elisha he revived and stood up on his feet' (2 Kgs. 13:21). [This was the old prophet of Beth El, so the wicked man was not to be buried with a righteous one (Shachter, p. 311, n. 9)]."

E. Said R. Pappa to him, "But perhaps it was to carry out [the request of Elisha to Elijah], 'Let a double portion of your spirit be upon me' (2 Kgs. 2:9)? [Since Elijah had raised one person from the dead, Elisha wanted to raise two, but he had only raised the son of the Shunamite. Then the desired proof is not at hand.]"

F. He said to him, "If that is the case, what is the sense of the following, that is taught on Tannaite authority:

G. "'He rose on his feet but he did not go home'?"

H. "Then how do you deal with, 'Let a double portion of your spirit be upon me'? Where did he resurrect [two people]?"

I. He said to him, "Said R. Yohanan, 'It is that he healed the leprosy of Naaman, which is accounted as equivalent to death.

J. "'For it is said, "Let her not, I pray you, be as one who is dead"' (Num. 12:12)."

K. And just as they do not bury a wicked person next to a righteous person, so they do not bury a grossly wicked person next to a mildly wicked person.

X.

A. And why not set up four burial grounds [to cover the four modes of execution]?

B. <u>Two burial grounds</u> is what has been learned as the tradition in this case.

XI.

A. Said Ulla said R. Yohanan, "if one [inadvertently] ate forbidden fat, and, [in penance,] set aside an animal for an offering, but [before actually sacrificing the beast] apostasized, and then repented, once the sacrifice has been put off, it has been put off [it is invalidated since apostates cannot offer sacrifices], and remains so. [It cannot now be used for the original, inadvertent sin.]"

B. It has been stated on Amoraic authority along these same lines:

C. Said R. Jeremiah said R. Abbahu said R. Yohanan, "If one [inadvertently] ate forbidden fat and in penance set aside an animal for an offering, but then lost his sanity, and then regained his sanity, once the sacrifice that has been put off, it has been put off [it is invalidated, since the man, when not in command of his senses, cannot bring the offering], and remains so [and cannot now be used for the original, inadvertent sin]."

D. And it is necessary [to have both teachings]. For had we learned only the former, we might have concluded that, because the man himself is responsible, through his own actions, for the sacrifice's being put off, [the animal cannot again be used], but here, where the animal has been set aside in the natural course of events, I might say that it is as if the man who had set it aside was merely sleeping [and in no way bears responsibility for the postponement of the use of the animal in expiation for his sin]. [So the beast may be used.]

E. And if we had learned only the present case, it is because the man has not the power to recover, but in the first case, where the man has the power to revert, one might hold [that the animal has] not [been permanently invalidated].

F. Accordingly, it is necessary to have both rulings.

XII.

A. Said R. Joseph, "We too have learned on Tannaite authority [the same point as has just now been made, namely]:

B. **"If in [the apostate city] there were offerings intended for use on the altar, they are left to die. Things which are consecrated for the upkeep of the house are to be redeemed [T. San. 14:5A-B].**

C. "And in that connection we reflected as follows: Why should they be left to die? If [the inhabitants of the apostate town] are put to death, do they not have atonement? So let the animals [afterward] be offered to the Most High! Then [the reason that they are not offered up] surely is that, once they have been put off [and not offered up, the animals at the moment belonging to the apostate town], they are permanently put off [and may not be offered at all, just as Yohanan has said in the foregoing]."

D. Said Abayye to him, "And do you think that if a wicked person dies in his wicked state, he gains atonement through his death? If he dies in his wicked state, he does not gain atonement through his death.

E. "For R. Shemaiah taught, 'Is it possible [to suppose] that, if a priest's parents left the ways of the community, he should contract corpse uncleanness [in order to bury them, although he otherwise may not contract corpse-uncleanness]?

F. "'Scripture states, 'Among his people,' Lev. 21:2. The rule [that the priest may contract corpse-uncleanness in connection with the burial of his parents] applies to [a parent] who had performed deeds appropriate to his people.' [This would indicate that merely because a person has died, he does not gain expiation for is sins. The parent after death remains a sinner. There has to be penitence.]"

G. Said Raba to [Abayye], "And you will compare the case of one who is put to death in his wicked state to that of one who died in his wicked state? In the case of the one who dies in his wicked state, since he dies in a natural way, he does not have atonement on that account. By contrast, if he is put to death in his wicked state, he does have atonement on that account.

H. "You may know that that is the case, for it is written, 'A psalm of Asaph. O God, the heathen are come into your inheritance, they have defiled your holy temple, they have given the dead bodies of your servants to be food for the fowl of the heaven, the flesh of your saints to the beasts of the earth' (PS. 79:1-2).

I.   "Who are these servants and saints? Is the meaning of 'saints' not those who actually are your saints?

J.   "Those who are referred to as 'your servants' are those who to begin with were liable to be put to death, and, once they have been put to death, are now called 'servants'?"

K.   Said Abayye to [Raba], "Do you propose to compare [47B] those who have been put to death by the government to those who have been put to death by an [Israelite] court?

L.   "As to those who have been put to death by the government, since they have been put to death without a proper trial, [their death] serves as atonement for them.

M.   "But those who have been put to death by an Israelite court, since they have received a proper trial, when they are put to death, [their death] does not serve as atonement for them.

N.   "You may know that that is the case, for we have learned in the Mishnah: They did not bury the felon in the burial grounds of his ancestors [M. 6:5E]. Now if you maintain that once such a one has been put to death, it serves as atonement, then let him be buried [in the family burial plot]."

O.   [He replied] "We require both execution and [shameful] burial [to attain atonement]."

P.   R. Ada bar Ahbah objected, "And they did not go into mourning. But they observe a private grief, for grief is only in the heart [M. 6:6D-E]. Now if you maintain that once [the felon] has been buried [in a shameful manner], that serves as suitable atonement, then let the relatives mourn!"

Q.   [He replied] "We require that the flesh rot [before we concede that there has been expiation of sins], for note that the passage goes on: When the flesh had rotted, they then collect the bones and bury them in their appropriate place [M. 6:6A]."

R.   That is decisive proof of the proposition.

XIII.

A.   R. Ashi said, "At what point do the rites of mourning commence? It is from when the grave is closed with the grave-stone.

B.   "When is atonement achieved? When the body has seen a bit of the pain of the grave.

C.   "Therefore, if [the rites] have been suspended [as in the case of the convicted felon], they are suspended [and not required].

D.   "If so, why must the flesh be consumed [before secondary burial]? [as stated at M. 6:6A]?

E.   "Because to do otherwise is not possible. [One cannot get at the bones before the flesh is destroyed.]"

XIV.

A.   As to the grave of Rab, people would take dirt from it for an attack of fever on the first day.

B. They came and informed Samuel. He said to them, "They do quite properly. It is ordinary dirt, and ordinary dirt does not become forbidden [as something belonging to the dead,] for it is written, 'And he cast the dust thereof on the graves of common people' (2Kgs. 23:6).

C. "The dirt of the grave of ordinary people is compared to idolatry. Just as, when an idol is attached to the ground, it is not forbidden, for it is written, 'You shall utterly destroy all the places where the nations that you are to dispossess served their gods, upon the high mountains' (Deut. 12:2), meaning, gods upon the high mountains, but not mountains which themselves serve as their gods,

D. "so here too what is attached [to the ground] is not forbidden."

E. An objection was raised [based on the following]: He who digs a grave for his father and who then went and buried him elsewhere -- lo, this one [who dug the grave] may never be buried in [that grave]. [The grave was prepared for a particular corpse and cannot be used for someone else. It is then assumed that the dirt of the grave is subject to the same prohibition and may not be used for any other purpose. That would represent an objection to Samuel, C-D].

F. Here, with what sort of case do we deal? With a grave that is built up [and is not part of the ground at all. The reason the grave is prohibited at E is simply that it was prepared by the man for his father. It would be disrespectful to use it for some other purpose.]

G. Come and take note: A new grave [not assigned to any particular corpse] is permitted [to be used] for benefit. But if an abortion has been placed there, it is forbidden [to be used] for benefit. [And the parallel is that even natural soil is forbidden in this context (Shachter, p. 316, n. 1)].

H. Here too we deal with a grave that is built up [and not part of the ground at all].

I. Come and take note.

J. It comes out that one may say, there are three kinds of graves: a grave that is discovered, a grave that is known, and a grave that inconveniences the public.

K. A grave that is discovered -- one may empty it out. [Once] one has emptied it out, its place is clean, and it is permitted for benefit.

L. A grave that is known -- one may not empty it out. [If] one has emptied it out, it is unclean, and it is forbidden [to be used] for benefit [T. Dh. 15:9].

M. A grave that inconveniences the public -- one may empty it out. Once one has emptied it out, its place is clean, but it is forbidden for benefit.
    [This proves that natural soil can also be forbidden (Shachter, p. 316, n. 11)].

N. Here too we deal with a grave that is built up.

O. But is it permitted to empty out a grave that is discovered? It may be that a neglected corpse is buried there, and a neglected corpse takes possession of the place in which it is buried.

P. The case of a neglected corpse is different, because it is subject to public knowledge [once it is found and buried].

XV.

A. It has been stated on Amoraic authority:

11018

B. He who weaves a shroud for a corpse --

C. Abayye said, "It is forbidden [to use for some other purpose]."

D. Raba said, "It is permitted.

E. Abayye said, "It is forbidden [to use for some other purpose, because] designating [an object for a given purpose] matters. [Shachter, p. 316, n. 15: Mere designation for the dead subjects it to the same law as though it has actually been employed for the purpose]."

F. Raba said, "It is permitted, [because] designating [an object for a given purpose] does not matter."

G. What is the scriptural basis for the view of Abayye?

H. He establishes an analogy based on the use of the word "there" both here [in connection with the deceased, "And Miriam died there and was buried there" (Num. 20:1)] and there, in the case of the heifer whose neck was broken [on account of the discovery of a neglected corpse, Deut. 21:4, "And he shall break the heifer's neck there"].

I. Just as in the case of the rite of the heifer whose neck is to be broken, once the act of designation [for the present purpose] has taken place, a prohibition [affects whatever has been designated, e.g., the heifer], so in the case of what is designated [for the dead, the mere act of designation] imposes a prohibition [so that what is designated for the dead cannot be used for some other purpose.]

J. And Raba derives the meaning of the word, "there," [used with reference to Miriam, Num. 20:1], from the meaning of the use of the word "there" in connection with idolatry. [In the latter case it is as follows: "You shall surely destroy all the places there where the nations which you are to dispossess serve their gods" (Deut. 12:2).] Just as, in the case of what is used for idolatry, mere designation for that purpose does not impose a prohibition on what is designated, so here the mere act of designation does not impose a prohibition.

K. And what is the reason that Raba does not derive the sense of the word from the case of the heifer whose neck is to be broken?

L. He will say to you, "[48A] We derive the rule governing objects that are actually used, and not merely designated, from the rule covering equivalent objects [and objects designated for idolatry are not affected by the designation, but are affected only by actual use], so we must exclude the case of the heifer whose neck is to be broken, which itself [by mere designation] falls into the category of what is sanctified."

M. And what is the reason that Abayye does not derive the sense of the word from the case of idolatry?

N. He will say to you, "We derive the rule for ordinary usage from a matter of ordinary usage, and we do not derive the rule for ordinary usage from idolatry, which is uncommon. [Ordinary usage involves what is permitted by law, and that would include both the preparation of shrouds for the dead and also the rite of breaking the heifer's neck, but it would not include idolatry.]" [Shachter, p. 317, n. 7: Mere designation in connection with idolatry does not impose a prohibition, because, since it is abnormal (forbidden), one may repent and never use it for the purpose. But in the case of the other two, if permitted (and certainly if obligatory), once they are designated for that purpose they will certainly be used, unless unforeseen circumstances intervene. Therefore the mere designation suffices to give them the same status as though they had actually been used.]

O. An objection was raised on the basis of the following:

P. A head-wrap, which is susceptible to become unclean with midras-uncleanness [imparted through pressure of standing, lying, or sitting upon an object by a person afflicted with the modes of uncleanness specified at Lev. 15], and which [a woman] put on a scroll [and so will not be used for sitting, lying, or standing, by such a person and therefore serves a different purpose entirely] is then rendered insusceptible of midras-uncleanness [by the shift in the use to which the object is put] but falls into the category of susceptibility to uncleanness [on account of corpse-uncleanness or other uncleanness]. [The head-wrap will no longer serve for sitting, so it loses its former susceptibility. But it remains susceptible to other forms of uncleanness.] [M. Kel. 28:5A]. [What this proves is that designation of an object for a given purpose does matter, and that supports Abayye's view and contradicts Raba's.]

Q. I [Raba] may reply, [That is the case if she actually assigned it and also put it on [tied it around] the scroll.

R. Why both assigning it and tying it around the scroll? [Why not merely the former of the two actions?]

S. The answer is in accord with what R. Hisda said.

T. For R. Hisda said, "As to a scarf which one designated for use in tying up phylacteries, if one tied up phylacteries in it, it is forbidden to tie up coins in it. If one designated it for that purpose but did not tie anything up in it, or tied something up in it but did not designate it for that purpose, [it is permitted for to use it for coins].

U. As to the position of Abayye, who holds that an act of designation matters, if one designated it for use for phylacteries, even though he did not tie something up in it, or if he tied something up in it, [and] if he also designated it for that purpose, it is indeed forbidden. But if he did not designate it for that purpose, it is not forbidden.

V. Come and take note:

W. As to a sepulchre which one built for a person still alive -- it is permitted to derive benefit from it.

X. If one added to it a single row of stones for a deceased person, it is forbidden to derive benefit from it. [The row of stones is not of consequence, hence the original designation mattered.]

Y. Here with what case do we deal? With a case in which the corpse was actually buried.

Z. If so, what does it matter that one added a row of stones? Even if he had not added a row of stones, one could not make use of the sepulchre.

AA. It is necessary to indicate that item, to show that even if the body was removed, [the prohibition remains valid].

BB. Rafram b. Papa said R. Hisda said, "If one can pick out that particular row of stones, he takes away the stones and it is permitted to use the tomb again."

CC. Come and take note:

DD. He who digs a grave for his father and went and buried him in another grave -- lo, this person may not be buried there ever. [This shows that mere designation matters.]

EE. The reason is [not designation but] the honor owing to the father. That is surely reasonable, for are not the concluding lines of the same passage:

FF. Rabban Simeon b. Gamaliel says, "Even in the case of one who hews stones for the burial of his father and then goes and buries him somewhere else -- lo, this one may not be buried in a grave using those stones ever."

GG. Now if you say that the operative consideration is the honor owing to the father, there are no problems.

HH. But if you say that it is because of the principle that designation matters [and so affects the stones at hand], would someone take the view that yarn spun for weaving a shroud [is forbidden? Surely not!] [Shachter, p. 319, n. 10: For Abayye only maintains that if a shroud is actually woven and so fit for its purpose, it is forbidden through mere designation. But what yarn is spun, although its ultimate destiny is to be woven into a shroud, is not forbidden, since, as yarn, it is useless for its purpose. Similarly, when stones are prepared for building a tomb, they should not become forbidden. Hence the prohibition must be on account of filial respect, not designation.]

II. Come and take note:

JJ. As to a newly-dug grave, it is for permitted [to be used] for benefit [in some other context]. If one placed an abortion in it, it is forbidden [to be used] for benefit.

KK. If one placed an abortion there, it is indeed [forbidden], but if one did not <u>do</u> so, it is not forbidden. [Hence mere designation for use as a grave does not make any difference.]

LL. [No, that is not the correct conclusion]. The same law applies if one has not placed an abortion in the grave. But matters are so formulated to exclude the view of Rabban Simeon b. Gamaliel, who has said, "Abortions do not take possession of the grave into which they are placed."

MM. Thus, matters are so formulated as to make clear that they do.

NN. Come and take note:

OO. <u>The surplus of money collected for burying the dead is used for the dead.</u>

PP. <u>The surplus of money collected for a particular deceased person is used for his heirs</u> <u>[M. Sheq. 2:5/O-P]</u>. [The surplus funds collected for burying a poor man must be used for other poor deceased. What is collected for a specific person may be used by the heirs for any other purpose, once the costs of the funeral are met. Hence designation does not matter.]

QQ. Here with what case do we deal? With a case in which the funds were collected while the man was yet alive.

RR. But the Mishnah-passage at hand does not say so, [for it says: The surplus of money collected for burying the dead is used for the dead. The surplus of money collected for a particular deceased person is used for his heirs [M. Sheq. 2:5/O-P].

SS. But it was taught on Tannaite authority in that connection:

TT. If they collected for the dead without further specification, this would constitute the surplus of funds collected for the dead, which is assigned to other deceased in need. If they collected for a particular deceased person, this is money the surplus of which goes to the heirs.

UU. But in accord with your reasoning, let me cite the concluding passage [which shows that designation does make a difference]:

VV. R. Meir says, "The surplus of money collected for a particular deceased person is left over until Elijah comes."

WW. R. Nathan says, "With surplus of money collected for a particular deceased person, they build a sepulchre on his grave. [M. Sheq. 2:5Q-R].

XX. "Or they sprinkle perfume before his bier" [T. Sheq. 1:120].

YY. But Abayye explains [this passage] in accord with his view, and Raba explains [this passage] in accordance with his view.

ZZ. Abayye explains this passage in accord with his view, maintaining that all parties concur that designation makes a difference. The first of the three authorities holds that what is needed by the deceased falls into the domain of the deceased, and what is not needed by the deceased does not fall into the domain of the deceased.

AAA. [And, Abayye continues,] R. Meir is in doubt whether or not that latter money falls into the domain of the deceased, on which account no one should touch that money until Elijah comes.

BBB. And R. Nathan finds it self-evident that the excess does fall into the domain of the deceased, on which account one builds a sepulchre on his grave.

CCC. Raba explains matters in accord with his basic principle. All parties concur that designation makes no difference. The first of the three authorities maintains that while [the people who collect the funds] have humiliated [the deceased] [by making a public collection for burying him], he forgives the embarrassment for the sake of his heirs [so they may benefit from the surplus].

DDD. R. Meir is in doubt about whether or not the deceased forgives the humiliation [of a public collection for his burial], on which account no one should touch the money until Elijah comes.

EEE. R. Nathan finds it self-evident that the deceased does not forgive the humiliation, on which account one should purchase a sepulchre for his grave or perfume to scatter before his bier.

FFF. Come and take note:

GGG. If the deceased's father and mother were putting clothing on the corpse [as an expression of grief] it is a religious duty for others to save them [so that they not go to waste]. [But here we have designation of the objects for the corpse, and as we see, it does not make a difference].

HHH. [48B] [But that is not really designation at all,] because what they did in that case they did out of grief.

IIL. If so, take account of that which is taught in this regard on Tannaite authority:

JJJ. Rabban Simeon b. Gamaliel said, "Under what circumstances? In a case in which the clothing has not actually touched the bier. But if the clothing has actually touched the bier, it is forbidden [to remove it]." [If the act occurred only because of grief, there has been no formality of designation at all. Why should they be forbidden? This challenges the explanation just now offered.]

KKK. Ulla explained the passage, "This statement speaks of a bier that is buried with the corpse, [and the clothing is forbidden] because it might be confused with the shrouds of the deceased."

LLL. Come and take note: In the case of a bag which one made for phylacteries, it is forbidden to put money into it. If one put phylacteries into [a bag not made for that purpose], it is permitted to put money into it. [Designation makes a difference in the former case.]

MMM. I read the passage to mean, If he made it and put phylacteries in it, then it is forbidden to put money into it, and this accords with the position of R. Hisda [requiring both designation and actual use].

NNN. Come and take note:

OOO. **If one says to a craftsman, "make me coverings for a [holy] scroll or a bag for phylacteries,**

PPP. **before one has made use of them for the Most High, one is permitted to make secular use of them.**

QQQ. **Once one has made use of them for the Most High, one is no longer permitted to make secular use of them.** [Mere designation makes no difference, contrary to Abayye's view.]

RRR. In point of fact, there is a dispute among Tannaite authorities, for it has been taught on Tannaite authority:

SSS. If one covered phylacteries with gold or attached to them the hide of an unclean beast, the phylacteries are invalid.

TTT. If one attached to them the hide of a clean beast, they are valid.

UUU. That is the case, even though one did not tan the hide for that purpose.

VVV. Rabban Simeon b. Gamaliel says, "Even in the case of the hide of a clean beast, the phylacteries are invalid unless one tanned the hide for the purpose of the use of phylacteries. [In the mind of the anonymous authority, designation makes no difference, so there is no reason to require it. That would be Raba's position. Simeon b. Gamaliel takes the view that designation does make a difference, and that is Abayye's view.

WWW. Said Rabina to Raba, "Is there any locale in which people set the corpse aside while weaving shrouds for it?"

XXX. He said to him, "Indeed so, in the case, for example, of the deceased of Harpania."

YYY. Maremar gave an exposition, "The decided law accords with the view of Abayye."

ZZZ. And rabbis say, "The decided law accords with the view of Raba."

AAAA. And the decided law accords with the view of Raba.

XV.

A. Our rabbis have taught on Tannaite authority:

B. Those put to death by the court -- their property goes to their heirs.

C. But those put to death by the king -- their property goes to the king.

D. And R. Judah says, "Those put to death by the king -- their property goes to their heirs."

E. They said to R. Judah, "It says, 'Behold he [Ahab] is in the vineyard of Naboth, where he has gone down to take possession' (I Kgs. 21:18)."

F. He said to them, "It was because he was the son of his father's brother, [and] it was appropriate [to come] to him as an inheritance."

G. "And did [Naboth] not have many children?"

H. He said to them, "And did he not kill both him and his children,

I. "as it is said, 'Surely I have seen yesterday the blood of Naboth and the blood of his sons, says the Lord; and I will requite you in this plat, says the Lord' (II Kgs. 9:26)."

J. And as to rabbis [how do they deal with the statement that they were killed]?

K. That refers to the sons who would have come forth from him.

L. Now from the viewpoint of him who has said that their property goes to the king, that is in line with the following verse of Scripture: "Naboth cursed God and the king" (1 Kgs. 21:13). [Shachter, p. 324, n. 1: This points to his culpability for treason to the king in addition to blasphemy, which is punished by the court; hence his estate would fall to the crown].

M. But from the viewpoint of him who has said that their property goes to the heirs, why specify that he cursed the king too?

N. And in accord with your reasoning, why mention that he had cursed God? But it was to outrage [the judges], and here too, it was to outrage [the judges] [Shachter, p. 324, n. 8: to make the crime appear more heinous].

O. From the viewpoint of him who has said that the estate goes to the king, that is in line with the following verse of Scripture: "And Joab fled to the tent of the Lord and caught hold of the horns of the altar" (1 Kgs. 2:28), and it is said, "And he said, No, but I will die here" (1 Kgs. 2:30). [Shachter, p. 324, n. 10: He declined to be tried by the king so that his estate might not be confiscated].

P. But from the position of him who says that the estate goes to the heirs, what difference did it make to him?

Q. It would be to gain time. [Shachter, p. 324, n. 11: He wished to gain the time which it would require to take his message to the king and bring back an answer.]

R. "And Benaiah brought back word to the king saying, Thus said Joab and thus he answered me" (1 Kgs. 2:30):

S.   He said to him, "Go tell him, 'You will not do two things to this man [me]. If you kill me, you have to accept the curses with which your father cursed me [for the murder of Abner, 2 Sam. 3:29. That curse then was to be Joab's punishment (Shachter, p. 324, n. 14)].

T.   "But if you [Shachter:] are unwilling to submit thereto, you must let me live and suffer from your father's curses against me."

U.   "And the king said to him, Do as he has said, and fall upon him and bury him" (1 Kgs. 2:21). [Solomon thus accepted the curses (Shachter)].

XVI.

A.   Said R. Judah said Rab, "All of the curses which David issued against Joab were carried out on David's own descendants.

B.   "'Let there not fail from the house of Joab one who has an issue or is a leper or leans on a staff or falls by the sword or lacks bread' (2 Sam. 3:29).

C.   "'One who has an issue' pertains to Rehoboam, for it is written, 'And king Rehoboam made the effort to get up on his chariot to flee to Jerusalem' (1 Kgs. 12:18), and it is written, 'And what chariot one who has an issue rides on shall be unclean' (Lev. 15:9).

D.   "'A leper' pertains to Uzziah, for it is written, 'But when he was strong, his heart was lifted up so that he did corruptly and he trespassed against the Lord his God, for he went into the Temple of the Lord to burn the incense upon the altar of incense' (2 Chr. 26:6) and it is written, 'And the leprosy broke forth on his forehead' (2 Chr. 26:19).

E.   "'He who leans on his staff' refers to Asa [2 Kgs. 15:8], for it is written, 'Only in the time of his age he suffered from his feet' (1 Kgs. 15:23)."

F.   In this regard R. Judah said R. Said, "He had gout."

G.   Mar Zutra, son of R. Nahman, asked R. Nahman, "What is it?"

H.   He said to him, "It is like a needle in raw flesh."

I.   How did he know it?

J.   If you wish, I may propose that he had personally felt it; and if you wish I shall say that he had learned it from his master; and if you wish, I shall say, because "The secret of the Lord is with those who fear him, and his covenant to make them know it" (Ps. 25:14).

K.   [Resuming Judah's statement in Rab's name,] "'Josiah, as it is written, 'And the archers shot at king Josiah' (2 Chr. 35:23)."

L.   In this regard said R. Judah said Rab, "They turned his entire body into a sieve."

M.   [Resuming Judah's statement in Rab's name,] "'Who lacks bread' refers to Jechoniah. For it is written, 'And for his allowance, there was a continual allowance given him by the king' (2 Kgs. 25:30)."

N.   Said R. Judah said Rab, "This is in line with what people say: '[49A] Be cursed but do not curse [someone else].'"

XVII.

A.   [Reverting to XV U:] They brought Joab to court. [Solomon] said to him, "Why did you call Abner?"

B.   He said to him, "I was redeemer of the blood [shed by him] of Asahel [his brother],
      [Shachter, p. 326, n. 5: Joab's brother, who pursued Abner when he fled for his life,
      after having been defeated by Joab at Gibeon while fighting for Ishbosheth, Saul's
      surviving son, 2 Sam. 2:23]."

C.   He said to him, "Asahel was in pursuit, [since Abner killed him in self-defense, 2
      Sam. 2:8-32 (Shachter)]."

D.   He said to him, "He should have saved himself by cutting off one of his limbs, [but
      he did not have to kill him.]"

E.   He said to him, "He could not do it."

F.   He said to him, "Now if at exactly the fifth rib he had the capacity [to take aim], as
      it is written, 'Abner with the hinder end of the spear smote him at the waist' (2
      Sam. 2:23),

G.   (on which R. Yohanan said, "It was at the fifth rib, where the gall bladder and liver
      are suspended" [Shachter]),

H.   "should he not have been able to aim at one of his limbs [instead of killing him]?"

I.   [Solomon] said, "Let us move on from the case of Abner. Why did you kill Amasa [2
      Sam. 17:25, 19:14]?"

J.   He said to him, "Amasa had rebelled against the throne, for it is written, 'Then said
      the king to Amasa, Call me the men of Judah together within three days ... So
      Amasa went to call the men of Judah together, but he tarried' (2 Sam. 20:   )."

K.   [Solomon] said to him, "Amasa made an exegetical basis out of the particles 'but'
      and 'only.'

L.   "[How so?] He came upon them as they commenced their study of a tractate. He
      said, 'It is written, "Whoever he be that shall rebel against your commandments and
      shall not hearken to your words in all that you command him shall be put to death'
      (Josh. 1:18).

M.   "'Is it possible that that is the case even with respect to study of the Torah [so that
      the violation of the king's commandment incurs death even if it is ignored so as to
      continue Torah-study]?

N.   "'Scripture says, "Only be strong and of good courage" (Josh. 1:18). [Shachter, p.
      327, n. 2: Hence the duty to fulfill the king's command does not apply where one is
      engaged in the study of the Torah. According to the view held by Amasa, God's law
      seemed more important to him than the will of the king, and no transgression was
      involved in waiting until they had finished their study.]'

O.   "But you yourself are the one who rebels against the king, for it is written, 'And the
      tidings came to Joab, for Joab had turned after Adonijah, though he had turned not
      after Absalom' (1 Kgs. 2:28)."

P.   What is the sense of "though he had turned not ..."?

Q.   Said R. Judah, "He proposed to turn after him but did not do so."

R.   What is the reason that he did not turn after him?

S.   Said R. Eleazar, "David was still vigorous."

T.   R. Yose b. R. Hanina said, "The star of David still was ascendant."

U. For R. Judah said Rab said, "David had four hundred sons, all children of beautiful captive women. They all had long locks and would march at the head of retinues. They were the influential men in David's regime."

V. [What has been said about Joab] contradicts what was said by R. Abba bar Kahana.

W. For R. Abba bar Kahana said, "Were it not for David, Joab could not have made war, and were it not for Joab, David could not have engaged in the study of Torah.

X. "For it is written, 'And David executed justice and righteousness for all his people, and Joab, the son of Zeruiah, was in charge of the host' (2 Sam. 8:15-16).

Y. "What is the reason that 'David executed justice and righteousness for all his people'? It was because 'Joab, son of Zeruiah, was in charge of the host.'

Z. "And what is the reason that 'Joab was in charge of the host'? It was because 'David executed justice and righteousness for all his people.'"

AA. "When Joab was come out from David, he sent messengers after Abner and they brought him back from Bor-Sira" (2 Sam. 3:26).

BB. What is "Bor Sira"?

CC. Said R. Abba bar Kahana, "Bor [a well, hence, a pitcher of water] and a 'thorn bush' caused Abner to be killed." [Shachter, p. 328, n. 4: The explanation of this statement is found in J. Sotah I, where one of the reasons given for Abner's death was his indifference to the effecting of a reconciliation between Saul and David, instead of seeking which, he rather endeavoured to increase their hatred. He did not take advantage of the following two occasions when he might have brought about the reconciliation: One, when Saul entered the cave of En-Gedi where David and his band were hidden, and the latter, though he could have destroyed his pursuer, contented himself with merely cutting of the skirt of his robe (I Sam. 24:4). The second time, in the wilderness of Ziph, when David found Saul sleeping and took the spear and jug of water from beside his head (ibid. 24:12ff.) subsequently reproaching Abner for not watching better over the King. Abner, however, made nought of this generous treatment of Saul by David, contending that the jug of water might have been given to David by one of the servants, whilst the skirt of the robe might have been torn away by a thorn-bush, and left hanging. These two incidents are hinted at in the words Bor (well, i.e., a jug of water), and Sira (a thorn-bush)].

DD. And Joab took him aside into the midst of the gate to speak with him quietly" (2 Sam. 3:27):

EE. Said R. Yohanan, "He judged him in accord with the rule of the sanhedrin.

FF. "He said to him, 'Why did you kill Asahel?'

GG. "'Asahel was in pursuit.'

HH. "'You should have saved yourself from him through one of his limbs.'

II. "'I could not do it to him that way.'

JJ. "'Now you were able to aim directly at the fifth rib, yet could you not aim at one of his limbs?'"

KK. "To speak with him quietly" (2 Sam. 3:27):

LL. Said R. Judah said Rab, "It concerned the pulling off of the shoe." [Shachter, p. 328, n. 8: The word is here derived from NSL, to draw or pull off. Joab is supposed to have inquired from Abner in what way a one-armed woman would loosen the shoe in the ceremony of halisah (v. Deut. 25:9). On his replying that she would do it with her teeth (cf. Yeb. 105a), he asked him to demonstrate it, and as he stooped low to do so, he smote him. This incident is hinted at in David's words of farewell to Solomon: "He (sc. Joab) shed the blood of war in peace, -- and put the blood of war in the shoes that were on his feet" (1 Kgs. 2:3)].

MM. "And he smote him there at the waist" (2 Sam. 3:27):

NN. Said R. Yohanan, "At the fifth rib, where the gall-bladder and liver are suspended."

OO. "And the Lord will return [Joab's] blood upon his own head, because he fell upon two men more righteous and better than he" (1 Kgs. 2:32):

PP. "Better" because they interpreted the particles that indicate "but" and "only" while he did not interpret those particles.

QQ. "Righteous" because they were commanded by word of mouth [to kill the priests of Nob], and they did not do it, while he was commanded only in a letter, and he did it.

RR. "But Amasa did not beware of the sword that was in Joab's hand" (2 Sam. 20:10):

SS. Said Rab, "Because he was not suspicious of him."

TT. "'And he was buried in his own house in the wilderness" (1 Kgs. 2:23):

UU. Was his house a wilderness?

VV. Said R. Judah said Rab, "It was like a wilderness. Just as the wilderness is free for everyone, so Joab's house was free for everyone [who wanted hospitality].

WW. "Another interpretation: 'Like a wilderness'. 'Just as the wilderness is free of robbery and fornication, so the house of Joab was clean of robbery and fornication."

XX. "And Joab kept alive the rest of the city" (1 Xhe. 11:8):

YY. Said R. Judah, "Even fish soup and fish hash he would taste and then divide up [to the poor]."

There are two sizable, autonomous discussions, imparting to the Talmud at hand special interest. The first is on the principle of whether merely designating something for a given purpose produces concrete consequences. The second is the rather lengthy discourse on Joab. While both constructions certainly came into being independent of any interest in Mishnah-exegesis, the latter, at least, hardly gives the appearance of being merely tacked on. The exegesis of the Mishnah-paragraphs at hand is carried out systematically, with attention first to the biblical basis for the rule, units I, II, and then further comments on M. 6:4S, unit III, M. 6:5A, unit IV, M. 6:5C, unit V. There is a secondary accretion for unit V at unit VI. Unit VII, on the purpose of burial, is tacked on, since the Mishnah does not raise the issue. But its pertinence lies at M. 6:5's interest in the burial of the felon. Unit VIII, which continues unit VII, guarantees that fact, since it makes explicit reference to M. 6:5D. Unit IX proceeds to M. 6:5E-F, and unit X deals with the same clause. Since units XI-XII form a continuous composite, we may be sure that XII P, which cites M. 6:6D-E, accounts for the inserting of the whole into the present construction of the Talmud. I assume that unit XIII D, which alludes to M. 6:6A, is introduced on the same redactional principle. Units XIV-XV, on whether or not designation makes a difference, go over the disposition of corpses and the like. I see no obvious point of intersection with the Mishnah-paragraphs before us. The composition itself is sustained and completely persuasive, but I am puzzled on why it was found appropriate here. My best guess is that the theme of burial rites satisfied the redactor who chose it for the present Talmud. Unit XVI, by contrast, clearly belongs -- and with it in its wake, units XVI-XVII -- because the basic issue is the disposition of the estates of those put to death by the court. That issue is tangential to our Mishnah-paragraph. Once Joab makes his appearance, the rest follows.

CHAPTER FOUR
BAVLI SANHEDRIN CHAPTER SEVEN

7:1

A. Four modes of execution were assigned to the court, [listed in order of severity]:

B. (1) stoning, (2) burning, (3) decapitation, and (4) strangulation.

C. R. Simeon says, "(2) Burning, (1) stoning, (4) strangulation, and (3) decapitation" [M. 9:3].

D. This [procedure considered in Chapter Six,] is [how] the religious requirement of stoning [is carried out].

I.

A. Said Raba said R. Sehora said R. Huna, "Any passage stated by sages in numerical order in fact does not list matters in order of priority or posteriority except for the matter of the seven substances.

B. "As we have learned in the Mishnah:

C. "Seven substances do they pass over a bloodstain [to see whether it is blood or dye]: tasteless spit, water from boiled grits, urine, nitre, soap, Cimolian earth, and lion's leaf [M. Nid. 9:6A-B].

D. "And it is taught at the end of the same passage: If one rubbed them on out of order, or if one rubbed on all seven substances at once, he has done nothing whatsoever [M. Nid. 9:7K]."

E. R. Papa, the elder, in the name of Rab stated, "The same principle pertains also to the catalogue of four modes of execution. Since R. Simeon disputes the sequence, it indicates that the framer of the passage for his part has listed them in precise order."

F. And the contrary position [Raba's view, that omits reference to M. San. 7:1]?

G. [When he made his statement,] it did not include passages subject to dispute [but only those in which the list is stated anonymously and hence in the name of the collegium of sages].

H. R. Papa said, "Also the order of rites on the Day of Atonement [is meant to be exact].

I. "For we have learned in the Mishnah: The entire rite of the Day of Atonement is stated in accord with its proper order. If one did one part of the rite before its fellow, he has done nothing whatsoever [M. Yoma 5:7A-B]."

J. And the contrary position?

K. That statement merely imposes an additional stringency.

L. R. Huna, son of R. Joshua, said, "Also the order of the daily whole offering, about which it is taught on Tannaite authority: This is the correct order of the daily whole offering [M. Tamid 7:3].

M.   And the contrary position?

N.   That statement is meant merely to describe the proper way of doing things [but not an indispensable sequence of actions].

O.   [Raba's statement that a listing by number bears no significance] serves to exclude the conduct of the rite of removing the shoe [Deut. 25:5-10]. [which does no have to follow a given sequence of steps].

P.   For we have learned in the Mishnah:

Q.   The proper conduct of the rite of removing the shoe [is as follows]: He and his deceased childless brother's widow come to court. And they offer him such advice as is appropriate for him, since it says, "Then the elders of the city shall call him and speak to him" (Deut. 25:8). And she shall say, "My husband's brother refuses [to raise up for his brother a name in Israel. He will not perform the duty of a husband's brother to me]" (Deut. 25:7). And he says, "I do not want to take her" (Deut. 25:7). And [all of this] they say in the Holy Language. "Then his brother's wife come to him in the presence of the elders and removes his shoe from his foot and spits in his face" (Deut. 25:9) -- spit which is visible to the judges. And she answers and says, "So shall it be done to the man [who does not build up his brother's house]" (Deut. 25:10) [M. Yeb. 12:6A-I].

R.   And R. Judah said, "The proper conduct of the rite of removing the shoe is that the woman makes her statement, then the man makes his statement, then the woman removes the shoe and spits and makes her statement."

S.   And we reflected on that statement: What exactly does he wish to tell us? The order is made explicit by our Mishnah-paragraph itself!

T.   This is what he wishes to tell us: this is precisely how the religious duty should be carried out, but if one reverses the order, we have no objection on that account.

U.   So too it has been taught on Tannaite authority:

V.   Whether the removing of the shoe came before the spitting or the spitting before the removing of the shoe, what is done is valid.

W.   [Raba's statement] further excludes that which we have learned in the Mishnah:

X.   The high priest serves in eight garments and an ordinary priest in four: tunic, breeches, head-covering, and girdle. The high priest in addition wears the breastplate, apron, upper garment and frontlet [M. Yoma 7:5A-C].

Y.   And it has been taught on Tannaite authority:

Z.   How do we know that nothing should come before the breeches?

AA.   As it is said, "He shall put on the holy linen tunic, and the linen breeches shall be upon his flesh" (Lev. 16:4).

BB.   And what is the reason that the Tannaite authority of the passage lists the tunic first?

CC.   Because Scripture lists it first.

DD.   And why does Scripture list it first?

EE.   Because it covers the whole of the body, which is better for him. [But that is not the order in which the priest puts on the garments, as is now clear.]

II.

A. Stoning, burning [M. 7:1B]:

B. Stoning is a more severe [mode of execution] than burning [as listed in sequence at M. 7:1B, against Simeon's order at M. 7:1C].

C. because it is assigned to the blasphemer and idolator.

D. Why is this a more severe offense? Because [the guilty party] has laid hands on the principle [i.e., the basis of the faith].

E. To the contrary, burning is the more severe [mode of execution], because it is assigned to the daughter of a priest who fornicated.

F. And why is that a more severe offense? Because she thus profanes her father['s genealogical sanctity].

G. [50A] Rabbis [behind the passage as it stands before us] take the view that [a priest's daughter who is] a married woman is taken out to be burned [and not strangled, as are others] but not a betrothed maiden. [An Israelite's daughter who commits adultery while in the status of a betrothed maiden is stoned, and the same penalty should apply to the priest's daughter. She is not an exception.] Since the All-Merciful, however, has singled out the priest's daughter who is in the status of a betrothed maiden, to declare that she shall be executed by stoning, this indicates that stoning is the more severe mode [of execution].

H. Stoning is a more severe [mode of execution] than decapitation, for it is assigned to the blasphemer and the idolator.

I. And why is this a more severe offense?

J. It is as we have already stated.

K. To the contrary, decapitation is the more severe [mode of execution], for it is assigned to the men of an apostate town. And what more severe penalty applies to them [in addition]? That their property is destroyed [along with them].

L. But now say, what power is greater, that of the one who entices another to sin, or that of the one who is enticed? You have to agree that it is the power of the one who entices.

M. And it has been taught on Tannaite authority:

N. Those who entice the apostate town [to apostasy are put to death] through stoning [which then proves that] stoning is the more severe [mode of execution, as compared to decapitation].

O. Stoning is a more severe mode of execution than strangulation, for it is assigned to a blasphemer and idolator.

P. And why is this a more severe offense?

Q. It is as we have already stated.

R. To the contrary, strangulation is the more severe [mode of execution], for it is assigned to one who strikes his father or mother.

S. And why is that a more severe offense? Because the honor owing to them is deemed analogous to the honor owing to the Omnipresent.

T.   But since the All-Merciful singled out the betrothed girl of the Israelite caste, separating her from the category of the married woman of Israelite caste [who has fornicated], assigning the penalty of strangulation rather than stoning, that proves that stoning is the more severe mode of execution.

U.   Burning is a more severe [mode of execution] than decapitation, for it is assigned to a priest's daughter who fornicated.

V.   And why is this a more severe offense? Because she profanes her father'[s genealogical sanctity].

W.   To the contrary, decapitation should be deemed the more severe, for it is assigned to the men of the apostate town.

X.   And what more severe penalty applies to them [in addition]? That their property is destroyed [along with them].

Y.   "Her father" is stated in connection with stoning [Deut. 22:2], the betrothed girl who fornicated is stoned because she has played the whore in her father's house], and "her father" is stated in connection with burning [a priest's daughter who fornicated is burned with fire, so Lev. 21:9, for having "profaned her father"].

Z.   Just as, when "her father" is stated with reference to stoning, stoning is deemed more severe than decapitation, so when "her father" is stated with reference to burning, burning is deemed more severe than decapitation.

AA.   Burning is a more severe mode [of execution] than strangling, because it is assigned to the daughter of a priest who fornicated.

BB.   And why is this a more severe offense?

CC.   It is as we have already stated.

DD.   To the contrary, strangulation is the more severe [mode of execution], for it is assigned to one who hits his father or his mother.

EE.   And why is this a more severe crime?

FF.   Because the honor owing to them is deemed analogous to the honor owing to the Omnipresent.

GG.   Since the All-Merciful singled out the case of a married woman, daughter of a priest, from the case of married women of Israelite caste, who had committed adultery, assigning the penalty of burning rather than strangulation, that indicates that burning is the more severe [mode of execution]. [Freedman, p. 335, n. 5: since the priest's daughter profanes her father in addition to disgracing herself].

HH.   Decapitation is a more severe [mode of execution] than strangulation, for it is assigned to the men of the apostate town.

II.   And what more severe penalty applies to them [in addition]? That their property is destroyed [along with them].

JJ.   To the contrary, strangulation is the more severe [mode of execution], for it is assigned to one who strikes his father or his mother.

KK.   And why is this a more severe offense?

LL.   Because the honor owing to them is deemed analogous to the honor owing to the Omnipresent.

MM. Nonetheless, one who lays hands on the principle [i.e., the basis of the faith] is guilty of a more severe offense [as is the case with the execution of the inhabitants of an apostate town.

III.

A. R. Simeon says [M. 7:1C]:

B. Burning is a more severe [mode of execution] than stoning, for it is assigned to a priest's daughter who fornicated.

C. And why is this a more severe offense? Because she has profaned her father's [genealogical sanctity].

D. To the contrary, stoning is the more severe [mode of execution], for it is assigned to the blasphemer and the idolator.

E. And why is this a more severe offense? Because such a one has laid hands on the principle [i.e., the basis of the faith].

F. R. Simeon is consistent with his views expressed elsewhere, for he has said, "All the same are the betrothed girl and the married woman [who have committed adultery]. They are taken out and burned. But since the All-Merciful has singled out the priest's daughter who was betrothed and assigned her a different penalty, namely, burning, rather than the stoning [that applies to an Israelite's daughter in the same status], this proves that burning is the more severe [mode of execution].

G. Burning is a more severe [mode of execution] than strangulation, for it is assigned to a priest's daughter who fornicated.

H. And why is this a more severe offense?

I. It is as we have stated.

J. To the contrary, strangulation is the more severe [mode of execution], for it is assigned to one who strikes his father or his mother.

K. And why is this a more severe offense? Because the honor owing to the parents is deemed analogous to the honor owing to the Omnipresent.

L. Since the All-Merciful singled out the married woman who is the daughter of a priest from the married women who is of Israelite caste and assigned her a different penalty, namely, burning rather than strangulation, thus proves that burning is the more severe [mode of execution].

M. Burning is a more severe [mode of execution] than decapitation, for it is assigned to the daughter of a priest who has fornicated.

N. And why is this a more severe offense?

O. It is as we have already stated.

P. To the contrary, decapitation is the more severe [mode of execution], for it is assigned to the men of an apostate down.

Q. And what more severe penalty applies to them [in addition]?

R. That their property is destroyed [along with them].

S. So now say: Which is the greater power, the power of the one who entices [others to commit idolatry] or the power of the one who is enticed? [50B] You must say it is the power of the one who entices.

T. And this yields an argument a fortiori:

U. If burning is more severe than strangulation, which is more severe than decapitation, which is a less severe mode of execution,

V. is it not an argument a fortiori [that burning is a more severe mode of execution than decapitation]?

W. Stoning is a more severe [mode of execution] than strangulation, for it is assigned to a blasphemer and an idolator.

X. And why is this a more severe offense?

Y. It is as we have already said.

Z. To the contrary, strangulation is the more severe [mode of execution], for it is assigned to the one who strikes his father or his mother.

AA. And why is this a more severe offense?

BB. Because the honor owing to them is deemed analogous to the honor owing to the Omnipresent.

CC. Since the All-Merciful has singled out a betrothed girl of Israelite caste who fornicated, from a married women of Israelite caste, assigning the penalty of stoning rather than strangulation, thus proves that stoning is a more severe [mode of execution].

DD. Stoning is a more severe [mode of execution] than decapitation, for it is assigned to the blasphemer, etc.

EE. To the contrary, decapitation is the more severe, since it is assigned to the men of an apostate town.

FF. And what more severe more severe penalty applies to them [in addition]? That their property is destroyed [along with them].

GG. So now say: which is more powerful, the one who entices or the one who is enticed? You must say it is the power of the one who entices.

HH. And this yields an argument a fortiori:

II. If stoning is more severe than strangulation, which is more severe than decapitation, which is a less severe mode of execution,

JJ. is it not an argument a fortiori [that stoning is a more severe mode of execution than decapitation]?

KK. Strangulation is a more severe [mode of execution] than decapitation, for it is assigned to the one who strikes his father or his mother.

LL. And why is this a more severe offense?

MM. It is as we have said.

NN. To the contrary, decapitation is the more severe [mode of execution], for it is assigned to the men of an apostate town.

OO. And what more severe penalty applyies to them [in addition]?

PP. It is that their property is destroyed [along with them].

QQ. So now say: Which power is greater, the power of the one who entices [another to commit idolatry], or the power of the one who is enticed? One must say it is the power of the one who entices.

RR. And it has been taught on Tannaite authority:

SS. Those who entice the apostate town [to idolatry are executed] by stoning.

TT. R. Simeon says, "By strangulation."

IV.

A. A pearl in the mouth of R. Yohanan:

B. **A betrothed girl, a priest's daughter, who committed adultery [is executed] by stoning.**

C. **R. Simeon says, "By burning."**

D. **If she committed adultery with her father, she is [executed] by stoning.**

E. **R. Simeon says, "By burning" [T. San. 12:2].**

F. What does this passage teach us?

G. In the view of the rabbis, it is that a married woman [who is daughter of a priest and commits adultery] goes forth to be burned, but not a betrothed girl.

H. From the viewpoint of R. Simeon, all the same are a betrothed girl and a married woman [daughters of priests, who commit adultery]. In both cases they go forth to be burned.

I. And what is the reason?

J. It is that, in the view of rabbis, stoning is the more severe [mode of execution], and, in the view of R. Simeon, burning is the more severe [mode of execution].

K. The practical difference [of all this] is that if someone is declared liable to the death penalty on two different counts, each with its [mode of execution], he is condemned in accord with the more severe of the two penalties.

V.

A. What [evidence is there concerning the view of] R. Simeon [that the daughter of a priest, whether betrothed or married, is executed for the crime of adultery by burning]?

B. It is accord with that which has been taught on Tannaite authority:

C. R. Simeon says, "Two encompassing principles have been stated with reference to the priest's daughter." [Freedman, p. 338, n. 3: One encompassing principle refers to a betrothed girl, the other to a married woman. When the Torah states, "And the man who commits adultery with another man's wife, even he who commits adultery with his neighbor's wife, the adulterer and the adulteress shall surely be put to death" (Lev. 20:10). This is a general law regarding a married woman, in which a priest's daughter should be included. Likewise the law in Deut. 22:23f.: "If a damsel that is a virgin be betrothed to a husband, and a man find her in the city and lie with her, then you shall bring them both out to the gate of the city and stone them." This is a general principle for an adulterous betrothed girl, which should embrace the priest's daughter too.]

D. [Do you mean to say that these rules speak] of a priest's daughter and not an Israelite's daughter?

E. I should say, "Also to a priest's daughter."

F.   Now Scripture has singled out the married [priest's daughter] from the [category of the] married [Israelite's daughter], and the betrothed [priest's daughter] from the [category of the] betrothed [Israelite's daughter].

G.   Now if the reason for singling out the married [priest's daughter] from the [category of the] married [Israelite's daughter] was [Scripture's wish] to impose a stricter penalty upon the priest's daughter, so too when Scripture singled out the betrothed [priest's daughter] from the [category of the] betrothed Israelite's daughter], it was to impose a stricter penalty on her.

H.   But false witnesses [who testify] against a married woman who is a priest's daughter [and claim she has committed adultery when she has not, and so are subjected to the same penalty that they proposed to inflict on her], fall into [exactly the same] category as false witnesses against a married woman who is an Israelite's daughter.

I.   And false witnesses who testify against the betrothed daughter of a priest fall into the same category as false witnesses against the betrothed daughter of an Israelite.

VI.

A.   Our rabbis have taught on Tannaite authority:

B.   "And the daughter of any priest, if she profane [herself]" (Lev. 21:9):

C.   Might one think [that that is the case] even if she had profaned the Sabbath?

D.   Scripture states, "by playing the whore" (lev. 21:9):

E.   It is concerning the profanation that involves whoredom that Scripture speaks.

F.   Might one think [that that is the case] even if she were unmarried?

G.   [No, that cannot be the case, for] "her father" is stated in the present context (Lev. 21:9), and "her father" is stated elsewhere (at Deut. 22:21).

H.   Just as in the latter passage [at issue] is an act of prostitution by a woman tied to a husband, so too here [at issue] is an act of prostitution by a woman tied to a husband.

I.   But perhaps the [analogous] usage of "her father" is intended to exclude everyone else? [Freedman, p. 340, n. 1: Only if she committed incest with her father is she punished by burning, but not for playing the harlot with others.]

J.   When Scripture states, "She profanes [herself]" (Lev. 21:9), it must mean that that act may take place with any man.

K.   How then am I to interpret [the use of] "her father"?

L.   "Her father" is stated here [at Lev. 21:9) and "her father" is stated elsewhere [at Deut. 22:21).

M.   Just as in the latter passage [at issue] is an act of prostitution by a woman tied to a husband, so here too [at issue] is an act of prostitution by a woman tied to a husband.

VII.

A.   If in the latter case (Deut. 22:21) [Scripture states] "a maiden," and she is merely betrothed, so here (Lev. 21:9) [does not Scripture imply] "a betrothed maiden" [who is a priest's daughter]?

B.   How do I know [from Scripture, that the death penalty for prostitution applies equally to a priest's daughter who is] a married maiden [i.e., a married girl under the age of twelve-and-a-half], or [a priest's daughter who is] an adult betrothed woman, or [a priest's daughter who is] an adult married woman, or even [a priest's daughter who is] an old woman [beyond her child-bearing years, hence cannot produce an illegitimate child]?

C.   Scripture states, "And the daughter of any priest (Lev. 21:9) -- under all circumstances.

VIII.

A.   "The daughter of a priest" (Lev. 21:9):

B.   [51A] I know only that that rule applies if she is married to a priest [as will be explained].

C.   If she is married to a Levite, an Israelite, an idolator, one of impaired priestly stock, one born of a union of a couple not legally permitted to wed at all, or to a Temple slave, how do we know [that the same rule applies]?

D.   "And the daughter of a man who is a priest" (Lev. 21:9) -- even if she is not herself married to a priest.

IX.

A.   "And the daughter of a priest, if she profanes herself by playing the harlot, she profanes her father; she shall be burned in fire" (Lev. 21:9).

B.   [Interpret the latter phrase to mean as follows:] She shall be burned but the man who had intercourse with her shall not be burned.

C.   She shall be burned, but the witnesses who testify falsely against her shall not be burned.

D.   R. Eliezer says, "[Since the verse says she profanes her father one may derive the following in conclusion:] If [she had intercourse] with her father, she shall be burned. But if [she had intercourse] with her father-in-law, she is stoned."

E.   A master said, "Is it possible [the above Scriptural verse] also refers to her [profaning herself by] profaning the Sabbath?

F.   "[No, that is impossible, for] profaning the Sabbath invokes stoning [whereas the above verse specifies only burning]."

G.   Said Raba, "Who holds the view [that she shall be burned for violating the Sabbath]?

H.   "It is R. Simeon, [for he] said that burning is a more severe [punishment than stoning]."

I.   [Simeon] might reason that since the Merciful One treated priests more strictly than Israelites by giving [the former] more commandments [than the latter], then God would invoke a more severe penalty if a priest violated the Sabbath than if an Israelite had violated the Sabbath. Thus, one might conclude that if a priest violates the Sabbath, he or she incurs burning, whereas if an Israelite violates the Sabbath, he or she incurs the less severe penalty of stoning.]

J.   [Scripture indicates this line of reasoning is incorrect; for it states,] "if she play the harlot" [that is only for harlotry does a priest's daughter invoke burning, not for the profanation of the Sabbath."

K.   But what difference is there between a woman priest and a male priest [so that Scripture specifically indicates that a woman priest does not invoke burning?]

L.   [Had Scripture not mentioned a woman of priestly descent] I might have arrived at
      the following incorrect conclusion. I might think a priest is punished by the less
      severe punishment of stoning because he is permitted to work on the Sabbath in the
      Temple service; but since a woman of priestly origins is not permitted to do so, her
      punishment should be stoning. [The Scriptural verse thus] teaches us [that that is
      not the case]."

M.   "Might one think that that is the case even if she was unmarried?"

N.   Lo, it is written, "By playing the harlot"? [So why should that have been an issue,
      since an unmarried woman does not commit whoredom if she has sexual relations.]

O.   The passage is framed in accord with the view of R. Eliezer, who gas said, "If an
      unmarried man had sexual relations with an unmarried woman, not intending thereby
      to effect a marital bond, he has turned her into a whore."

X.

A.   "But perhaps the force of the analogous usage is to indicate that only 'her father' is
      meant, so excluding everyone else"?

B.   What would be the sense of the passage? Is it that she had an incestuous sexual
      relationship with her father? Then why specify that this is the daughter of a
      priest? Even if it were the daughter of an Israelite, the rule would be the same.

C.   It would accord with what Raba said, "R. Isaac bar Abodimi said to me, 'The word
      "they" occurs in two related passage, so too the word "wickedness." [Freedman, p.
      342, n. 1: In Lev. 18:10 it is stated: The nakedness of thy son's daughter, or of they
      daughter's daughter, even their nakedness thou shalt not uncover: for they (hennah)
      are thine own nakedness. Further it is written (ibid. XVIII, 17): Thou shalt not
      uncover the nakedness of a woman and her daughter, neither shalt thou take her
      son's daughter, or her daughter's daughter, to uncover her nakedness; for they
      (hennah) are her near kinswomen: it is wickedness (zimmah). Just as in the latter
      verse, intercourse with one's wife's daughter is treated as with her granddaughter,
      so in the former case, incest with one's daughter is the same offense as with one's
      granddaughter. Though this is not explicitly stated, it is deduced from the fact that
      hennah occurs in both cases. Further, in Lev. 18:17 it is staed: And if a man take a
      wife and her mother, it is wickedness (zimmah); they shall be burnt with fire. The
      use of zimmah in Lev. 18:17 and Lev. 18:10 show that burning by fire is the penalty
      in both cases; and the use of hennah in Lev. 18:17 and Lev. 18:10 shews that in Lev.
      18:10 too the penalty is burning (cf. the Euclidean axiom: the equals of equals are
      equal. Thus we see that incest between a man, even an Israelite, and his daughter is
      punished by burning. How then could we assume that the verse under discussion,
      which decrees burning as a penalty for whoredom by a priest's daughter (implying
      the exclusion of an Israelite's daughter), refers to incest with one's father, and
      consequently what need is there for the deduction from she profaneth?]

D.   "It was necessary to state the verse as is, [Freedman, p. 342:] For I would think that
      this whole passage treats of incest with one's father and the penalty of burning is
      prescribed here intentionally to obviate Raba's deduction." [Freedman, p. 342, n.2:

show that only a _priest's_ daughter, who is differently punished. In that case, the identical phrasing of the verses cited by Raba would have to be otherwise interpreted].

E.   So we are informed that that is not the case.

XI.

A.   "'The daughter of a priest' (Lev. 21:9):

B.   "I know only that the rule applies if she was married to a priest. If she was married , to a Levite, an Israelite, an idolator, one of impaired priestly stock, one who was born of a union of a couple not legally permitted to wed at all, or to a Temple slave, how do we know that the same rule applies?

C.   "Scripture says, 'And the daughter of a man who is a priest' (Lev. 21:9) -- even though she is herself not of the priestly caste."

D.   Merely because the girl is married to one of these, does she cease to be the daughter of a priest?

E.   And furthermore, does it say, "A priest's daughter married to a priest [in particular]"?

F.   It might have entered your mind to suppose that, when the All-Merciful said, "If she profane herself by playing the whore," at issue was solely a girl who to begin with does so. But in this case, since she is already in the situation of one who has profaned her status [the rule should not pertain].

G.   For a master has said, "'If the priest's daughter is married to a non-priest [she may not eat of an offering of holy things] (Lev. 22:12) [this verse teaches that] if she has sexual relations with one who is unfit for her, he disqualifies her [from eating food in the present status].

H.   "If she marries a Levite or an Israelite that is also the case, for it is said, '[But if a priest's daughter be a widow or divorced and have no child] and returns to her father's house, as in her youth, [she shall eat of her father's meat]' (Lev. 22:13)."

I.   That bears the implication that when she is with him [the Levite or Israelite], she was not eating such food.

J.   I might then have supposed that, under those same circumstances, she should not suffer the penalty of burning.

K.   Accordingly, the cited verse indicates that that is not the case.

XII.

A.   The ruling [that a priest's daughter married to the offspring of a union of parents who cannot legally married is put to death through burning] does not accord with the view of R. Meir [who says the penalty is by strangling].

B.   For we have learned in the Mishnah:

C.   "The daughter of a priest who married an Israelite and afterwards [unintentionally] ate heave-offering pays the principal, but does not pay the [added] fifth.

D.   "And [if she commits adultery] her death is by burning.

E.   "[If] she married any person who is ineligible [for marriage to priestly stock, e.g., a bastard (M. Yeb. 6:2), and then unintentionally ate heave-offering],

F. she pays the principal and the [added] fifth.

G. "And [if she commits adultery] her death is by strangling," -- the words of R. Meir.

H. But sages say, "Both of these [women] pay the principal, but do not pay the [added] fifth,

I. "and [if they commit adultery] their death is by burning," [M. Ter. 7:2, trans. Alan J. Avery-Peck]. [Avery-Peck explains: The daughter of a priest who marries an Israelite. While such a woman is of priestly lineage, because of the marriage she becomes an outcast and loses the right she had while living in her father's house to eat holy things. The problem is whether such a woman still is treated as a person of priestly status, or whether she is treated as an ordinary Israelite. The issue is disputed by Meir, C-G, and sages, H-I. The key to the exegesis of the pericope is in what on the surface appears to be a secondary dispute at D+G vs. I. Meir distinguishes between a priest's daughter who marries an Israelite of unimpaired stock, and one who marries an Israelite who is not fit for marriage to priests. His point is made through the contrast. Upon divorce or widowhood the woman at D returns to her father's house and regains her previously held priestly rights. It follows for Meir that she is treated like a person of priestly status. If she commits adultery, she is executed by burning, as are all women of priestly caste who commit adultery (Lev. 21:9, M. San. 9:1). This is not the case at G. where the woman has married an Israelite of impaired lineage. Such a woman never may return to her father's house. Meir holds, therefore, that she is treated under the law as an Israelite. If she is unfaithful, her death is by strangulation, as it is for all Israelite women who are unfaithful (M. San. 11:1). On this basis we readily can interpret Meir's view regarding the restitution these women pay if they unintentionally eat heave-offering. The priest's daughter who marries an Israelite of unimpaired stock is treated like a person of priestly status. If she eats heave-offering she does not pay the added fifth, which is paid only by non-priests. Since she had no right to eat the heave-offering, however, she must replace it, as would any priest who ate heave-offering belonging to some other priest. For this reason she pays the principal. This is not the case at F. Since here the woman is treated like an Israelite, if she eats heave-offering, she must pay both the principal and the added fifth. Sages reject Meir's distinction. By birth the woman is of priestly stock. This is not changed by her marriage to a non-priest, even one of impaired lineage. After her marriage she does not have the right to eat heave-offering. If she does so anyway, since she is of priestly stock, she need not pay the added fifth required of non-priests. If she commits adultery, her death is by burning, as it is in the case of all unfaithful priestly women.]

XIII.

A. R. Eliezer says, "If she committed adultery with her father, she is put to death through burning, and is if she did so with her father in law, it is through stoning."

B. What is the meaning of the foregoing statement?

C. Should one propose that "her father" means that she committed adultery with her father, and "with her father in law" means that she committed adultery with her father in law, then why address in particular the case of the daughter of a priest?

D. Even if it were the daughter of an Israelite, the penalty of committing adultery with the father is punishable by burning, and with the father-in-law, by stoning.

E. But the phrase, "with her father" means "in the domain of her father," and "with her father in law" means in the domain of her father in law. [The former, then, is betrothed, the latter fully wed.]

F. In accord with whose view is the statement of Eliezer made, then? It cannot be in accord with the view of rabbis, for have they not said that a married woman [who committed adultery] goes forth to execution through burning?

G. And that penalty could not apply, then, to the betrothed girl [as Eliezer claims].

H. It furthermore cannot accord with the view of R. Simeon, for has he nor said that the same penalty, namely, burning, applies to both the betrothed girl and the married woman?

I. And it could also not accord with R. Ishmael, for has he not said [in a passage given below XV B-C] that the betrothed girl [who commits adultery] goes forth to execution through being burned, but not a married woman, so that, when in the domain of her father in law [as a married woman, should she commit adultery,] she is put to death by being strangled [and not through stoning]?

J. Rabin sent word in the name of R. Yose b. R. Hanina, "This is the sense of the teaching [of Eliezer].

K. "In point of fact it accords with rabbis. And this is the sense of what he has said:

L. "In any case in which the penalty of a woman who has committed adultery is more lenient than that inflicted on her father for incest [with his daughter]

M. "and what would such a case be? It is the case of an Israelite's daughter, for, if the Israelite's daughter is married [and commits adultery], she would be put to death through strangling [while her father is put to death through burning]

N. "then in the present case, namely, that of the priest's daughter, she would be put to death in the same way as the father, namely through burning.

O. "But in any case in which the mode of execution of the woman who has committed adultery is more stringent than that inflicted of her father [for incest with his daughter]

P. "and what would such a case be? It is the case of an Israelite's daughter who is betrothed [and commits adultery], for an Israelite's daughter who is betrothed would be put to death through stoning

Q. "then in the present case, namely that of the priest's daughter, she would be put to death in the mode of execution that would apply to her father-in-law should he commit incest, and that is, through stoning."

R. To this interpretation R. Jeremiah objected, "But does the passage at hand speak of penalties that are more or less stringent than one another? [Obviously not. The explanation is a complete fabrication.]"

S.   Rather, said R. Jeremiah, "[51B] The statement of Eliezer] accords with the position of R. Ishmael.

T.   "This is the sense of his statement:

U.   "'With her father' means that when she is in the domain of her father [as an engaged girl, and commits adultery], she is put to death through burning, while 'with her father-in-law' means that if she commits adultery [literally] with her father-in-law, she is put to death through stoning.

V.   "If, on the other hand, she committed adultery with anyone else, she is put to death through strangling."

W.   Said Raba, "How can there be a distinction in the reading of the two halves of his statement? Either both clauses refer to literal [incest], or both refer to the domain in which she is located [that is to say, as an engaged or married woman, respectively]."

X.   Rather, said Raba, "The passage accords with the position of R. Simeon [in line with his view that burning is the most severe mode of execution].

Y.   "R. Eliezer takes the view that the married woman is in the same category as the betrothed woman.

Z.   "Just as, with an engaged girl [who commits adultery], [the penalty imposed upon a priest's daughter who commits adultery] is raised one step [over that applicable to an Israelite's daughter who commits adultery], that is to say, from death by stoning to death by burning, so in he case of a married woman [who commits adultery], we raise the severity of the mode of execution [should such a woman commit adultery] by one step, that is to say, from strangulation to stoning."

AA.   To this explanation R. Hanina objected, "But R. Simeon takes the view that both categories of woman [should they commit adultery] are put to death through burning."

BB.   Rather, said Rabina, "In point of fact [Eliezer] accords with rabbis. The assigned views, however, have to be exchanged, so that if she commits adultery while in her father's house [as a betrothed girl], she is put to death through stoning, and if it is in her father-in-law's domain [as a married woman], it is through burning.

CC.   "And as to [Eliezer's] use of the phrase, 'with her father,' it is simply a common usage."

DD.   Said R. Nahman said Rabbah bar Abbuha said Rab, "The decided law accords with the message that was sent by Rabin in the name of R. Yose b. R. Hanina."

EE.   Said R. Joseph, "That is a legal decision that will only apply to the times of the Messiah [since the law is not carried out at this time in he modes of execution specified by the Mishnah]!"

FF.   Said Abayye to him, "If that is the case, then people should not repeat the laws governing the cultic slaughter of animals designated as Holy Things, since these two are laws that will be applicable only after the Messiah comes [and rebuilds the Temple].

GG.   "But the principle is to expound these laws and receive a reward for doing so, and here too, we expound the laws and receive a reward for doing so."

HH. [He replied], "This is the sense of what I said: What do I need a decision on the practical law? As the discussion went on, for what purpose would anyone have stated a concrete legal decision?"

XIV.

A. [As to the statement above, XIV I], what is the source for R. Ishmael's statement?

B. It has been taught on Tannaite authority:

C. "'And the daughter of any priest, if she profanes herself by playing the whore' (Lev. 21:9):

D. "Scripture speaks of a girl who is betrothed.

E. "You say that Scripture speaks of a girl who is betrothed, but perhaps it refers even to one who is married.

F. "Scripture says, 'And the man who commits adultery with another man's wife, even he who commits adultery with his neighbor's wife, both the adulterer and the adulteress shall be put to death' (Lev. 20:10).

G. "All categories of persons are encompassed within the terms 'adulterer' and 'adulteress.' Now Scripture has singled out the daughter of an Israelite [who commits adultery,] who is to be put to death through stoning, and the daughter of a priest [who commits adultery], who is to be put to death through burning.

H. "Now, when Scripture made explicit references to the daughter of an Israelite, who, if she committed adultery, was to be put to death through stoning, it then specified that it was a betrothed girl and not a married woman.

I. "So too when Scripture singled out the daughter of a priest [who committed adultery], it indicated that she was to be put to death through burning. Scripture thus referred to a betrothed girl and not a woman.

J. "Perjured witnesses and the lover [of a married woman, who committed adultery] also were encompassed within the verse, 'If a false witness rise up against any man to testify against him that which is wrong ...] then you shall do to him as he had conspired to do to his brother' (Deut. 19:16-19).

K. "Now what aspect of a conspiracy to commit perjury can apply to the lover?

L. "Rather: The penalty to be inflicted on a conspiracy of perjury against the woman had fallen into the category of the death penalty to be inflicted on the lover [of the married woman], in line with the simple statement of Scripture, 'And you shall do to him as he had conspired to do to his brother' (Deut. 19:19) -- to his brother and not to his sister," the words of R. Ishmael. [Freedman, p. 347, n. 2: When a priest's daughter commits adultery, she is burned, but her lover is stoned; hence if witnesses testified falsely on such a charge, they are to be stoned, not burned.]

M. R. Aqiba says, "The same rule applies both to the betrothed girl and to the married woman [who have committed adultery]. They go forth to be put to death through burning.

N. "Is it possible that that is the case even if the woman is unmarried?

O. "Here it is stated, 'Her father,' and elsewhere the same word is used. Just as in the latter case an act of whoredom applies only if the woman is subject to a husband, so here too the act of whoredom is punishable only if she is subject to a husband."

P.   Said R. Ishmael to him, "Just as, in that latter passage, she is a girl who is betrothed, so here, she is a girl, and she is betrothed, [but if she is a married woman, the punishment she should be different]."

Q.   Said R. Aqiba to him, "Ishmael, by brother, I explain the language, 'and the daughter' where it would have sufficed to say merely 'the daughter.' [This additional word, and, serves to encompass the married woman]."

R.   He said to him, "And because you interpret the additional use of the word 'and' in connection with the daughter, should we take out this woman and [impose a more stringent mode of execution and so burn her [as a penalty]?

S.   "If the use of the word 'and' serves to encompass the married woman, then why not encompass within the law also the unmarried woman [instead of freeing her from all penalty]?

T.   "And if the use of the superfluous 'and' serves to exclude the unmarried woman [from all penalty], then let it serve also to omit all reference even to the married woman."

U.   And R. Aqiba's view? The argument by analogy serves to exclude reference to the unmarried woman, and the use of the additional word, "and," with reference to the daughter, serves to encompass the married woman.

V.   And R. Ishmael? He takes the view that since [Aqiba] has said to him that the exegesis was based on the superfluous use of the word, "and," it bore the further implication that he had retracted the argument by analogy.

W.   And how does R. Ishmael interpret the superfluous "and" with reference to the daughter?

X.   He requires it to serve the purposes of the teaching on Tannaite authority of the father of Samuel bar Abin: "Is it possible to suppose that just as the Scripture has made distinctions among male priests between those who are unblemished and those who bear blemishes [who cannot participate in the Temple cult],

Y.   "so we should distinguish among the daughters of priests [along the same lines, e.g., with regard to an act of adultery, punishing blemished daughters of the priestly caste who commit adultery as if they were of the Israelite caste and not burning them as their mode of execution]?

Z.   "Scripture uses the word" 'and' where it is not needed [to serve the purpose of proving that all daughters of the priestly caste, whatever their physical condition, are put to death by burning should they commit adultery]."

AA. And R. Aqiba? [How does he prove the same proposition]?

BB. He derives it from the verse, "[For the offerings of the Lord made by fire and the bread of their God] they do offer; therefore they shall be holy" (Lev. 21:6). [Freedman, p. 348, n. 6: "Therefore they shall be holy" is an emphatic assertion of their holiness, implying that they do not lose it even if blemished.]

CC. And R. Ishmael?

DD. If I had to derive proof from that passage, I should have reached the conclusion that the statement applies to them, but not to their daughters. So we are informed [by the use of the extra "and" that the daughters are included as well].

EE. And as to R. Ishmael, [52A] how does he deal with the verse, "She profanes her father" (Lev. 21:9)?

FF. He interprets it along the lines of that which has been taught on Tannaite authority:

GG. R. Meir would say, "What is the meaning of the statement, 'She profanes her father' (Lev. 21:9)?

HH. "If [her father] had been treated as holy, now he is treated as ordinary.

II. "If he had been paid honor, now he is treated with disgrace.

JJ. "They say, 'Cursed is he who produced such a child, cursed is he who raised her, cursed is he who brought her forth from his loins.'"

KK. Said R. Ashi, "In accord with whom do people call a wicked man, 'Son of a wicked man,' even if it is a wicked man who is son of a righteous man?

LL. "It is in accord with the Tannaite authority just now cited."

XV.

A. This procedure is how the religious requirement of stoning is carried out [M. 7:1D]:

B. What is the sense of the Tannaite authority in saying, This procedure is how the religious requirement of stoning is carried out?

C. It is because, just prior, it has been taught:

D. When the trial is over, they take him out to stone him. The place of stoning was well outside the court ... [M. 6:1A-B].

E. Now since the framer of the passage planned to make reference to the religious duty of inflicting the death penalty through burning, he made reference, also, to the religious duty of inflicting the death penalty through stoning.

While the Talmud at hand is somewhat protracted, it is remarkably cogent, taking up only a few problems and treating them at some length. So once more the impression that the document is somewhat prolix turns out, upon closer analysis, to be inaccurate. Unit I sets the stage, because it raises the question of the issue between the anonymous ruling and Simeon's revised order and asks why the difference. Units II, III then explain the reasoning behind the two positions, each one working its way step by step through the four items at hand. So sustained and beautifully executed a construction cannot fail to win admiration. Unit IV then moves on to the diverse circumstances in which the penalty of stoning as against burning may be inflicted, explicitly bringing us back to the dispute at hand at M. 7:1. Unit V carries forward the foregoing discussion. Unit VI then begins what turns out to be a long and intricate, but completely unified construction, running on through unit XV, an amazingly thorough and sustained discourse. The relevance of the entire set is established at unit V, so the bulk of the Talmud at hand, from unit II to unit XVI, turns out to form a composite from a single hand. Unit XVI then explains the sense of M. 7:1D.

7:2

A. The religious requirement of burning [is carried out as follows]:

B. They would bury him up to his armpits in manure, and put a towel of hard material inside one of soft material, and wrap it around his neck.

C.   This [witness] pulls it to him from one side, and that witness pulls it to him at the other side, until he opens up his mouth.

D.   And one kindles a wick and throws it into his mouth, and it goes down into his bowels and burns his intestines.

E.   R. Judah says, "Also this one: if he died at their hands [through strangulation], they will not have carried out the religious requirement of burning [in the proper manner].

F.   "But: They open his mouth with tongs, against his will, kindle a wick, and throw it into his mouth, and it goes down into his bowels and burns his intestines."

G.   Said R. Eleazar b. Sadoq, "There was the case of a priest who committed adultery.

H.   "And they put bundles of twigs around her and burned her."

I.   They said to him, "It was because the court of that time was not expert [in the law]."

I.

A.   What is a wick [M. 7:2D]?

B.   Said R. Mattenah, "It is a strip of lead."

II.

A.   How do we know [that death through burning is carried on in this way, rather than in that posited at M. 7:2H]?

B.   We establish an analogy between the meaning of the word "burning" used in the context of the death penalty [Lev. 21:9], and the meaning of the word "burning" used in connection with the congregation of Korach [Num. 17:4].

C.   Just as, in that latter case, it involved burning the soul, with the body intact, so in the present case, it involves burning the soul, with the body intact.

D.   R. Eleazar said, "We establish an analogy governing the word 'burning' in the present context from the meaning of the word 'burning' in the case of Aaron's sons.

E.   "Just as in that case [Lev. 10:6] it involved burning the soul, with the body intact, so here there must be burning of the soul with the body intact."

F.   What is the scriptural basis for the position of the one who derives evidence from the congregation of Korach?

G.   It is because it is written, "[Speak to Eleazar ... that he take up the censers out of the burning ...], the censers of these sinners against their own souls" (Lev. 17:2), indicating that their souls were burned while the body was intact.

H.   And the other party?

I.   He maintains that that passage refers, literally, to burning. And what is the sense of "against their own souls"? That they incurred liability to the burning of the souls on account of matters having to do with their souls.

J.   This accords with the view of R. Simeon b. Laqish.

K.   For R. Simeon b. Laqish said, "What is the meaning of the verse, 'With hypocritical mockers in feasts, they gnashed upon me with their teeth' (Ps. 35:16)?

L.   "On account of the hypocrisy that they showed to Korach on account of the banquet [that he laid out for them], the prince of Gehenna sharpened his teeth against them."

M.   Now as to the view of him who derives the meaning of the passage from the case of the sons of Aaron, on what scriptural basis does he reach his view?

N.   It is because it is written, "And they died before the Lord" (Lev. 10:12), that is, death of an ordinary character.

O.   And the other party?

P.   That passage alludes to burning, literally.

Q.   And what is the sense of the statement, "They died before the Lord"? It began within, as is the case with an ordinary death.

R.   That accords with what has been taught on Tannaite authority:

S.   Abba Yose b. Dosetai says, "Two streams of fire spurted forth from the house of the holy of holies and divided into four and entered the two nostrils of this one and the two nostrils of that one and burned them up [internally]."

T.   But lo, it is written, "And the fire devoured them" (Lev. 10:12) -- [them, and not another thing, so what is excluded]?

U.   "Them" -- and not their garments.

V.   And why not derive [the mode of inflicting the death penalty through burning] by analogy to the disposition of the bulls that are to be burned up [Lev. 4:12ff.]? Just as in that case, burning is meant literally, so here, burning should be meant literally.

W.   It is more reasonable to derive the analogy to a case involving a human being, for in the case of a human being [there are the following shared traits]: it is a human being, the act involves a sin, the human being has a soul, and in a human being there is no issue of an improper motive's rendering the death invalid [while for a sacrificial beast, if a priest forms the intention of eating the meat after the prescribed limits, the sacrifice is invalidated].

X.   To the contrary, it would be better to derive the matter from the analogy supplied by the bulls that are to burned, for [while the cases of Aaron's sons and the congregation of Korach were one-time events only], the mode of killing in the case of the bulls that are to be burned serves for generations to come [Freedman: permanency. Freedman, p. 351, n. 6: The law of execution by fire, as that of sacrifices, was of permanent validity, whereas in the other two cases their deaths were unique, the result of miracles confined to particular times.]

Y.   The former consideration [Y] are more numerous.

Z.   As to the one who derives the analogy from the case of the congregation of Korach, what is the reason that he did not derive the analogy from the death of the sons of Aaron?

AA.   That case involved burning in a literal sense.

BB.   And why not derive the analogy from that case anyhow?

CC.   Said R. Nahman said Rabbah bar Abbuha, "Scripture has said, 'But you shall love your neighbor as yourself' (Lev. 19:18), meaning, choose for him a form of execution that is easy [and the burning of the body is painful]."

DD. But if there is the exegesis provided by R. Nahman, what need do I have for the argument by analogy at all?

EE. Were it not for the argument by analogy, I might have concluded that the burning of the soul with the body left intact is not a mode of burning at all.

FF. And if the principle derived solely from the exegesis, "You shall love your neighbor as yourself" (Lev. 19:18), then one should collect many bundles of twigs, so that the victim will burn up quickly.

GG. So we are informed [of the appropriate mode of burning].

III.

A. Now Moses and Aaron were walking on the way, and Nadab and Abihu were walking behind them, with all Israel after them. Said Nadab to Abihu, "When will these two elders die, so that you and I may become leaders of the generation?"

B. Said the Holy One, blessed be he, to them, "Now let us see who will bury whom."

C. Said R. Pappa, "That is in line with what people say: 'There are many old camels bearing the hides of young camels.'"

IV.

A. Said R. Eleazar, [52B] "What is a disciple of a sage like in the view of an ordinary person?

B. "At the outset he is like a gold ladle.

C. "If he talks with him, he is like a silver ladle.

D. "If he accepts some sort of benefit from him, he is like an earthenware ladle.

E. "Once it is broken, it cannot ever be repaired." [Freedman, p. 352, n. 4: This passage is inserted here because the assembly of Korach has just been mentioned, who were scholars (Num. 16:2). These, becoming overfamiliar with Korach and accepting gifts from him, lost his esteem, until ultimately he incited them to support him in his revolt against Moses.]

V.

A. Imrata, daughter of Teli, was the daughter of a priest who committed an act of adultery.

B. R. Hama bar Tubiah had her surrounded by twigs and burned.

C. Said R. Joseph, "You erred in two matters.

D. "You erred in the matter of R. Mattenah [on how the execution through burning was to be done].

E. "And you erred in that which has been taught on Tannaite authority:

F. "'And you shall come to the priests, Levites, and judge that shall be in those days' (Deut. 17:9). This verse teaches that when there is a priest [at the altar], there is judgment [of capital cases in the Jewish courts, including inflicting capital punishment], but when there is no priest, there is no such judgment.'"

VI.

A. Said R. Eleazar b. Sadoq, "There was the case of the daughter of a priest who committed adultery ..." [M. 7:2G]:

B. Said R. Joseph, "It was a court made up of Sadduccees."

C. Did [Eleazar] say this to them, and did they answer him in this way?

D. And has it not been taught on Tannaite authority:

E. **Said R. Eleazar bar Sadoq, "I was a child, and I was riding on my father's shoulders, and I saw the daughter of a priest who had committed adultery, and they put bundles of twigs around her and burned her" [M. 7:2G-H].**

F. **They said to him, "You were a child, and a child has no evidence [to contribute to our discussion]" [T. San. 9:11A-B].**

G. [Since the argument in the cited passage is different from the one at M. 7:2I, one must explain that] there were two separate cases [about which he reported].

H. Which one did he report first of all?

I. If one should propose that it was this first one [cited at M. 7:2I] that he reported to them first, the one that took place when he was an adult, and they paid no attention to him, would he then have told them a story of what happened when he was a minor and expect to have them pay attention to him?

J. Rather, it was this one [at T. San. 9:11A-B] that he told them first, and when they said to him, "You were a child" then he told them the story of what happened when he was an adult, and they said to him, "It was because the court of that time was not expert in the law" [M. 7:2I].

The Talmud closely follows its usual program of Mishnah-interpretation. It begins, unit I, with a comment on a word-choice, and then proceeds, as usual, to an extensive account of the basis, in Scripture -- here, scriptural analogies -- for the rule in the Mishnah. Units III and IV develop materials on one of the analogies investigated in unit II. Units V and VI then proceed to materials pertinent to M. 7:2G-I, as indicated.

7:3A-F

A. The religious requirement of decapitation [is carried out as follows]:

B. They would cut off his head with a sword,

C. just as the government does.

D. R. Judah says, "This is disgusting.

E. "But they put his head on a block and chop it off with an ax."

F. They said to him, "There is no form of death more disgusting than this one."

I.

A. It has been taught on Tannaite authority:

B. **Said R. Judah to sages, "I too recognize that it is a disgusting form of death, but what shall I do?**

C. **"For lo, the Torah has said, 'You will not follow their ordinances' (Lev. 18:3)" [T. San. 9:11C-H].**

D. And rabbis? [They reply], "Since execution through the sword is written in the Torah, it is not a matter of learning [our rules] from what [gentiles] do.

E.   "And if you do not concede that point, as to that which we have learned on Tannaite authority, **They make burnings in honor of deceased kings, and this is not forbidden on the count of being one of the ways of the Amorites [T. Shab. 7:18]**, how can we make such a pyre? And lo, it is written, 'You will not follow their ordinances' (lev. 18:3)!

F.   "But since the matter of a funeral pyre is written in the Torah, as it is written, 'But you shall die in peace and with the burning of your fathers ... so shall they burn for you' (Jer. 34:5), it is not from [the gentiles] that we learn the practice.

G.   "Here too, since it is in the Torah that execution by the sword is written, it is not from the gentiles that we learn the practice."

II.

A.   And as to what we have learned in the Mishnah:

B.   And these are those who are put to death through decapitation: the murderer and the townsfolk of an apostate town [M. San. 9:1D-E], [What is the scriptural basis for decapitation in these crimes]?

C.   Now with respect to the apostate town, it is written, "You shall surely smite the inhabitants of that town with the edge of the sword" (Deut. 13:18).

D.   But how do we know that that is the case for the murderer?

E.   As it has been taught on Tannaite authority:

F.   "He shall surely be avenged" (Ex. 21:20).

G.   I do not now the form of this vengeance. When Scripture says, "I will bring a sword upon you, that shall execute the vengeance of the covenant" (Lev. 26:25), one has to say that this form of vengeance is through the sword.

H.   And might I say that one has to pierce the man through?

I.   It is written, "With the edge of the sword."

J.   Then might I say that one cuts the felon in half [lengthwise]?

K.   Said R. Nahman said Rabbah bar Abbuha, "Scripture has said, 'You shall love your neighbor as yourself' (Lev. 19:18), meaning that you should choose for him a form of death that is easy."

L.   [Since the context of Ex. 21:20 is vengeance for the death of a slave], we have found that when one has killed a slave [he is put to death through decapitation].

M.   How do we know that if one killed a free man, the same rule applies?

N.   Is it not an argument a fortiori?

O.   If one kills a slave, he is put to death through decapitation. If he killed a free man, should it be merely through strangulation [that he is put to death]?

P.   That argument poses no problem to the view of him who has said that strangulation is the lighter form of execution. But in the view of him who has said that strangulation is the more severe form, what sort of argument can you supply?

Q.   It derives from that which has been taught on Tannaite authority:

R.   "So you shall put away the built of the innocent blood among you" (Deut. 21:9)

S.   The case of all those who shed blood is compared to the case of the heifer whose neck is to be broken.

T. Just as in that case, the execution takes places with a sword at the neck, so here the execution takes place with a sword at the neck.

U. If one should propose that, just as in that case, it is done with an ax at the nape of the neck, so here too it should be done with an at at the nape of the neck, [the answer derives from the argument already given].

V. Namely, said R. Nahman said Rabbah bar Abbuha, "Scripture has said, 'You will love your neighbor as yourself' (Lev. 19:18), meaning to choose for him a form of death that is easy."

Unit I expands upon the Mishnah's argument. Unit II then supplies the proof, on the basis of Scripture, to which unit I refers.

7:3G-J

G. The religious requirement of strangulation [is carried out as follows:]

H. They would bury him in manure up to his armpits, and put a towel of hard material inside one of soft material, and wrap it around his neck.

I. This [witness] pulls it to him from one side, and that witness pulls it to him at the other side,

J. until he perishes.

I.

A. Our rabbis have taught on Tannaite authority:

B. ["And the man who commits adultery with another man's wife, even he who commits adultery with his neighbor's wife, the adulterer and the adulteress shall surely be put to death" (Lev. 20:10)]. "A man" -- excluding a minor.

C. "... who commits adultery with another man's wife" -- excluding the wife of a minor.

D. "His neighbor's wife -- excluding the wife of others [idolators]."

E. "' ... shall surely be put to death' -- through strangulation.

F. "You say that it is through strangulation.

G. "But perhaps it is only through one of any of the other modes of inflicting the death penalty that are stated in the Torah?

H. "Now do you say so? In any passage in which there is reference in the Torah to 'death-penalty' without further specification, you do not have the right to impose the death penalty in a stringent manner but only in a lenient manner," the words of R. Josiah.

I. R. Jonathan says, "It is not because this is the mot lenient of the modes of execution, but because in any passage in the Torah in which there is reference to the death-penalty without further specification, it is to be inflicted only through strangulation."

J. [In support of this same proposition] Rabbi says, "There is reference to death inflicted at the hand of heaven and there is reference to death inflicted at the hand of man.

K.   "Just as death inflicted at the hand of heaven is such that there is no physical mark [on the body], so death inflicted at the hand of man [in the same sort of passage] is death in which there is no physical mark [on the body], [and that is strangulation]."

L.   And might I say that that is burning [in the manner described just now]?

M.   Since the All-Merciful has specified that the daughter of a priest]who commits adultery] is put to death through burning, it must follow that adultery under discussion here is <u>not</u> punished by the death penalty inflicted through burning [but in some other way than that specified at the counterpart]."

N.   [53A] Now there are no problems from the viewpoint of R. Jonathan, since Rabbi has already provided an explanation of his reasoning.

O.   But as to R. Josiah, on what basis do we know that the death penalty is inflicted through strangulation in any event? Might I say it is through decapitation?

P.   Said Raba, "We have a tradition that there are four modes of inflicting the death penalty [M. 7:1A]."

Q.   What is the sense of the statement, "It is not because it is the most lenient form of the death penalty" [at I, above]?

R.   The dispute follows the lines of that between R. Simeon and rabbis [at M. 7:1].

II.

A.   Said R. Zira to Abayye, "As to the rest of those who are put to death through stoning, in connection with those cases Scripture does not explicitly specify that stoning is the mode of inflicting the death penalty, so that stoning is the choice mode of execution is a proposition we derive by analogy to the case of the necromancer or wizard [put to death through stoning], on the basis of which relevant phrase [of those specified at B] do we derive that fact?

B.   "Do we derive that fact from the phrase, 'They shall surely be put to death'? Or do we derive it from the phrase, 'Their blood shall be upon them' (Lev. 20:27)?" [The relevant verse is as follows: 'A man or a woman who has a familiar spirit or who is a wizard they shall surely be put to death; they shall stone them with stones; their blood shall be upon them.'] [Freedman, p. 357, n. 7: In the case of all other malefactors who are stoned, though stoning is not explicitly stated, the two phrases, 'They shall surely be put to death' and 'their blood shall be upon their head' occur.]

C.   He said to him, "We derive the fact that they are put to death through stoning from the phrase, common to those other cases as well as to the case of the wizard or necromancer, 'Their blood shall be upon them.'

D.   "For if we should derive the matter from the phrase, 'They shall surely die,' what need do I have for the phrase concerning 'their blood'?

E.   "But what is the purpose of the repeated use of the statement about 'their blood'? It is to supply the needed analogy to tell us that stoning applies in both cases.

F.   "What need do I have, then, for the phrase, 'They shall surely die'"

G.   "It accords with that which has been taught on Tannaite authority:

H.   "'He who smote him shall surely die. He is a murderer' (Num. 35:21).

I.   "'I know only that that applies to a mode of execution that is specified in Scripture in his regard.

J. "'How do I know that, if you cannot put him to death through the mode of execution that is specified in his connection in Scripture, you may put him to death through any means of inflicting death that you can use?

K. "'Scripture says, "He who smote him shall surely die" (Num. 35:21), meaning, by any means at all.'"

L. Said R. Aha of Difti to Rabina, "As to deriving the proof from the phrase, 'He shall surely die,' what was the difficulty that troubled him [leading him to raise the question at all]?

M. "Should I propose that the difficulty lay in the case of the penalty to be inflicted on the married woman who committed adultery [who, we know, suffers the death penalty through strangulation]?

N. "That is to say, one should derive the mode of execution in her case from the analogy of the words, 'He shall surely die' used in connection with the necromancer and wizard, so that, just in that case, the penalty is inflicted through stoning, so here it is inflicted by stoning. [Freedman, p. 358, n. 5: Instead of regarding it as an unspecified death penalty, why not treat it as explicit, in virtue of the phrase, 'They shall surely be put to death,' written also in the case of adultery with a married woman?]

O. "But since the All-Merciful made it explicit that the betrothed girl who committed adultery is put to death through stoning, it must follow that the married woman who committed adultery would not be put to death through stoning, [so that problem really is null].

P. "Rather, it was the fact that he who his father or mother [is put to death through strangulation] that troubled him.

Q. "[This is the difficulty:] one should derive proof from the case of the necromancer or wizard [that he is stoned. Why? Because the phrase at hand, 'He shall surely be put to death' is used of the one who hits his mother or father as well, at Ex. 21:15].

R. "But rather than deriving the mode of execution in the case of the necromancer or wizard, why not derive it from the case of a married woman [who is put to death through strangulation], for you do not have the right to derive a stringent mode of execution for him when you can derive a lenient mode of execution from him. [So what was the problem that led to his question?] [Freedman, p. 358, n. lo: For the same phrase occurs in the three places, namely, the necromancer, put to death through stoning, the married woman, put to death through strangulation, and he hits his father or mother, which has to be deduced from the one or the other. It follows that one must incline to leniency. So even if the dedication were made from the phrase, 'They shall surely be put to death,' it would be still correct to say that one who hits his father or mother is strangled.]"

S. He said to him, "What troubled him was the case of all of the others who are put to death through stoning. For if it is from the phrase, 'They shall surely be put to death,' that we derive the fact that the mode of executing them is through stoning, why derive that fact from the case of the necromancer or wizard? Derive it from the case of the married woman who committed adultery [on the principle that we impose the more lenient form of the death penalty]."

Unit I contributes the information of who is put to death through the mode of execution at hand, with the not-incidental information of why death is inflicted in just this way, namely, there is no mark on the body. Unit II then presents a much more complex problem of the scriptural basis for imposing the death penalty in this way, linked, as is clear, to unit I's proof on the basis of the adultery of the woman. So the composition is quite cogent, even though the two units are entirely distinct from one another -- a fine piece of construction.

7:4 A-R

A. These are [the felons] who are put to death by stoning:

B. He who has sexual relations with his mother, with the wife of his father, with his daughter-in-law, with a male, and with a cow;

C. and the women who brings an ox on top of herself;

D. and he who blasphemes, he who performs an act of worship for an idol, he who gives of his seed to Molech, he who is a familiar spirit, and he who is a soothsayer;

E. he who profanes the Sabbath,

F. he who curses his father or his mother.

G. he who has sexual relations with a bethrothed maiden,

H. he who beguiles [entices a whole town to idolatry],

I. a sorcerer,

J. and a stubborn and incorrigible son.

K. He who has sexual relations with his mother is liable on her account because of her being his mother and because of her being his father's wife [Lev. 18:6-7, 20:11].

L. R. Judah says, "He is liable only on account of her being his mother alone."

M. He who has sexual relations with his father's wife is liable on her account because of her being his father's wife and because of her being a married woman,

N. whether this is in the lifetime of his father or after the death of his father,

O. whether she is only betrothed or already married [to the father].

P. He who has sexual relations with his daughter-in-law is liable on her account because of her being his daughter-in-law and because of her being another man's wife,

Q. whether this is in the lifetime of his son or after the death of his son [Lev. 20:12,

R. whether she is only betrothed or already married [to the son].

I.

A.   It has been taught on Tannaite authority:

B.   **R. Judah says, "If his mother was not fit to be married to his father, he is liable only on the count of her being his mother [but not on the count of her being a married woman], [T. San. 10:1A].**

C.   What is the meaning of his statement **if she was not fit to be married to his father**?

D.   Should we say that it is a marriage forbidden on pain of liability to extirpation and liability to the death penalty at the hands of a court? [That is, the father is subject to the death penalty either at the hands of heaven or at human hands on account of his marriage to this woman]. Then it would follow that the rabbis take the view that even though the woman is not fit for the father, [there is a twofold penalty]. But [given the penalties of death] the father in point of fact has no sacramental bond to his woman at all! [So how can the son incur the penalty of having sexual relations with a married woman, when in point of fact she is not a married woman?]

E.   It must follow that [Judah's sense is that she is not fit for the father because the couple falls into the category of those who, if they marry], are subject to the penalty for violating a negative commandment [but not to the penalty of extirpation or execution by a court].

F.   Then it follows that R. Judah concurs with R. Aqiba, who held that there is no sacramental bond between a couple who, [if they wed,] are subject to liability for violating a negative commandment.

G.   To this proposition, R. Oshaia raised the objection,

H.   "[A general rule did they lay down in regard to the levirate woman, widow of a deceased childless brother: any sister-in-law who is prohibited as one of the forbidden degrees of Leviticus Chapter Eighteen neither executes the rite of removing the shoe, specified at Deut. 25:5-10, nor is taken into levirate marriage.] [If she is prohibited to her brother-in-law by reason of a prohibition on account of a commandment or a prohibition on account of sanctity, she executes the rite of removing the shoe but is not taken in levirate marriage. [54B] A prohibition on account of a commandment is a secondary grade of forbidden degrees on account of the rulings of scribes [M. Yeb. 2:3, 2:4A].

I.   "Now why do they call such [marriages] 'prohibited on account of a commandment as a secondary grade of forbidden degrees on account of rulings of scribes'? Because it is a commandment to obey the teaching of sages.

J.   **"A prohibition on account of the sanctity of the levir is a widow married to a high priest, or a divorcee or a woman who has executed the rite of removing the shoe married to an ordinary priest [M. Yeb. 2:4B].**

K.   "And why do they call such marriages 'prohibited on account of the sanctity of the levir' Because it is written, 'The priests shall be holy unto their God' (Lev 21:6).

L.   "And in this connection it has been taught on Tannaite authority: R. Judah reverses these definitions. [T. Yeb. 2:4J: R. Judah says, 'A widow wed to a high priest, or a divorcee or a woman who has undergone the rite of removing the shoe wed to an ordinary priest, fall into the category of those prohibited on account of a commandment. A secondary grade of forbidden degrees (listed at Leviticus Chapter Eighteen) on account of rulings of scribes constitutes a prohibition on account of sanctity.']

M.   "Now while he reverses the definition, for both categories he nonetheless requires the rite of removing the shoe, [hence recognizing that a marital bond of some sort existed between the priest and the woman improperly wed to him, that is, in violation of the negative commandment that such a woman not be wed to a priest.]

N.   "If, then, you maintain the view that R. Judah accords with R. Aqiba, then, since in R. Aqiba's view, couples who, if they wed, are liable for violating a negative commandment are in the status of couples who, if they wed, are subject to extirpation, and couples who, if they wed, become liable to the penalty of extirpation do not fall into the category of a marriage sufficiently strong to impose the obligation to undergo the rite of removing the shoe, let alone the obligation of levirate marriage should the husband die childless [there being no valid and legal connection between this man and this woman at all], [how could Judah concur that there is any obligation, in the present context, to undergo the rite of removing the shoe? Aqiba would never impose such an obligation, as we see l.]"

O.   [The reply:] [Judah] made his statement in accord with the position of the anonymous authority of the Mishnah-paragraph at hand but, in point of fact, he does not concur with the premises of that authority. [Judah maintains that there is no requirement of either removing the shoe or levirate marriage.]

II.

A.   When R. Isaac came, he repeated the Mishnah passage as we have learned it: 'R. Judah says, "He is liable only on account of her being his mother" [M. 7:4L].'

B.   [He then said,] "And what is the scriptural basis for his view [that the rule applies not only when she is forbidden to the father, but under all circumstances?]'

C.   Said Abbaye, "It is because Scripture has said, '[The nakedness of your father or the nakedness of your mother you shall not uncover;] she is your mother' (Lev. 18:7).

D.   "It is because she is his mother that you impose liability, and you do not impose liability because she is a married woman."

E.   How then do you deal with the following: "The nakedness of your father's wife you shall not uncover; it is your father's nakedness," (Lev. 18:8)? [Surely it means] you impose liability because she is his father's wife, and you do not impose liability [in this case] because she is his mother [his step-mother]?

F.   Rather, in the present case, we deal with his mother who is his father's wife, then [Freedman:] one verse implies the exclusion of maternal incest [as the offense], and the other excludes incest with his father's wife [as the offense]. [Freedman, p. 362, n.1]: thus leaving no grounds for punishment at all.]

G. Now if she is his mother but not his father's wife, he is liable, and, if she is his father's wife but not his mother, he is liable. But if she is his mother and also his father's wife, will he not be liable at all? [That is absurd!]

H. And furthermore, from the viewpoint of rabbis too, is it not written, "She is your mother" (Lev. 18:7)?

I. Rather, they require that verse to make the point of R. Shisha, son of R. Idi [given presently].

J. R. Judah also requires the same verse to make the point of R. Shisha, son of R. Idi.

K. [We shall now prove the sought point from the viewpoint of rabbis, that a double-liability is incurred, in line with M. 7:4K and against Judah's view at M. 7:4L:] The matter is in line with what R. Aha, son of R. Iqa, said, "Scripture has stated, '[...you shall not uncover] her nakedness' (Lev. Lev. 18:8). On one count of nakedness you impose liability, and you do not impose liability on two counts of nakedness."

L. How then do you deal with the following verse: "You shall not uncover the nakedness of your daughter-in-law; she is your son's wife; you shall not uncover her nakedness" (Lev. 18:15). In this case, too, do we maintain that only on one count of nakedness you impose liability, but you do not impose liability on two counts of nakedness? But have we not learned in the Mishnah: He who has sexual relations with his daughter-in-law is liable on her account because of her being his daughter-in-law and because of her being another man's wife, whether this is in the lifetime of his son or after the death of his son [M.7:4P]. And here R. Judah does not differ! [So what has K contributed?]

M. But since she is one person, even though there are prohibitions on two counts, it is written, "...her nakedness...," and here too, since she is one person, even though there are prohibitions on two counts, it is written, "...her nakedness...."

N. Rather, [since the proposed proof does not work,] Raba said, "R. Judah takes the view that 'The nakedness of your father' refers to [the prohibition of sexual relations with] one's father's wife. Then, through the argument by analogy, he deduces that that is the case whether she is his father's wife who is also his mother, or his father's wife who is not also his mother.

O. "How, further, do we know that the penalty applies if he has sexual relations with his mother who is not his father's wife? Scripture says, '... the nakedness of your mother you will not uncover, she is your mother' (Lev. 18:8). [Then Judah concludes], 'On the count of her being his mother you impose liability upon him, and you do not impose liability upon him on the count of her being his father's wife." [Freedman, p. 362, n. 1, states: Thus, Raba agrees with Abbaye that R. Judah's reason is the limitation implied in the phrase 'she is thy mother'. But he disposes of the consequent difficulty, viz., that of the verse, it is thy father's nakedness, in the following way: The dictum, The nakedness of thy father shalt thou not uncover, refers to his father's wife, whether his mother or not; and so far, (without an additional limiting phrase) it is implied that in both cases the interdict is on account of paternal, not maternal consanguinity. Hence, when the following verse states, (The nakedness of thy father's wife thou shalt not uncover:) it is thy father's nakedness, it cannot mean that guilt is incurred only on account of paternal, but not maternal relationship, since that has already been implied in the preceding verse, the nakedness of thy father ... shalt thou not uncover. Therefore the limitation undoubtedly intended by the latter verse must be otherwise interpreted. (This is done further on.) Now, since the nakedness of thy father would imply that whether she is his mother or not he is penalised on account of paternal consanguinity, it follows that when the same verse inserts a limiting clause, 'she is thy mother', the limitation must apply to that which has already been expressed, viz., that the father's wife, if also one's mother, is forbidden on account of maternal, not paternal, consanguinity.]

P.   [54A]: In support of Raba's view it has been taught on Tannaite authority to the same effect:

Q.   "[And the man who lies with his father's wife has uncovered his father's nakedness; both of them shall surely be put to death; their blood shall be upon them" (Lev. 20:11)]; "A man" excludes a minor.

R.   "...who lies with his father's wife ..." bears the implication that that is whether it is his father's wife who is his mother, or his father's wife who is not his mother.

S.   How then do I know that the rule applies to his mother who is not his father's wife?

T.   Scripture states, "He who has uncovered his father's nakedness." And that phrase bears no meaning on its own [since its point is self-evident], and so it is available to establish an analogy, from which the law may be derived on the basis of [Freedman]: identity of meaning [which will be spelled out in a moment]

U.   "They shall surely be put to death" -- through execution by stoning.

V.   You maintain that it is execution by stoning, but perhaps it means only execution by any one of the modes of execution that are prescribed in the Torah?

W.   Here it is stated, "Their blood shall be upon them" and in the case of the necromancer or wizard, it is stated, "Their blood shall be upon them" (Lev. 20:27).

X.   Just as in that passage, the mode of execution is stoning, so here the mode of execution is stoning.

Y.   Now we have deduced the penalty [to be inflicted]. Whence do we derive an admonition [indicating that the act is forbidden to begin with? The verse at hand serves to impose a penalty, but not to prohibit the deed.]

Z.   Scripture states, "The nakedness of your father you shall not uncover" (Lev. 18:7).

AA.   "The nakedness of your father" refers to the wife of your father.

BB.   You say that it refers to the wife of your father. But perhaps it refers literally to the nakedness of your father? [The prohibition then is against having sexual relations with one's father.]

CC. Here is it stated, "The nakedness of your father you shall not uncover" (Lev. 18:8) and elsewhere it is stated, "The nakedness of his father he has uncovered" (Lev. 20:1).

DD. Just as in that passage Scripture speaks of sexual relations between man and woman, so here too it is of sexual relations between man and woman that Scripture speaks.

EE. And the implication is that that is the case whether it is his father's wife who also is his mother, or his father's wife who is not his mother.

FF. Then how do I know that the prohibition applies also to his mother who is not his father's wife?

GG. Scripture says, "The nakedness of your mother you shall not uncover" (Lev. 18:7).

HH. I thus deduce only that one is admonished not to do so, for Scripture has treated his mother who is not his father's wife as equivalent to his mother who is also his father's wife.

II. How then do I know from in Scripture the penalty [to be inflicted for such a deed]?

JJ. Here it is stated, "You shall not uncover the nakedness of your father" (Lev. 18:8) and elsewhere it is written, "The nakedness of his father he has uncovered" (Lev. 20:11).

KK. Just as, in the [matter of the] admonition, the Scripture has treated his mother who is not his father's wife as equivalent to his mother who is his father's wife, so with respect to the penalty [to be inflicted], the Scripture treats his mother who is not his father's wife as equivalent to his mother who is his father's wife.

LL. "She is his mother" teaches that it is on account of her being his mother that you impose liability upon him, and you do not impose liability upon him because she is his father's wife [as Judah would have it].

MM. And rabbis? this refers literally to his father's nakedness.

NN. But that prohibition surely derives from the statement, "You shall not lie with mankind as with womankind" (Lev. 18:22).

OO. On the basis of that verse, a penalty on two counts is incurred [in the case of relationship between father and son].

PP. And that accords with the view of R. Judah.

QQ. For R. Judah has said, "A 'gentile' who has sexual relations with his father is liable on two counts."

RR. "One who has sexual relations with his uncle is liable on two counts."

SS. Said Raba, "It stands to reason that this statement of R. Judah speaks of an Israelite, [who has committed] an unwitting act, and [refers to the issue of] an offering. The reference to a gentile serves merely as a euphemism.

TT. "For if you maintain that he referred literally to a gentile, then the penalty for the act is death, and you surely are not going to execute him twice! [So the point that there are two counts of liability is senseless, unless it refers, as Raba says, to an Israelite, an unwitting act, and the issue of the number of sin-offerings he must bring.]"

UU. So too it has been taught on Tannaite authority:

VV. He who has sexual relations with his father is liable on two counts. He who has sexual relations with his uncle is liable on two counts.

WW. There are those who maintain that that statement does not accord with the position of R. Judah [of our Mishnah] [for obvious reasons] and there are those who maintain that that statement accords even with R. Judah.

XX. [As to the view of the latter:] He derives evidence [of a twofold penalty in this case] on the basis of an argument a fortiori derived from the case of the father's brother.

YY. Now if in the case of the father's brother, who is [merely] a relative of the father, he is liable on two counts, in the case of the father will he not all the more so be liable on two counts? [Freedman, p. 35, n. 3: The liability of the son on account of sexual relations with the father's brother is deduced from the verse, "You shall not uncover the nakedness of your father's brother, you shall not approach his wife" (Lev. 18:14). Since his wife is specifically prohibited, the first half of the verse must be understood literally. Consequently, it is twice prohibited, for it is also included in the prohibition of Lev. 17:22, and hence a double penalty is incurred.

ZZ. And at issue is the dispute of Abbaye and Raba [on the issue of whether we impose penalties merely on the basis of logical argument].

AAA. One authority holds that we do impose penalty for a crime merely on the basis of a logical argument [such as just now has been given].

BBB. And the other party maintains the view that we do not impose a penalty on the basis of a logical argument.

CCC. [Reverting to the issue at hand:] in the view of rabbis, how do we derive an admonition not to commit adultery with the wife of one's father [since they interpret "the nakedness of your father" literally (Freedman, p. 365, n. 6)]?

DDD. They derive it from the statement, "The nakedness of your father's wife you shall not uncover" (Lev. 18:8).

EEE. And R. Judah? He takes the view that that verse serves to admonish one not to have sexual relations with the father's wife after the father has died.

FFF. And the rabbis? They derive that point from the end of the verse at hand: "It is your father's nakedness [even after death]."

GGG. And R. Judah? He derives from that statement the fact that one is penalized on the count of her being his father's wife, but he is not penalized on the count that she is a married woman.

HHH. But lo, we have learned in the Mishnah:

III. He who has sexual relations with his father's wife is liable on her account because she is his father's wife and also, because she is a married woman, whether this is in the lifetime of his father or after the death of his father [M. 7:4M-N].

JJJ. And R. Judah does not express disagreement with that statement. [So how can be take the position just now imputed to him?]

KKK. Said Abbaye, "He does not dispute it in the external teaching on Tannaite authority [but not in the Mishnah's version of the same matter].

LLL. And how do rabbis derive from Scripture that one who has sexual relations with his father's wife after his father's death is punished?

MMM. Now from the viewpoint of R. Judah, there is no problem, for he finds evidence in an argument by analogy. But how do the rabbis prove the same point?

NNN. They will say to you, "'He has uncovered his father's nakedness' (Lev. 20:11), on the basis of which R. Judah establishes his argument by analogy, from our viewpoint serves to prove that one is punished if he has sexual relations with his father's wife after his father's death."

OOO. And how do rabbis prove that he is punished if he has sexual relations with his mother who is not his father's wife?

PPP. Said R. Shisha, son of R. Idi, "Scripture has said, 'She is your mother' (Lev. 18:7). This shows that Scripture has treated his mother who is not his father's wife as equivalent to his mother who is his father's wife [on the basis of the analogy of the word mother.]"

III.

A. He who has sexual relations with his daughter-in-law (M. 7:4P).

B. [While the Mishnah imposes liability on the count of her being his daughter-in-law and on the count of her being another man's wife,] why not in addition impose a penalty on the count of her being his son's wife?

C. Said Abbaye, "Scripture began its statement by referring to his daughter-in-law [at Lev. 28:15:'You shall not uncover the nakedness of your daughter-in-law...she is your son's wife, you shall not uncover her nakedness'] and then concluded with a reference 'to his son's wife,' to tell you that his daughter-in-law falls into the same category as his son's wife, [and so a single count is involved]."

Unit I presents a different version of Judah's position, M. 7:4L, since the Mishnah does not introduce the issue of her not being "fit to be married" to the father, while the external Tannaite version does add that consideration. That issue then carries in its wake the question of the grounds on which the woman is not fit to be married to her husband. So the exegetical interest lies in the explanation of the Tosefta's version. Unit II introduces the more complicated question of the number of counts on which a person is going to be punished, the scriptural basis for the several views, and the diverse issues emerging on the basis of those facts. The discussion is substantial, but continuous and cogent. Unit III then briefly raises the same question for M. 7:4P. So the Talmud ignores the bulk of the Mishnah's materials and deals principally with one clause only.

7:4 S-V

S. He who has sexual relations with a male [Lev. 20:13, 15-16], or a cow, and the woman who brings an ox on top of herself.

T. if the human being has committed a sin, what sin has the beast committed?

U.   But because a human being has offended through it, therefore the
      Scripture has said, "Let it be stoned."

V.   Another matter: So that the beast should not amble through the market
      place, with people saying, "This is the one on account of which Mr.
      So-and-so got himself stoned."

I.

A.   How do we know [on the basis of Scripture] that the penalty of pederasty is stoning?

B.   It is in line with what our rabbis have taught on Tannaite authority:

C.   ["If a man lies with a man, as the lyings of a woman, both of them have committed
      an abomination; they shall surely be put to death; their blood shall be upon them"
      (Lev. 20:13)]: "A man" -- excluding a minor.

D.   "...lies also with a man..." -- whether adult or minor.

E.   "...as the lyings of a woman..." -- Scripture thus informs you that there are two
      modes of sexual relations with a woman.

F.   Said R. Ishmael, "Lo, this comes to teach a lesson but is itself subject to a lesson.
      [Freedman, p. 367, n. 5: For the phrase "the lyings of a woman" is redundant
      insofar as it teaches that even unnatural pederasty is punishable, since all
      pederasty is such. Hence its teaching is thrown back upon itself, viz., that
      unnatural cohabitation is punishable when committed incestuously.]"

G.   "They shall surely be put to death" -- by stoning.

H.   You say that it is by stoning. But perhaps it is by one of the other modes of
      inflicting the death penalty prescribed in the Torah.

I.   Here it is stated, "Their blood shall be upon them," and in the case of the
      necromancer and the wizard, it is stated, "Their blood shall be upon them" is. Just
      as in that passage, the mode of execution is stoning, so here the mode of execution
      is stoning.

J.   [54B] Accordingly, we have deduced the mode of execution. Whence do we derive
      an admonition [that the act is forbidden to begin with]?

K.   Scripture states, "You shall not lie with mankind as with womankind; it is an
      abomination" (Lev. 18:22).

L.   From this passage we derive the admonition that applies to the one who lies [with
      the male].

M.   Where in Scripture do we find an admonition that applies to the passive partner?

N.   "Scripture states, 'There shall be no sodomite among the sons of Israel' (Deut.
      23:18), and it is said, 'And there were also sodomites in the land, and they did
      according to the abominations of the nations which the Lord has cast out before
      the children of Israel,' (1 Kgs. 14:24). [Freedman, p. 368, n. 1: Just as abomination
      applies to sodomy in the latter verse, so it applies to it in the former too; thus it is
      as though the former verse read, 'There shall be no sodomite among the sons of
      Israel, it is an abomination.' And just as the 'abomination' implicit here applies to

both parties, so the 'abomination' explicitly stated in Lev. 18:22 refers to both]," the words of R. Ishmael.

O.   R. Aqiba says, "It is not necessary [to derive proof in that way]. Lo, Scripture says, 'You shall not lie with mankind as with womankind' (Lev. 20:13). Read it as, 'You shall not be lain with....'"

II.

A.   How on the basis of Scripture do we know that the rule applies to a beast?

B.   It is in accord with that which our rabbis have taught on Tannaite authority:

C.   ["And if a man lie with a beast, he shall surely be put to death, and you shall slay the beast" (Lev. 20:15)]: "A man" -- excludes a minor.

D.   "...lie with a beast" -- whether young or mature.

E.   "He shall surely be put to death" -- by stoning.

F.   You say that it is by stoning. But perhaps it is by one of the other modes of inflicting the death penalty that are prescribed in the Torah.

G.   Here it is stated, "And you shall kill the beast," and elsewhere it is stated, "You shall surely kill him [and you shall stone him with stones]" (Deut. 13:10).

H.   Just as, in that passage, the mode of execution is stoning, so here, too, the mode of execution is stoning.

I.   In this way we have learned how the penalty is inflicted on one who has sexual relations [with a beast].

J.   Whence do we learn that the same penalty applies to [the beast] who is so treated?

K.   Scripture says, "Whosoever lies with a beast shall surely be put to death" (Ex. 22:18).

L.   Now since this passage is not required to deal with the one who has sexual relations with the beast [who is dealt with in the passage just now cited], then apply it to the beast with which a man has sexual relations.

M.   So we have derived the penalty applying both to the active and to the passive party.

N.   Whence do we derive an admonition [that one not to do so]?

O.   Scripture states, "Neither shall you lie with any beast to defile yourself with it" (Lev 18:23).

P.   In this passage we derive an admonition for the one who as sexual relations with a beast.

Q.   Whence do we derive an admonition against permitting a beast to have sexual relations with a human being?

R.   Scripture says, 'There shall be no sodomite of the sons of Israel, (Deut. 23:18), and elsewhere it is stated, 'And there were also sodomites in the land...' (1 Kgs. 14:24), the words of R. Ishmael.

S.   R. Aqiba says, "This proof is not necessary. Lo, Scripture says, 'You shall not lie with any beast', meaning, you shall not permit any sort of lying."

III.

A.   He who has sexual relations with a male or serves as a passive partner of a male --

B. Said R. Abbahu, "In the view of R. Ishmael, he is liable on two counts, one on the count of, 'You shall not lie with mankind,' and the other on the count, 'There shall not be a sodomite of the sons of Israel.

C. "But on the view of R. Aqiba, he is liable on only one count, 'You shall not lie' and 'you shall not be lain with' constitute a single statement [each one based on revocalization of a single passage]."

D. He who has sexual relations with a beast and he who serves as a passive partner of a beast --

E. "Said R. Abbahu, "In the view of R. Ishmael, he is liable on two counts, one based on, 'You shall not lie with any beast,' and the other based on, 'There shall be no sodomite of the sons of Israel.'

F. "But in the view of R. Aqiba, he is liable only on one count, since, 'your lying' and 'your being lain with', constitute a single admonition."

G. Abbaye said, "Even in the view of R. Ishmael, one is liable on only one count. For 'There shall be no sodomite' speaks of sexual relations among men [not beasts]."

H. Then what is the scriptural basis, in R. Ishmael's view, for an admonition against playing the passive partner [with a beast]?

I. One may derive it from the following verse: "Whosoever lies with a beast shall surely be put do death" (Ex: 23:18).

J. Now if this does not refer to one who takes the active part [since that matter is covered by Lev. 18:23], apply it to the one who takes the passive role.

K. The All-Merciful thus refers to the passive partner in the language applying to the active partner, so indicating that, just as the active partner is subject to a penalty and an admonition, so the passive partner is subject to a penalty and an admonition.

IV.

A. He who is a passive partner for a male and for a beast --

B. Said R. Abbahu, "In the view of R. Aqiba, he is liable on two counts, one on the count of, 'You shall not lie [with mankind]' (Lev. 18:2), and the other on the count, 'You shall not lie [with any beast]' (Lev. 18:23).

C. "But in the view of R. Ishmael, he is liable on only one count, both items deriving from the verse, 'There shall be no sodomite' (Deut. 23:18)."

D. Abayye said, "Even in the view of R. Ishmael, he is liable on two counts, for it is written, 'Whosoever lies with a beast shall surely be put to death' (Ex. 22:18). If this does not refer to the active partner [since that is dealt with elsewhere], apply the verse to the passive partner.

E. "And the All-Merciful has singled out the passive partner with a phrase referring to the active partner to indicate that, just as the active partner is subject to a penalty and an admonition, so the passive partner is subject to a penalty and an admonition."

F. But one who has sexual relations with a male or serves as a passive partner for him, and one who has sexual relations with a beast or serves as a passive partner for him, whether in the view of R. Abbahu and whether in the view of Abbaye,

G.   so far as R. Ishmael is concerned is liable on three counts,

H.   and so far as R. Aqiba is concerned, is liable on two counts.

V.

A.   Our rabbis have taught on Tannaite authority:

B.   As to sexual relations with a male, sages have not treated a minor boy as equivalent to an adult, but as to sexual relations with a beast, sages have treated a minor girl as equivalent to an adult.

C.   What is the meaning of "sages have not treated a minor boy as equivalent to an adult?"

D.   Said Rab, "They have not treated sexual relations of a male less than nine years old as equivalent to sexual relations of a male of nine years [or older]."

E.   And Samuel said, "They have not treated sexual relations with a minor girl less than three years as equivalent to sexual relations with a minor girl of three years [or older]."

F.   What principle is under dispute?

G.   Rab takes the view that whoever is subject to laws governing sexual relations with another is subject to the laws governing a passive partner, and whoever is not subject to the laws governing sexual relations with another is not subject to the laws governing a passive partner. [The nine-year-old is able to have sexual relations so is subject to the prohibition of serving as a passive partner].

H.   And Samuel takes the view that what is written is "...as with the lyings of a woman" (Lev. 18:22, [which take effect from the age of three years].

I.   It has been taught in accord with the view of Rab on Tannaite authority:

J.   A male nine years and one day old [55A] who has sexual relations with a beast, whether vaginally or anally, and a woman who serves as passive partner to a beast, whether in vaginally or anally, is liable.

VI.

A.   R. Nahman son of R. Hisda expounded, "In the case of a woman there are two ways in which sexual relations may take place, but in the case of a beast, only one." [Freedman, p. 372, n.1: The reference is to bestiality. If a woman allows herself to be made the subject thereof, whether naturally or not, she is guilty. But if a man commits bestiality, he is liable only for a connection in a natural manner, but not otherwise. - Thus Rashi. Tosaf., more plausibly, explains it thus: If one commits incest or adultery with a woman, whether naturally or not, guilt is incurred; but bestiality is punishable only for a connection in a natural manner, but not otherwise.]

B.   R. Pappa objected, "To the contrary, in the case of a woman, since it is the natural thing, one is liable only on account of normal sexual relations, but as to 'some other thing' one should not be liable. In the case of a beast, in which the entire procedure is not natural, one should be liable on account of having sexual relations with any orifice at all." [Freedman, p. 372, n.2: The meaning according to the interpretation of Tosafoth is clear. Yet R. Pappa's objection is not made in order to prove that unnatural incest is not culpable (which, in fact, it is), but that if a distinction is to be drawn, unnatural bestiality is far more likely to be liable than unnatural incest. On Rashi's interpretation, R. Pappa's objection is explained thus: Since a woman is naturally the passive object of sexual intercourse, it follows that she should be punished for bestiality only when the connection is carried out in a natural way. But as man is the active offender in an unnatural crime he should be punished even for unnatural connection. It must be confessed that this is not without difficulty, and hence Tosaf. rejects Rashi's explanation, which is based on a slightly different reading.]

VII.

A.   It has been taught on Tannaite authority:

B.   A male nine years and one day old who has sexual relations with a beast, whether via the vagina or the anus,

C.   And a woman who has sexual relations with a beast, whether via the vagina or the anus, is liable.

VIII.

A.   Said Rabina to Raba, "As to him who commits the first stage of sexual relations with a male, what is the law?"

B.   What is the law? He who commits the first stage of sexual relations with a male falls into the category of the verse of Scripture, "...with mankind as with womankind" (Lev. 18:20)[1]

C.   But as to one who commits the first stage of sexual relations with a beast, what is the law?

D.   He said to him, "Since [Freeman:] the culpability of the first stage of incest, which is explicitly stated with reference to one's paternal or maternal aunt, is redundant there, for it is likened to the first state of intercourse with a menstruating woman, apply its teaching to the first stage of bestiality [as being punishable]. [Freedman, p. 372-3, n.6: In respect of one's paternal or maternal aunt, Scripture states, 'And you shall not uncover the nakedness of your mother's sister or of your father's sister, for he uncovers his near kin' (Lev. 20:19). The word for 'he uncovers' is understood as meaning the first stage of sexual intercourse, and this verse teaches that this is a culpable offense. But this teaching is superfluous, for in the preceding verse the same is taught of a menstruating woman, which serves as a model for all forbidden human sexual intercourse. Hence the teaching, being redundant, here is applied to the first stage of bestiality.]"

E.   Now since sexual relations with a beast constitute a crime punishable by death at the hands of a court, why should Scripture treat the commission of the first stage of such an act as subject to liability to extirpation? [That is the punishment for sexual relations with an aunt.] It should rather have been stated with respect to crimes punishable by death at the hand of a court, so that one might derive liability to the death penalty in a court from a crime which is likewise subject to the death liability.

F.   Since the entire verse at hand [Lev. 20:19, on sexual relations with an aunt] is stated for the purpose of deriving new rulings, another such derivation is included in the verse.

IX.

A.   R. Ahadboi bar Ammi asked R. Sheshet, "He who reaches the first stage of sexual activity through masturbation -- what is the law?"

B.   He said to him, "You disgust us."

C.   Said R. Ashi, "What is the issue that troubles you? In the case at hand it is not possible. Where it is possible is where one has sexual relations with a flaccid penis.

D.   "In the view of him who ruled that he who has sexual relations, with a flaccid penis, with consanguineous relations is exempt from all penalty, here too such a one is exempt.

E.   "And in the view of him who ruled that such a one is liable, here too he is liable, on two counts, since he is [Freedman:] simultaneously the active and passive partner of the deed."

X.

A.   The question was asked of R. Sheshet, "As to an idolator who had sexual relations with a beast -- what is the law? [For the stoning of the beast], we require both a stumbling stock and disgrace, and while the beast indeed is a stumbling block, there is no consideration of disgrace [since gentiles do this sort of thing routinely].

B.   "Or perhaps if there is a stumbling block even though there is no consideration of disgrace, [the beast is put to death]."

C.   Said R. Sheshet, "You have learned on Tannaite authority: 'If trees, which neither eat nor drink nor breathe, are subject to the decree of the Torah to be destroyed and burned up [at Deut. 12:3, "And you shall burn their groves with fire"], because they have served man as a stumbling block, he who diverts his fellow from the paths of life to the paths of death how much the more so!' [The beast, then, should be destroyed.]"

D.   In that case, what about the case of an idolator who worships his beast? Should it not be forbidden and put to death?

E.   But is there anything which is not forbidden for an Israelite but is forbidden for a gentile? [If an Israelite worships his cow, it is not forbidden. So there surely can be no prohibition if a gentile worships it.]

F.   But if an Israelite worshipped it, it should be forbidden, along the lines of a beast that is subjected to sexual relations by a man.

G.   Said Abbaye, "In that case [that of an act of bestiality], the disgrace is great, while in this case [animal worship] the disgrace is little."

H.   But take the case of trees [as above, Deut. 12:3], in which the disgrace is slight, and the Torah has said that they are to be burned and destroyed.

I.   We speak of the case of animate creatures, on which the All-Merciful has had pity. [Freeman, p. 275, n.2: Hence, only where there is much degradation, as in bestiality, is an animal destroyed; but trees are destroyed even when the disgrace is not great.]

J. Raba said, "The Torah has said that it is because the animal derived benefit from the sin that it is to be put to death."

K. But lo, the trees did not derive benefit from the sin, and the Torah has said that they are to be burned and destroyed.

L. We speak of the case of animate creatures, for the All-Merciful has had pity on them.

M. [Answering the question with which we began,] come and take note:

N. Another matter: So that the beast should not amble through the market place, with people saying, "This is the one on account of which Mr. So-and-so got himself stoned: [M. 7:4V).

O. Now since this second reason [55B] involves both a stumbling block and disgrace, does the first reason [at M. 7:4U, "Because a human being has offended through it"] involve a stumbling block with disgrace, for instance, when a gentile has sexual relations with a beast?

P. No, the considerations in the second of the two reasons involve both a stumbling block and disgrace.

Q. And as to the first of the two reasons, what is proposes to tell us is that, even in a case where there is disgrace without a stumbling block, there also would be liability.

R. What would that involve? It would be the case of an Israelite who by inadvertence had sexual relations with a beast, in accord with the inquiry of R. Hamnuna. [Freedman, p. 375, n.7: When bestiality is committed in ignorance, one has not sinned, yet he has greatly degraded himself.]

S. For R. Hamnuna raised the question, "In the case of an Israelite who inadvertently had sexual relations with a beast, what is the law?

T. "We require both a stumbling block and disgrace, and here, while we do have a matter of disgrace, we do not have a stumbling block.

U. "Or perhaps it suffices that there be disgrace even though there is no consideration of a stumbling block."

V. Said R. Joseph, "Come and take note: A girl three years and one day old is betrothed by intercourse. And if a Levir has had intercourse with her, he has acquired her. And one can be held liable on her account because of the law prohibiting intercourse with a married woman. And she imparts uncleanness to him who has intercourse with her when she is menstruating, to convey uncleanness to the lower as to the upper layer [of what lies beneath]. If she was married to a priest, she may eat food in the status of priestly rations. If one of those who are unfit for marriage with her had intercourse with her, he has rendered her unfit to marry into the priesthood. If any of those who are forbidden in the Torah to have intercourse with her had intercourse with her, he is put to death on her account, but she is free of responsibility [M. Nid. 5:4].

W. "Any of those who are forbidden -- even a beast! And lo, in this case there is disgrace, but there is no consideration of a stumbling block, and yet it is taught that such a one is put to death on her account."

X.   In that case, since the girl does it intentionally, there also is the consideration of a stumbling block, but it is the All-Merciful who has had pity on her -- on her, not on the beast.

Y.   Said Raba, "Come and take note: A boy nine years and one day old who had intercourse with his childless brother's widow has acquired her. But he cannot give her a writ of divorce until he comes of age. And he is made unclean by a menstruating woman, to convey uncleanness to the lower as to the upper layer. And he disqualifies, but does not render a woman qualified to eat heave-offering. And through bestiality he spoils a beast for use on the altar, and it is stoned on his account. And if he had intercourse with any of all the prohibited relationships stated in the Torah, they are put to death on his account. But he is free of responsibility [M. Nid. 5:5].

Z.   "Now here is a case where there is disgrace but no stumbling block, and it is taught that it is stoned on his account!"

AA.   Since it was a deliberate act, it also was a stumbling block, and it is the All-Merciful that had pity on him -- on him the All-Merciful had pity, but not on the beast.

BB.   Come and take note: Another matter: So that the beast should not amble through the market place, with people saying, "This is the one on account of which Mr. So-and-so got himself stoned" [M. 7:4V].

CC.   Now is it not the case that, since the second of the two reasons deals with a case in which there was a stumbling block and also disgrace, in the first of the two reasons we have a disgrace without a stumbling block?

DD.   And what would such a case involve? An Israelite who inadvertently had sexual relations with a beast.

EE.   No, the second of the two reasons involves a stumbling block and a disgrace, and the first involves a stumbling block without disgrace.

FF.   And what would such a case involve? An idolator who had sexual relations, along the lines of the question addressed to R. Sheshet.

Unit I provides a scriptural basis for the law of M. 7:4S, that stoning applies to the sin at hand. Unit II goes on to the execution of the cow of M. 7:4S. Unit III then raises a secondary question, flowing from unit II, and unit IV is continuous with unit III. Units V-IX develop themes pertinent to the rule at hand but in no way constructed to serve as exegesis or amplification for that rule. Unit X is inserted because it intersects with our Mishnah-paragraph.

7:5

A.   He who blasphemes [M. 7:4D1] [Lev. 24:10] is liable only when he has fully pronounced the divine Name.

B.   Said R. Joshua b. Qorha, [56A] "On every day of a trial they examine the witnesses with a substituted name, [such as], 'May Yose smite Yose.'

C.   "[Once] the trial is over, they would not put him to death [on the basis of
      evidence given] with the substituted euphemism, but they clear the court
      and ask the most important of the witnesses, saying to him, 'Say, what
      exactly did you hear [in detail]?'

D.   "And he says what he heard.

E.   "And the judges stand on their feet and tear their clothing, and never
      sew them back up.

F.   "And the second witness says, 'Also I [heard] what he heard.'

G.   "And the third witness says, 'Also I [heard] what he heard.'"

I.

A.   A Tannaite authority [states], "... When he has cursed the divine Name by Name."

B.   What is the source of this rule?

C.   Said Samuel, "It is because Scripture has stated, 'And he who blasphemes the name
      of the Lord...when he blasphemes the name of the Lord shall be put to death' (Lev.
      24:16). [Freeman: The repetition shows that the Divine Name must be cursed by
      the Divine Name.]:

D.   How do we know that the word, "blaspheme" means curse?

E.   Because it is written, "How shall I curse [using the same root] whom God has not
      cursed" (Num. 23:8).

F.   The admonition not to do so derives from here: "You shall not curse God" (Ex.
      22:27).

G.   And might I suggest that the same word means "to pierce," [so that one may not rip
      up a piece of paper on which the divine Name is written]"

H.   For it is written, "[So Jehoiada the priest took a chest] and [using the same root]
      pierced a hole in the lid of it" (2 Kgs. 12:10).

I.   And the admonition would derive from here: "You shall destroy the names of the
      [idols] out of that place. You shall not do so to the Lord your God" (Deut. 12:3-4).

J.   We require that the Name be cursed by use of the divine Name, and that is not
      present [in the cited passage].

K.   But perhaps what is involved is placing two slips with the divine Name together,
      and piercing both of them?

L.   Then that would be a case in which one pierced the one and only then pierced the
      other [not piercing one with the other simultaneously].

M.   And might I suggest that what is involved is engraving the divine Name on the point
      of a knife and with that knife piercing [a slip on which the divine Name is written]?

N.   But then it is the point of the knife that does the piercing.

O.   And might I suggest that what is involved is the pronunciation of the Name. For it
      is written, "And Moses and Aaron took these men who were identified [using the
      same root] by their names" (Num. 1:17), with the admonition against doing so in the
      following: "You shall fear the Lord your God" (Deut. 6:13)?

P.   First , we require cursing of the Name by the use of the Name, and that is absent. Furthermore, you have here the case of an admonition in the form of an affirmative commandment, and an admonition in the form of an affirmative commandment does not fall into the category of an admonition at all.

Q.   If you like, I shall suggest that Scripture has said, "And the Israelite woman's son blasphemed and cursed" (Lev. 24:11), indicating that blasphemy takes the form of a curse.

R.   Than perhaps the prohibited deed involves doing both [blaspheming and cursing]?

S.   Do not let it enter your mind, for it is written, "Bring forth him who has cursed" (Lev. 24:14), and it is not written, "Bring forth him who blasphemed and cursed." [That proves that only a single action is involved.]

II.

A.   Our rabbis have taught on Tannaite authority:

B.   ["Any man who curses his God shall bear his sin" (Lev. 24:15)]": [It would have been clear had the text simply said,]"A man." Why does it specify, "Any"?

C.   It serves to encompass idolators, who are admonished not to curse the Name, just as Israelites are so admonished.

D.   And they are put to death only by decapitation, for the sole form of inflicting the death penalty in the case of the sons of Noah is by decapitation.

E.   How do we deduce from the cited verse [that idolators are not to blaspheme]?

F.   It derives from the following verse: "The Lord" (Gen. 2:16) [each word of the verse at hand being subjected to an exegetical exercise, as we shall see below] signifies that cursing the divine Name [is forbidden for gentiles as much as for Israelites].

G.   Said R. Isaac the Smith, "The phrase cited earlier ['any man'] serves to encompass even the use of euphemisms, and it is framed in accord with the principle of R. Meir."

H.   For it has been taught on Tannaite authority:

I.   "'Any man who curses his God shall bear his sin' (Lev. 24:15).

J.   "Why is this passage stated? Is it not already said, 'And he who blasphemes the name of the Lord shall surely be put to death' (Lev. 24:16)?

K.   "Since that passage specifies, '...blasphemes the Name....,' one might think that a person is liable only on account of cursing the ineffable Name. How do I know that encompassed within the prohibition are also euphemisms?

L.   "Scripture states, 'Any man who curses his God' -- in any manner whatsoever," the word of R. Meir.

M.   And sages say, "On account of using the ineffable Name, one is subject to the death penalty, but as for euphemisms, one is subject to the admonition [not to do so, but not to the death penalty if he does so]."

N.   [Isaac's view] differs from that of R. Miasha.

O.   For R. Miasha said, "A son of Noah who cursed the Name by using euphemisms in the opinion of rabbis is liable [to the death penalty].

P. "What is the scriptural basis for that claim? Scripture has said, 'As well the stranger as he that is born in the land [when he blasphemes the name of the Lord shall be put to death]' (Lev. 24:16). So in the case of the proselyte or the homeborn [before we inflict the death penalty] we require cursing by the use of the divine Name in particular, but in the case of the idolator, even if he uses only a euphemism [he is subject to the death penalty]."

Q. Then how [within this theory] does R. Meir interpret the words, "as well the stranger as he that is born in the land"?

R. The proselyte and the homeborn [who are guilty of blasphemy] are put to death by stoning, but the idolator [who is guilty of blasphemy] is put to death by decapitation.

S. One might have supposed that, since the law was extended to encompass them, it encompassed them for all purposes. So we are informed that that is not the case.

T. And as to the theory of R. Isaac the Smith vis a vis rabbis, how are we to interpret the phrase, "as well the stranger as he that is born in the land"?

U. We require that phrase to indicate that [in the case of an Israelite, guilt is incurred only if he curses] the divine Name by using the divine Name, while in the case of the idolator, we do not require the use of the divine Name in cursing the divine Name [before we impose a penalty].

V. Why then has Scripture used the phrase, "When any man..."? The Torah speaks in the language used by ordinary men.

III.

A. Our rabbis have taught on Tannaite authority:

B. Concerning seven religious requirements were the children of Noah commanded: setting up courts of justice, idolatry, blasphemy, [cursing the Name of God], fornication, bloodshed, thievery, and cutting a limb from a living beast [T. A.Z. 8:4].

C. [56B] R. Hananiah b. Gamaliel says, "Also on account of blood deriving from a living beast."

D. R. Hidqa says, "Also on account of castration."

E. R. Simeon says, "Also on account of witchcraft."

F. R. Yose says, "On account of whatever is stated in the pericope regarding the children of Noah are they subject to warning, as it is said, 'There shall not be found among you any one who burns his son or his daughter as an offering, any one who practices divination, a soothsayer or an augur or a sorcerer or a charmer or a medium or a wizard or a necromancer' (Deut. 18:10-11).

G. "[T.:1] Is it possible then that Scripture has imposed a punishment without imparting a prior warning.?

H. "But it provides a warning and afterward imposes the punishment.

I. "This teaches that he warned them first and then punished them."

J. R. Eleazar says, "Also as to mixed seeds, it is permitted for a child of Noah to sow seeds which are mixed species and to wear garments of mixed species of wool and linen. But it is prohibited to breed a hybrid beast or to graft trees" (T. A.Z. 8:6K-O, 8:7, 8:8].

K. What is the scriptural basis for this rule?

L. Said R. Yohanan, "It is in the following verse of Scripture: 'And the Lord God commanded Adam saying, Of every tree of the garden you may freely eat' (Gen. 2:16).

M. "'And he commanded' — this refers to setting up courts of justice, for Scripture says, 'For I know him, that he will command his children and his household after him, and they shall keep the way of the Lord, to do justice and judgment'(Gen. 18:19).

N. "'The Lord' — this refers to blasphemy, and so it is written, 'And he who blasphemes the name of the Lord shall surely be put to death' (Lev. 24:16).

O. "'God' — this refers to idolatry, as it is written, 'You shall have no other gods before me' (Ex. 20:3).

P. "'Adam' — this refers to murder, as it is written, 'Whoever sheds the blood of a man, by man shall his blood be shed' (Gen. 9:6).

Q. "'Saying' — this refers to adultery, as it is written, 'They say, If a man put away his wife and she go from him and became another man's (Jer. 3:1). [Freedman, p. 383, n.5: Thus 'saying' is used in connection with adultery.]

R. "'Of every tree of the garden' -- but not of robbery. [A person may not eat what does not belong to that person. Freedman, p. 383, n. 6: Since it was necessary to authorize Adam to eat of the trees of the garden, it follows that without such authorization--when something belongs to another--it is forbidden.]

S. "'You may freely eat' -- but not a limb cut from a living animal."

T. When R. Dimi came, he repeated matters in reverse:

U. "'God' -- this refers to courts of justice."

W. Surely "God" refers to courts of justice, for it is written, "And the householder will come near to God" (Ex. 22:7).

X. But on what basis do we conclude that, "And he commanded" refers to idolatry?

Y. R. Hisda and R. Isaac bar Abedimi: One said, "'They have turned aside quickly out of the way which I commanded them; they have made them a molten calf' (Ex. 32:8)."

Z. The other said, "'Ephraim is oppressed and broken in judgment, because he willingly walked after the commandment' (Hos. 5:11) [in which context, 'commandment' speaks of idolatry]."

AA. What is at issue between them?

BB. At issue is the case of an idolator who made an idol but did not bow down to it.

CC. In the view of him who has said that [the prohibition of gentiles' idol-worship is in the verse,] "They have made them a golden calf,"] one is liable from the time of the making of the idol [even without worshipping it].

DD. In the view of him who has said that the source of the prohibition is in the verse, "Because he willingly walked after the commandment," one is liable only after he has followed the idol and worshipped it.

EE. Said Raba, "And is there anyone who maintains that if an idolator merely makes an idol but does not worship it, he is liable?

FF. "Has it not been taught on Tannaite authority:

GG. **"On account of things for which an Israelite court inflicts the death penalty, the children of Noah are subject to warning. If the Israelite court does not inflict a death penalty, the children of Noah are not admonished concerning such actions [cf. T. A.Z. 8:4G].**

HH. "What then is excluded by that statement? Is it not to exclude the case of an idolator who made an idol but did not bow down to it [an act for which a court will not inflict the death penalty on an Israelite]?"

II. Said R. Pappa, "No, it serves to exclude the acts of embracing and kissing idols [which actions are not punishable]."

JJ. Embracing and kissing what sort of idols? If I should say that it refers to doing so with an idol that is usually worshipped in this way, then such a one is subject to the death penalty anyhow. Rather, it serves to exclude [punishment for doing so with idols that are] not usually worshipped in this way.

KK. **Setting up courts of justice:** Are the children of Noah subject to a commandment in this regard?

LL. And has it not been taught on Tannaite authority"

MM. The Israelites were given ten commandments at Marah, seven of which the children of Noah had already accepted, to which were added [for Israel] the laws of setting up courts of justice, observing the Sabbath, and honoring father and mother.

NN. Courts of justice, as it is written, "There [at Marah] he made for them a statute and an ordinance" (Ex. 15:25).

OO. Sabbath observance, and honoring of father and mother, as it is written, "as the Lord thy God commanded thee" (Deut. 5:15 and 5:16). [The term "commanded thee," used in both the fourth and fifth commandments, suggests that both of these had been given before the giving of the Decalogue at Sinai. These must therefore constitute the statute and ordinance of Marah.]

PP. Said R. Judah, "'As he commanded thee' refers to the events at Marah."

QQ. Said R. Nahman in the name of Rabbah bar Abbuha, "[The commandment at Marah] served to institute trial by an assembly of judges, with witnesses and formal admonition."

RR. If so, why say "to which courts of justice were added" [since that addition involved only legal procedure and not actual laws]?

SS. Rather, said Raba, "[The commandment at Marah] served to institute penal fines."

TT. But even so, should it not have been said, "and courts of justice were added"?

UU. Rather, said R. Aha b. Jacob, "[The commandment at Marah] served to indicate that they must establish courts in every district and town."

VV. But were not the children of Noah already commanded to do this?

WW. And has it not been taught on Tannaite authority:

XX. Just as Israelites are commanded to call into session in every district and town courts of justice, so the sons of Noah were commanded to call into session in every district and town courts of justice (T. A.Z. 8:4D).

YY. Rather, said Raba, "The Tannaite authority at hand [who claims that the requirement to establish courts of justice in gentile communities was added at Marah, and not earlier] is a Tannaite authority of the house of Manasseh, who omits references, in the list of the commandments to the sons of Noah, to courts of law and to blasphemy, and instead adds to the list the prohibitions of emasculation and mixing seeds.

ZZ. "For a Tannaite authority of the house of Manasseh [said], 'Seven commandments were assigned to the children of Noah: the prohibition of idolatry, adultery, murder, robbery, cutting a limb from a living creature, emasculation, and mixing seeds.'

AAA. "R. Judah says, 'The first man was commanded only concerning idolatry, for it is said, "And the Lord God commanded Adam" (Gen. 2:16).'

BBB. "R. Judah b. Baterah says, '"Also concerning cursing the divine Name."'

CCC. "And there are those who say, '"Also concerning setting up courts of justice."'

DDD. In accord with which authority is the following statement that R. Judah said Rab said, "[God said to Adam,] 'I am God. Do not curse me. I am God. Do not exchange me for another. I am God. Let my fear of me be upon you [and so establish justice].

EEE. In accord with whom? It is in accord with "there are those who say."

FFF. Now if the Tannaite authority of the house of Manasseh interprets the verse, "And God commanded..." (Gen. 2:16), then even these other [commandments, listed earlier, also should be on his list, and not only the ones he includes]. If he does not interpret the verse, "And God commanded..." (Gen. 2:16), then what is the scriptural basis for the items he does include?

GGG. Indeed he does not interpret the cited verse, and he derives each item from a verse of its own.

HHH. As to idolatry and adultery, [57A] it is written, "The earth also was corrupt before God" (Gen. 6:11), and a Tannaite authority of the house of R. Ishmael [taught], "In every passage in which it is stated, 'was corrupt,' the reference is always to adultery and idolatry.

III. Adultery, as it is said, 'For all flesh had corrupted its way upon the earth' (Gen. 5:11).

JJJ. Idolatry, for it is written, 'Lest you corrupt yourselves and make you a graven image...' (Deut. 4:16).

KKK. And the other party [who interprets the verse, "And the Lord commanded..." (Gen. 6:11)]?

LLL. The cited verse simply reveals the way they did things.

MMM. Murder, as it is written, "Whoever sheds a man's blood..." (Gen. 9:6).

NNN. And the other party?

OOO.   The verse at hand simply indicates that [murderers] are to be executed.

PPP.   Robbery, as it is written, "As the wild herbs, have I given you all things" (Lev. 9:3), and R. Levi said, "As the wild herbs and not as garden herbs [which belong to private individuals]."

QQQ.   And the other party? The cited verse serves the purpose of permitting people to eat meat.

RRR.   Cutting a limb from a living animal, as it is written, "But flesh with the life thereof, which is the blood thereof, shall you not eat" (Gen. 9:4).

SSS.   And the other party? That verse serves to permit people to eat creeping things.

TTT.   Emasculation, as it is written, "Bring forth abundantly in the earth and multiply therein" (Gen. 9:4).

UUU.   That verse serves merely to speak of a blessing in general.

VVV.   Mixing seeds, as it is written, "Of fowl after their kind" (Gen. 6:20).

WWW.   And the other party? That refers to mating [indicating merely that the species mate more readily with one another than with outsiders.

IV.

A.   Said R. Joseph, "[Disciples] of the house of one master said, 'On account of [violating] three religious duties are children of Noah put to death: on account of adultery, murder, and blasphemy.'"

B.   To this statement, R. Sheshet objected, "There is no problem with regard to murder, for it is written, 'Whoever sheds the blood of man by man shall his blood be shed' (Gen. 9:6).

C.   "But what is the source for the other two? If one derives them from the matter of murder, then all of them should also be subject to the death penalty, and not only those listed.

D.   "If it is because they are included through the reference to 'any man' (Lev. 24:15, Lev. 18:6, thus covering blasphemy and adultery], then they should also encompass idolatry [from the use of the phrase, 'any man [at Lev. 20:2]."

E.   Rather, said R. Sheshet, "[Disciples] of the house of one master have said, 'On account of four commandments a son of Noah may be put to death [on account of idolatry, plus those listed at A]."

F.   And is a son of Noah put to death on account of idolatry?

G.   And has it not been taught with reference to idolatry:

H.   **Because of matters on account of which an Israelite court inflicts the death penalty, the children of Noah are subject to warning [T. A.Z. 8:4G].**

I.   They are subject to warning, but they are not put to death.

J.   Said R. Nahman bar Isaac, "A warning that pertains to them constitutes also a sentence of death."

V.

A.   R. Huna, R. Judah, and all the disciples of Rab say, "On account of seven commandments a son of Noah is put to death. The All-Merciful revealed that fact of one of them, and the same rule applies to all of them."

B.   Is a son of Noah put to death on account of robbery?

C.   And has it not been taught on Tannaite authority:

D.   **Concerning robbery: if one has stolen or robbed and so too in the case of stealing a beautiful captive woman and in similar cases, a gentile doing so to a gentile, or a gentile doing so to an Israelite — it [what is stolen] is prohibited. And an Israelite doing so to a gentile -- it [what is stolen] is permitted [T. A.Z. 8:5C-E].**

E.   Now if matters were [as you say], should it not teach, "One is <u>liable</u>," [not "permitted", treating only the stolen object]!

F.   It is because the framer of the passage wished to repeat at the end, **"An Israelite doing so to a gentile -- it [the stolen object] is permitted,"** that he used the language in the opening clause, **It is prohibited.**'

G.   But in every passage in which there is liability to a penalty, it is made explicit, for the opening clause states: **Concerning bloodhsed, a gentile who kills a gentile, and a gentile who kills an Israelite are liable, but an Israelite who kills a gentile is exempt [T. A.Z. 8:5A-B].**

H.   In that passage how else might the framer of the passage expressed matters? Could he have said, "It is forbidden..it is permitted..."? [Surely not.]

I.   And has it not been stated on Tannaite authority:

J.   **Gentiles and shepherds of small cattle and those who raise them make no difference one way or the other [in figuring out whose lost object to seek first] [T. B.M. 2:33A].**

K.   **And similar acts, in the case of robbery:** what would be an example?

L.   Said R. Aha bar Jacob, "It is necessary only to cover the case of a worker in a vineyard [who munches as he eats]."

M.   But when would this be culpable? If it is at the time that the work is complete, then it is permitted. If it is not at the time that the work is complete, it is a perfectly standard form of robbery.

N.   Rather, said R. Pappa, "It is necessary to take account of robbery of something of value of less than a <u>perutah</u>."

O.   If that is the case, why should it be stated that if **a Samaritan does so to an Israelite, it is forbidden [to keep the object]?** Does [the Israelite] not write off the object?

P.   Granted that afterward he indeed does write off the object, at the time that [the theft] takes place, it does give distress to the owner.

Q.   [Now you say that] the commission of such an act by one Samaritan against another falls into the same category of <u>similar acts</u>. But since [we assume that] the Samaritan will not write off the object, it again is a perfectly standard form of robbery.

R.   But R. Aha the son of R. Iqa says it covers the case of one who withholds the wages of a hired man. A gentile who does so to a gentile, or a gentile who does so to an Israelite, are liable. But an Israelite who does so to a gentile is exempt.

S.   And similar acts in the case of a beautiful captive woman: what would be an example?

T.   When R. Dimi came, he said R. Eleazar said R. Hanina said, "A son of Noah who designated a slave-girl for his slave-boy and [thereafter] had sexual relations with her is put to death on that account."

U.   And similar acts in the case of murder is not listed at all in the Tannaite teaching.

V.   Said Abbaye, "If it were found to have been taught on Tannaite authority, then it would represent the view of R. Jonathan b. Saul."

W.   For it has been taught on Tannaite authority:

X.   R. Jonathan b. Saul says, "[If a man] pursues his fellow to kill him, and [the pursued] could save himself by lopping off one of the [pursuer's] limbs and did not do so [but rather killed him], [57B] he is put to death on his account."

VI.

A.   R. Jacob bar Aha found that it was written in the book of the lore of the house of Rab, "A son of Noah is put to death by a court consisting of a single judge,

B.   "on the testimony of a single witness,

C.   "not after appropriate admonition,

D.   "on the testimony of a man but not on the testimony of a woman,

E.   "but even if the witness is a relative."

F.   In the name of R. Ishmael it is said, "He is put to death even for the murder of an embryo."

G.   What is the source of this statement?

H.   Said R. Judah, "Scripture says, '"And surely the blood of your lives will I require". (Gen. 9:5)

I.   "[The fact that it is I who shall require" indicates that] it may be a court made of of even one judge alone.

J.   "'At the hand of every thing will I require it' (Gen. 9:5) -- even without admonition.

K.   "'And at the hand of man' (Gen. 9:5) -- even a single witness.

L.   "'At the hand of man' (Gen. 9:5) -- not at the hand of a woman.

M.   "'His brother' -- even a relative."

N.   In the name of R. Ishmael it is said, "He is put to death even for the murder of an embryo."

O.   What is the scriptural basis of the view of R. Ishmael?

P.   Since it is written, "Whoever sheds the blood of a man within a man [B'DM], his blood shall be shed" (Gen. 9:6).

Q.   What sort of "man" is located "within a "man"?

R.   One must say it is the embryo in the mother's womb.

S.   And the former of the two authorities [who reject as Ishmael's view]?

T.   He is a Tannaite authority of the house of Menasseh, who has said, "As to all death penalties that pertain to sons children of Noah, they are carried out in all cases only by strangulation." He then assigns the phrase, "within a man" to the concluding part of the verse at hand, and he interprets it in this way: "By man [B'DM] his blood will be shed."

U.   What then is the form of bloodshed of a human being which takes place in such a way that [the blood remains] within the man's body? One must say it is strangulation.

V.   R. Hamnuna objected [to the proposition that gentile women do not have to impose justice and so may not testify, as stated at D,L], "And is a woman not subject to the same commandment? Lo, it is written, 'For I know him that he will command his sons and household after him, and they shall keep the way of the Lord to exercise charity and judgment' (Gen. 18:19) [and the household includes women]."

W.   [Hamnuna] raised the question and he settled it: "'His sons' -- to impose justice, and 'his household' -- to do righteousness [that is, acts of charity]."

VII.

A.   Said R. Abia the elder to R. Pappa, "Might I propose that a daughter of Noah who committed murder should not be put to death?

B.   "'At the hand of man [who committed murder] '-- and not the hand of woman' is what is written [at Gen. 9:6]."

C.   He said to him, "This is what R. Judah said, "'He who sheds the blood of man' -- under any circumstances."

D.   "May I propose that a daughter of Noah who committed adultery should not be put to death, for it is written, 'Therefore shall a man forsake his father and mother and cleave to his wife' (Gen. 2:24), meaning, a man and not a woman?"

E.   He said to him, "This is what R. Judah said, "'And they shall be as one flesh" (Gen. 2:24), so that Scripture went and treated the two as one [applying the statement to both parties].'"

VIII.

A.   Our rabbis have taught on Tannaite authority:

B.   "[A man, a man shall not approach any who is near of kin to him, to uncover their nakedness" (Lev. 18:6):] As to the word, "A man," why does Scripture say it twice? It serves to encompass Samaritans [gentiles], indicating that they are admonished, just like Israelites, against sexual relations with close relatives.

C.   Does that proposition derive from the present passage? Surely it derives from the following: "'[And the Lord commanded...,] saying...'(Gen. 2:16) [as interpreted above, 56B] -- this refers to adultery."

D.   That passage refers to adultery within their own group, the present passage refers to adultery with our group.

E.   For it has been taught on Tannaite authority at the end of the passage at hand:

F.   If [a Samaritan (gentile)] had sexual relations with an Israelite, he is tried in accord with the laws governing israelites.

G.   What practical difference does this law make [since the penalty in both cases is death]?

H. Said R. Nahman said Rabbah bar Abbuha, "It is necessary only [to indicate] that there must be a 'congregation' of judges [twenty-three], appropriate testimony, and admonition."

I. Is this act [of adultery] with a Jewish woman a lesser offense [that the protection of Jewish law should be accorded to him]? [Had the act been committed with a Samaritan woman, he would not enjoy the protection of the provisions in the foregoing list.]

J. Said R. Yohanan, "The law is necessary only to cover the case of [his committing adultery with] a betrothed girl, for in their law, there is no such category. In that case we try by him by our law."

K. But as to [his adultery with] a married woman, do we try him in accord with their law?

L. Has it not been taught on Tannaite authority:

M. If he had sexual relations with a betrothed girl, he is put to death by stoning. If with a married woman, he is put to death by strangulation.

N. Now if he is judged in accord with their law, he should be put to death by decapitation.

O. Said R. Nahman bar Isaac, "What is the sense of 'a married woman' in the passage at hand? It would be a case in which the woman had entered the marriage canopy but the marriage had not been consummated. In their law, there is no such category [as a capital crime], so he is judged in accord with our law [as though she were fully married]."

P. For R. Hanina taught on Tannaite authority: "The category of a married woman who has had sexual relations exists to their legal system, but the category of a married woman who has entered the marriage canopy but not yet had sexual relations does not exist in their legal system."

IX.

A. It has been taught on Tannaite authority in accord with the view of R. Yohanan: [T]

B. "In the case of any form of prohibited sexual relationship for which an Israelite court inflicts the death penalty, the children of Noah are subject to warning. If an Israelite court does not inflict the death penalty in the case at hand, a son of Noah is not subect to warning with respect to it," the words of R. Meir.

C. And sages say, "There are many prohibited relationships with respect to which an Israelite court does not inflict the death-penalty, and the children of Noah are warned with respect to them. If one has had sexual relations with a woman prohibited by Israelite law, he is tried in accord with Israelite law. If he had sexual relations in violation of Noahide law, he is judged in accord with Noahide law.

D. "But only the prohibition of sexual relations with a betrothed maiden [=VIIIJ] falls into the category at hand, in which Israelite law prohibits such a relationship and Noahide law does not]" [T. A.Z. 8:G-I].

E. But [included in that last category, in which Israelite law prohibits a type of relationship gentile law permits] is the case, also, of the woman who has entered the marriage canopy but not had sexual relations [and who, by Jewish law, is regarded as a married woman]?

F. This Tannaite authority is the one of the house of Manasseh, who has said that in the case of every death penalty imposed on Noahides, the mode of execution is strangulation, and both for Israelite and for foreign law, in the present case, the mode of execution is the same, namely strangulation.

G. And does R. Meir maintain that in the case of any form of prohibited sexual relationship for which an Israelite court inflicts the death penalty, the children of Noah are subject to warning?

H. And lo, it has been taught on Tannaite authority:

I. A proselyte [58A] whose mother, when she conceived him, was not in a state of sanctification but who [because, while pregnant, the mother had converted to Judaism] was [then] born in a state of sanctification, is subject to the laws of consanguinity on his mother's side, but he is not subject to the laws of consanguinity on his father's side.

J. How so? If he married his sister on his mother's side [a half-sister, born of his mother and a different father], he must divorce her. [If it was] a [half-] sister on his father's side [born of a different mother], he may keep her [as his wife].

K. If it was his father's sister by his father's mother, he must put her away. If it was his father's sister by his father's father, he may remain wed to her. If it was his mother's sister by her mother, he must put her away.

L. If it was his mother's sister by her father, R. Meir says, "He must put her away."

M. But sages say, "He may keep her."

N. For R. Meir held, "In the case of any consanguineous relationship on the mother's side, he must put away [such a woman]. If it is on his father's side, he may keep her. [Freedman, p. 394, n. 1: The guiding principle in all this is: 'a proselyte is as a new born babe', who stands in absolutely no relationship to any pre-conversion relation. Consequently, his brothers and sisters, father, mother, etc. from before his conversion lose his relationship on his conversion. Should they too subsequently become converted, they are regarded as strangers to him, and he might marry, e.g., his mother or sister. This is the Biblical law. But since heathens themselves recognized the law of incest in respect of maternal relations, the Rabbis decreed that this should hold good for a proselyte too, i.e., that he is forbidden to marry his maternal relations who were forbidden to him before his conversion, so that it should not be said that he abandoned a faith with a higher degree of sanctity than the one he has embraced (since he cannot be expected to understand the principle of complete annulment of relationships). In this case, since he was born in sanctity, he is really not a proselyte at all, He is so styled because he too is legally a stranger to all his father's and mother's pre-conversion relations. As for his mother's paternal sister, R. Meir held that since she is partly maternally related, she is forbidden, as otherwise it would be thought that a proselyte is permitted to marry his maternal relations. But the Rabbis held that there was no fear of this, and since the relationship is in its source paternal, it is not forbidden].

O. "And he is permitted to marry his brother's wife [Freedman, p. 394, n.3: even his brother by his mother], his father's brother's wife, and all other relations deemed consanguineous by affinity of marital ties are permitted to him,

P. Including the wife of his father.

Q. "If he has [already] married a woman and her daughter, he may consummate the marriage with one of them and put away the other. But to begin with, he should not do so at all.

R. "If his wife died, he may marry his mother-in-law."

S. Others say [in his view], "He may not marry her." [Freedman, p. 384, n. 5: Now in this Baraita a number of relations forbidden to Jews on pain of death, e.g., his father's wife and his mother-in-law, are permitted to the proselyte, and hence to heathens in general; whilst a number of relations not forbidden on pain of death, e.g., his sister, his paternal and maternal aunts, are prohibited to him. This, taught in R. Meir's name, contradicts his other ruling that all forbidden degrees of consanguinity punishable by death are forbidden to heathens.]

T. Said R. Judah, "There is no contradiction between the one passage and the other. The one has R. Meir presenting the matter in accord with the view of R. Eliezer, the other has R. Meir presenting the matter in accord with the view of R. Aqiba."

U. For it has been taught on Tannaite authority:

V. "Therefore shall a man leave his father and his mother" (Gen. 2:24).

W. R. Eliezer says, "'His father' means the sister of his father, 'his mother' means the sister of his mother,' [whom he may not marry]."

X. R. Aqiba says, "'His father' means his father's wife [by another marriage, for example], and 'his mother' refers literally to his mother.'"

Y. "And he shall cleave" -- and not to a male.

Z. "To his wife" -- and not to his fellow's wife.

AA. "And they shall become one flesh" -- one with whom one can become one flesh [in an offspring], excluding domesticated beasts and wild beasts, who cannot produce an offspring with man. [Freedman, p. 395, n. 5: Hence (since this rule applies to Noahides) Meir's dictum that heathens are forbidden those relations which are prohibited to Jews on pain of death, e.g., the father's wife, reflects Aqiba's teaching, while his ruling in the Baraita that a proselyte may marry his father's wife is the view of Eliezer, who does not interpret 'his father' as his father's wife.]

BB. A master has said [in expanding upon the foregoing], "R. Eliezer says, "'His father" means his father's sister.'"

CC. But might I say it means literally, his father?

DD. That is covered by the statement, "'And he will cleave' -- and not to a male."

EE. Might I say it means, "His father's wife?" That is covered by "'his wife' and not the wife of his fellow.'"

FF. Might I say that this would apply after death?

GG. It is similar to the prohibition of his mother. Just as his mother [Freedman] is not a relation by marriage, so "his father" must refer to a non-marriage relationship.

HH. "His mother" refers to his mother's sister. But might I say that it refers literally to his mother?

II. That is covered by the reference to "'His wife' and not to the wife of his fellow."

JJ. And might I say that it would apply even after death?

KK. It is similar to the prohibition of "his father." Just as "his father" is not literally so, so "his mother" is not literally so.

LL. "R. Aqiba says, "'His father' means his father's wife.'"

MM. But might I say that it refers literally to his father?

NN. This is covered by the statement "And he shall cleave' -- and not to a male."

OO. If that is the mode of argument, then may we invoke the proof already given, namely, "'His wife' -- and not the wife of his fellow?"

PP. The passage at hand teaches that even after death [the father's wife] is forbidden to him."

QQ. "His mother is literally his mother."

RR. But is this not covered by, "'To his wife' and not to his fellow's wife?"

SS. At issue is his mother [who is related to his father because] his father had raped her [but not married her].

TT. At what point is there a dispute?

UU. R. Eliezer maintains the view that [58B] [Freedman:] only by referring to collateral relations can "his father" and "his mother" bear similar interpretations. [Freedman, p. 396, n. 2: For they cannot both be literal, since his father is prohibited by "and he shall cleave," nor can they both refer to relationship by marriage, since his mother is a blood-relation.]

VV. R. Aqiba takes the position that it is better to refer the phrase of "his father" to his father's wife, who is covered by the reference [at Lev. 18:8] to "the nakedness of his father," and not to his father's sister, who falls merely in the category [at Lev. 18:12] of "his father's kin" and not his father's nakedness.

WW. Come and take note: "And Amram took Jochebed, his aunt, as his wife" (Ex. 6:20):

XX. Was this not his aunt on his mother's side [as against Eliezer's view]?

YY. No, it was his aunt on his father's side. [His father's maternal sister would have been forbidden (Freedman)].

ZZ. Come and take note: "And yet indeed she is my sister, she is the daughter of my father but not of my mother" (Gen. 20:12).

AAA. Would this not contain the implication that the daughter of the mother is forbidden [as against Aqiba's view?] [Freedman, p. 396, n. 8: For since he interprets the verse as referring to his father's wife and his mother, who are forbidden on pain of death, he evidently regards those who are forbidden under penalty of excision as permissible, and his mother's daughter is only thus forbidden, but not on pain of death.]

BBB. But do you think so? Was she his sister? She was the daughter of his brother, and since that was the case, there is no difference whether this was his brother by the same father or by the same mother, being permitted in either case.

CCC.   But his is the sense of what [Abraham] said to [Abimelech], "I have a relationship with her as a sister on my father's side [she is the daughter of my half-brother by my father], but not on my mother's side. [Freedman, p. 396, n. 10: Not that she would have been forbidden in that case, but this was stated merely for the sake of exactness.]"

DDD.   Come and take note: On what account did Adam not marry his daughter? It was so that Cain would be able to marry his sister, as it is said, "For I said the world shall be built up by grace" (Ps. 89:2). But were it not the case [that it was an act of grace,] she would have been forbidden [to Cain, because one cannot marry a paternal sister].

EEE.   [To the contrary,] once that relationship was permitted, it remained so.

FFF.   Said R. Huna, "A Samaritan is permitted to marry his daughter."

GGG.   "And if you say, 'On what account did Adam not marry his daughter?' It was so that Cain would be able to marry his sister, so that 'the world shall be built up by grace' (Ps. 89:2)."

HHH.   There are those who say, Said R. Huna, "A Samaritan may not marry his daughter.

III.   "You may know that that is the fact, for Adam did not marry his daughter."

JJJ.   But that is not the correct implication to draw. The reason in that case was so that Cain could marry his sister, so that "the world shall be built up by grace" (Ps. 89:2).

X.

A.   Said R. Hisda, "A slave is permitted to marry his mother and permitted to marry his daughter,

B.   "for he has ceased to fall into the category of the Samaritan [gentile] and has not yet entered the category of Israelite."

XI.

A.   When R. Dimi came, he said R. Eliezer said R. Hanina said, "A Noahide who set aside a slave-girl for his slave-boy and then had sexual relations with her is put to death on her account."

B.   From what point [is she so designated]?

C.   Said R. Nahman, "From the time that he referred to her as the girl friend of so-and-so."

D.   When is she no longer bound to him?

E.   Said R. Huna, "From the time that she walks about in the market with her head uncovered."

XII.

A.   Said R. Eleazar said R. Hanina, "A son of Noah who had anal intercourse with his wife is liable, for it is said, 'And he shall cleave' (Gen. 2:24) -- [by vaginal] and not by anal intercourse."

B.   Said Raba, "Is there anything on account of which an Israelite is not liable and a Samaritan is liable?"

C.   Rather, said Raba, "A son of Noah who had anal intercourse with the wife of his fellow is exempt."

D.   What is the scriptural basis for that view?

E.   "' ... to his wife' and not to the wife of his fellow, 'And he shall cleave ...' [by vaginal] and not by anal intercourse."

XIII.

A.   Said R. Hanina, "An idolator who hit an Israelite is liable to the death penalty.

B.   "For it is said, 'And he looked this way and that way, and when he saw that there was no man, he slew the Egyptian' (Ex. 2:12). [Freedman, p. 398, n. 6: Thus Moses slew the Egyptian for striking an Israelite, proving that he had merited it.]"

C.   And R. Hanina said, "He who hits an Israelite's jaw is as if he hits the jaw of the Presence of God.

D.   "For it is said, 'One who smites man [an Israelite] attacks the Holy One' (Prov. 20:25)."

XIV.

A.   Said R. Simeon b. Laqish, "He who raises his hand against his fellow, even though he did not actually hit him, is called a wicked man.

B.   "For it is said, 'And he said to the wicked man, Why would you smite your fellow' (Ex. 2:13).

C.   "It does not say, 'Why did you smite,' but rather, 'Why would you smite.' Thus, even though he had not actually hit him, he is called a wicked man."

D.   Said Zeiri said R. Hanina, "He is called a sinner, as it is said, 'But if not, I will take it by force' (1 Sam. 2:16), and it is written, 'Wherefore the sin of the young men was very great before the Lord' (1 Sam. 2:16)."

E.   R. Huna said, "His hand should be cut off, for it is said, 'The uplifted arm should be broken' (Job 38:15)."

F.   R. Huna ordered a hand to be cut off.

G.   R. Eleazar says, "His only remedy is burial, for it is written, 'And as for a man of uplifted arm, for him is the earth' (Job 22:8) [Freedman]."

H.   And R. Eleazar said, "The ground has been given over only for strong-armed men, as it is said, 'But as for the strong-armed man, for him is the earth' (Job 22:8)."

XV.

A.   And R. Simeon b. Laqish said, "What is the meaning of the verse of Scripture, 'He who serves his land [meaning: tills his plot] shall be satisfied with bread' (Prov. 12:11)?

B.   "If a man turns himself into a slave for his property, he shall have enough bread, and if not, he shall not have enough bread."

XVI.

A.   And R. Simeon b. Laqish said, "An idolator who keeps the Sabbath incurs the death penalty,

B.   "for it is said, 'And a day and a night they shall not rest' (Gen. 8:22).

C.   "And a master has said, 'The very admonition concerning them carries with it the death penalty.'"

D.   Said Rabina, "Even if he observed Monday as the Sabbath [he is liable]."

E.   And why is this not included in the seven Noahide commandments?

F.   Included there are laws which one observes by abstention, not by positive action.

G.   [59A] And lo, establishing courts of justice is a matter of taking positive action, and that item is included in the list!

H.   That is both a positive commandment and commandment involving abstention [from injustice].

XVI.

A.   And R. Yohanan said, "An idolator who takes up study of the Torah incurs the death penalty.

B.   "For it is said, 'Moses commanded the Torah for us, an inheritance' (Deut. 33:4) -- for us an inheritance, and not for them."

C.   And why is this not included in the seven Noahide commandments?

D.   If we read the word as "inheritance," then he is subject to prohibition against stealing it, and if we read it as "a betrothed girl" [by changing the pronunciation of the Hebrew word], then [Torah] falls into the category of a betrothed girl, and one who violates her is punished by stoning.

E.   An objection was raised:

F.   R. Meir says, "Whence do we know that even an idolator, should he take up study of the Torah, is equivalent to a high priest?

G.   "For it is said, '[You shall therefore keep my statutes and my judgments,] which, if a man do them, he shall live by them' (Lev. 18:5); priests, Levites, and Israelites are not specified, but only a man.

H.   "From that formulation you learn that even an idolator, should he engage in study of the Torah, is equivalent to a high priest."

I.   The reference [to a gentile's study of Torah] is among the seven commandments that apply to them.

XVII.

A.   R. Hanina says, "Also [children of Noah must not eat] blood drawn from a living beast."

B.   Our rabbis have taught on Tannaite authority:

C.   "But flesh with the life thereof, which is the blood thereof, you shall not eat" (Gen. 9:4).

D.   This refers to not eating a limb cut from a living beast.

E.   R. Hanina b. Gamaliel says, "It refers also to blood drawn from a living beast."

F.   What is the scriptural basis for the view of R. Hanina b. Gamaliel?

G.   He reads the cited verse in this way: "Flesh with its life you shall not eat, blood with its life you shall not eat."

H.   And rabbis? That verse serves to permit the eating of creeping things.

I.   Along these same lines, you may say: "Only be sure that you do not eat the blood, for the blood is the life, and you may not eat the life with the flesh" (Deut. 12:23) [Freedman, p. 401, n. 2: Thus the blood being equated with the life, it may not be eaten while "the life is with the flesh," that is, while the animal remains alive.]

J.   And rabbis? They interpret the verse to refer to the blood of the arteries, with which the soul flows out. [That blood is forbidden too.]

XVIII.

A.   Why was it necessary to state [the commandments just cited] to the sons of Noah and then to repeat them at Sinai?

B.   The answer accords with what R. Yose b. R. Hanina said.

C.   For R. Yose b. R. Hanina said, "Every religious duty that was stated to the children of Noah and then repeated at Sinai applies both to this group [the gentiles] and to that group [the Israelites].

D.   "If it was stated to the children of Noah and not repeated at Sinai it is intended for the Israelites, not for the children of Noah.

E.   "And [in that category] was have only the prohibition of [meat containing] the sciatic nerve, speaking in accord with the view of R. Judah, [who holds that it was forbidden to the children of Jacob]."

F.   Said a Master, "Every religious duty that was stated to the children of Noah and then repeated at Sinai applies both to this group and to that group."

G.   To the contrary, since the law was repeated at Sinai, surely it was stated to Israel and not to the children of Noah!

H.   Since the practice of idolatry was stated at Sinai and we find that idolators are penalized on its account, it follows that that prohibition [and hence others in its category] was stated both to this group and to that group.

I.   "If it was stated to the children of Noah and not repeated at Sinai, it is for the Israelites, not for the children of Noah."

J.   To the contrary, since it was not stated at Sinai, it was addressed to the children of Noah and not to Israel.

K.   There is nothing that is permitted to Israelites and forbidden to idolators.

L.   There is nothing? Lo, there is the case of the beautiful captive woman.

M.   The reason in that case is that the gentiles are not permitted to make conquests anyhow.

N.   And there is the theft of something worth less than a penny [which gentiles treated as a crime but Israelites do not].

O.   The idolators are not forgiving [and so regard such a paltry sum as of value, so if someone steals such a sum, he is punished. Israelite courts would not punish a theft of such a sum.]

P.   "Every religious duty that was stated to the children of Noah and then repeated at Sinai applies both to this group and to that group."

Q.   [59B] Lo, there is the case of circumcision, which was stated to the children of Noah, for it is written, "You shall keep my covenant" (Gen. 17:9), and it was repeated at Sinai: "And in the eighth day the flesh of his foreskin shall be circumcised" (Lev. 12:3). Now that commandment was addressed to Israel and <u>not</u> to the sons of Noah.

R. That [repetition of the rule] served the purpose of permitting [the observance of the rite on the Sabbath. [How so?]

S. "By day" -- even [if the eighth day falls] on the Sabbath.

T. And lo, there is the commandment to be fruitful and multiply, which was stated to the children of Noah, for it is written, "And you, be fruitful and multiply (Gen. 9:7), and was repeated at Sinai, as it is written, "Go say to them, get you into your tents again" (Deut. 5:27).

U. Yet the religious duty to be fruitful and multiply applies to Israel and not to the children of Noah.

V. The latter statement serves to indicate that in any matter adopted by a vote [of sages], another vote is necessary for repeal. [Deut. 5:27 is taken to allow people to resume sexual relations that had been suspended, as described at Ex. 19:15, three days before the giving of the Torah.]

W. If so, then each of the Noahide laws may be explained away as serving another purpose.

X. This is the sense of the statement at hand: "As to the admonition, what need was there to go and repeat it?"

Y. "And in that category we have only the instance of the prohibition of [meat containing] the sciatic nerve, stated in accord with the view of R. Judah."

Z. But [circumcision and procreation] also were not repeated [at Sinai]. [Freedman, p. 403, n. 5: For ... their repetition being for a definite purpose is not a repetition at all.]

AA. [Freedman:] These two were repeated, though for a purpose, but this [other item] was not repeated at all.

BB. [As to the question about stating the rule of circumcision to the Noahides and repeating it at Sinai], if you wish, I shall explain as follows:

CC. As to circumcision, to begin with it was addressed to Abraham by the All Merciful [and not to the children of Noah]: "You shall keep my covenant therefore, you and your seed after you in their generations" (gen. 17:9) -- you and your seed will do so, but others need not do so.

DD. Then how about the sons of Ishmael? They too should be liable.

EE. [Not so, for the verse states,] "For in Isaac shall your seed be called" (Gen. 21:22).

FF. Then the children of Esau should be liable?

GG. "<u>In</u> Isaac," but not all [descendants of] Isaac.

HH. R. Oshaia objected, "But how about the children of Keturah. They then should not be liable [to circumcise but they are liable to do so]."

II. Has not R. Yose bar Abin, and some say, R. Yose bar Hanina, said, "'[And the uncircumcised child, the flesh of whose foreskin is not circumcised, that soul shall be cut off from his people;] he has broken my covenant' (Gen. 17:14) -- serving to encompass the children of Keturah"?

XIX.

A. Said R. Judah said Rab, "As to the first man, he was not permitted to eat meat.

B. "For it is written, 'Therefore I have given you all the herbs], to you it shall be for food and to all the beasts of the earth' (Gen. 1:29-30) -- [herbs], and the beasts of the earth shall not be for you [to eat].

C. "And when the children of Noah came, [God] permitted [meat] to them.

D. "For it is said, '[Every moving thing that lives shall be meat for you;] even as the green herb [now] have I given you all things' (Gen. 9:3).

E. "Is it possible to suppose that the prohibition of cutting a limb from a living beast should not apply to [the children of Noah]?

F. "Scripture says, 'But flesh with the life thereof, which is the blood thereof, you shall not eat' (Gen. 9:4).

G. "Is it possible that the rule applies even to creeping things?

H. "Scripture says, 'But' [implying a limitation on the applicability of the rule at hand]."

I. What is the basis of that conclusion?

J. Said R. Huna, "' ... the blood thereof ...' refers to a creature whose blood is distinct from the flesh. That then excludes creeping things, whose blood is not distinct from the flesh."

K. It was objected [to Rab's proposition about Adam as a vegetarian]:

L. "And rule over the fish of the sea" (Gen. 1:28): Is this not for purposes of eating?

M. No, it is for purposes of work.

N. And do fish work?

O. Indeed so, in accord with the inquiry of Rahbah.

P. For Rahbah raised the question, "If one drove a wagon with a goat and a shibbuta-fish [would this involve a violation of the rule not to plow with an ox and an ass together, Deut. 22:10]?"

Q. Come and take note: " ... and over the fowl of the heaven" (Gen. 1:28): Is this not for the purposes of eating?

R. No, it is for purposes of work.

S. And do fowl work?

T. Indeed so, in accord with the inquiry of Rabbah b. R. Huna, "If one has threshed [grain] using geese or cocks, in the view of R. Yose b. R. Judah [who rules on Deut. 25:4, not muzzling the ox while it treads out grain], what is the rule?"

U. Come and take note: "... and over every wild beast that crawls on the earth" (Gen. 1:28): That statement serves to encompass even the snake.

V. It is in line with that which has been taught on Tannaite authority:

W. R. Simeon b. Menassia says, "Woe for the valuable servant that has perished from the earth.

X. For had the snake not been cursed, every Israelite would have assigned to him two valuable snakes. One would he send to the north and one he would send to the south, to bring back to him gemstones, precious stones, and pearls.

Y. "And not only so, but they should tie a strap under its tail, with which it would produce earth for the gardens and untilled ground [of the Israelites]."

Z. An objection was raised [to the foregoing claim that Adam was not permitted to eat meat]:

AA. R. Judah b. Tema would say, "The first man reclined in the Garden of Eden, and the ministering angels roasted meat for him and strained wine for him. The snake looked in and saw all of this glory [that was coming to Adam] and envied him."

BB. That refers to meat that came down from heaven.

CC. And is there such a thing as meat that comes down from heaven?

DD. Indeed so, in line with the following:

EE. R. Simeon b. Halafta was walking along the way. Lions met him and growled at him. He cited the verse, "The young lions roar for prey" (Ps. 104:21).

FF. Two pieces of meat came down [from him]. One they ate, the other they left. He took it along and came to the school house. He asked about it, "Is this an unclean thing or is it a clean [and edible] one?"

GG. They said to him, "Nothing unclean comes down from heaven."

HH. R. Zira asked R. Abbahu, "If something came down from heaven in the form of an ass, what is the law?"

II. He said to him, "You screeching jackal! Lo, they have said to him, 'Nothing unclean comes down from heaven.'"

XX.

A. R. Simeon says, "Also witchcraft [is forbidden to the children of Noah]" [T. A.Z. 8:6M]:

B. What is the scriptural basis for the view of R. Simeon?

C. It accords with what is written in Scripture: [60A] "You shall not permit a witch to live" (Ex. 22:17), and thereafter: "Whoever lies with a beast shall surely be put to death" (Ex. 22:18).

D. Whoever falls into the category of "whoever lies with a beast" [thus including the children of Noah] falls into the category of "You shall not permit a witch to live."

XXI.

A. R. Eleazar says, "Also as to mixed seeds" [T. A.Z. 8:8A]:

B. What is the scriptural basis for this position?

C. Said Samuel, "Scripture states, 'You shall keep my statutes ... ' (Lev. 19:19), meaning the statutes that I have already ordained for you, hence: 'You shall not let your cattle gender with a diverse kind; you shall not sow your field with mixed seed' (Lev. 19:19).

D. "Just as for your beast, the prohibition is against hybridization, so in respect to your field, the prohibition is against hybridization.

E. "Just as the prohibition applies to your beast whether in the Land or outside of the Land, so with respect to your field, the prohibition applies whether it is in the Land or outside of the Land."

F. Then how do you deal with the following:

G. "You shall therefore keep my statutes" (Lev. 18:26)? Does this too refer to statutes that I have already ordained? [In that case the children of Noah have to keep all the commandments.]

H. There it means, "You shall keep my statutes [which I already have given]". Here, "You shall keep my statutes" -- meaning, statutes which to begin with [I now give] you shall keep. [The version of Lev. 19:19 places "statutes" first in the verse, that is, those already in hand, but in Lev. 18:26, "You shall keep" comes first, so "the statutes that follow" are beginning at that point (Freedman, p. 407, n. 1)].

XXII.

A. Said R. Joshua b. Qorha ... [M. 7:5B]:

B. Said R. Aha bar Jacob, "One is liable only if he curses the name made up of four letters, thus excluding a name made up of two letters, which is not subject to a curse [and use of which is not punishable]."

C. That is self-evident, since we have learned May Yose smite Yose [M. 7:5B] [in which "Yose" stands for the four-lettered name of God].

D. What might you have supposed? That the framer of the passage chose a phrase at random? So we are informed that that is not the case [and Yose stands for the four-lettered name of God].

E. There are those who report as follows:

F. Said R. Aha bar Jacob, "That implies that the four-lettered name of God also falls into the category of a name of God."

G. That is self-evident. Have we not learned in the Mishnah, May Yose smite Yose [M. 7:5B]?

H. What might you have supposed? That the penalty for cursing God applies only if one makes use of the great name of God [containing forty-two letters], and the framer of the passage has chosen a phrase at random?

I. So we are informed that that is not the case.

XXIII.

A. Once the trial is over [M. 7:5C]:

B. How do we know that [the judges] rise to their feet [M. 7:5E]?

C. Said R. Isaac bar Ammi, "Scripture has said, 'And Ehud came to him, and he was sitting in a summer room, which he had for himself alone, and Ehud said, I have a message from God to you. And he rose out of his seat' (Judges 3:20).

D. "Now is it not an argument a fortiori? If Eglon, king of Moab, who was a gentile and knew God only by a nickname, rose up, in the case of an Israelite, involving the Ineffable Name, now much the more so!?

E. And how do we know that they tear their clothing [M. 7:5E]?

F. From the following: "Then came Eliakim, the son of Hiliah, who was superintendent of the household, and Shebna the scribe, and Joah the son of Asaph the recorder, to Hezekiah, with their clothes torn, and told them the words of Rab-Shakeh" (2 Kgs. 18:37).

G.   And never sew them back up [M. 7:5E]:

H.   How do we know this?

I.   Said R. Abbahu, "We derive an analogy on the basis of the use of the word 'tear.'

J.   "Here it says, 'With their clothes torn' (2 Kgs. 18:37).

K.   "And elsewhere it is said, 'And Elisha saw [Elijah's ascension] and he cried, My father, my father, the chariot of Israel and the horsemen thereof.' And he saw him no more; and he took hold of his own clothes and tore in them two shreds' (2 Kgs. 2:12).

L.   "Since it says, 'tore them in two,' would I not know that they were shreds? Why then does Scripture specify, 'tears'? It teaches that they were to remain torn forever."

XXIV.

A.   Our rabbis have taught on Tannaite authority:

B.   All the same are the one who actually hears [the blasphemy] and the one who hears it from the one who heard it. Both are liable to tear their garments.

C.   But the witnesses are not liable to tear their garments, for they already did so at the moment when they heard the original blasphemy.

D.   But if they did so at the moment when they heard the original blasphemy, what difference does that make? Lo, they are now hearing it again!

E.   Do not let that argument enter your mind, for it is written, "And it came to pass, when King Hezekiah heard it, that he tore his clothes? (2 Kgs. 18:37).

F.   King Hezekiah tore his clothes, but they did not tear their clothes.

G.   Said R. Judah said Samuel, "He who hears the name of God [blasphemed] by an idolator does not have to tear his clothes,

H.   And should you ask about Rab Shakeh [who was an idolator, and on account of whose blasphemy the king and court tore their clothes], in point of fact, he was an Israelite apostate.

I.   And R. Judah said Samuel said, "People tear their clothes only on account of the four-lettered name of God [used as a curse]."

J.   That then would exclude hearing a euphemism, on account of which one does not [tear clothes].

K.   And this differs from the view of R. Hiyya in two matters.

L.   For R. Hiyya said, "He who hears the name of God blasphemed these days is not liable to tear his clothes, for if you do not take that position, it will result that peoples' entire garments will be full of rents [Freedman: one's garments would be reduced to tatters]."

M.   Now from whom [would one hear these curses]? Should you say that it is from Israelites, are the Israelites so wanton?

N.   Rather, it is clear that he assumes the curses come from idolators.

O.   And if you should propose that what they are saying is that four-lettered name of God, do they know it?

P.   Does it not, rather mean, that they curse by using a euphemism?

Q. And it further follows that he speaks of the present age, in which one is not liable, but in olden times, one was liable.

R. That proves it.

XXV.

A. And the second witness says, "Also I heard what he heard" [M. 7:5F]:

B. Said R. Simeon b. Laqish, "It follows from this rule that the language, 'Also I heard what he heard,' is valid in property cases as well as in capital cases.

C. "But rabbis imposed a stricter rule [in requiring each witness to speak for himself].

D. "But here, because it is not possible [to allow the second to repeat what the first has said], rabbis established the practice as permitted by the law of the Torah.

E. "For if it should enter your mind that this is an invalid mode of testimony, then merely on account of the notion that it is not possible [to do things otherwise], are we going to put a man to death? [Surely not.]"

XXVI.

A. And the third witness says, "Also I heard what he heard" [M. 7:5G]:

B. The unattributed statement at hand accords with the principle of R. Aqiba, who treats three witnesses as equivalent to two.

The Talmud at hand is made up of two essentially distinct units, and the connection between them is casual at best. If we isolate the group of materials that take up the Mishnah-paragraph, we see clearly that that other group follows its own plan and program. The former is found at units I-II, XXIII-XXVI, a rather brief but appropriate treatment of the Mishnah paragraph. The enormous insertion of units III-XXII is formed around a theme and added on account of the issue of whether gentiles who curse God are punished on that account. Unit II introduces that question. Unit II is a logical next step and explains why unit II seemed entirely à propros. One of the seven Noahide commandments was to refrain from blasphemy. The cited passage of Tosefta then is subjected to a systematic analysis in what follows, right down to units XX and XXI, which take up III E.J. I can think of no more persuasive evidence that the entire construction represents a compositor's theory of how matters should be compiled and arranged. Once we deal with the Tosefta-passage, we proceed to follow up each of its elements, e.g., IV H as part of the inquiry of unit IV,and so on throughout. The topic of the Noahide commandments draws in its wake interest in the rights and obligations of gentiles in general, as well as in the status of the first man. So, in all, we have what elsewhere might fill up half a chapter of Talmud, all composed in a rather orderly way and inserted whole on a rather trivial pretext. As a subdivision, however, we can readily explain the flow of argument and therefore the rather solid logic of composition.

7:6

A. [60B] He who performs an act of worship for an idol [M. 7:4D] --

B. all the same are the one who performs an act of service, who [actually] sacrifices, who offers up incense, who pours out a libation offering, who bows down,

C.   and the one who accepts it upon himself as a god, saying to it, "You are my god."

D.   But the one who hugs, it, kisses it, polishes it, sweeps it, and washes it,

E.   anoints it, puts clothing on it, and puts shows on it, [merely] transgresses a negative commandment [Ex. 20:5].

F.   He who takes a vow in its name, and he who carries out a vow made in its name transgress a negative commandment [Ex. 23:13].

G.   He who uncovers himself to Baal Peor [is stoned, for] this is how one performs an act of service to it.

H.   He who tosses a pebble at Merkolis [Hermes] [is stoned, for] this is how one performs an act of service to it.

I.

A.   What is the meaning of all the same are the one who performs an act of service ... [M. 7:5B]?

B.   Said R. Jeremiah, "This is the sense of the passage:

C.   "All the same are the one who performs an act of service in the proper manner, [and] the one who sacrifices, the one who offers incense, the one who pours out a libation, and the one who bows down, even if [these other actions] are not the usual way [in which this particular statue is worshipped]."

D.   And why not take account, also, of tossing blood [of an animal to the god]?

E.   Said Abayye, "'Tossing blood' falls into the category of a libation.

F.   "For it is written, 'Their drink libations of blood will I not offer' (Ps. 16:4). [So it is covered.]"

II.

A.   What is the biblical source [for the fact that these acts of worship impose guilt]?

B.   It is in accord with what our rabbis have taught on Tannaite authority:

C.   If Scripture had stated, "He who sacrifices shall be utterly destroyed" (Ex. 22:19) [without adding the words, "to any god,"] I might have reached the concussion that Scripture speaks of one who sacrifices Holy Things outsides of the Temple.

D.   Accordingly, Scripture states, " ... to any gods," indicating that Scripture speaks of any sort of idolatry.

E.   I know only that penalty applies to one who sacrifices. How do I know that there is a penalty for offering incense, making a libation offering [and the like]?

F.   Scripture says, " ... except to the Lord alone" (Ex. 22:19), by which Scripture limited these forms of worship [regarding them as legitimate only when performed] for the divine name.

G.   Now since there is specific reference to "sacrificing," supplying an analogy to all other acts of service that are performed within the Temple, how do I know that subject to the same prohibition of worship of other gods is an act of prostration? [That is, Deut. 17:2-5 refers to various acts of service in general. Ex. 22:19 speaks of sacrifice in particular. So one particular act of service is specified among the many covered by Deut. 17:3, thus defining what falls into that latter category by means of analogy to what is specified in the former. Whatever bears the traits of the specific items then falls into its category (Freedman, p. 411, n. 9).]

H.   [To encompass prostration, not performed in the Temple as part of an act of service], Scripture says, "And he went and served other gods and prostrated himself before them" (Deut. 17:3), followed by, "You shall bring forth that man or that woman and you shall stone them with stones" (Deut. 17:4).

I.   We have thereby derived evidence of the penalty for that action. How do we know to begin with that there is an admonition against doing it?

J.   Scripture states, "For you shall not prostrate yourself to any other god" (Ex. 34:14).

K.   Might I think that subject to the same rule are such actions as embracing the idol, kissing it, or putting on its shows [so that these acts too should be subject to the death penalty]?

L.   Scripture says, "He who sacrifices ... " (Ex. 22:19).

M.   The act of sacrifice was included in the general rule [specified at Deut. 17:2ff.], and why was it singled out? It was to draw an analogy on the basis of that action and to indicate that, just as the act of sacrifice is distinctive in that it is an act of service performed within the Temple, and it is an act of service on account of which people are liable to the death penalty [should they violate its taboos], so any act of service [performed for an idol] which is analogous to one that is carried on within the Temple and produces the death-penalty, is encompassed, thus excluding such actions as prostratrating oneself to the idol.

N.   Prostration, accordingly, was singled out to testify to itself, while the act of sacrifice was singled out to impart its traits on all those actions that would fall into its category.

III.

A.   A master has said, "I might have reached the conclusion that Scripture speaks of one who sacrifices Holy Things outside of the Temple [rather than of idolatry] [=II C].

B.   But one who sacrifices Holy Things outside of the Temple is subject to the penalty of extirpation [while in the passage at hand, the penalty is death, so how could someone have reached such a conclusions?]

C.   It might have entered your mind to maintain that if people gave him a warning, he is subject to a death penalty [as Scripture states], while if they did not give him a warning, he is subject to extirpation [in which case the passage could well speak of sacrificing Holy Things outside of the cult, not sacrificing to an idol].

D.   So we are informed that that is not the case.

IV.

A.   Said Raba bar R. Hanan to Abayye, "Might I say that prostration is subjected to explicit discussion to impose its traits on the general rule at hand [as against II N, above, that claims prostration was singled out to testify to its own traits, not to impose its traits on the definition of other culpable actions]?

B. "And should you propose to reply that, in that case, why was the act of sacrifice singled out, my answer is that it was to make a point about itself."

C. "Specifically we take account of the intention that a priest forms while performing one act of sacrifice, namely, one for God, to carry out that act of sacrifice with the intention of serving an idol. [That is, by referring at the passage at hand to an act of sacrifice, Scripture makes this point: If one is offering a beast to God and forms the intention of sprinkling its blood for the sake of an idol, that improper intention is taken into account and the priest is subject to punishment, even though the one sacrifice is to God and the other is to an idol.]

D. "For it has been taught on Amoraic authority:

E. "He who slaughters a beast, forming the intention of tossing its blood in honor of an idol and burning its fat in honor of an idol [even if he then properly slaughtered the beast with appropriate intent and did not sprinkle the blood or burn the fat in honor of an idol, so that the original, improper intent, is not actually effected in a concrete deed at all],

F. "R. Yohanan said, [61A] 'The carcass of the beast [thereafter] is forbidden [because of the original, improper intent. He thus invokes the rule that applies to an offering made with improper intent for the sake of God and applies it equally to an offering made with improper intent for the sake of an idol.]'

G. "And R. Simeon b. Laqish said, 'The carcass of the beast is permitted.'

H. "[Now, to continue Raba bar R. Hanan's question,] there is no problem from the viewpoint of R. Yohanan. [Freedman, p. 413, n. 2: Since Yohanan draws an analogy in respect to the animal itself, he can apply the same analogy to the offender. That is, an idolatrous intention in respect of one service is punishable, even though made in another act. Consequently, if prostration was singled out in order to illumine the entire law, the special statement of sacrificing is super-fluous. Hence we are forced to the conclusion that prostration was singled out only for itself].

I. "But from the viewpoint of R. Simeon b. Laqish, the verse of Scripture is required [to prove the point at hand, that prostration was singled out in order to throw light upon the general law]. [Freedman, p. 413, n. 3: Since Simeon b. Laqish does not accept the analogy, we can argue thus: prostration was singled out to illumine the whole. Sacrificing was singled out to teach that though an unlawful intention in respect of one act of service made in the course of another does not affect the animal's fitness for use, it is nevertheless punishable.]"

J. R. Pappa raised an objection, "And from the viewpoint of R. Yohanan, is there no need for a verse of Scripture? One might argue that R. Yohanan to be sure imposes a prohibition on use of the carcass of the beast, but the man who forms the improper intention is not liable to be put to death. Then the verse comes along [and is needed] to impose upon him the liability to the death penalty."

K. R. Aha, son of R. Iqa, objected, "And from the viewpoint of R. Simeon b. Laqish, is a verse of necessary actually required for the stated purpose at all?

L.   "So far as R. Simeon b. Laqish rules that it is permitted, that ruling applies only to the use of the carcass of the beast. But as to the status of the man who has formed the improper intention, he assuredly is subject to the death penalty.

M.   "In this ruling, then, there would be a parallel to the case of one who prostrates himself to a mountain. The mountain remains permitted [for ordinary use and enjoyment] but the one who worships it nonetheless is put to death through decapitation."

N.   Said R. Aha of Difti to Rabina, "Now let us take up the question of Raba, bar R. Hanan, to Abayye, 'Might I say that prostration is subjected to explicit discussion to impose its traits on the general rule at hand?'

O.   "[If so,] then as to the verse, '[Take heed to yourself ... that you do not seek after their gods, saying,] How did these nations serve their gods? [Even so I will do the same]' (Deut. 12:30) [A verse that implies that only the normal way of serving these gods is forbidden], what acts of service are excluded by the cited verse? [For if we claim that prostration serves to indicate that even acts of service outside of the Temple are punished, then what further acts are forbidden by the verse at hand? We already know the point that it evidently wishes to make (Freedman, pp. 413-4, n. 5)].

P.   "And should you say that it serves to exclude the act of showing one's behind to those idols that are ordinarily served by having sacrifices made to them, that point derives, in fact, from the reference to prostration.

Q.   "Just as prostration is an act of honoring the idol, so every act that is interpreted as an honor [would be punished, thus excluding showing one's behind to the idol]."

R.   [The reply:] Rather, it serves to exclude one who shows his behind to a statue of Mercury.

S.   You might have thought that one should rule, since its appropriate act of worship is an act of disgrace, so some other act of disgrace falls into the same category [and is punishable].

T.   So we are informed that that is not the case.

U.   Then what about the statement of R. Eliezer: "How do we know that one who sacrifices a beast to Mercury is liable?

V.   "For it is said, 'They shall not more offer their sacrifices to demons' (Lev. 17:7).

W.   "Now if it cannot speak of a mode of worship that is the ordinary and accepted one, since it is already stated, 'How did these nations serve their gods ...' (Deut. 12:30) [proving that routine modes of worship are penalized if done for idols], apply it to an unusual mode of worship of those gods. [In that case, such an abnormal mode of worship is subject to punishment.]"

X.   [Reverting to Raba's thesis that the reference to prostration imposes the traits of that action on all others, with the result that abnormal modes of worship are punishable], surely an act of worship not in accord with the usual procedure would derive from the reference to prostration [and we know from that reference that such an act is punishable. We do not need to provide the proof that Eliezer gives. Would then Eliezer's proof not show therefore that Raba's thesis is wrong?'

Y.   The verse at hand proves that one who makes a sacrifice [to Mercury] merely for spite [to God] [without regarding Mercury as a god] [nonetheless is subject to penalty.] [So Raba's question is not obviated by the proof at hand and valid.]

V.

A.   R. Hamnuna's oxen got lost on him. [While searching for them] he met Rabbah and laid out for him two passages of the Mishnah which he deemed to contradict one another: "We have learned in the Mishnah: he who performs an act of worship for an idol [M. 7:6A], meaning that if he actually performed such an act, he is [liable] but if he merely said, 'I shall do it,' he is not liable.

B.   "But we have also learned in the Mishnah: He who says, 'I am going to worship,' 'I shall go and worship,' 'Let's go and worship' [M. 7:10N]. [This bears the implication that merely saying, not doing, also is penalized.]"

C.   He said to him, "The former passage speaks of one who says, 'I shall not accept it upon me as a god until I perform an act of worship' [so that passage, too, speaks of incurring liability only by making a statement]."

D.   Said R. Joseph, "You have simply taken views at random of two Tannaite authorities [and not all Tannaite authorities are in agreement]."

E.   It is, in point of fact, a dispute among Tannaite authorities.

F.   For it has been taught on Tannaite authority:

G.   He who says, "Come and worship me" --

H.   R. Meir declares him liable [for enticing people to commit idolatry].

I.   And R. Judah declares him exempt.

J.   But in a case of their actually bowing down [to that man], all parties concur, for it is said, "You shall not make for yourself any idol" (Ex. 20:4). [Freedman, p. 415, n. 1: Hence, since they worshipped him, he is guilty as a seducer to idolatry].

K.   Where there is a dispute, it concerns a case in which what is involved is merely a statement.

L.   R. Meir takes the view that a mere statement is consequential [and hence one is liable on that account, as a M. 7:10N], and R. Judah maintains that a mere statement is null [in lines with M. 7:6A].

M.   [Having made reference to the present dispute], R. Joseph retracted and said, "What I said is of no consequence, for even R. Judah concurs that a mere statement may well impose liability [without its being accompanied by a concrete action].

N.   "For it has been taught on Tannaite authority:

O.   "R. Judah says, 'Under no circumstances is one liable until he says, "I am going to worship," "I shall go and worship," "Let's go and worship" [M. 7:10N. [This would then concur with Meir's position, that a statement without action in the matter of encitement to idolatry is penalized.]

P.   "At issue in the dispute [between Meir and Judah] is a case in which he incited others to worship him himself, and the people replied that they would do so.

Q.   "One party maintains that if one incites people to worship himself, the others do pay attention to him, and when they said 'Yes,' they were telling the truth [and so, Meir holds, he is liable].

R.   "The other party takes the view that when one incites people to worship himself, they do not pay attention to him, for people say, '[61B] what difference is there between him and us?' So when they say 'Yes,' they [are not telling the truth but] making fun of him.

S.   "Now [to reconcile the two versions of the law], the Mishnah-rule refers [at M. 7:10N] to an individual who is reenticed to commit idolatry, while the one at hand refers to a community that was enticed to commit idolatry.

T.   "Since an individual will not change his mind, he will certainly go in error after [the seducer to idolatry] [and hence the mere statement matters, as at M. 7:10N],

U.   "but the community as a whole will surely change their minds and not go in error after him [hence the mere statement does not matter at M. 7:6A]."

V.   Said R. Joseph, "How do I know that [a mere statement attempting to incite an individual, not accompanied by a concrete deed, brings a penalty in the case of an individual]?

W.   "As it is written, "[If your brother ... entice you ...], you shall not consent to him nor hearken to him' (Deut. 13:9).

X.   "Lo, if one had consented and hearkened to him, he would be liable."

Y.   To this proof, Abayye objected, "And is there any difference between a case in which an individual is enticed and a case in which the community is enticed [to idolatry]?

Z.   "Has it not been taught on Tannaite authority:

AA.   "'If your brother, son of your mother, entice you' (Deut. 13:7) -- all the same is the case in which an individual is enticed and the case in which the community is enticed.

BB.   "But the Scripture has made particular reference to an individual, as distinct from the community, and to the community, as distinct from the individual.

CC.   "The reason that the individual is singled out from the community is so as to impose a strict penalty on the man's body and a lenient penalty on his property [which, in the case of an entire community, is destroyed along with the individual].

DD.   "The reason that the community is distinguished from the individual is to impose a lenient rule on the penalty applicable to their bodies] since they are decapitated, not stoned] but a more strict penalty on their property [which is destroyed].

EE.   "Now [Abayye continues], it is in that particular aspect that the case of the individual and that of the community are distinguished from one another. In all other aspects they are identical to one another, [and hence the proposed distinction of Joseph is null]."

FF.   Rather, said Abayye, "The one passage speaks of one who is enticed to commit idolatry by what he himself says, the other passage speaks of one who is enticed to commit idolatry by what someone else says.

GG.   "In the case of one who is enticed by what he himself says, he may change his mind [so that he actually does something, he is not subject to a penalty], but if he is enticed by what some else says, he will follow the other [and so is not likely to change his mind, so he is penalized for what he says, without actually doing a thing]."

HH. Said Abayye, "How do I know it? Because it is written, 'You shall not consent to him nor hearken to him' (Deut. 13:9). Lo, if one consented and hearkened [by agreeing with what a third party had to say], he is liable."

II. Raba said, "Both this passage and that passage refer to a case of one who is enticed by what someone else says.

JJ. "The one speaks of a case in which one has said to him, 'This is what it it eats, this is what it drinks, this is the good it does, this is the bad it does.' The other passage speaks of a case in which one has not said to him, 'This is what it eats, this is what it drinks, and so on.' [If one does not make the second set of statements, the hearer may reconsider, so we impose punishment only when he actually does an act of worship (Freedman, p. 416, n. 5).]"

KK. Said Raba, "How do I know it? As it is written, '[If your brother entice you ... saying, let us go and serve other gods ...,] namely, of the gods of the people who are round about you, near to you or far from you' (Deut. 13:8).

LL. "What difference does it make to me whether they are near or far?

MM. "But this is what he said to him, 'From the quality of the ones that are near, you may learn the quality of those that are far.'

NN. "Does this then not refer to a case in which one said to him, 'This is what it eats, this is what it drinks, this is the good that it does, this is the bad that it does'?"

OO. That indeed proves the case.

PP. R. Ashi said, "The latter of the two passages of the Mishnah refers to an Israelite apostate [who is punished merely for what he says, not for what he does, since we assume he will do what he says. A loyal Israelite may change his mind.]"

QQ. Rabina said, The two passages mean to indicate 'not only this but even that.' [Freedman, p. 417, n. 4: The first Mishnah-Passage states that the death penalty is imposed for engaging in idol worship; the second adds that this is so not only for actually worshipping idols but also for the mere statement of intention.]"

VI.

A. It has been stated on Amoraic authority:

B. He who does an act of worship for an idol, whether from love or from fear,

C. Abayye said, "He is liable."

D. Raba said, "He is exempt."

E. Abbaye said, "He is liable, for lo, he has worshipped it."

F. Raba said, "He is exempt. If he had accepted it upon himself as a god, he would be liable, but if not, he would not be liable."

G. Said Abayye, "And on what basis do I take this position? It is in accord with what we have learned in the Mishnah: He who performs an act of worship for an idol -- all the same are the one who performs an act of service, etc. [M. 7:6A-B].

H. "Does this not mean, "All the same are he who worships out of love and he who worships out of fear'?"

I.   And Raba will tell you, "No, it is as R. Jeremiah has explained matters [at I A-C]."

J.   Said Abayye, "And on what basis do I take this position? For it has been taught on Tannaite authority:

K.   "'You shall not prostrate yourself to them" (Ex. 20:5) --

L.   "'To them you may not prostrate yourself, but you may prostrate yourself to a man such as yourself.

M.   "'Is it possible that one may do so even to one who is worshipped like Haman?

N.   "'Scripture says, "You will not worship them" (Ex. 20:5).'

O.   "Now Haman was worshipped on account of fear. [So, it follows, one may not worship an idol whether from love or fear, and even though one has not accepted it upon himself as a god.]"

P.   And [what is] Raba's [view]? [He maintains that one may not bow down to one] like Haman or not like Haman: One may not bow down to one like Haman, because he himself was an idol.

Q.   And not like Haman, because Haman was worshipped on account of fear, while the verse at hand speaks of worship not on account of fear."

R.   Said Abayye, "And on what basis do I take this position? For it has been taught on Tannaite authority:

S.   "'As to the case of an anointed high priest who has unwittingly worshipped an idol,

T.   "'Rabbi says, "[He is liable] if the action was done inadvertently."

U.   "'And sages say, "He is liable only if the very principle [that one may not worship an idol] was forgotten by him." [The high priest is liable for entire ignorance that the prohibition against idolatry exists, not merely for inadvertently doing the action while knowing it should not be done.]

V.   "'And they concur that so far as his sacrifice in atonement is concerned, it is a she-goat, just as is brought by an individual.

W.   "'And they further concur that he does not have to bring a suspensive guilt-of-fering.'

X.   "Now as to inadvertently carrying out an act of idolatry, what sort of action can have been contemplated?

Y.   "If [the high priest] inadvertently imagined that [a temple] was a synagogue and he prostrated himself to the [idol's temple] on that account, then his heart was directed to heaven [and there is no sin here at all].

Z.   "Rather, we deal with a case in which he saw a statue of a man and prostrated himself to it.

AA.   "Now is he had accepted the idol as his god, then what he did was deliberate [and does not fall into the present category at all].

BB.   "[62A] If he did not accept the idol as his god, then what he did was null.

CC.   "Rather, is it not a case in which it was done out of love and dear [Freedman, p. 419, n. 4: without knowing that this is idol worship. This constitutes inadvertency in respect of the action, but not forgetfulness or ignorance of the law, since he knows that idolatry per se is forbidden. Hence the passage supports Abayye's ruling.]"

DD. And Raba? He will say to you, "Is it not a case in which the man says that it is permitted [to carry out such an act]?"

EE. but if it is a case in which the man says that it is permitted to carry out such an act, what we have is nothing other than a situation in which the very principle that idolatry per se is forbidden has been forgotten.

FF. The present passage speaks of a case in which the person holds that it is entirely permitted to carry out such an action, while a case in which the principle that the act is prohibited is forgotten deals with a matter in which part of the action is to be carried out and part not carried out. [Freedman, p. 419, n. 5: If the priest declares that sacrificing and offering incense to idols are forbidden but prostration is permitted, that is called ignorance of the law; if he declares that idolatry is not prohibited at all, in Raba's opinion it is regarded as inadvertency of action.]

VII.

A. R. Zakkai repeated on Tannaite authority before R. Yohanan, "If a person sacrificed, burned incense, poured out a libation, and prostrated himself [to an idol] in one spell of inadvertence [not knowing that any form of service to an idol is forbidden], he is liable on only one count."

B. He said to him, "Go and repeat this in public."

C. Said R. Abba, "That which R. Zakkai has stated in point of fact represents a dispute between R. Yose and R. Nathan.

D. "For it has been taught on Tannaite authority:

E. "'The prohibition of lighting a fire [on the Sabbath, which is covered under the general prohibition not to work on the Sabbath, Ex. 20:10, and did not require specification], was singled out so as to indicate that it is [merely] a negative [commandment],' the words of R. Yose.

F. "R. Nathan says, 'It was singled out to signify that it is treated as distinct [from other actions, so showing that, overall, if on the Sabbath in a single spell of inadvertence one carried out a number of prohibited actions, he is liable on each count, and not solely on the single count covering all of them.]' [This would place Zakkai in Yose's position, with Nathan rejecting the basic principle.]

G. "From the viewpoint of him who has said that the specific reference to kindling a flame was to indicate that that commandment was simply a negative one, the specific reference to prostration before an idol serves the same purpose, namely to place that act into the category of a negative commandment.

H. "In the viewpoint of him who has said that the explicit prohibition of kindling a flame served to show that one is liable on each count of a number of actions in violation of the Sabbath done in a single spell of inadvertence, the same principle applies to the act of prostration, also singled out, so that if one does a number of distinct actions of service to an idol in a single spell of inadvertence, he is liable on each count."

I. To this proposition R. Joseph objected, "But it may well be that R. Yose maintains that the specific reference to kindling a fire was made so as to place that act in the category of a negative commandment only because he is able to prove the other principle on the strength of a different proof-text altogether. Specifically, the fact that one should make distinctions among other acts of labor on the Sabbath [and impose liability for each one when many of them are done in a single spell of inadvertence] derives, in his view, from the verse, ' ... of one of them ...' (Lev. 4:2).

J.   "For it has been taught on Tannaite authority:

K.   "R. Yose says, '"[If a soul shall sin through ignorance against any of the command-ments of the Lord, concerning things which ought not to be done,] and shall do one of them (Lev. 4:2) indicates that there are occasions on which is liable on one count for all actions, and there are occasions on which one is liable for each act individually.'"

L.   "And R. Jonathan said, 'What is the scriptural basis for R. Yose's view? It is because it is written, "and shall do of one of them" (Lev. 4:2).'" [Freedman, p. 421, n. 3: This is a peculiar construction. The Scripture should have written, 'and shall do one (not of) of them,' or, 'and do of them' (one being understood), or, 'and shall do one' (of them being understood). Instead of which, a partitive preposition is used before each. Hence each part of the pronoun is t o be interpreted separately, teaching that he is liable for the transgression of 'one' precept; and for part of one (i.e., for 'of one'): for 'them' (explained as referring to the principal acts); and for the derivatives 'of them' (acts forbidden because they partake of the same nature as the fundamentally prohibited acts); also, each pronoun reacts upon the other, as explained in the discussion.

M.   [What follows, to the end of this paragraph, is Freedman's translation, pp. 423-425, reproduced with only minor changes:] This teaches that liability is incurred for one complete act of violation [i.e., 'one']; and for one which is but a part of one [i.e., 'of one']; and for transgressing actions forbidden in themselves [i.e., 'them'], and for actions [the prohibited nature of which is derived] from others [i.e., 'of them']; further, that open transgression may involve liability for a number of sacrifices [i.e., 'one' = 'them'], whilst many offenses may involve but one sacrifice [i.e., 'them' = 'one']. Thus: 'one complete act of violation,' -- the writing [on the Sabbath] of Simeon; 'one which is but a part of one,' -- the writing of Shem as part of Simeon, 'actions forbidden in themselves' [i.e., 'them'] -- the principal acts of labor forbidden on the Sabbath; 'actions [the prohibited nature of which is derived] from others [i.e., "of them"]' -- the derivatives; 'one transgression may involve liability for a number of sacrifices [i.e., "one" = "them"] -- e.g., if one knew that it was the Sabbath [and that some work is forbidden on the Sabbath], but was unaware that these particular acts are forbidden; 'many offenses may involve but one sacrifice [i.e., "them" = "one"]' -- e.g., if he was unaware that it was the Sabbath, but knew that his actions are forbidden on the Sabbath. But here [in idol worship], since separation of actions is not derived from elsewhere, may we not say that all agree [even R. Yose] that prostration was singled out to indicate 'separation'? [But this is so?] May not 'separation' of acts in the case of idolatry too be deduced from 'of one of them'? Thus, 'one complete act of idolatry' -- sacrificing [to idols]; a part of one [i.e., 'of one'] -- the cutting of one organ. 'Actions forbidden in themselves' [i.e., 'them'] -- principal acts, i.e., sacrificing, burning, incense, making libations, and prostration; 'actions derived from others' [i.e., 'of them'] the derivatives of these -- e.g., if he broke a stick before it; 'one transgression may involve liability for a number of sacrifices,' [i.e., 'one' = 'them'], e.g., when one knows that it is an idol [and that idolatry is forbidden], but is unaware that the particular acts in question constitute idol-worship; many offenses may involve but one sacrifice, [i.e., 'them' = 'one']; if he is unaware that it is an idol, but knows that these acts are forbidden in idol worship.

N.   As to an act of idolatry done in inadvertence, how would it be defined?

O.   If one should suppose that he was worshipping a synagogue when he bowed down to [a temple of an idol], lo, his heart was directed to heaven.

P.   Rather, he saw a statue of a man and bowed down to it.

Q.   But if he had accepted it as a god, then what he did was a deliberate violation of the law.

R.   And if he had not accepted it as a god, then what he did was null.

S.   Hence what he did was out of love and fear.

T.   That poses no problems to Abayye, who has held that one is liable on that account.

U.   But from the viewpoint of Raba, who has said that one is exempt, what is there to be said?

V.   It is that the man maintained that it is permitted [to worship an idol]. [Freedman, p. 423, n. 6: Though this does not constitute unawareness that a particular thing is an idol worship, yet it is a case where many transgressions involve but one sacrifice.]

W.   On that basis you may work out the problem posed by Raba to R. Nahman: "If one is responsible for forgetting the principle of both [the Sabbath as a day on which labor is prohibited, and also that the given act of labor is prohibited on the Sabbath], what is the law?"

X.   One may reach the conclusion that one is liable on only one count. [Freedman, p. 424, n. 2: For if one declared that idolatry is permissible, it is as though he were unaware that a particular things was an idol. Hence if we deduce from the verse that in idolatry only one sacrifice is needed for such inadvertence, the same must apply to the Sabbath. At this stage of the discussion it is assumed, however, hat this deduction is impossible, as otherwise Raba would not have propounded his problem. Consequently the verse cannot be applied to idolatry, and Abba is justified in regarding kindling and prostration as interdependent both in interpretation and in the resultant laws and Zakkai's statement is admissible as correct -- according to R. Yose.]

Y.   That is no objection. If you can solve the problem, solve it. [What difference does it make?]

Z. But can you interpret the verse at hand to speak of idolatry? The cited verses speak of idolatry, while the verses under discussion concern sacrifices brought on account of the anoited priest, that is, a bullock; for the chief, a he-goat; and for an individual, a she-goat or lamb.

AA. In regard to idolatry, we have learned: they concur that his sacrifice is a she-goat, as in the case of a private individual.

BB. There is nothing further [to be said. Freedman, p. 424, n. 8: Consequently this verse cannot teach separation of idolatrous actions.]

CC. When R. Samuel bar Judah came, he said, [62B] "This is what [Zakkai] taught on Tannaite authority before [Yohanan]: 'There is a more strict rule that applies to the Sabbath than applies to other religious duties, and there is a more strict rule that applies to other religious duties that does not apply to the Sabbath.

DD. "'For in the case of the Sabbath, if one has done two forbidden actions in a single spell of inadvertence, he is liable for each one separately, a rule that does not apply to other religious duties.

EE. "'The more strict rule applying to other religious duties is that if one has performed a forbidden action inadvertently, without prior intention, he is liable, which is not the rule for the Sabbath.'"

FF. A master has said, "In the case of the Sabbath, if one has done two forbidden actions ...":

GG. How shall we illustrate that statement? If one should propose that a person did an act of reaping and one of grinding, then, in respect to other religious duties, it would be similar to eating both forbidden fat and blood. In such a case, one is liable on two counts, just as here he is liable on two counts.

HH. Then with respect to other religious duties, what sort of case would yield the result that one is liable on only a single count?

II. If one ate forbidden fat and then more forbidden fat.

JJ. In a parallel case involving the Sabbath it would be if one performed an act of reaping and then another act of reaping.

KK. In that case, however, in the one context [eating forbidden fat] he is liable on only one count, and in the other context, he also is liable on only one count.

LL. That is why [R. Yohanan] said to him, "Go and repeat your tradition outside.

MM. But what is the real problem at hand? Perhaps one may say to you that, as to the acts of reaping and grinding, subject to a rule distinct from other religious duties, the reference [to "other religious duties"] is specifically to idolatry, and it accords with what R. Ammi said.

NN. For R. Ammi said, "If one has sacrificed, offered incense, and poured out a libation, all in a single spell of inadvertence, he is liable on only a single count," [while in the case of the Sabbath, as we see, one is liable on more than a single count].

OO. You cannot assign the statement only to idolatry, for the end of the same sentence reads: "The more strict rule applying to other religious duties is that, if one has performed a forbidden action inadvertently, without prior intention, he is liable, which is not the rule for the Sabbath."

PP. Now what, in reference to idolatry, can possibly fall into the category of an action that has been performed inadvertently, without intention?

QQ. If one supposed that a temple of an idol was a synagogue and prostrated himself to it, lo, his heart was directed to heaven.

RR. Rather, he saw a statue of a man and bowed to it.

SS. If, then, he accepted it as a god, what he did was done deliberately.

TT. If he did not accept it as a god, then what he did was null.

UU. Rather, what he did was out of love and awe.

VV. That poses no problems to Abayye, who has said that, in such a case, he is liable.

WW. But as to the view of Raba, who has said that he is exempt, what is there to be said?

XX. Rather, it is one who has the view that such an action is permitted. [Freedman, p. 425, n. 3: And since he has never known of any prohibition, it is not regarded as unwitting, but as unintentional too.]

YY. Then this is what is not the case for the Sabbath, for, in a similar circumstance, one would not be liable at all.

ZZ. [But surely that conclusion is not possible], for when Raba poses his question to R. Nahman as to the rule governing a single spell of inadvertence in each of the two contexts, it is only whether one is liable on one count or on two counts. But it never entered his mind that one would be entirely exempt from all liability.

AAA. What difficulty is at hand? Perhaps one may say to you indeed that the first clause speaks of idolatry and the remainder of other religious duties.

BBB. The case of inadvertence, without intention, would be one in which one had the view that [when he found there was forbidden fat in his mouth], he thought that it was spit and swallowed it [rather than spitting it out], a rule which, in a parallel case on the Sabbath, would produce the ruling of non-liability. [How so?] If one had the intention of lifting up something that was already harvested but turned out to cut something yet attached to the ground, he is exempt. [Freedman, p. 426, n. 2: Cutting or tearing out anything growing in the earth is a forbidden labor on the Sabbath. His offense was both unwitting and unintentional for (i) he had no intention of tearing out anything and (ii) he did not know that this was growing in the soil. Now, had he known that it was growing in he soil and deliberately uprooted it in ignorance of the forbidden nature of that action, his offense would have been unwitting but intentional. By analogy, had he intended to eat the melted fat, thinking that it was permitted, his offense would be regarded as unwitting but intentional. Since, however, he did not intend eating it at all, but accidently swallowed it, thinking at the same time that it was spittle, his offense was both unwitting and unintentional.]

CCC. This is in line with what R. Nahman said Samuel said, "He who gets involved with forbidden fat or consanguineous sexual relationships is liable, for he derived benefit from the act. [That is, if one planned to eat permitted fat but inadvertently ate forbidden fat, or planned to have sexual relations with his wife but inadvertently had them with his sister, he is liable.] If by contrast one was involved in a forbidden action on the Sabbath [and thereby did what he did not intend to do], he is exempt, for it is a deed involving full deliberation that the Torah has prohibited."

DDD. R. Yohanan is consistent with his views expressed elsewhere, for he does not wish to apply one paragraph of a Mishnah-teaching to one circumstance, and a later paragraph to a difference circumstance." [We now have an example of that same approach of consistency.]

EEE. For R. Yohanan said, "For whoever explains for me the Mishnah-paragraph of 'a barrel' in such a way that it accords with the position of a single Tannaite authority, I shall carry his clothes to the baths." [Freedman, p. 427, n. 2: This reference is to a Mishnah on B.M. 40b: If a barrel was entrusted to a man's keeping, a particular place being assigned to it, and this man moved it from the place where it was first set down, and it was broken -- Now, where it was broken whilst he was handling it, then if he was moving it for his own purposes (e.g., to stand on it), he must pay for it; if for its sake (e.g, if it was exposed to harm in the first place), he is not liable. But if it was broken after he had set it down, then in both cases he is not liable. If the owner, however, had assigned a place to it, and this man moved it, and it was broken, whether whilst in his hand or after he had set it down: if he moved it for his sake, he is liable; if for its own, he is not. The Talmud then proceeds to explain that the first clause is in accordance with R. Ishmael, who maintained that if one stole an article and returned it without informing its owner, he is free from all further liability in respect of it. Consequently, if he moved the barrel for his own purpose (which is like stealing), and set it down elsewhere, no particular place being assigned to it, his liability have ceased. But the second clause agrees with R. Aqiba's ruling that if an article is stole and returned, the liability remains until the owner is informed of its return. Consequently, if he moved it for his own purpose, he remains liable even after it is set down. But R. Johanan was dissatisfied with this explanation, holding that both clauses should agree with one Tanna. Now, the Talmud does actually explain that it can agree with one Tanna, viz., by assuming that in the first clause the barrel was subsequently returned to its original place, but that in the second clause it was not. Consequently, it concurs entirely with R. Ishmael, but his liability continues in the second instance because he did not return it to its first place. But R. Johanan rejects this explanation, not deeming it plausible to conceive of such different circumstances in the two clauses of the Mishnah. For the same reason, when R. Zakkai taught that sometimes the Sabbath is more stringent than other precepts, and sometimes it is the reverse, R. Johanan would not accept an interpretation whereby 'other precepts' in the first clause means idolatry, whilst in the second it referred to forbidden fat.]

FFF.   Returning to the body of the text just now cited:

GGG.   [63A] Said R. Ammi, "If one sacrificed to an idol, burned incense, and poured out a libation to it, in a single spell of inadvertence, he is liable on only a single count."

HHH.   Said Abayye, "What is the scriptural basis for the view of R. Ammi? '[You shall not bow down to them] nor serve them' (Ex. 20:5), by which formulation Scripture has treated all of them as a single act of service."

III.   But did Abayye make such a statement?

JJJ.   And has not Abayye said, "Why is reference in three settings made to the prohibition of bowing down for an idol [at Ex. 20:5]?

KKK.   "One covers doing so in the proper way, one covers doing so not in the proper way, and the third serves to impose a distinct liability for each act of doing so [so that if one does so three times in a single spell of inadvertence, he is liable on three counts]"?

LLL.   [Abayye's statement] was in fact a report of R. Ammi's viewpoint, but [Abayye] does not concur with that viewpoint.

MMM.   Returning to the text just now cited:

NNN.   Said Abayye, "Why is reference made to the prohibition of bowing down for an idol in three settings [at Ex. 20:5]? One covers doing so in the proper way, one covers doing so not in the proper way, and the third serves to impose a distinct liability for each act of doing so."

OOO.   But as to doing so in the proper way, is this not derived from the verse, "[How did these nations serve their gods? Even so will I do likewise]" (Deut. 12:30)?

PPP.   Rather: "one of the references to prostration deals with a case in which one worships the idol in a normal but somewhat unusual way, one deals with the case in which one worships it not in its normal way at all, and the third serves to impose a distinct liability for each act of doing so."

VIII.

A.   The one who accepts it upon himself as a god, saying to it, "You are my god" [M. 7:6C]:

B.   Said R. Nahman said Rabbah bar Abbuha said Rab, "Once one has said to it, 'You are my god,' he is liable."

C.   "For what? If it is for the death penalty, that is the explicit statement of the Mishnah-passage.

D.   Rather, it is for an offering. But is that even from the viewpoint of rabbis?

E.   For has it not been taught on Tannaite authority:

F.   One is liable only on account of something which is of practical consequence, such as sacrificing, burning incense, pouring out a libation, or prostrating oneself [T. 10:3B].

G.   And in this connection R. Simeon b. Laqish said, "Who is the Tannaite authority who includes the matter of prostration [which is hardly a concrete action in the category of a sacrifice]? It is R. Aqiba, who maintains the view that we do not require that there be a concrete deed at all [to impose liability for idolatry].

H.   It surely must follow that rabbis take the view that we do require a concrete deed [and Rab's statement would then not represent the position of rabbis but only of an individual authority].

I.   When Rab made that statement, it was from the viewpoint of R. Aqiba.

J.   But if it was from the viewpoint of R. Aqiba, that is a self-evident fact. The person at hand falls into the category of a blasphemer.

K.   What might you have said? R. Aqiba imposes the requirement of bringing an offering only in the case of a blasphemer, in which case Scripture makes explicit reference to extirpation.

L.   But here, in which case there is no explicit reference in Scripture to extirpation, I might have said that that was not the case.

M.   So we are informed that there is an analogy to be drawn [between saying "You are my god" and blasphemy,] for it is written, "They have made a molten calf and have worshipped it and have sacrificed to it and have said, '[These are your gods, O Israel who brought you up out of the land of Egypt]" (Ex. 32:8). [So sacrificing and declaring that this is one's god are regarded as analogous actions, as Aqiba maintains].

N.   Said R. Yohanan, "Were it not for the indication of the plural in the verb, 'who have brought you up,' the Israelites would have become liable to destruction. [The calf then is not the sole god, the Israelites' language indicating that God also was a divinity.]

O.   This is subject to a dispute on Tannaite authority:

P.   Others say, "Were it not for the indication of the plural in the verb, 'who have brought you up,' the Israelites would have become liable to destruction."

Q.   Said to him R. Simeon b. Yohai, "Is it not the case that whoever joins together the Name of heaven and the name of 'something else' [an idol] is uprooted from the world, as it is said, 'He who sacrifices to any god, save to the Lord alone, shall be utterly destroyed' (Ex. 22:19)?

S.   "What is the meaning of the plural verb?

T.   "It indicates that they desired many gods."

IX.

A.   But the one who hugs it, kisses it, polishes it, sweeps it... [M. 7:6D]:

B.   When R. Dimi came [from Palestine], he said R. Eleazar [said], "On account of all [of the actions listed at M. 7:6Dff.] one is given a flogging, except for the one who takes a vow in its name or who carries out a vow made in its name [M. 7:6R]."

C.   What distinguishes one who takes a vow in its name or who carries out a vow made in its name that such a one is not flogged?

D.   It is because that constitutes a violation of a negative commandment that does not involve a concrete action.

E.   The other items also constitute prohibitions based on a negative commandment phrased in general terms, and people do not administer a flogging for the violation of a prohibition based on a negative commandment phrased in general terms.

F.   For it has been taught on Tannaite authority:

G.   How do we know that if someone eats meat from a beast before it has died, he violates a negative commandment?

H.   Scripture says, "You shall not eat anything with the blood" (Lev. 19:26).

I.   Another matter: "You shall not eat anything with the blood" means you shall not eat meat while the blood is still in the bowl [and not sprinkled].

J.   R. Dosa says, "How do we know that people do not provide a mourners' meal on account of those who are executed by a court? Scripture says, 'You shall not eat anything for one whose blood has been shed.'"

K.   R. Aqiba says, "How do we know that a sanhedrin who put someone to death should not taste any food all that day?

L.   "Scripture says, 'You shall not eat anything with bloodshed.'"

M.   R. Yohanan says, "How do we know that there is an admonition against the wayward and rebellious son? Scripture says, 'You shall not do anything to cause bloodshed' (Lev. 19:26) [Freedman's translation]."

N.   And said R. Abin bar Hiyya, and some say, R. Abin bar Kahana, "In the case of all of these, one is not flogged, for each of these constitutes a prohibition based on a general principle."

O.   But when Rabin came [from Palestine], he said R. Eleazar [said], "In the case of all of them, one is not flogged, except for the case of one who takes an oath by [the idol's] name or carries out an oath made in its name.

P.   "What is the reason that these are differentiated so that one is not flogged?

Q.   "It is because these items constitute prohibitions based on a negative commandment phrased in general terms."

R.   But these other items constitute violations of a negative commandments that do not involve concrete actions.

S.   The rule follows the view of R. Judah, who has said, "As to a negative commandment that does not involve a concrete action, the court nonetheless administers a flogging on account of a violation of such a commandment."

T.   For it has been taught on Tannaite authority:

U.   "'You shall let nothing of it remain until the morning, and that which remains of it until the morning you shall burn with fire' (Ex. 12:10).

V.   "In framing matters this way, the Scripture has stated a positive commandment following a negative commandment, [63B] so as to indicate to you that the court does not inflict a flogging on that account," the words of R. Judah.

W.   R. Jacob says, "That is not the principle at hand. Rather it is because what we deal with is a negative commandment that does not contain a concrete deed, and on account of the violation of a negative commandment that does not involve a concrete deed, the court does not inflict a flogging."

X.   It must follow that R. Judah takes the view that, on such an account, the court does inflict a flogging.

X.

A.   He who takes a vow in its name and he who carries out a vow made in its name transgress a negative commandment [M. 7:6F]:

B.   How do we know that this is the case for him who vows in its name or who carries out a vow made in its name?

C.   As it has been taught on Tannaite authority:

D.   "And you shall make no mention of the name of other gods" (Ex. 23:13):

E.   **This means that one should not say to his fellow, "Wait for me by the idol of so and so,"**

F.   **or, "I'll wait for you by the idol of such-and-such"** [T. A.Z. 6:11A-C].

G.   "And neither let it be heard of your mouth" -- that one should not take a vow or carry out a vow made by its name, nor should he cause others [gentiles] to take a vow by its name or to carry out a vow by its name.

H.   Another matter: "Let it not be heard out of your mouth" -- this is an admonition against one who incites or entices Israelites to practice idolatry.

I.   But the matter of inciting is stated explicitly, for it is written in that connection, "And all Israel shall hear and fear and shall do no more any such wickedness as this is among you" (Deut. 13:12).

J.   This is an admonition against one who causes Israelites to practice idolatry.

K.   "Nor should he cause others [gentiles] to take a vow by its name:"

L.   This supports the viewpoint of Samuel's father.

M.   For Samuel's father said, "It is forbidden for a person to form a partnership with an idolator, lest he become liable to take an oath to him and have to take thee oath by his idol.

N.   "For the Torah has said, 'Neither let it be heard out of your mouth' (Ex. 23:13)."

XI.

A.   When Ulla came, he stayed at the City of Nebo. Said Raba to him, "And where did the master lodge?"

B.   He said to him, "In the City of Nebo."

C.   He said to him, "Is it not written, 'And do not mention the name of other gods' (Ex. 23:13)?"

D.   He said to him, "This is what R. Yohanan has said, 'It is permitted to mention the name of any idol that is written in the Torah."

E.   "And where is this one written?"

F.   "As it is written, 'Bel bows down, Nebo stoops' (Is. 46:1)."

G.   And if it is not written in the Torah, may one not mention it?

H.   To that proposition R. Mesharshia objected, "If one saw a flux as profuse as three, which is sufficient for one to go from Gad Yon to Shiloah, which is time enough for two immersions and two dryings, lo, this one is entirely a zab [M. Zab. 1:5A-D]. [Clearly, the framer of the Mishnah was willing to refer to a town named for an idol.]"

I.   Said Rabina, "Gad too is mentioned in the Torah: 'That prepare a table for Gad' (Is. 65:2)."

XII.

A. Said R. Nahman, "Any form of mockery is forbidden except for mockery of idolatry, which is permitted.

B. "For it is written, 'Bel bows down. Nebo stoops... they stoop, they bow down together, they could not deliver the burden' (Is. 46:1).

C. "And it is written, 'They have spoken: the inhabitants of Samaria shall fear because of the calves of Beth Aven; for the people therefore shall mourn over it, and the priests thereof that rejoiced on it for the glory thereof, which is departed from it' (Hos. 10:5).

D. "Do not read 'its glory' but 'his weight.'"

XIII.

A. Said R. Isaac, "What is the meaning of the following verse of Scripture: 'And now they sin more and more and have made for themselves molten images of their silver and idols in their image' (Hos. 13:2)?

B. "What is the meaning of 'idols in their image'? This teaches that each one of them made an image of his god and put it in his pocket. When he called it to mind, he took it out of his pocket and embraced it and kissed it."

C. What is the meaning of, "Let the men that sacrifice kiss the calves" (Hos. 13:2)?

D. Said R. Isaac of the house of R. Ammi, "The servants of the idols would look enviously at wealthy men. They would starve the calves and make images of [the rich men] and set them up at the side of the cribs and then bring the calves out. When the calves would see the men, they would run after them and nuzzle them. [The servants] would say to the men, 'The idol wants you. Let him come and sacrifice himself to him.' [Freedman, p. 433, n. 7: Thus the verse is translated: They sacrifice themselves in their homage to the calves.]"

E. Said Raba, "Then the verse, 'Let the men that sacrifice kiss the calves' should read, 'Let the calves kiss the men that sacrifice.'"

F. Rather said Raba, "'Whoever sacrifices his son to an idol would have the priest say to him, "You have offered a great gift to it. Come and kiss it."'"

XIV.

A. Said R. Judah said Rab, "'And the men of Babylonia made Succoth-benoth' (2 Kgs. 17:30) [among idols brought by gentiles who resettled Samaria after the deportation].

B. "What was it? It was a chicken.

C. "'And the men of Cuth made Negral (NRGL)' (2 Kgs. 17:30).

D. "What was it? It was a cock (TRNGL).

E. "'And the men of Hamath made Ashima' (2 Kgs. 17:30).

F. "What was it? It was a bald buck.

G. "'And the Avites made Nibhaz an Tarak' (2 Kgs. 17:30).

H. "What are these? A dog and an ass.

I. "'And the Sepharvites burned their children in fire to Adrammelech and Anammelech, the gods of Sepharvaim' (2 Kgs. 17:30).

J.   "What were they? A mule and a horse.

K.   "'Adrammelech' means that [the mule] honors its master in carrying its load.

L.   "'Anammelech' means that the horse answers its master in battle.

M.   "Also the father of Hezekiah, king of Judah, wanted to do the same to him [namely, to burn him in fire], but his mother covered him with salamander [blood and so made him fire-proof]."

XV.

A.   Said R. Judah said Rab, "The Israelites know that idolatry was of no substance and did not perform acts of idolatry except with the intent of allowing themselves publicly to engage in consanguineous sexual relations."

B.   R. Mesharsheyya objected, "'As those who remember their children, so they longed for their altars, and their graves by the green trees' (Jer. 17:2).

C.   "And R. Eleazar said, 'It was like a man who yearned for his son.' [So their belief in idols was sincere.]"

D.   This was after they had cleaved to idolatry [and gotten used to it].

E.   Come and take note:

F.   "And I will cast your carcasses upon the carcasses of your idols" (Lev. 26:30):

G.   They say: Elijah, the righteous man, was searching among those who are starving in Jerusalem. One time he found a child who was starving and who was thrown into a dung heap. He said to him, "From what family do you come?"

H.   He said to him, "From such and such a family do I come."

I.   He said to him, "Has anyone survived from that family?"

J.   He said to him, "No one but me."

K.   He said to him, "If I teach you something by which you will live, will you learn it?"

L.   He said to him, "Yes."

M.   He said to him, "Say every day, 'Hear O Israel, the Lord our God, the Lord is one.'"

N.   He said to him, "[64A] Be silent, so as not to make mention of the name of the Lord.'

O.   It was because his father and mother had not taught him [the worship of the Lord]. He forthwith took out his little idol from his bosom and began to hug it and kiss it, until his stomach burst and his idol fell to the ground, and he fell on it.

P.   This was to carry out that which is said, "And I shall cast your carcasses upon the carcasses of your idols" (Lev. 26:30). [Thus we see that the Israelites were sincere in their idolatry.]

Q.   This came after they had cleaved to idolatry [and gotten used to it.]

R.   Come and take note:

S.   "And they cried with a loud voice to the Lord their God" (Neh. 9:4) [when the Israelites came back to Zion in the time of Ezra].

T.   What did they say?

U.   Said R. Judah, and some say, R. Jonathan, "'Woe, woe, this is what destroyed the house and wiped out the temple, killed the righteous and caused Israel to go into exile from its land, and it still is dancing among us. Is it not so that you put it among us only so that we could gain a reward [for resisting it]. We don't want it, we don't want the reward for resisting it!'" [So they were deeply attracted to the idolatry.]

V.   This came after they had cleaved to idolatry.

W.   [Judah continues,] "They sat in a fast for three days and prayed for mercy. A message came down from the firmament, with the word 'truth' written on it."

X.   Said R. Hanina, "This proves that the seal of the Holy One, blessed be he, is truth."

Y.   [Judah goes on,] "Something in the shape of a lion's whelp made of fire came forth from the house of the Holy of Holies and said to the prophet to Israel, 'This is the tempter of idolatry.' While they held it, its hairs fell out of it, and its roar could be heard for four hundred parasangs. They said, 'What shall we do? Perhaps from heaven there will be mercy for it.'

Z.   "The prophet said to them, 'Throw it into a lead pot and cover it with lead to stifle its voice.'

AA.   "For it is written, 'And he said, This is wickedness, and he cast it into the midst of the ephah and he cast the weight of lead upon the mouth of it' (Zech. 5:8).

BB.   "They said, 'Since it is a propitious time, let us pray for mercy about the tempter of sin [so we may be saved from it].'

CC.   "They prayed for mercy, and it was given into their hands, and they imprisoned it for three days.

DD.   "People went looking for a fresh egg for a sick person and could not find it. [All sexual activity had ceased.]

EE.   "They said, 'What should we do? If we ask for half-and-half [so that the power of temptation be limited by half], it will not be granted to us.'

FF.   "They blinded its eye with rouge, so that a man will not lust for his close female relations."

XVI.

A.   Said R. Judah said Rab, "There was the case of a gentile woman who was very sick. She said, 'If that woman [I] survive this illness, she will go and worship every idol in the world.'

B.   "She recovered from the illness and went and worshipped every idol in the world.

C.   "When she came to Peor, she asked its keepers how people worship this idol.

D.   "They said to her, 'People eat beets and drink beer and then show their behinds before it.'

E.   "She said, 'It would be better for that woman [me] to fall sick again but not to worship that idol in such a way.'

F.   [Rab continues], "But you, house of Israel, were not this way, 'who were joined to Baal Peor' (Num. 25:5) -- joined like a tightly fitting seal.

G.   "'But you who cleave to the Lord your God' (Deut. 4:4) -- like two dates that are stuck together."

H.   In a Tannaite passage it is taught:

I.   "That were joined to Baal Peor" (Num. 25:5) -- like a woman's bracelet.

J.   "And you who cleave to the Lord your God" (Deut. 4:4) -- literally <u>cleaving</u>.

XVII.

A.   Our rabbis have taught on Tannaite authority:

B.   There is the case of Sabta of Eles, who hired his ass to a gentile woman. When she came to Peor, she said to him, "Wait for me while I go in and come out."

C.   After she came out, he said to her, "Now you wait for me while I go in and come out."

D.   She said to him, "Aren't you a Jew?"

E.   He said to her, "And what difference does it make to you?"

F.   He went in, showed his behind to the idol and wiped himself on its nose, and the servants of the idol praised him, saying, "There never has been a person who served it in such a way."

G.   [That is line with M. 7:6G, thus] <u>He who shows his behind to Baal Peor -- lo, this is the way it is served</u>, even though the person who does so has the intent of committing a disgrace against it.

H.   <u>He who throws a pebble at Mercury [M. 7:6H] -- lo, this is the way it is served</u>, even though the person who does so has the intent of stoning it.

XVIII.

A.   R. Menassia was going along to Be Torta. They pointed out to him, "There is an idol standing here."

B.   He took a stone and threw it at it.

C.   They said to him, "It is Mercury."

D.   He said to them, "What we have learned in the Mishnah is: <u>He who tosses a pebble at Merkolis [M. 7:6H]</u>."

E.   He came to the school house and asked [whether he had committed a sin, having intended to express contempt].

F.   They said to him, "We have learned in the Mishnah: <u>He who tosses a pebble at Merkolis [M. 7:6H]</u> -- even though one's intent is to stone it."

G.   He said to them, "Then I shall go and take it away [the heap of stones that constitutes the idol]."

H.   They said to him, "All the same are the one who takes a stone away and the one who places a stone on it -- both are liable, for each one [removed] leaves room for another stone."

Unit I clarifies the sense of the Mishnah's language. Unit II then seeks the biblical source for the Mishnah's rule. The inquiry proceeds through units III, IV. Unit V then takes up the contradiction in the implications of M. 7:6A and M. 7:10N. Units VI-VII are inserted because of the clarification of M. 7:6A-B. I cannot claim to have done justice to unit VII and, as indicated, rely upon Freedman's exposition of the passage as well as on his translation. Unit VIII brings us to M. 7:6C, unit IX to M. 7:6D, unit X to M. 7:6F. Unit XI carries forward the theme of unit X, as do units XII, XIII, XIV, and XV. Units XVI-XVIII take up M. 7:6G-H. So despite the diffuse appearance of sizable components

of the composition at hand, the bulk of the materials are put together systematically to
clarify the Mishnah's statements.

7:7A-E

A. He who gives of his seed [child] to Molech [M. 7:4D] [Lev. 20:2] is liable
    only when he will both have given him to Molech and have passed him
    through fire.

B. [If] he gave him to Molech but did not pass him through fire,

C. passed him through fire but did not give him to Molech,

D. he is not liable --

E. until he will both have given him to Molech and have passed him through
    fire.

I.

A. The Mishnah [at M. 7:4] refers to both idolatry in general and giving to Molech in
    particular [treating them as separate. This would imply that giving a child to
    Molech is not an act of idolatry.]

B. Said R. Abin, "Our Mishnah-passage is framed in accord with him who has said that
    Molech is not an idol."

C. For it has been taught on Tannaite authority:

D. **One is liable for [worshipping] Molech or any other idol.**

E. **R. Eleazar b. R. Simeon says, "One is liable for doing so for Molech, and exempt
    for doing so not for Molech" [T. San. 10:5D-E].**

F. Said Abayye, "R. Eleazar b. R. Simeon and R. Hanina b. Antigonos have said the
    same thing.

G. "R. Eleazar b. R. Simeon has said that which we have just now cited.

H. "R. Hanina b. Antigonos, as it has been taught on Tannaite authority:

I. "R. Hanina b. Antigonos says, 'On what account did the Torah use the word Molech
    [with the same root as the word for king]? It is to indicate that the prohibition
    pertains to any sort of thing which people have made a king over themselves, even
    a pebble or a splinter. [Freedman, p. 438, n. 1: This shows that he too regards any
    fetish as a Molech.]'"

J. Said Raba, "At issue between [Eleazar and Hanina] is the case of a Molech of a
    temporary character. [Freedman, p. 438, n. 3: Anything which was only
    temporarily worshipped as Molech, such as a pebble, which would obviously not be a
    permanent idol. According to Hanina, one is liable, and Eleazar applies the law
    only to a permanent idol worshipped as Molech.]"

II.

A. [64B] Said R. Yannai, "One is liable only if he hands his son over to the worshippers
    of an idol.

B. "For it is said, 'And you shall not give of your seed to pass through the fire to
    Molech' (Lev. 18:21). [Freedman, p. 438, n. 5: This proves that the offense

consists of two parts, formal delivery to the priests and causing the seed to pass through the fire.]"

C. So too it has been taught on Tannaite authority:

D. Is it possible to suppose that <u>if one passed his son through fire but did not give him to Molech</u> [M. 7:7C], he might be liable?

E. Scripture states, "You shall not give" (Lev. 18:21).

F. Is it possible to suppose that <u>if he handed his son over but did not pass him through fire</u> [M. 7:7B], he might be liable?

G. Scripture states, "To pass through...."

H. If he handed over his son [to the priests] and passed him through fire, but not to Molech, is it possible that he might be liable?

I. Scripture says, "...to Molech."

J. If one handed his son over and passed him to Molech, but not through fire, is it possible that he might be liable?

K. Here it is said, "to pass through...," and elsewhere it is said, "There shall not be found among you any one who makes his son or daughter pass through fire" (Deut. 18:10).

L. Just as in that passage it must be through fire, so in the present case it must be through fire.

M. Just as in the present case it must involve Molech, so in that case it must involve Molech.

III.

A. Said R. Aha, son of Raba, "If one passed all of his children through fire, he is exempt.

B. "For it is said, '<u>Of</u> your seed,' but not all your seed."

IV.

A. R. Ashi raised the question, "If one passed a blind son through fire, what is the law?

B. "If he passed through a son who was asleep, what is the law?

C. "If he passed through the son of his son or the son of his daughter, what is the law?"

D. In any event one may solve one of these questions.

E. For it has been taught on Tannaite authority:

F. "Because he has given of his seed to Molech" (Lev. 20:2).

G. What is the sense of Scripture here?

H. Since it is said, "There shall not be found among you any one who makes his son or his daughter pass through the fire" (Deut. 18:10), I know only that the law applies to one's own son or daughter. How do we know that it encompasses the son of his son or the son of his daughter?

I. Scripture says, "When he gives of his seed to Molech" (Lev. 20:4).

J. The Tannaite authority opens with the verse, "Because he has given of his seed" (Lev. 20:2) and concludes with the verse, "When he gives of his seed" (Lev. 20:4). This serves to provide the occasion for yet another interpretation. [Freedman, p. 439, n. 8: From the first verse we learn that the law applies to one's grandsons too; "When he gives" is stated in order that another law may be deducted.]

K.   So "Because he has given of his seed" (Lev. 20:2):

L.   I know that the rule applies to giving one's legitimate children.

M.   How do I know that the law encompasses also invalid offspring?

N.   Scripture says, "When he gives of his seed" (Lev. 20:4) [a superfluous statement leading to the inclusion of the other sort of offspring].

V.

A.   Said R. Judah, "One is liable only when he will have passed him through fire in the usual way [T. 10 San. 10:4B]."

B.   What would this mean?

C.   Said Abayye, "A pile of bricks was in the middle, with fire on one side and on the other side."

D.   Raba said, "It was like the bouncing about on Purim."

E.   There is a Tannaite teaching in accord with the view of Raba:

F.   And he is liable only when he will have passed him through fire in the usual way.

G.   [If] he passed him through fire by foot, he is exempt.

H.   And he is liable, moreover, only on account of those who are his natural children [T. San. 10:4B-D].

I.   How so? If it was his son or daughter, he is liable.

J.   [He who passes] his father, mother, or sister through fire [for Molech] is exempt.

K.   He who passes through himself is exempt.

L.   R. Eleazar b. R. Simeon declares him liable.

M.   All the same is doing so for Molech and for any other idol: one is liable.

N.   And R. Simeon says, "He is liable only on account of Molech alone" [T. San. 10:5A-E].

O.   Said Ulla, "What is the scriptural basis for the view of R. Eleazar b. R. Simeon?

P.   "Scripture says, 'There shall not be found among you' (Deut. 18:10) -- 'among you' meaning 'within you.'"

Q.   And rabbis? They do not interpret the clause, "Within you."

R.   But have we not learned in the Mishnah:

S.   If one has to choose between seeking what he has lost and what his father has lost, his own takes precedence [M. B.M. 2:11A-B].

T.   And in this connection, we said, "What is the Scriptural basis for that view?"

U.   And R. Judah said, "Scripture has said, 'Save that there shall be no poor among you' (Deut. 15:4), meaning that what is among you [personally, your own family] takes precedence over what belongs to anyone else." [So rabbis do interpret the word "among you."]

V.   That follows the exclusionary phrase, "Save that...."

VI.

A.   Said R. Yose bar Hanina, "The three references to extirpation on account of idolatry serve what purpose? [These are at Lev. 20:2-5, 'Whoever gives of his seed to Molech will I cut off from among his people,' 'And if the people of the land kill him not, then I will set my face against that man... and will cut him off,' and, at

Num. 15:30: 'But the soul that does something presumptuously... shall be cut off from among his people.']

B.   "One serves to state the penalty for worship in the normal way, one serves to state the penalty for idol worship not in the normal way, and one states the penalty for worship of Molech."

C.   And in the view of him who has said that Molech falls into the general category of idolatry, what need is therefore a specific reference to extirpation as the penalty for serving Molech?

D.   It states the penalty for him who passes his son through fire but not in the normal way.

E.   And as to him who has said that the blasphemer falls into the category of one who has served an idol, what need is there to specify that extirpation applies to the blasphemer [at Num. 15:30]?

F.   It is in accord with that which has been taught on Tannaite authority:

G.   "'That soul, being cut off, shall be cut off' (Num. 15:30).

H.   "'Being cut off' in this world; 'shall be cut off,' in the world to come," the words of R. Aqiba.

I.   Said R. Ishmael to him, "And has it not already been said, 'That soul shall be cut off' (Num. 15:30). Are there then three worlds?

J.   "Rather: 'And that soul shall be cut off' in this world; 'he is to be cut off' in the world to come.

K.   "The repetition is because the Torah uses ordinary human speech [and bears no further meaning at all]."

Unit I takes up M. 7:4A, and the clarification of the Mishnah is worked out at units II, III. Unit IV raises some secondary questions based on the foregoing. Unit V goes over the Tosefta's complement, and unit VI deals with the scriptural relevant verses. So the entire construction follows the established exegetical program.

7:7F-I

F.   [65A] He who has a familiar spirit [M. 7:4D4] [Lev. 20:27] -- this is a ventriloquist, who speaks from his armpits;

G.   and he who is a soothsayer [M. 7:4D5] -- this is one whose [spirit] speaks through his mouth --

H.   lo, these are put to death by stoning.

I.   And the one who makes inquiry of them is subject to a warning [Lev. 19:31, Deut. 18:10-11].

I.

A.   What is the reason that, in the present passage, the framer of the passage refers to both one who has a familiar spirit and also a soothsayer [at M. 7:7F, G], while at the list of those who are put to their death through extirpation, the one who has a familiar spirit is included in the list, but the one who is a soothsayer is omitted [at M. Ker. 1:1]?

B.   Said R. Yohanan, "It is because both of them are encompassed in a single negative commandment [at Lev. 19:31, 'Do not recognize those who have familiar spirits or soothsayers']."

C.   R. Simeon b. Laqish said, "The soothsayer is omitted [at M. Ker. 1:1], because there is no concrete deed that he does."

D.   And as to R. Yohanan, why did the framer [of the passage at M. Ker. 1:1] refer to one who has a familiar spirit [and leave out the other item]?

E.   Because it is with that one that Scripture [Lev. 19:31] began discourse.

F.   And as to R. Simeon b. Laqish, why does he not explain matters as does R. Yohanan?

G.   Said R. Pappa, "Because the two [categories of sorcerer] are treated distinctly when it comes to the specification of the death penalty [at Lev. 20:27: 'A man who has a familiar spirit _or_ a soothsayer will surely be put to death.' The 'or' distinguishes the two.]"

H.   And R. Yohanan? Deeds that are distinct when they are stated in a verse that prohibits them are regarded as truly distinct, while distinctions in the expression of the death penalty applying to such deeds do not impose a difference.

I.   And why does R. Yohanan not explain matters in accord with the view of R. Simeon b. Laqish?

J.   He will reply to you that the Mishnah-paragraph of tractate Keritot represents the position of R. Aqiba, who has taken the view that we do not require a concrete deed [to impose the penalty of having to bring a sin-offering for an unwitting act of idolatry]. [He includes the blasphemer on the list of M. Ker. 1:1, as against the view of rabbis, who would omit the blasphemer because he is one who has not performed a concrete deed.]

K.   And R. Simeon b. Laqish?

L.   Granted that R. Aqiba does not require a substantial deed [for imposition of liability], he does require some sort of slight action [before he will require the bringing of a sin-offering for an inadvertent act of blasphemy].

M.   But as to the blasphemer, what sort of action is involved?

N.   The use of the lips constitutes an action.

O.   And what sort of action does a one who has a familiar spirit perform?

P.   He flaps his arms [so that the voice of the dead appears to come from his armpits], and that constitutes an action.

Q.   Is this the case even from the viewpoint of rabbis? But it has been taught on Tannaite authority:

R.   **One is liable only for something that involves a concrete deed, such as sacrificing, offering incense, pouring out a libation, or prostrating oneself [T. San. 10:3B-C].**

S.   In this regard Simeon b. Laqish said, "What Tannaite authority stands behind the inclusion of prostration? It is R. Aqiba, who has said that we do not require a concrete deed [to impose liability, as before]."

T.   And R. Yohanan said, "You may even maintain that it is the viewpoint of rabbis, since bending one's body in rabbis' view constitutes a deed."

U.   Now in R. Simeon b. Laqish's view of rabbis' opinion, so far as rabbis are concerned, bending one's body in prostration does <u>not</u> constitute a deed, while flapping one's arms, as done by a person who has a familiar spirit, does constitute a concrete deed! [What difference can there be between these obviously similar acts?]

V.   When R. Simeon b. Laqish made his statement [that the one who has a familiar spirit carries out an action], it was within the context of the viewpoint of R. Aqiba, but so far as rabbis are concerned, that is not the case.

W.   If so, then [the Mishnah-passage at M. Ker. 1:1 should specify that just as a blasphemer does not have to bring a sin-offering for inadvertent blasphemy, there being no action, so too] the one who consults a familiar spirit likewise should be excluded [from those required to bring a sin-offering] [there being no concrete action involved in what he has done either].

X.   Rather, said Ulla, "We deal with one who has a familiar spirit who burned incense to a demon [and that involves a concrete action]."

Y.   Said Raba to him, "But burning incense to a shade constitutes an act of idolatry. [That is a separate item on the list and cannot be subsumed within the reference to one who has a familiar spirit.]"

Z.   Rather, said Raba, "The passage [at M. Ker. 1:1] refers to one who has a familiar spirit who burned incense as a charm."

AA. Said Abayye to him, "Burning incense as a charm constitutes merely an act of charming, [and that is merely prohibited by a negative precept (Freedman)]."

BB. Indeed so, and the Torah has said that one one who acts as a charmer is put to death through stoning. [Freedman, p. 444, n. 2: Consequently, for unwitting transgression a sin offering is due.]

CC. Our rabbis have taught on Tannaite authority:

DD. "There shall not be found among you... a charmer" (Deut. 18:11):

EE. All the same are the one who charms large objects and the one who charms small objects, and even snakes and scorpions.

FF. Said Abayye, "Therefore one who seals up wasps or scorpions [using charms to do so], even though he intends only that they not do harm to anyone, violates a prohibition."

GG. And why does R. Yohanan maintain that bending over in prostration constitutes a concrete action in rabbis' view, while in their view moving the lips does not constitute a concrete action?

HH. Said Raba, "The case of the blasphemer is different, because the issue there is what is in the heart."

II. [65B] [To this explanation of what is at issue] R. Zira objected, "'A conspiracy of perjurers is excluded [from the list at M. Ker. 1:1, those obligation to a sin-offering for inadvertent offense] because there is no concrete deed involved in what they have done.' Now why should this be the case? Lo, is the issue there not what is in the heart?"

JJ.   Said Raba, "That case, involving a conspiracy of perjurers, is different, since there it is a matter of speech ['the voice']."

KK.   And in R. Yohanan's view, does not an act of speech constitute an act?

LL.   Lo, it has been stated on Tannaite authority: If one frightened a beast by his act of speech or drove off animals by his act of speech, R. Yohanan said, "He is liable." R. Simeon b. Laqish said, "He is exempt."

MM.   R. Yohanan said liable [because in his view] the movement of the lips constitutes a concrete deed.

NN.   R. Simeon b. Laqish said, "Exempt [because in his view] the movement of the lips does not constitute a concrete action."

OO.   Rather, said Raba, "The case of the conspiracy of perjurers is different, since they are subject to having caused an offense by what they have seen [in using their eyes, and there there is no concrete action whatsoever]."

II.

A.   Our rabbis have taught on Tannaite authority:

B.   He who has a familiar spirit -- this is one who has a ventriloquist which speaks [M. 7:7F] from between his joints and from between his elbows.

C.   A soothsayer [M. 7:7G] -- this one who has the bone of a familiar spirit in his mouth, and it speaks on its own [T. San. 10:6A-B].

D.   The following objection was raised: "And your voice shall be as of one who has a familiar spirit, out of the ground" (Is. 29:4).

E.   Does this not mean that it speaks in a natural way?

F.   No, it comes up and takes a seat between his joints and speaks

G.   Come and take note: "And the woman said to Saul, I saw a god-like form ascending out of the earth" (1 Sam. 28:13).

H.   Does that not mean that it speaks in a natural way?

I.   No, it took a seat between her joints and then spoke.

III.

A.   Our rabbis have taught on Tannaite authority:

B.   He who inquires of the dead (Deut. 18:11) -- all the same are the one who raises up the dead by divining and the one who makes inquiry of a skull.

C.   What is the difference between one who makes inquiry of a skull and one who raises up the dead by witchcraft?

D.   For the one who raises up the dead by witchcraft -- the ghost does not come up in his normal way and does not come up on the Sabbath.

E.   But the one who makes inquiry of a skull -- [the spirit] comes up in the normal way and comes up on the Sabbath [T. San. 10:7A-D].

F.   It goes up -- but where to? Lo, [the skull (E)] is lying before him.

G.   Rather say, It answers in the normal way and it answers on the Sabbath.

IV.

A.   And so too did Turnusrufus ask R. Aqiba, "What distinguishes one day [the Sabbath] from all other days?"

B.   He said to him, "What distinguishes one man from all other men?"

C.   "Because that is what my lord [the emperor] wants."

D.   "As to the Sabbath, too, that is what my Lord wants."

E.   He said to him, "What I meant to ask you was this: Who tells you that this particular day is the Sabbath?"

F.   He said to him, "The Sabbation river will prove the matter, the one who has a familiar spirit will prove the matter, your father's grave will prove the matter, from which no smoke goes up on the Sabbath."

G.   He said to him, "You have shamed, disgraced, and cursed him."

V.

A.   One who asks a question of a familiar spirit -- it this not the same as one who seeks after the death?

B.   So it has been taught on Tannaite authority:

C.   "Or who consults the dead" (Deut. 18:11):

D.   This refers to one who fasts and goes and spends the night in a cemetery, so that the unclean spirit will come to rest on him.

E.   Now when R. Aqiba would come to this verse of Scripture, he would cry, "And if one who fasts so as to have rest on him an unclean spirit succeeds so that an unclean spirit does rest on him, he who fasts in order that a clean spirit will come to rest on him -- how much the more so [should he succeed]!

F.   "But what can I do? For our sins have caused us [to be unable to fast with such a result], for it is said, 'But your iniquities have separated between you and your God' (Is. 59:2)."

G.   Said Raba, "If they wanted, the righteous could create a world for it is said, 'But your iniquities have distinguished' (Is. 59:2)."

H.   Rabbah created a man. He sent it to R. Zira, who talked with him, but he did not answer him.

I.   He said to him, "You have come by means of enchantment, go back to the dust you came from."

J.   R. Hanina and R. Oshaia went into session every Friday afternoon and took up the study of the Book of Creation. They made a third-grown calf and ate it.

VI.

A.   Our rabbis have taught on Tannaite authority:

B.   One who observes the times (Deut. 18:10) --

C.   R. Simeon says, "This is one who rubs the semen of seven sorts of men in his eyes."

D.   And sages say, "This is one who holds peoples' eyes [giving them hallucinations]."

E.   R. Aqiba says, "This is one who reckons the times and hours, saying, 'Today is a good to go out.' 'Tomorrow is a good day to make a purchase.' 'The wheat that ripens on the eve of the Seventh Year usually is sound.' 'Let beans be pulled up to save them from becoming wormy'" [T. Shab. 7:14].

F.   Our rabbis have taught on Tannaite authority:

G.   [In T's version] Who is an enchanter?

H.   One who says, "My staff has fallen from my hand."

I.   "My bread has fallen from my mouth."

J.   "Mr. So-and-so has called me from behind me."

K.   "A crow has called to me."

L.   "A dog has barked at me."

M.   "A snake has passed at my right and a fox at my left."

N.   [66A] "Do not begin with me, for lo, it is dawn."

O.   "It is a new moon."

P.   "It is Saturday night" [T. Shab. 7:13].

Q.   Our rabbis have taught on Tannaite authority:

R.   "You shall not use enchantments or observe times" (Lev. 19:26):

S.   This speaks of those who use enchantment through weasels, birds, or fish.

Unit I deals with the relationship between M. San. 7:7 and M. Ker. 1:1. Units II, III-IV take up the Tosefta's complement to our Mishnah. Units V and VI define various pertinent categories of law-violators in the present context.

7:8A

A.   He who profanes the Sabbath [M. 7:4E] -- in regard to a matter, on account of the deliberate doing of which they are liable to extirpation, and on account of the inadvertent doing of which they are liable to a sin-offering.

I.

A.   This statement bears the implication that there is a form of profanation of the Sabbath on account of which people are not liable to a sin-offering should they do it inadvertently, or to extirpation if they do it deliberately.

B.   What would it be?

C.   It is violation of the law of boundaries, in the view of R. Aqiba,

D.   or of the law against kindling a fire, in the view of R. Yose.

The Talmud lightly clarifies the implications of the Mishnah's statement.

7:8B-E

B.   He who curses his father and his mother [M. 7:4F] is liable only when he will have cursed them by the divine Name.

C.   [If] he cursed them with a euphemism,

D.   R. Meir declares him liable.

E.	And sages declare him exempt.

I.

A.	Who are the sages [of M. 7:8E]?

B.	They represent the view of R. Menahem, son of R. Yose.

C.	For it has been taught on Tannaite authority:

D.	R. Menahem, son of R. Yose, says, "'When he blasphemes the name of the Lord, he shall be put to death' (Lev. 24:16).

E.	"Why is 'the Name' stated here [since the verse earlier refers to it, 'And he who blasphemes the Name of the Lord shall surely be put to death']?

F.	"The usage teaches that the one who curses his father and mother he is liable only if he curses them with the divine Name."

II.

A.	Our rabbis have taught on Tannaite authority:

B.	"[For any man that curses his father of his mother shall surely be put to death; his father and his mother he has cursed; his blood shall be upon him" (Lev. 20:9).] Why does Scripture say "any man"?

C.	It serves to in encompass a daughter, one of undefined sexual traits, and one who exhibits the traits of both sexes.

D.	"'Who curses his father or his mother' -- I know only that the law covers his father and his mother. How do I know that it covers his father but not his mother, or his mother but not his father?

E.	"Scripture says, 'His father and his mother he has cursed; his blood shall be upon him' (Lev. 20:9), that is, 'he has cursed his father,' 'he has cursed his mother,'" the words of R. Josiah.

F.	R. Jonathan says, "The verse bears the implication that it speaks of the two of them simultaneously, and it bears the implication that it speaks of each by himself or herself, unless the text explicitly treats the two of them together."

III.

A.	"He shall surely be put to death" (Lev. 20:9). That is, by execution through stoning.

B.	You say that it is through stoning. But perhaps it is by any one of the other modes of execution that are listed in the Torah.

C.	Here the Scripture states, "His blood shall be upon him" (Lev. 20:9), and elsewhere it states, "[A man... who has a familiar spirit or a wizard shall surely be put to death; they shall stone them with stones;] their blood shall be upon them" (Lev. 20:27).

D.	Just as in that latter passage the mode of execution is through stoning, so in the present passage the mode of execution is through stoning.

E.	We thereby have derived evidence on the character of the penalty. Whence do we find evidence of an admonition [against the act itself]?

F.	Scripture states, "You shall not curse the judges nor curse the ruler of your people" (Ex. 22:27).

G. If [the wayward's son's] father was a judge, he is covered by the general statement, "You shall not curse the judges."

H. If he was the chief, he is covered in the statement, "Nor curse the ruler of your people."

I. But if he is neither a judge nor a leader, how do we know [that he is not to be cursed]?

J. This is how to proceed: Lo, you must construct an argument based on the definitive traits of each of the two parties, for the traits of the chief are not the same as the traits for the judge, and the traits of the judge are not the traits of the chief.

K. The definitive traits of the judge are not the same as those of the chief, for lo, in the case of a judge, you are commanded concerning his decision [that is, to obey his decision], which is not the case for the chief.

L. The definitive trait of the chief is that you are commanded not to rebel against him, which is not the case of the judge, in which instance you are not commanded against rebelling against him.

M. The shared definitive trait of both types is that they fall into the category of "your people," and you are admonished not to curse them.

N. So I introduce the case of "your father" who also is "among your people," and you are thus admonished not to curse him.

O. [Arguing against this proposition], what indeed is the shared definitive trait [of the judge and the chief] is that both of them derive the [honor owing to them] from their high position.

P. [No, that cannot be the consideration,] for the Torah has said, "You shall not curse the deaf" (Lev. 19:14), and so [in connection with the prohibition against cursing], Scripture speaks of the most humble who are "among your people."

Q. But the distinctive trait of the deaf person is that his deafness has caused [him to be given special status, namely, protection against being cursed].

R. The cases of the chief and the judge will prove to the contrary.

S. The special trait of the chief and the judge is that their high position has caused them [to enjoy immunity from cursing]. A deaf person will prove to the contrary.

T. Then the circular argument continues on its merry way, for the definitive trait of the one is not the same as the definitive trait of the other, and the definitive trait of the other is not the same as the definitive trait of the one.

U. The shared trait among them all is that all of them fall into the category of "among your people," and you are admonished not to curse them.

V. And I then introduce the cases of "your father" who is "among your people," and in his case too you are admonished against cursing him.

W. [Not at all,] for what the several categories have in common is that they are distinguished [from the common people]. [The one set is distinctive because of its high position, the other because of deafness.]

X. If that were the case, Scripture should have said either, "The judges and the deaf..." or "the chief and the deaf."

Y. Why was it necessary to make references to "the judges"?

Z. If it is not necessary to make a point concerning itself [since the judges could have been covered by the reference to the chief], apply it to another matter entirely, specifically, to the case of his father.

AA. That argument suffices for him who maintains that the word used for judges [which also is the word for God] is secular [and means a judge], but what is there to be said from the viewpoint of him who maintains that the word here means God and is used in a sacred sense [That is, "You should not curse God"]?

BB. That is in accord with the following Tannaite teaching:

CC. "The word that serves for both God and the judges is used in a secular sense, for judges," the words of R. Ishmael.

DD. R. Aqiba says, "The word is used in a sacred sense, for God."

EE. And it further has been taught on Tannaite authority:

FF. R. Eliezer b. Jacob says, "Where in Scripture do we find an admonition against cursing the Name of God?

GG. "Scripture says, 'You shall not curse God' (Ex. 22:27)."

HH. From the viewpoint of the one who has said that the word is used in a secular sense, we may derive the case of the sacred from the secular usage.

II. In the viewpoint of him who has said that the word is used in a sacred sense, we derive the rule covering the secular setting from the rule covering the sacred one.

JJ. Now from the viewpoint of him says that the word is used in a secular sense and one derives the rule covering the sacred from the secular, there are no problems [since we have a simple argument a fortiori].

KK. But from the viewpoint of him says that the word is used in the sacred sense and that one may derive the rule covering the secular setting from the one covering the sacred, perhaps there is an admonition against cursing the sacred [Judge], but there is no admonition against cursing the secular [judge]?

LL. If so, Scripture should have written, "You shall not revile God" [spelling the word in a less emphatic way].

MM. [66B] Why say, "You shall not curse..." [spelling the word in a more emphatic way]?

NN. It is to imply the rule covering both circumstances.

Unit I seeks the authority behind the rule at hand, and units II-III uncover the scriptural basis for that rule.

7:9

A. He who has sexual relations with a betrothed maiden [M. 7:4G] [Deut. 22:23-4] is liable only if she is a virgin maiden, betrothed, while she is yet in her father's house.

B.   [If] two different men had sexual relations with her, the first one is put to death by stoning, and the second by strangulation. [The second party, B. has not had intercourse with a virgin (M. 11:1). The maiden is between twelve years and one day and twelve years six months and one day old.]

I.

A.   Our rabbis have taught on Tannaite authority:

B.   "If a girl that is a virgin is betrothed to a husband" (Deut. 22:23): "Girl" and not [either a minor, under twelve years, or] a mature woman.

C.   "A virgin" -- and not one who has had sexual relations.

D.   "Betrothed" and not one in a fully consummated marriage.

E.   "In her father's house" -- excluding a case in which the father has given the girl over to the agent of the husband.

F.   Said R. Judah said Rab, "[The Mishnah-paragraph before us] represents the view of R. Meir, but sages say that subject to the law of a betrothed girl is even a minor [and not only a girl from twelve years to twelve years six months and one day, such as is ordinarily subsumed under a reference to a 'girl.']"

G.   Said R. Aha of Difti to Rabina, "How do we know that the Mishnah passage represents the view of R. Meir, and that the reference to 'girl' serves to exclude a minor?

H.   "Perhaps it represents the view of rabbis, and the reference to 'girl' serves to exclude a mature woman but no other category of woman?"

I.   He said to him, "[If that were the case, then the formulation], ...is liable only if she is a virgin, a maiden, betrothed, [while she is yet in her father's house] [M. 7:9A], should be, '...is liable only if she is a virgin-maiden and betrothed.' And nothing further is needed [to prove the case]."

II.

A.   R. Jacob bar Ada asked Rab, "If one has had sexual relations with a minor who was betrothed, in R. Meir's view, what is the law?

B.   "Does he exclude such an act entirely from any sort of punishment or is it from the penalty of stoning that he excludes the action [by the exegesis given at unit I]?"

C.   He said to him, "It stands to reason that he excludes the felon from the penalty of stoning."

D.   "But is it not written, '[If a man be found lying with a woman married to a husband,] then both of them shall die' (Deut. 22:22), meaning that a penalty is imposed only if both of them are treated in the same way?"

E.   Rab remained silent [having no answer to this argument. The implication of the argument is that if both are not penalized -- and the minor girl is not penalized -- then neither is penalized at all. Hence the intent of Meir should be to exclude the felon from punishment of any sort whatsoever.]

F. Said Samuel, "Why should Rab had remained silent? He should have said to him, 'But if a man find a betrothed damsel in the field...] then the man <u>only</u> who lay with her shall die' (Deut. 22:25). [Sometimes the man alone is punished, even when the betrothed consented, that is, if she was a minor (Freedman, p. 453, n. 3)]."

III.

A. The foregoing follows the lines of the following dispute among Tannaite authorities:

B. "'Then they shall both of them die' (Deut. 22:22) means that a penalty is imposed only when the two of them are equal," the words of R. Josiah.

C. R. Jonathan says, "'Then the man only that lay with her shall die' (Deut. 22:25)."

D. And as to the other party [Jonathan], how does he deal with the statement, "Then they shall both of them die" (Deut. 22:22)?

E. Said Raba, "It serves to exclude a case of mere petting [in which the woman does not reach orgasm]." [Both must enjoy sexual gratification (Freedman, p. 453, n. 5)].

F. And as to the other party? A case of mere petting bears no consequences whatever [and is not penalized by the court].

G. And as to the other party [Josiah], how does he deal with the reference to "the man only"?

H. It accords with that which has been taught on Tannaite authority:

I. **It ten men had intercourse with her and she remained yet a virgin, all of them are put to death by stoning.**

J. **Rabbi says, "The first is put to death by stoning, and the others by strangulation" [T. San. 10:9C-D].**

K. Our rabbis have taught on Tannaite authority:

L. "And the daughter of any priest, if she profane herself by playing the whore" (Lev. 21:9).

M. Rabbi says, "[The verse refers to] the first [such action]."

N. "And so it is written, 'Then the man <u>only</u> who lies with her shall die' (Deut. 22:25)."

O. What is the sense of this statement?

P. Said R. Huna, son of R. Joshua, "Rabbi accords with the view of R. Ishmael.

Q. "[Ishmael] has said, 'A betrothed girl [daughter of a priest] is distinguished in that her death penalty [should she commit adultery] is through burning, but that penalty does not apply to a married woman [a priest's daughter, who committed adultery].'

R. "And this is the sense of his statement: 'If the first act of sexual relations [of the priest's daughter, who was betrothed] is one of adultery, then she is put to death through burning. But if it is any later sexual act [and not the first,] she is put to death through strangulation.'

S. "And what is the sense of, 'And so...'?

T. "'Just as, in that other passage, Scripture speaks of her first act of sexual relations, so here too the same applies. [Freedman, p. 454, n. 2: Just as a betrothed maiden is excepted from the punishment of a married woman, that is, strangulation, being stoned instead, which exception applies to her seducer too, and that only for the first coition, so also in the case of the priest's daughter, the exception is made only for her first coition, that is, if she is a betrothed girl and not a married woman.'"

U.   Said R. Bibi bar Abayye to him, "But this is not what the master (and who is it? it is R. Joseph) said.

V.   "Rather, Rabbi accords with R. Meir, who has said, If the priest's daughter married one of those who is invalid for marriage into the priesthood, she would be put to death through strangulation [M. Ter. 7:2].

W.   "In this connection Rabbi says, 'If her first act of sexual relations constitutes profanation through adultery, she is put to death through burning, and thereafter it is through strangulation.

X.   "And what is the sense of, 'And so...'?

Y.   [67A] "It serves only to call to mind [that under discussion is something done for the first time. There is no further intent to draw an analogy.]"

Unit I proves that the authority at hand is Meir, and units II, III then at greater depth explore Meir's views. So the entire composition is unitary and sustained.

7:10A-N

A.   He who beguiles others to idolatry [M. 7:4H] -- this [refers to] an ordinary fellow who beguiles some other ordinary fellow.

B.   [If] he said to him, "There is a god in such a place, who eats thus, drinks thus, does good in one way, and harm in another" --

C.   against all those who are liable to the death penalty in the Torah they do not hide witnesses [for the purposes of entrapment] except for this one.

D.   [If] he spoke [in such a way] to two, and they serve as witnesses against him,

E.   they bring him to court and stone him.

F.   [If] he spoke [in such a way] to [only] one person, [the latter then] says to him, "I have some friends who will want the same thing."

G.   If he was clever and not prepared to speak in [the friends'] presence,

H.   they hide witnesses on the other side of the partition,

I.   and he says to him, "Tell me what you were saying to me now that we are by ourselves."

J.   And the other party says to him [what he had said], and then this party says, "Now how are we going to abandon our God who is in Heaven and go and worship sticks and stones?"

K.   If he repents, well and good.

L.   But if he said, "This is what we are obligated to do, and this is what is good for us to do,"

M.   those who stand on the other side of the partition bring him to court and stone him.

N.   [He who beguiles others is] one who says, "I am going to worship," "I shall make an offering," "I shall offer incense," "I shall go and offer incense,"

"Let's go and offer incense," "I shall make a libation," "I shall go and make a libation," "Let's go and make a libation," "I shall bow down," "I shall go and bow down," "Let's go and bow down."

I.

A. The one who beguiles others is an ordinary fellow [M. 7:10A] [so he is put to death through stoning].

B. But if he were a prophet, he would be put to death through strangulation.

II.

A. Who beguiles some other ordinary fellow [M. 7:10A]:

B. The point is that he is an individual.

C. But if it had been a community, he would have been put to death through strangulation.

D. In accord with which authority is the Mishnah-paragraph before us?

E. It is R. Simeon.

F. For it has been taught on Tannaite authority:

G. A prophet who enticed people to commit idolatry is put to death through stoning.

H. R. Simeon says, "Through strangulation."

I. Those who entice a town to apostasy are put to death through stoning.

J. R. Simeon says, "Through strangulation."

K. Let us turn to the concluding passage of the same Mishnah-paragraph: He who beguiles others is one who says, Let's go and worship..." [M. 7:10N], on which R. Judah said Rab said, "What is subject to discussion here is those who beguile a town to apostasy."

L. So the passage accords with rabbis [who hold that those who beguile a town to apostasy are stoned to death, not strangled].

M. Accordingly, does the opening part of the Mishnah-passage accord with the view of R. Simeon, and the closing part with rabbis?

N. Rabina said, "The entirety accords with the view of rabbis, and the point is to say, 'not only this but also that.'" [Freedman, p. 456, n. 1: When the Mishnah states, He who beguiles an individual, it is not intended to exclude a multitude, but merely to commence with the universally agreed law. Then the next Mishnah adds that the same applies to the seduction of a multitude, though this is not admitted by all.]

II.

A. R. Pappa said, "When the Mishnah says, He who beguiles others refers to an ordinary fellow who beguiles some other ordinary fellow, [M. 7:10A], it is for the purpose of entrapment."

B. So it has been taught on Tannaite authority:

C. Against all those who are liable to the death penalty in the Torah they do not use procedures of entrapment, except for the one who beguiles others to idolatry [M. 7:10C].

D. How do they do it?

E.   They hand over to him two disciples of sages, [who are put] in an inside room, and he sits in an outside room.

F.   And they light a candle, so that they can see him.

G.   And they listen to what he says.

H.   But he cannot see them.

I.   And this one says to him, "Tell me what you were saying to me now that we are by ourselves."

J.   And the other party says to him what he had said, and then this party says, "Now how are we going to abandon our God who is in heaven and worship an idol?"

K.   If he repents, well and good. But if he said, "This is what we are obligated to do, and this is what is good for us to do," then the witnesses, who hear outside, bring him to court and stone him [T. San. 10:11].

Unit I seeks the authority behind the Mishnah, and unit II then amplifies the Mishnah with Tosefta's complement.

7:10O-7:11

O.   He who leads [a whole town astray] [M. 10:4H] is one who says, "Let's go and perform an act of service to an idol."

M. 7:10O

A.   The sorcerer [M. 7:41] -- he who does a deed is liable,

B.   but not the one who merely creates an illusion.

C.   R. Aqiba says in the name of R. Joshua, "Two may gather cucumbers. One gatherer may be exempt, and one gatherer may be liable.

D.   "[Likewise:] He who does a deed is liable, but he who merely creates an illusion is exempt."

M. 7:11

I.

A.   Said R. Judah said Rab, "Subject to the present statement of the Mishnah are those who entice a whole town to apostasy."

II.

A.   The sorcerer -- he who does a deed is liable [M. 7:11A]:

B.   Our rabbis have taught on Tannaite authority:

C.   "[You shall not permit] a sorceress [to live]" (Ex. 22:17).

D.   The same rule applies to a sorcerer and to a sorceress. Why then does Scripture speak of a sorceress?

E.   It is because it is mainly women who practice sorcery.

III.

A.   How are they put to death?

B.   R. Yose the Galilean says, "Here it is stated, "'You shall not permit a sorceress to live' (Ex. 22:17) and elsewhere it is written, 'You shall not allow anything that breathes to live' (Deut. 20:17).

C.   "Just as in that context [the Canaanite nations], everything is put to death through decapitation, so here it is through decapitation."

D.   R. Aqiba says, "Here it is stated, 'You shall not permit a sorceress to live' (Ex. 22:17), and elsewhere it is stated, '[There shall not a hand touch it, but he shall surely be stoned or shot through], whether it be beast or man it shall not live' (Ex. 19:13).

E.   "Just as in that passage [having to do with the avoidance of Sinai before the giving of the Torah], the penalty is through stoning, so here too the penalty is through stoning."

F.   Said R. Yose to him, "I have drawn an analogy based on the use in two passages of the language, 'You shall not permit to live...' But you have drawn an analogy between 'It shall not live' and 'You shall not permit to live...,' [so that the language is not exactly the same in the verses that you cite]."

G.   Said R. Aqiba to him, "I have drawn an analogy for the penalty to be inflicted on an Israelite from the case of an Israelite, in which setting Scripture has provided several different modes of execution, while you have drawn an analogy for the death penalty to be inflicted on an Israelite from the case of idolators, in which context Scripture has not specified a number of different modes of execution, [67B] but only a single mode of inflicting the death penalty."

H.   Ben Azzai says, "It is stated, 'You shall not suffer a sorceress to live' (Ex. 22:17), and immediately beyond, 'Whosoever lies with a beast shall surely be put to death' (Ex. 22:18).

I.   "The juxtaposition of the two topics is to indicate that, just as one who lies with a beast is put to death through stoning, so a sorceress also is put to death through stoning."

J.   Said to him R. Judah, "And merely because one matter is juxtaposed to the next, shall we take this person out for execution through stoning?! [There must be better proof.]

K.   "Rather, those who divine by a ghost or by a familiar spirit fall into the classification of of sorcery. Why were they singled out? It was so as to drawn an analogy to them, so as to tell you, 'Just as those who divine by a ghost or by a familiar spirit are put to death through stoning, so a sorceress who is to be executed is put to death through stoning.'"

L.   But from the viewpoint of R. Judah's arguments, we have in the case of the one who divines by the ghost and the one who consults a familiar spirit two verses of Scripture that say the same thing, and in a case of two verses of Scripture that say the same thing, one cannot derive lessons for some other matter entirely.

M.   Said R. Zechariah, "In respect to that matter, R. Judah indeed maintains that two verses of Scripture that say the same thing do serve to teach yet another lesson entirely."

IV.

A.   R. Yohanan said, "Why are they called sorcerers?

B.   "Because they deny the power of the family above [a play on the word for sorcery]."

C.   "There is no one else besides him" (Deut. 4:25):

D.   R. Hanina said, "Even as to sorcery, [Freedman, p. 459, n. 5: Not even sorcerers have power to oppose his decree.]"

E.   There was a woman who tried to make dirt from under the feet of R. Hanina.

F.   He said to her, "If it works out for you, go do it. [But] 'There is no one else besides him' (Deut. 4:25) is what is written."

G.   Can this be so [that Hanina made such a statement]?

H.   But did not R. Yohanan say, "Why are they called sorcerers? Because they deny the power of the family above"?

I.   R. Hanina was in a special category, because he had a great deal of merit.

J.   Said R. Aibu bar Nigri said R. Hiyya bar Abba, "'With their sorcery' (Ex. 7:22) refers to magic through the agency of demons, 'with their enchantments' (Ex. 7:11) refers to sorcery without outside help."

K.   "So it is said, 'And the flame of the sword that turns of itself' (Gen. 3:24) [thus an action taking place of itself, similarly, the word at hand connotes sorcery performed without extraneous aid (Freedman, p. 459, n. 10)]."

VI.

A.   Said Abayye, "If [the sorcerer] uses exact methods, it is through a demon.

B.   "If the sorcery does not work through exact methods, it is through enchantment."

C.   Said Abayye, "The laws of sorcery are like the laws of the Sabbath.

D.   "There are some actions that are punished by execution through stoning, some for which there is no penalty but which are forbidden, and some that are permitted to begin with.

E.   "He who does a deed is punishable by stoning, but he who merely creates an illusion does what is forbidden but is exempt from punishment [M. 7:11D].

F.   "And as to what is permitted to begin with, it accords with the matter involving R. Hanina and R. Oshaia.

G.   "Every Friday afternoon they would study the laws of creation and make for themselves a third-grown calf and they would eat it."

VII.

A.   Said R. Ashi, "I saw the father of Qarna blow his nose hard and ribbons of silk came out of his nostrils."

VIII.

A.   "Then the magicians said to Pharaoh, This is the finger of God" (Ex. 8:19).

B.   [Since the reference is to the creation of lice, which the Egyptian sorcerers could not do,] said R. Eleazar, "On the basis of that statement we learn that a demon cannot make a creature smaller than a barley seed."

C.   R. Pappa said, "By God, he cannot make a creature as large as a camel.

D.   "But these he can collect and those he cannot collect."

E. Said Rav to R. Hiyya, "I myself saw a Tai-Arab take a sword and chop up a camel, then he rang a bell and the camel arose."

F. He said to him, "After this was there blood or dung? [If not], it was merely an illusion."

G. Zeira went to Alexandria in Egypt. He bought an ass. When he went to give it water, it dissolved, and in place arose a landing board.

H. They said to him, "If you were not Zeiri, we should not give you back your money. Is there anyone who buys something here without testing it with water?"

IX.

A. Yannai came to an inn. He said to them, "Give me some water to drink." They brought him a flour-and-water drink.

B. He saw that the woman's lips were moving. He poured out a little of the drink, and it turned into scorpions. He said to them, "I drank something of yours, now you take a drink of mine."

C. He gave her something to drink and she turned into an ass. He mounted her and went out to the market place.

D. Her girl-friend came and nullified the charm, so he was seen riding around on a woman in the market place.

X.

A. "And the frog came up and covered the land of Egypt" (Ex. 8:6):

B. Said R. Eleazar, "It was one frog, and it multiplied into a swarm and filled the whole land of Egypt."

C. That accords with a Tannaite dispute:

D. R. Aqiba says, "It was one frog and filled the whole land of Egypt."

E. Said to him R. Eleazar b. Azariah, "Aqiba, what have you to do with matters of lore? Stop this talking of yours and go to discuss the laws of nega-spots and tents.

F. "It was a single frog, and it croaked for the others, and they came."

XI.

A. R. Aqiba says in the name of R. Joshua [M. 7:11D]:

B. Did R. Aqiba learn his knowledge of magic from R. Joshua? And have we not learned in a Tannaite teaching [that he learned his magic from R. Eleazer]?

C. When R. Eleazer fell ill, R. Aqiba and his colleagues came in to visit him. He was sitting on his bed, and they sat in the antechamber. That day was a Friday, and Hyrcanus, his son, came in to remove his father's phylacteries. [Eliezer] grew angry with him and he went out in distress.

D. He said to them, "It appears to me that father's mind is deranged."

E. [Aqiba] said to them, "His [your] mind and your mother's mind are deranged. How will one ignore a matter that is prohibited on pain of stoning and take up a matter that is prohibited merely by reason of Sabbath rest [on the authority of rabbis]. [Freedman, p. 462, n. 1: The wife had not yet kindled the Sabbath lights nor put away the Sabbath meal to keep it hot. Both of these, if done on the Sabbath, are punishable by stoning, while the wearing of phylacteries indoors is forbidden only by rabbinical ordinance. Therefore he rebuked his son and wife.]"

F. Since sages observed that [Eliezer's] mind was at ease, they went in and sat before him at a distance of four cubits. [This was because he had been excommunicated, so they were prohibited from coming closer than that distance.]

G. He said to them, "Why have you come?"

H. They said to him, "To study Torah we have come."

I. He said to them, "And up to now why have you not come?"

J. They said to him, "We did not have free time."

K. He said to them, "I should be surprised if you people die natural deaths."

L. R. Aqiba said to him, "What will my death be?"

M. He said to him, "Your death will be the most difficult of all."

N. He raised his two arms and laid them on his heart and said, "Woe for you, these two arms of mine, for they are like to scrolls of the Torah that have been rolled up [and have not been opened and read].

O. "I learned much Torah, I taught much Torah.

P. "I learned much Torah, but I did not take away from my masters even so much as a dog licks up from the water of the ocean.

Q. "I taught much Torah, but my disciples did not take away from me so much as an eye-brush takes of eye-shadow.

R. "And not only so, but I can repeat three hundred rules concerning a bright spot [Lev. 13:2], and no one ever asked me a thing about them.

S. "And not only so, but I can repeat three hundred laws (and some say, three thousand laws), about the planting of cucumbers, and no one has ever asked me a thing about those laws, except for Aqiba, son of Joseph.

T. "Once he and I were walking along the way, and he said to me, 'Rabbi, teach me something about planting cucumbers.'

U. "I said something and the whole field was filled with cucumbers.

V. "He said to me, 'Rabbi, you have taught me how to plant them. Now teach me how to pull them up.'

W. "I said something and all of them were collected into a single place."

X. They said to him, "As to the ball, shoemaker's last, amulet, leather bag containing pearls, and small weight [M. Kel. 23:1], what is the law? [Are they susceptible as receptacles or not susceptible?]

Y. He said to them, "They are susceptible to uncleanness." But they can regain insusceptibility to uncleanness just as they are."

Z. "As to a shoe on the last, what is the law?"

AA. He said to them, "It is [insusceptible to uncleanness and so] pure," and his soul went forth as he said the word, "pure."

BB. R. Joshua stood on his feet and said, "The vow is released, the vow is released."

CC. At the end of the Sabbath, R. Aqiba met his [bier] as it went from Caesarea to Lud. He beat his flesh until blood flowed to the ground. He began his eulogy for the line of mourners saying, "'My father, my father, the chariot of Israel and the horsemen thereof' (2 Kgs. 2:12).

DD. "I have many coins but there is no money-changer to straighten them all out."

EE. Therefore it was from R. Eleazer that [Aqiba] learned [the rules cited in the Mishnah-paragraph].

FF. He learned them from R. Eleazer but did not learn the reasoning about them, and then he went and learned them from R. Joshua, who taught them how to reason about them.

GG. And how, to begin with, did [Eliezer] do any such thing? And lo, we have learned in the Mishnah: He who does a deed is liable [M. 7:11D]!

HH. If it is to practice learn so as to teach about the subject, it is a different matter, for a master has said, "'You shall not learn to do after the abominations of these nations' (Deut. 18:9).

II. "You may not learn in order to do, but you may learn in order to understand and to teach about it."

Units I, II deal with the formulation of the Mishnah's rule. Unit III takes up the mode of execution, which, after all, forms the topic at hand. Various little compositions on the practice of magic, units IV-X, fill out the topic, and unit XI reverts to the Mishnah-passage and supplies materials on the authority behind it.

CHAPTER FIVE
BAVLI SANHEDRIN CHAPTER EIGHT

8:1

A. A rebellious and incorrigible son [M. 7:4J] --

B. at what point [does a child] become liable to be declared a rebellious and incorrigible son?

C. From the point at which he will produce two pubic hairs, until the 'beard' is full --

D. (that is the lower [pubic], not the upper [facial, beard], but the sages used euphemisms).

E. As it is said, "If a man has a son" (Deut. 21:18) -- (1) a son, not a daughter; (2) a son, not an adult man.

F. And a minor is exempt, since he has not yet entered the scope of the commandments.

I.

A. How do we know on the basis of Scripture that a minor is exempt?

B. How do we know it! For it has been explicitly taught in the Mishnah-passage before us: since he has not yet entered the scope of the commandments [M. 8:1F].

C. And furthermore, where do we find that Scripture has imposed a penalty [on a minor] so that, in the present setting in particular, one should require a verse of Scripture to declare a minor to be exempt?

D. This is what we meant to say: Is a wayward and rebellious son put to death on account of a sin that he has actually committed? He is put to death on account of what he will end up doing. Since he will be put to death on account of what he will end up doing, then even a minor [might fall within the framework of the law].

E. And furthermore, "A son" implies, a son and not a man [M. 8:1E], hence a minor [so the supposition of the question is quite sound].

F. Said R. Judah said Rab, "It is because Scripture has said, 'When a man will have a son...' (Deut. 21:18) -- a son who is close to reaching the full strength of a man."

II.

A. Until the lower beard is full:

B. R. Hiyya taught on Tannaite authority, "Until it surrounds the corona."

C. When R. Dimi came, he said, "Surrounding the penis and not surrounding the testicles. [The former is an earlier point.]"

III.

A. Said R. Hisda, "If a minor male produced a child, his son is not subject [to the law] of a wayward and rebellious son, for it is said, 'If a man has a son' (Deut. 21:18), meaning, when a man has a son, and not 'when a son has a son.'"

B.   But that proof-text is needed for the proposition stated by R. Judah in the name of Rab [at I F].

C.   If so, Scripture should have said, "When a son will be born to a man."

D.   What is the sense of, "When a man has a son"?

E.   What is implied is in accord with what R. Hisda has said, [Freedman, p. 466, n. 4: By reversing the order, the manhood of the father when betting the son is emphasized. Only if a man beget a son, but not if a minor beget one, though he is already a man when his son transgresses.]

F.   May I then say that the entire verse serves only for the present purpose [excluding Rab's proposition entirely]?

G.   If so, Scripture should have written, "The son of a man." What is the sense of, "A man has a son"? It bears the proof for two propositions.

H.   The present proposition stands at variance with the view of Rabbah. For Rabbah has said, "A minor male cannot produce a child, for it is said, 'But if the man has no kinsmen to recompense the trespass to' (Num. 5:8).

I.   "Now [since all Israelites are related], is it possible that any Israelite would not have a redeemer?

J.   "But the Scripture here speaks of taking what belongs to the estate of a proselyte [who has no Israelite heirs, by definition]. [69A] And the All-Merciful thereby indicates by saying, 'A man,' that is in the case of a man that you have to go in search of a redeemer, to find out whether he has kinsmen, but if it is a minor, it is not necessary to search for kinsmen, for you may be certain that he does not have kinsmen. [That is because a minor cannot produce a child.]"

K.   Abayye objected, "'[And if any man lies carnally with a woman who is a bondmaid' (Lev. 19:20)]: 'A man' indicates that it must be an adult male.

L.   "How do we know that the law applies to a boy nine years and one day old who is capable of having sexual relations?

M.   "Scripture says, '<u>And</u> if a man....'"

N.   He said to him, "To be sure, he has [semen], but he cannot produce a child, such as with grain that is not yet a third grown [which has seed but, if sown, that seed cannot germinate]."

O.   A Tannaite authority of the house of Hezekiah [stated], "'But if a man came presumptuously (<u>MZYD</u>)...' (Ex. 21:14).

P.   "A man can [Freedman:] inflame his genitals and emit semen, but not a minor."

Q.   Said R. Mordecai to R. Ashi, "How do we know that the word (<u>MZYD</u>) at hand means 'heating'?

R.   "It is from the verse, 'And Jacob sod (<u>YZD</u>) pottage' (Gen. 25:29) [which uses the same root]."

IV.

A.   Now as to the Tannaite authority of the house of Ishmael, [who taught, 'If a man has a son'] (Deut. 21:18) means, a son but not a father [so that if the son is himself a father already, the law does not apply (Freedman, p. 467, n. 10)],

B.   how would such a case be possible? [We recall that the Mishnah has defined the period of liability as that interval between the appearance of two pubic hairs and the completion of the pubic corona, a relatively brief span of time.]

C.   Should one maintain that the wife became pregnant after the boy had produced two pubic hairs but produced the child before the lower beard had completed encircling the penis?

D.   Is there a sufficient interval [to permit the pregnancy to come to term]?

E.   And has not R. Keruspedai said, "The entire period of liability of a wayward and rebellious son is only three months alone."

F.   Rather, is it not a case in which the wife became pregnant prior to the husband's producing two pubic hairs and then gave birth before the beard had completely grown. [That is how the son would not be subject to the law at hand].

G.   That would then prove that a minor may produce a child.

H.   No, in point of fact his wife became pregnant after he had produced two pubic hairs and then gave birth after the lower beard was complete.

I.   And as to the problem of the saying in the name of R. Keruspedai [that there would not be done for the pregnancy to come to term while the boy was subject to the law of the wayward and rebellious son], when R. Dimi came, he said, "In the West they say, '"A son," and not one who is fit to be called a father.' [Freedman, p. 468, n. 1: Once his wife is impregnated, he is already fit to be called a father. But it is unnecessary to exclude him when he is already a father, for by then his hair must be fully grown, and he is automatically excluded by the limitations expressed in the Mishnah.]"

V.

A.   Reverting to the body of the foregoing: Said R. Keruspedai said R. Shabbetai, "The entire period of liability of a wayward and rebellious son is only three months alone."

B.   But lo, we have learned in the Mishnah: From the point at which he will produce two pubic hairs until the beard is full [M. 8:1C]. [Is that only in three months?]

C.   [This is the reply:] If the beard is full, even though three months have not passed, or if three months have passed, even though the beard is not full [he is no longer liable, and that is why Keruspedai's statement is valid under all circumstances.]

D.   R. Jacob of Nehar Peqod sat before Rabina, and, going into session, said in the name of R. Huna, son of R. Joshua, "From the statement of R. Keruspedai in the name of R. Shabbetai it follows that if a woman bears a child at seven months, her pregnancy will not be discernible at a third of its term.

E.   "For if you think that her pregnancy will be discerned at a third of term, why should the statement at hand specify three months? It would have sufficed to specify two and a half months. [Freedman, p. 468, n. 4: For the fetus being then discernible, the son is fit to be called a father and is no longer liable.]"

F.   He said to him, "Under all circumstances I should say to you that the fetus will be discernible at a third of term, [after three months, for in framing the law] we follow the majority [of cases]. [Most pregnancies go on for nine months, and the fetus is discerned at three months. That is then the point at which the son may be called a father and is no longer subject to the law of the wayward and rebellious son.]"

G.   They made this statement before R. Huna, son of R. Joshua, He said to him, "But in capital cases [such as this one] do we follow the majority? Has the Torah not said, 'Then the congregation shall judge and the congregation shall deliver the slayer' (Num. 35:25). [Freedman, p. 468, n. 6: This is taken to mean that in doubt the accused be given the benefit.] Can you then say that we follow the majority?"

H.   This statement was repeated before Rabina. He said to him, "But in capital cases do we not follow the majority?

I.   "Have we not learned in the Mishnah: If one of the witnesses says, 'It was on the second of the month,' and one of the witnesses says, 'It was on the third of the month,' their testimony stands, for one of them may know about the intercalation of the month, and the other one may not know about the intercalation of the month [M. 5:3A-B].

J.   "And if you maintain that we do not follow the majority, then we should rule in the present case that the witnesses testify in a precise way and so contradict one another. [Freedman, p. 469, n. 3: Since there is a minority that does not err in respect of the length of the month, why not assume that each knows the length of the preceding month?]

K.   "Rather, is it not because we do maintain that we follow the case of the majority, and the majority is likely to err in the matter of the intercalation of the month."

L.   Said R. Jeremiah of Difti, "We too have learned in the Mishnah:

M.   "A girl three years and one day old is betrothed by intercourse. And if a Levir has had intercourse with her, he has acquired her. And they are liable on her account because of the law prohibiting intercourse with a married woman. And she imparts uncleanness to him who has intercourse with her when she is menstruating, to convey uncleanness to the lower as to the upper layer. If she was married to a priest, she eats heave-offering. If one of those who are unfit for marriage has intercourse with her, he has rendered her unfit to marry into the priesthood. If one of all those who are forbidden in the Torah to have intercourse with her has intercourse with her, they are put to death on her account, but she is free of responsibility [M. Nid. 5:4A-H].

N.   "[69B] Now why should this be the case [that she should be regarded as legally married at all]?

O.   "I might invoke the possibility that she is barren, and it was in the supposition that she was barren, the husband would not have betrothed her [so that, in point of fact, should she prove to be barren, she is not regarded as betrothed at all].

P.   "Must we therefore not maintain that we follow the status of the majority, and the majority of women are not barren [and that is why the rule is as stated in the Mishnah]."

Q.   No, [that is not right, for] what is the sense of "liable on her account" as the Mishnah states matters? It is to an offering.

R. But lo, what it says is, They are put to death on her account!

S. At issue is her father's having sexual relations with her.

T. But it says, If one of all those who are forbidden in the Torah to have intercourse with her has intercourse with her [not just the father]!

U. So the Mishnah-rule speaks of a case in which the husband accepted her [whether or not she was barren, so the case does not make the besought point anyhow].

VI.

A. Our rabbis have taught on Tannaite authority:

B. A woman who commits lewdness with her minor son, who entered into the first state of cohabitation with her --

C. the House of Shammai invalidate her from marriage into the priesthood.

D. And the House of Hillel declare her valid [T. Sot. 5:7A-C].

E. Said R. Hiyya, son of Rabbah bar Nahmani, said R. Hisda, and some say, said R. Hisda said Zeiri, "All concur in the case of a son nine years and one day old, that his act of sexual relations is entirely valid.

F. "In the case of a child less than eight years of age, [all agree that] his act of sexual relations is null.

G. "The dispute pertains only to the case of a child eight years of age.

H. "For the House of Shammai take the view that we derive the law from the case of the earlier generations [when a boy of eight years could impregnate a woman], and the House of Hillel take the view that we do not derive the law from the case of the earlier generations."

I. And how on the basis of Scripture do we know that the earlier generations could produce a pregnancy [at the age of eight years]?

J. May we say that the proof is as follows:

K. It is written, "[And David sent and inquired after the woman, and one said,] 'Is not this Bath Sheba, daughter of Eliam, wife of Uriah the Hittite'" (2 Sam. 11:3).

L. And it is written, "Eliam, the son of Ahitophel the Gilonite" (2 Sam. 23:134).

M. And it is written, "And he sent by the hand of Nathan the prophet, and he called his name Jedidiah [Solomon later on] because of the Lord" (2 Sam. 12:25).

N. And it is written, "And it came to pass, after two full years [after Solomon was born] that Absalom had sheepshearers" (2 Sam. 13:23).

O. And it is written, "So Absalom fled and went to Geshur and was there three years" (2 Sam. 13:38).

P. And it is written, "So Absalom dwelt two full years in Jerusalem and did not see the king's face" (2 Sam. 14:28).

Q. And it is written, "And it came to pass after forty years that Absalom said to the king, I pray you, let me go and pay my vow which I have vowed to the Lord in Hebron" (2 Sam. 25:7).

R. And it is written, "And when Ahitophel saw that his counsel was not followed, he saddled his ass and arose and went home to his house, to his city, and he put his household in order, and hanged himself" (2 Sam. 17:23).

S.   And it is written, "Bloody and deceitful men shall not live out half their days" (Ps. 55:24). [This proves that Ahitophel did not reach the age of thirty-five].

T.   And it has been taught on Tannaite authority:

U.   The entire lifespan of Doeg was only thirty-four years, and of Ahitophel only thirty-three years.

V.   So how many years were they? Thirty-three. Then deduct the seven years, the age of Solomon at that time [that Ahitophel committed suicide], leaving twenty-six. Take off two years for three pregnancies, and it comes out that each one was eight years old when he produced a child. [Ahitophel must have been eight years at the conception of Eliam, Eliam eight years at the conception of Bath Sheba, Bath Sheba eight years at the conception of Solomon (Freedman, p. 471, n. 3)].

W.   But perhaps the two of them [Ahitophel and Eliam] were nine years old [when they produced conceptions], and Bath Sheba was only six years old when she conceived, for a woman is more vital. You may know that that is the case, for she had had a child earlier [before Solomon].

X.   The proof derives from here:

Y.   "Now these are the generations of Terah: Terah begat Abram, Nahor and Haran" (Gen. 11:27).

Z.   Abraham was a year older than Nahor, and Nahor was a year older than Haran. So Abraham was older than Haran by two years.

AA.   And it is written, "And Abraham and Nahor took wives for themselves, the name of Abram's wife was Sarai, and the name of Nahor's wife was Milcah, daughter of Haran, father of Milcah and father of Iscah" (Gen. 11:29).

BB.   (And R. Isaac said, "Iscah is the same as Sarai, and why was she called Iscah? Because she foresaw through the Holy Spirit [what would happen in the future], and this is in line with that which is written, 'In all that Sarah has said to you, hearken to her voice' (Gen. 21:12).")

CC.   (Another reason: Everyone looked at her beauty.)

DD.   It is written, "Then Abraham fell upon his face and laughed and said in his heart, [Shall a child be born to him who is a hundred years old? And shall Sarah, who is ninety years old, bear?]" (Gen. 17:17).

EE.   Now how much older was Abraham than Sarah? Ten years.

FF.   And he was older than her father by two years.

GG.   It turns out that Haran begat Sarah when he was eight years old.

HH.   But why should we reach this conclusion? Perhaps Abraham was the youngest of the three, and the brothers were ranked in wisdom.

II.   You may know that Scripture ranked them in accord with their wisdom, for it is written, "And Noah was five hundred years old, and Noah begat Shem, Ham and Japheth,"

JJ.   [If ranked by age,] Shem would be a year older than Ham, and Ham a year older than Japheth, so Shem was two years older than Japheth.

KK. It is written, "And Noah was six hundred years old when the flood of water was upon the earth" (Gen. 7:6), and it is written, "These are the generations of Shem. Shem was a hundred years old and begat Arphaxad two years after the flood" (Gen. 11:10).

LL. Now can he have been a hundred years old? He must have been a hundred and two years old. [Freedman, p. 472, n. 5: Since Noah was five hundred years old when Shem was born, and six hundred when the flood commenced, Shem must have been a hundred then. Consequently, two years later he was a hundred and two years old.]

MM. Rather, Scripture ranked them by wisdom, and here too, Scripture ranked them by wisdom.

NN. Said R. Kahana, "I stated this teaching before R. Zebid of Nehardea.

OO. "He said to me, 'You derive the fact from that passage. And this is the proof from which we derive the same proposition:

PP. "'To Shem, also, the father of all the children of Eber, brother of Japheth the elder, even to him were children born' (Gen. 10:21).

QQ. "[This indicates that] Japhath was the oldest of the brothers."

RR. How do we know [that in earlier generations a boy of eight years of age could produce a child]?

SS. It is from the following:

TT. "And Bezaleel, son of Uri, son of Hur, of the tribe of Judah" (Ex. 38:22).

UU. And it is written, "And when Azubah, [Caleb's wife], died, Caleb took Ephrath, who bore him Hur" (1 Chr. 2:19).

VV. And when Bezaleel made the tabernacle, how old was he?

WW. He was thirteen, for it is written, "And all the wise men, who wrought all the work of the sanctuary, came every man from his work which they made" (Ex. 36:4) [Freedman: he had must reached manhood].

XX. And it has been taught on Tannaite authority:

YY. In the first year [after the Exodus] Moses made the tabernacle, in the second he put up the tabernacle and sent out the spies.

ZZ. And it is written, "And Caleb said, I was forty years old when Moses, the servant of the Lord, [sent me from Kadesh-bernea to spy out the land]" (Jos. 14:7), "and now, lo, I am today eighty-five years old" (Josh. 14:10).

AAA. So how old was he? He was forty years old. Take off the fourteen years of Bezaleel's age at that time [since he was thirteen when he made the tabernacle, and this was a year later], leaving twenty-six years [as Caleb's age when Bezaleel was born].

BBB. Take off two years for three pregnancies [leaving twenty-four years], so each must have produced a child at the age of eight.

VII.

A. A son, not a daughter [M. 8:1E]:

B. It has been taught on Tannaite authority:

C. Said R. Simeon, "By strict law a daughter also should have been appropriate to fall into the category of the wayward and rebellious child, [70A] for everyone comes around to her to commit a sin [and she may turn out to be a whore].

D.   "But it is the decree of Scripture: <u>'a son,' not a daughter</u>" [T. San. 11:6C].

Despite the rather elaborate proof that fills up unit VI, the bulk of the materials at hand is framed around the interests of the Mishnah-paragraph. Units I, II provide proof texts or clarifications of the Mishnah's rule. Unit III expands upon the proof-text at hand. Unit IV is continuous with unit III. Unit V provides an important qualification of the law at hand. Unit VI remains within the same topical framework. Unit VII then reverts to the Mishnah-paragraph and expands upon is proof-text.

8:2

A.   At what point is he liable?

B.   Once he has eaten a tartemar of meat and drunk a half-log of Italian wine.

C.   R. Yose says, "A mina of meat and a log of wine."

D.   [If] he ate in an association formed for a religious duty.

E.   [if] he ate on the occasion of the intercalation of the month,

F.   [if] in Jerusalem he ate food in the status of second tithe,

G.   [if] he ate carrion and terefah-meat, forbidden things or creeping things,

H.   [if] he ate untithed produce, first tithe, the heave-offering of which had not been removed, second tithe or consecrated food which had not been redeemed [by money],

I.   [if] he ate something which fulfilled a religious duty or whereby he committed a transgression,

J.   [if] he ate any sort of food except meat, drank any sort of liquid except wine --

K.   he is not declared a rebellious and incorrigible son --

L.   unless he eats meat and drinks wine,

M.   since it is said, "A glutton and a drunkard" (Deut. 21:20).

N.   And even though there is no clear proof for the proposition, there is at least a hint for it,

O.   for it is said, "Do not be among the wine-drinkers, among gluttonous meat-eaters" (Prov. 23:20).

M. 8:2

I.

A.   Said R. Zira, "As to this tartemar, I do not know what it is, but since R. Yose doubles the measure applying to wine, it follows that he doubles the measure in regard to meat.

B.   "So it turns out that a tartemar is a half mina."

II.

A.   Said R. Hanan bar Moledah said R. Huna, "He is liable only if he buys meat cheaply [ZWL] and eats it, buys wine cheaply [ZWL] and drinks it, for it is written, 'He is a glutton [ZWLL] and a drunkard' (Deut. 21:20) [a play on words, since the root for 'glutton' yields 'cheap.']"

B. Said R. Hanan bar Moledah said R. Huna, "He is liable only if he eats raw meat and drinks undiluted wine."

C. Is this so?

D. And lo, both Rabbah and R. Joseph say, "If he ate raw meat and drank undiluted wine, he is not regarded as a wayward and rebellious son."

E. Said Rabina, "What is meant by undiluted wine is wine that is diluted but not diluted, and what is meant by raw meat is meat that has been cooked but not cooked.

F. "It is like charred meat that thieves eat [on the run]."

G. Both Rabbah and R. Joseph say, "If he ate salted meat and drank wine right from the vat [before it has matured], he cannot be treated as a wayward and rebellious son."

III.

A. We have learned there:

B. On the eve of the ninth of Ab a person should not eat two prepared dishes, nor should one eat meat or drink wine [M. Ta. 4:7D].

C. In this regard a Tannaite authority taught, "But one may eat salted meat and drink wine fresh from the vat.

D. As to salted meat, how long must it be salted?

E. Said R. Hanina bar Kahana, "So long as one might eat the meat of a peace-offering [two days and an intervening night].

F. And how long is wine regarded as fresh from the vat?

G. So long as it is in its first stage of fermentation.

H. And it has been taught on Tannaite authority:

I. Wine which still is fermenting -- as long as it is fermenting, it is not liable to the law of uncovered liquids. And how long is it deemed still to be fermenting? Three days [T. Ter. 7:15 (Avery-Peck)].

J. What is the law here [i.e. with regard to fermenting wine]?

K. There [with respect to not eating meat on the eve of the ninth of Ab] it is so as to diminish rejoicing. [So long as the meat is like the meat of a peace-offering, it gives the pleasure of fresh meat.]

L. Here it is because of its attractiveness, and even after a brief period, it is no longer attractive.

M. Wine for its part is attractive only after forty days have passed. [The son is liable only for eating and drinking what is very attractive, hence excluding meat a day old and wine less than forty days old (Freedman, p. 476, n. 2)].

IV.

A. Said R. Hanan, "Wine has created in this world only for comforting the bereaved and for requiting the wicked.

B. "For it is written, 'Give strong drink to him who is ready to perish [=the wicked], and wine to those of heavy heart' (Prov. 31:6).

C. Said R. Isaac, "What is the meaning of the statement of Scripture, 'Do not look upon wine when it is red' (Prov. 23:31)?

D.   Do not look upon wine, which makes the face of the wicked red in this world and white [with embarrassment] in the world to come."

E.   Raba said, "'Do not look upon wine when it is red' (Prov. 23:31) -- do not look upon wine, which ends up as blood."

F.   R. Kahana contrasted verses of Scripture, "It is written, Tirash, but we read, tirosh [for the word for wine].

G.   "If one had merit, he is made a head (rosh). If not, he becomes poor (rash)."

H.   Raba contrasted verses of Scripture, "It is written, 'And wine makes desolate the heart of man' but it is read, 'rejoices the heart of man.' If one has merit, wine makes him glad, if not, it makes him sad."

I.   And this is in line with what Raba said, "Wine and spice makes one wise."

V.

A.   Said R. Amram, son of R. Simeon bar Abba, said R. Hanina, "What is the meaning of the verse of Scripture, 'Who has woe? who has sorrow? who has contentions? who has babbling? who has wounds without cause? who has redness of eyes? They who tarry long at wine, they who go to seek mixed wine' (Prov. 23:29-30)?"

B.   When R. Dimi came, he said, "In the West they say, in respect to this verse, that one may interpret the second part in explanation of the first, or the first in explanation of the second. [Freedman, p. 477, n. 3: The second as explanatory of the first: who have all these evils? Those who tarry long. The second being the cause, the first the effect. Vice versa: For whom is it fitting to tarry long over wine? For the wicked only.]"

VI.

A.   Ubar, the Galilean, expounded as follows: "The word 'and' is stated thirteen times with respect to wine:

B.   "'And Noah began to be a husbandman, and he planted a vineyard, and he drank of the wine and was drunken, and he was uncovered within his tent. And Ham the father of Canaan saw the nakedness of his father and told his two brothers outside. And Shem and Japheth took a garment and laid it upon their shoulders and went backward and covered the nakedness of their father, and their faces [were backward, and they did not see their father's nakedness]. And Noah awoke from his wine and knew what his younger son had done to him' (Gen. 9:20-24). [Freedman: the conversive waw occurs thirteen times. The combination of waw yod means woe, thus there were thirteen woes; so great are the sorrows caused by drunkenness]."

C.   [On the reference to what the younger son had done to him,] Rab and Samuel [discussed the matter].

D.   One said, "He castrated him."

E.   And the other said, "He had sexual relations with him."

F.   The one who said that he castrated them holds that, since he cursed him by his fourth son [the sons of Ham, Cush, Mizraim, Phut, and, fourth, Canaan, and at Gen. 10:7, Noah cursed Canaan], he cursed him because of a fourth son [which Noah could not have].

G.   And the one who maintains that he had sexual relations with him compares the use of, "And he saw." Here: "And Ham the father of Canaan saw the nakedness of his father," and elsewhere: "And when Shechem, son of Hamor, saw her, [he took her and lay with her and defiled her]" (Gen. 34:2).

H.   Now from the viewpoint of him who says that he castrated him, that is why he cursed him as to his fourth son in particular.

I.   But as to him who maintains that he had sexual relations with him, why did he curse the fourth son in particular? Rather, he ought to have cursed him.

J.   In point of fact, both took place.

VII.

A.   "And Noah began to be a husbandman and he planted a vineyard" (Gen. 9:25):

B.   Said R. Hisda said R. Uqba, and some say, Mar Uqba said R. Zakkai said, "The Holy One, blessed be he, said to Noah, 'Noah, you should have learned from the first man, for whom it was only wine that was the cause [of all his troubles]."

C.   This accords with the view of him who has said that the tree from which the first man ate was the vine.

D.   That is in accord with what has been taught on Tannaite authority:

E.   R. Meir says, "As to the tree from which the first man ate [and was cursed],

F.   "It was a vine, [70B] for there is nothing that causes for man so much wailing as wine, [as it says, 'And he drank of the wine and got drunk' (Gen. 9:21)]."

G.   R. Judah says, "It was wheat, for a child does not know how to call his mother and father by name before he can taste wheat, [so wheat is the source of knowledge, hence the Tree of Knowledge]."

H.   R. Nehemiah says, "It was a fig tree, for the source of the curse proved also to be the remedy, as it is said, 'And they sewed fig leaves together' (Gen. 3:7)."

VIII.

A.   "The words of King Lemuel, the burden wherewith his mother admonished him" (Prov. 31:1):

B.   Said R. Yohanan in the name of R. Simeon b. Yohai, "This verse teaches that his mother had him bound on a post [to be flogged].

C.   "She said to him, 'What, my son? and what, the son of my womb? and what, the son of my vows?' (Prov. 31:1).

D.   "'What my son? Everybody knows that your father feared heaven, and now people will say that his mother was the cause of his [corruption].

E.   "'And what, the son of my womb? As to all the other wives of your father's harem, once they got pregnant, they did not see the face again. But I forced my way in so that I should have a vigorous and well-formed son. [Further acts of intercourse would make the foetus better looking.]

F.   "'And what, the son of my vows? All the other women in your father's harem would take vows, "May I have a son worthy of the throne," but I took a vow and said, "May I have a son that is vigorous and filled with Torah-learning and fit for prophecy."

G.   "'It is not for kings, O Lemuel, it is not for kings to drink wine [nor for princes to say, Where is a strong drink]' (Prov. 31:4).

H. "She said to him, 'What business do you have with kings who drink wine and get drunk and say, "What do we need God for?"'?

I. "'Nor for princes to say, Where is strong drink' (Prov. 31:4):

J. "'Should he to whom all the secrets of the world are self-evident drink and get drunk?'"

K. There are those who say, "Should he, to whom all the princes of the world rise early to come to his door, drink wine and get drunk?"

L. Said R. Isaac, "How do we know that Solomon repented and confessed that his mother [was right]?

M. "As it is written, 'I am more brutish than man and have not the understanding of a man' (Prov. 30:2).

N. "'I am more brutish than man' refers to Noah, of whom it is written, 'And Noah began to be a husbandman' (Gen. 9:20).

O. "'And have not the understanding of a man' — of Adam."

IX.

A. If he ate in an association formed for a religious duty [M. 8:2D]:

B. Said R. Abbahu, "He is liable only if he eats in an association that is made up entirely of louts."

C. But have we not learned in the Mishnah: If he ate in an association formed for a religious duty he is not declared a wayward and rebellious son [M. 8:2D]?

D. The reason is that such an association was formed for a religious duty.

E. Lo, if it was not formed to carry out a religious duty, even if the whole of the association was not made up of louts, he may be declared liable [and that is not limited to an association made up entirely of louts, as Abbahu has claimed].

F. So we are informed [by the Mishnah] that even if everyone in the association was a lout, since the association is taken up with carrying out a religious duty, he is not going to be led astray [and so penalized].

X.

A. If he ate on the occasion of the intercalation of the month [M. 8:2F]:

B. Does this bear the implication that on such an occasion they eat meat and wine?

C. And has it not been taught on Tannaite authority:

D. They go up for it only with a piece of wheat bread and pulse alone.

E. So we are informed that even though people do not come up [to testify] carrying more than a piece of wheat bread and pulse, if he brought up meat and wine and ate it, since he was involved in performing a religious duty, he is not led astray [and so is not penalized].

F. Our rabbis have taught on Tannaite authority:

G. Not less than ten come up for the rite of intercalating the month.

H. People come up only with a piece of wheat bread and pulse.

I. People come up only on the evening following the intercalation.

J. And they come up not by day but by night.

K. And has it not been taught on Tannaite authority:

L. They come up not by night but by day?

M.   This accords with what R. Hiyya bar Abba said to his sons, "Get up early and come
       out early, so people may know of your celebration. [But the rite took place at
       night.]"

XI.

A.   If in Jerusalem he ate food in the status of second tithe [M. 8:2F]:

B.   Since he eats it in the correct way, he will not be led astray.

XII.

A.   If he ate carrion and terefah-meat, forbidden things or creeping things [M. 8:2G]:

B.   Said Raba, "If he ate chicken, he is not condemned as a wayward and rebellious son."

C.   Lo, we have learned in the Mishnah: If he devoured carrion and terefah meat,
       forbidden things or creeping things [M. 8:2G] ... he is not declared a wayward and
       rebellious son [M. 8:2K]. Thus if he ate clean [and appropriate meat], he would be
       condemned as a wayward and rebellious son.

D.   The Mishnah speaks only of what completes the requisite volume. [If the whole
       measure was the meat of chicken, he would be exempt, but if it was mostly
       cow-meat and completed with a little chicken, he is liable.]

XIII.

A.   If he ate something which fulfilled a religious duty or whereby he committed a
       transgression [M. 8:2I]:

B.   Something which fulfilled a religious duty is a meal served to comfort mourners.

C.   Something whereby he committed a transgression is a meal on a public fast.

D.   And what is the scriptural basis for that view?

E.   Scripture has said, "He will not obey our voice" (Deut. 21:20) meaning, "our voice"
       and not the voice of the Omnipresent. [If he disobeys God, he does not fall into the
       category of a wayward and rebellious son.]

XIV.

A.   If he ate any sort of food except meat, or drank any sort of liquid except wine [M.
       8:2J]:

B.   If he ate any sort of food except meat -- ["meat" here is meant] to include even
       Keilah-figs.

C.   If he drank any sort of liquid except wine -- ["wine" here is meant] to include even
       honey and milk.

D.   For it has been taught on Tannaite authority:

E.   If one ate Keilah-figs or drank honey or milk, and then went into the Temple, [71A]
       he is liable [for entering the Temple after drinking wine.]

XV.

A.   He is not declared a rebellious and incorrigible son unless he eats meat and drinks
       wine [M. 8:2K-L].

B.   Our rabbis have taught on Tannaite authority:

C.   If he ate any sort of food but did not eat meat, drank any sort of liquid but did not
       drink wine, he is not declared a rebellious and incorrigible son, unless he eats meat
       and drinks wine, since it is said, "A glutton and a drunkard" (Deut. 21:20).

D. Even though there is no clear proof for the proposition, there is at least a hint for it, for it is said, "Do not be among the wine-drinkers, among gluttonous meat-eaters" (Prov. 23:20) [M. 8:2J-O].

E. And it says, "For the drunkard and glutton shall come to poverty, and drowsiness shall clothe a man with rags" (Prov. 23:21).

F. Said R. Zira, "Whoever sleeps in the school house will find that his learning of Torah is torn into rags,

G. "For it is said, 'And drowsiness shall clothe a man with rags'" (Prov. 23:21).

The Talmud is made up of two large compositions, one treating the Mishnah in particular, at units I, II, IX-XV, and a long inserted unit on the theme of wine. That unit, III-VIII, occasionally reverts to the topic at hand, e.g., at unit III J-M. But for the most part the theme explains the conglomeration of materials, and there is no point at which the Mishnah-paragraph plays a role.

8:3

A. [If] he stole something belonging to his father but ate it in his father's domain,

B. or something belonging to others but ate it in the domain of those others,

C. or something belonging to others but ate it in his father's domain,

D. he is not declared a rebellious and incorrigible son --

E. until he steals something of his father's and eats it in the domain of others.

F. R. Yose b. Judah says, "...until he steals something belonging to his father and his mother."

I.

A. If he stole something belonging to his father but ate it in his father's domain,

B. even though he has ready access [to what belongs to his father], he will be afraid [and not do this very often].

C. If he stole something belonging to others but ate it in the domain of those others,

D. even though he is not afraid, he does not have ready access [and so will not do this very often].

E. And all the more so if he stole something belonging to others but ate it in his father's domain,

F. in which case he does not have ready access, and, further, is afraid [so he will not do this often].

G. Until he steals something of his father's and eats it in the domain of others,

H. in which case he has ready access and will not be afraid [and so will make this theft a habitual practice].

II.

A. R. Yose b. Judah says, "...until he steals something belonging to his father and his mother [M. 8:3F]:

B.   Whence would his mother get domain over property? What a wife buys is as if her husband bought it.

C.   Said R. Yose b. R. Hanina, "It would involve something prepared for a meal for his father and for his mother."

D.   And has not R. Hanan b. Moladah said R. Huna said, "He is liable only if he will buy meat at a cheap price and drink wine acquired at a cheap price"?

E.   Rather, I may say, [he stole] funds for a meal designated for his father and his mother [Freedman, p. 482, n. 2: in which money the mother has an exclusive share, as alimentation is part of the husband's obligations to the wife].

F.   And if you wish, I shall propose that it was from property that a third party gave over to her, saying, "I give you this on the condition that your husband enjoy no domain over it."

The Talmud at unit I presents its underlying thesis on the purpose of the law and reads each clause in light of that thesis. Unit II clarifies an obvious problem in the Mishnah-paragraph.

8:4

A.   [If] his father wanted [to put him to judgement as a rebellious and incorrigible son] but his mother did not want to do so,

B.   [if] his father did not want and his mother did want [to put him to judgment],

C.   he is not declared a rebellious and incorrigible son --

D.   until both of them want [to put him to judgment].

E.   R. Judah says, "If his mother was unworthy of his father, he is not declared to be a rebellious and incorrigible son."

I.

A.   What is the sense of unworthy of his father [at M. 8:4E]? May I say that it was a marriage that produced liability to extirpation or even to the death penalty at the hands of an earthly court [e.g., an incestuous union]?

B.   But in any case his father remains his father and his mother, his mother.

C.   Rather, the sense is that he was not similar [in appearance] to his father.

D.   So too has it been taught on Tannaite authority:

E.   R. Judah says, "If his mother is not like his father in voice, appearance, and stature, he cannot be declared a wayward and rebellious son."

F.   What is the scriptural basis for that view?

G.   It is because Scripture has said, "He will not obey our voice" (Deut. 21:10).

H.   Since we require that the voice of the two be alike, so we require that they be alike in appearance and stature.

II.

A.   In accord with which authority is the following Tannaite teaching:

B.   There has never been, and there never will be, a wayward and rebellious son.

C.   So why has the passage been written? To tell you, "Expound and receive a reward" [T. San. 11:6A-B].

D.   In accord with whom? The foregoing surely accords with the theory of R. Judah.

E.   And if you wish, I shall propose that it accords with R. Simeon, for it has been taught on Tannaite authority:

F.   Said R. Simeon, "And because this one has eaten a tartemar of meat and drunk a half-log of Italian wine, will his father and his mother bring him out to be stoned?

G.   "But such a case has never been and will never be.

H.   "And why has it been written? It is to tell you, 'Expound and receive a reward.'"

I.   Said R. Jonathan, "I saw such a case and sat on his grave."

J.   In accord with whom is the following that has been taught on Tannaite authority:

K.   An apostate town never was and is not ever going to be. And why was the matter written? To say, Expound it and receive a reward [T. San. 14:1A-B, T.'s version.]

L.   In accord with whom? In accord with R. Eleazer.

M.   For it has been taught on Tannaite authority:

N.   R. Eleazer says, "Any town in which there is even a single mezuzah cannot be declared an apostate town."

O.   What is the scriptural basis for that view?

P.   Scripture has said, "And you shall gather all the spoil of it in the midst of the street thereof and shall burn them" (Deut. 13:17).

Q.   Now if there is even a single mezuzah, it is not possible to do so, for it is written, "And you shall destroy the names of them.... You shall not do so to the Lord your God" (Deut. 12:4).

R.   Said R. Jonathan, "I saw such a town and sat on its mound."

S.   In accord with what authority is the following that has been taught on Tannaite authority:

T.   A diseased house has never come into existence and is never going to come into existence. And why was the passage written? It was to tell you, Expound and receive a reward [T. Neg. 6:1A].

U.   In accord with what? It is in accord with R. Eleazar b. R. Simeon, for we have learned in the Mishnah:

V.   R. Eleazar b. R. Simeon says, "[A house is not declared unclean] until a spot the size of two split beans will appear on two stones on two walls in the corner; its length is two split beans and its width a split bean [M. Neg. 12:3G-H].

W.   What is the reason for the view of R. Eleazar b. R. Simeon? It is written, "Wall" (Lev. 14:37) and it is again written, "Walls" (Lev. 14:37). What is one wall that appears as two walls? It has to be at the angle at which walls meet.

X.   It has been taught on Tannaite authority:

Y.   Said R. Eleazar b. R. Sadot, "There was a place on the border of Gaza, and they called it, 'A quarantined ruin.'"

Z.   Said R. Simeon of Kefar Akkum, "Once I went in Galilee and I saw a place that is marked off by designated stones, and they said, 'They deposited diseased stones in this place'" [T. Neg. 6:1B-C].

Once Judah's qualification is offered, at unit I, the question obviously arises of whether such a case can ever come to court. Unit II, continuous with the foregoing, then explores that question in its own terms.

8:4F-O

F.   [If] one of them was maimed in the hand, lame, dumb, blind, or deaf,

G.   he is not declared a rebellious and incorrigible son,

H.   since it is said, "Then his father and his mother will lay hold of him" (Deut. 21:20) -- so they are not maimed in their hands;

I.   "and bring them out" -- so they are not lame;

J.   "and they shall say" -- so they are not dumb;

K.   "This is our son" -- so they are not blind;

L.   "He will not obey our voice" -- so they are not deaf.

M.   They warn him before three judges and flog him.

N.   [If] he went and misbehaved again, he is judged before twenty-three judges.

O.   He is stoned only if there will be present the first three judges, since it is said, "This, our son" -- this one who was flogged before you.

I.

A.   Does this passage prove that the Scripture must be read in a literal way, just as it is written?

B.   The present case is distinctive, [71B] for the entire verse of Scripture at hand is superfluous [and available for exposition such as is given here].

II.

A.   They warn him before three judges [M. 8:4M]:

B.   Why? Should two not suffice?

C.   Said Abayye, "This is the sense of the passage: 'They warn him before two judges and administer a flogging before three.'"

III.

A.   Whence is it stated that a wayward and rebellious son [is flogged]?

B.   It is in accord with what R. Abbahu has said. For R. Abbahu has said, "We have derived an analogy from 'And they shall chastise him' which occurs two times [Deut. 22:18, Deut. 21:18].

C.   "And the sense of that repeated phrase derives from the use of the word 'son,' with an analogy to the use of that same word in the phrase, 'And it shall be if the wicked man be worthy ["a son"] to be flogged' (Deut. 25:2)."

IV.

A.   If he went and misbehaved again, he is judged before twenty-three judges [M. 8:4/O]:

B.   Is the cited verse, "This our son..." not used to make the point [at M. 8:4K], "This is our son" -- so they are not blind?

C.   If so, the Scripture should have stated, "He is our son."

D.   Why: "This, our son"?

E.   It is to permit the deduction of two rules.

The Talmud systematically explains the Mishnah's clauses, providing a scriptural basis for the rules.

8:4P-Q

P.   [If] he fled before his trial was over, and afterward [while he was a fugitive,] the lower "beard" became full, he is exempt.

Q.   If after his trial was done he fled, and afterward the lower beard became full, he is liable.

M. 8:4

I.

A.   Said R. Hanina, "A son of Noah who cursed the divine Name and afterward converted to Judaism is exempt from penalty, since the mode of trying him has undergone a change, so too the mode of inflicting the death penalty."

B.   May I say that the following passage of the Mishnah supports [Hanina's view]?

C.   If he fled before his trial was over, and afterward the lower "beard" became full, he is exempt [M. 8:4P].

D.   What is the reason for this ruling? Is it not because we invoke the rule that, since he has changed [in one aspect of culpability], he has changed [in all others]?

E.   No, the present case is different from the other, because if he had done such a deed at this time, he would not be subject to the death penalty at all.

F.   Come and take note: If after his trial was done he fled, and afterward the lower beard became full, he is liable [M. 8:4Q]. [This would refute Hanina's view.]

G.   Now you have said, If after his trial was done. And if his trial is done, then he is already subject to the death penalty [so there is no parallel to Hanina's case].

H.   Come and take note: A son of Noah who hit his neighbor or had sexual relations with his neighbor's wife and then converted to Judaism is exempt. If he did so to an Israelite and then converted to Judaism, he is liable.

I.   Now why should this be the case? May we not invoke the rule that, since his status has changed, the liability affecting him also should change?

J.   We require a shift both in the mode of trying the man and also in the mode of inflicting the death penalty, and in this one's case, while the rules of trying him have changed, the mode of inflicting the death penalty has not changed.

K.   But in the case of this one, while the mode of trying him has changed, the mode of inflicting the death penalty has not changed.

L.   [How so?] While, to be sure, in the case of the murderer, to begin with he was subject to death through decapitation and he is now subject to death through decapitation, as to the one who commits adultery, to begin with he was subject to the death penalty through decapitation, but now he is subject to the death penalty through strangulation.

M.   But a pertinent parallel is provided by the betrothed girl, for in both instances [before, after conversion], the death penalty is the same, namely through stoning.

N.   But lo, the passage has been framed in the language of, "If he did so to an Israelite," parallel to the matter of "his neighbor's wife!" [Freedman, p. 487, n. 1: His neighbor's wife must refer to a married woman, since the sacredness of betrothal alone is not recognized by gentiles. Consequently, "if he did this to an Israelite" must refer to the case of a married woman.]

O.   [While we do indeed deal with a married woman, if one had had sexual relations with her before conversion, he would be put to death through decapitation; if it is after conversion, it is by stoning. Since stoning is a more lenient mode of execution, we maintain that] the lesser mode of execution is encompassed by the more severe [so the mode of execution cannot be said to have changed, that is, changed for the worse].

P.   That reply is suitable for one who maintains that decapitation is the more severe mode of execution.

Q.   But as to him who maintains, as does R. Simeon, that strangulation is the more severe mode of execution, what is there to say?

R.   R. Simeon takes the view of the Tannaite authority of the house of Manasseh, who has said, "All penalties of execution that apply to the sons of Noah take the form only of strangulation" [so the above argument is entirely valid].

S.   Now to be sure, in the case of a married woman [the argument remains valid, since] to begin with the mode of execution was through strangulation and it now remains strangulation.

T.   But in the case of the murderer, to begin with the mode of execution was strangulation, while now it is through decapitation.

U.   Just as before, the lesser mode of execution [decapitation] is encompassed by the greater [which is strangulation, and the rest follows].

V.   May I say that the following passage supports this argument?

W.   If a betrothed maiden went astray [committing adultery] and then reached puberty, she is subject to the death penalty through strangulation.

X.   But why should she not be subject to execution through stoning [as she would have been, had she remained a girl prior to puberty]? Is it not because, once the penalty changes, it changes [Freedman, p. 488, n. 1: Though here it does not exempt her entirely, since strangulation, to which the pubescent girl is liable, is included in stoning, the punishment for the prepubescent girl]. All the more so [in a case of blasphemy], where the mode of execution wholly changes.

Y.   Has not R. Yohanan said to the Tannaite authority [who stated the passage], "Repeat it in the form: She is put to death through <u>stoning</u>."

The Talmud in no way was composed to related to the Mishnah-passage at hand. It is inserted only because of its reference to the present passage. In fact it is the general principle that is at issue, not the Mishnah's rule in particular.

8:5

A.   A rebellious and incorrigible son is tried on account of [what he may] end up to be.

B.   Let him die while yet innocent, and let him not die when he is guilty.

C.   For when the evil folk die, it is a benefit to them and a benefit to the world.

D.   But [when the] righteous folk [die], it is bad for them and bad for the world.

E.   Wine and sleep for the wicked are a benefit for them and a benefit for the world.

F.   But for the righteous, they are bad for them and bad for the world.

G.   Dispersion for the evil is a benefit for them and a benefit for the world.

H.   But for the righteous, it is bad for them and bad for the world.

I.   Gathering together for the evil is bad for them and bad for the world.

J.   But for the righteous, it is a benefit for them and a benefit for the world.

K.   Tranquility for the evil is bad for them and bad for the world.

L.   But for the righteous, it is a benefit for them and a benefit for the world.

I.

A.   [72A] It has been taught on Tannaite authority:

B.   R. Yose the Galilean says, "And is it the case that merely because this one has eaten a _tartemar_ of meat and drunk a half-_log_ of Italian wine, the Torah has said that he should be taken to court and [tried for the penalty of] stoning?

C.   "Rather, it is because the Torah has plumbed the depths of the psychology of the wayward and rebellious son.

D.   "For in the end, he will use up his father's wealth and then will want to satisfy his gluttony. Not finding the means, he will go out to the crossroads and mug people.

E.   "The Torah has said, Let him die while yet innocent, and let him not die when he is guilty [M. 8:5B].

F.   "For when evil folk die, it is a benefit to them and a benefit to the world.

G.   "But when the righteous folk [die], it is bad for them and bad for the world.

H.   "Wine and sleep for the wicked are a benefit for them and a benefit for the world.

I.   "But for the righteous they are bad for them and bad for the world.

J.   "Tranquility for the evil is bad for them and bad for the world.

K.   "But for the righteous it is a benefit for them and a benefit for the world.

L.   "Dispersion for the evil is a benefit for them and a benefit for the world.

M.   "But for the righteous, it is bad for them and bad for the world. [M. 8:5C-L, in slightly different order].

N.   [B. lacks: Gathering together for the evil is bad for them and bad for the world.

O.   "But for the righteous, it is a benefit for them and a benefit for the world."]

The Talmud contributes Yose the Galilean's reason.

8:6

A.   He who breaks in [Ex. 22:1] is judged on account of what he may end up to be.

B.   [If] he broke in and broke a jug, if blood-guilt applies to him, he is liable.

C.   If blood-guilt does not apply, he is exempt.

I.

A.   Said Raba, "What is the reason [that the householder may kill] one who breaks in?

B.   "It is because we make the assumption that no one restrains himself when it comes to protecting his property.

C.   "And this one [the thief] must have taken the view, 'If I go there, the householder will resist me and not let me [take what I want], so if he resists, I shall kill him.'

D.   "And the Torah has said, 'If he comes to kill you, you kill him first' [cf. Ex. 22:1]."

E.   Said Rab, "He who breaks into a house and took utensils and got away is exempt [from having to pay for them].

F.   "What is the reason? He has acquired ownership of them by the risk of his life."

G.   Said Rabbah, "It stands to reason that the ruling of Rab applies to a case in which the utensils were broken and no longer available for restitution, but if one took them [and they remain available], that is not the case."

H.   By God! what Rab said applies even to a case in which he took them away.

I.   For even in a case in which if the householder had killed him, there would have been a consideration of blood guilt; if the utensils are damaged, he remains liable. Therefore the utensils fall into the robber's domain.

J.   Here too the utensils fall into the robber's domain. [Freedman, p. 490, n. 1: The reasoning is as follows: when something is stolen, it loses its first ownership and passes into that of the thief, who is therefore liable for having removed it from its owner's control as for an ordinary debt. Consequently, he is liable even if it is broken. For if it theoretically remained in its first ownership, the thief would not be liable for any damage done to it. Hence in this case, since the thief, by his act of breaking in, became liable to death, restoration cannot be demanded even if the pot is intact, for liability to monetary restoration is cancelled in the face of the greater liability to death.]

K.   But that is not the case. When the All-Merciful placed the utensils into the domain of the robber, it was as to damages, but as to ownership, the property remains in the domain of the original owner. This is parallel to the case of one who borrows property [which remains in the domain of the owner, though the borrower would have to pay for any damages done to the property while he holds on to it.]

L.   We have learned in the Mishnah: [He who breaks in] ...if he broke in and broke a jug, if blood-guilt applies to him, he is liable. If blood-guilt does not apply, he is exempt [M. 8:6].

M.   The reason then is that he broke it, so he is exempt when no blood-guilt would apply to him [should the owner kill him], but if he only took it, he is not exempt [as against Rab's view].

N.   The rule at hand [of exemption from having to pay for the jug] also applies if he took it. The reason the framer of the passage says, and broke a jug, is to inform us that, if the owner should be subject to blood-guilt, even if he [the robber] broke the jug, [the robber has to pay].

O.   That is self-evident. The robber has done damage.

P.   What the framer of the passage tells us is that even if it was not intentionally [broken, liability applies].

Q.   What then does that tell us? That a human being always is regarded as forewarned? That we have learned in following Tannaite teaching: A human being always is regarded as forewarned, whether he does something inadvertently or deliberately, under constraint or willingly [M. B.Q. 2:6].

R.   That is a problem.

S.   R. Bibi bar Abayye objected, "He who steals the purse of his fellow and took it out of his domain on the Sabbath -- lo, this person is liable for the theft, for he had already become obligated on account of the theft of the purse before it had gone forth. If he was dragging it along and so removed it from the domain of the other, he is exempt [as to the purse] since he did not make acquisition of the purse before he had also and simultaneously violated the Sabbath [T. B.Q. 9:19A-C]. [Freedman, p. 491, n. 1: Hence we see that though the purse is still in existence, he is not bound to return it. This refutes Rab's ruling.]"

T.   Not at all. The ruling applies to a case in which the thief threw the purse in the river [and so could not return it].

U.   Some rams were stolen from Raba in a break-in. The robbers returned them to him, but he would not accept them back. He said, "Since such a ruling has come forth from Rab, [it must be obeyed, and the thieves have acquired ownership of the rams.]"

II.

A.   Our rabbis have taught:

B.   "[If a thief be found breaking in, and he be smitten that he die,] there shall no blood be shed for him, if the sun be risen upon him" (Ex. 22:1-3).

C.   Did the sun rise on him alone?

D.   But if it is as clear to you as the sun that he was not at peace with you, then kill him, but if not, do not kill him [T. 11:9F-H].

E.   A further Tannaite teaching:

F.   "If the sun be risen upon him, there shall be blood shed for him:"

G.   And did the sun rise on him alone?

H.   But if it is as clear to you as the sun that he is at peace with you, do not kill him, but if not, kill him [T. 11:9F-H].

I.   There is a contradiction between one unattributed teaching and another unattributed teaching.

J.   There is no contradiction.

K.   [72B] The one speaks of a father robbing from his son, the other of a son robbing his father. [The former has more compassion for the son than does the son for the father. The son must not assume the father will kill him, but the father may assume the son will kill him (Freedman, p. 492, n. 2)].

III.

A.   Said Rab, "I would kill anyone who broke in on me, except for R. Hanina bar Shila."

B.   "What is the reason? Should I say that it is because he is a righteous man [and therefore no threat to life but], lo, in the cited possibility, he is by definition a housebreaker!

C.   "Rather, it is because I am confident in his regard that he would have mercy on me the way a father has mercy on a son."

IV.

A.   Our rabbis have taught on Tannaite authority:

B.   "[If the sun be risen upon him], there shall be blood shed for him" (Ex. 22:1):

C.   That is the case whether on a weekday or on the Sabbath.

D.   "[If the thief be found breaking in], there shall be no blood shed for him" (Ex. 22:2).

E.   That is the case whether on a weekday or on the Sabbath.

F.   Now there is no problem with the statement that there is no blood shed for him whether on a weekday or on the Sabbath. Such a statement was necessary. You might have thought that one might rule that the case may be compared to the one involving those put to death by a court, in which case, on the Sabbath we do not inflict the death penalty. Then we are taught that we do inflict the death penalty.

G.   But as to the statement, "There shall be no blood shed for him" whether on a weekday or on the Sabbath, now if we do not inflict the death penalty on a weekday, is there any question about not doing so on the Sabbath?

H.   Said R. Sheshet, "The statement nonetheless was necessary to deal with the case of removing a pile of dirt for the sake of such a person [who has dug his way into the house and been buried by a pile of dirt in his tunnel. We learn that the dirt must be removed even on the Sabbath, so as to safe the thief's life.]"

V.

A.   Our rabbis have taught on Tannaite authority:

B.   "[If a thief be found breaking in] and be smitten" (Ex. 22:1) -- by any one.

C.   "And he die" (Ex. 22:1) -- by any mode of death by which you can kill him.

D.   Now it was indeed necessary to teach, "'And be smitten' -- by any man." For it might have entered your mind to maintain that it is the householder alone who will take action against the man, because someone will not refrain from defending his property, but a third party will not do so.

E.   So we are informed that the housebreaker is a threat, and even a third party will put him to death [if he can].

F.   But as to the teaching, "'And he die' -- by any mode of death by which you can kill him," what need is there for that teaching? One may derive that same fact [that any way of killing the housebreaker is permissible] from the case of the murderer.

G.   For it has been taught on Tannaite authority:

H.   "He who smote him shall surely be put to death, for he is a murderer" (Num. 35:21).

I.   I know only that he may be put to death by the form of death that has been stated in his regard.

J.   How do I know that if you cannot put him to death in the mode of inflicting the death penalty that has been stated in his regard, you have the right to put him to death in by any means by which you can kill him?

K.   Scripture says, "He shall surely be put to death" -- by any means whatsoever.

L.   [One might say] that that case is different [from the present one], for it is written, "He shall surely be put to death" [a phrase not stated in the present context, and it follows that proof of the same proposition in the case at hand is necessary.]

M.   But why not derive the present rule from that case in any event.

N.   The reason is that the matter that treats the murderer and the redeemer of the blood derives from two verses that speak of the same topic, and in the case of two verses that treat the same topic, we cannot derive any further lessons [applicable to cases other than the one at hand]. [So the proof before us is required.]

VI.

A.   Our rabbis have taught on Tannaite authority:

B.   "If a thief be found breaking in" (Ex. 22:1):

C.   I know that only that the rule applies to a break-in [through one's walls]. How do I know that the same rule applies to a break-in through one's roof, courtyard, or outer buildings?

D.   Scripture says, "If the thief be found" -- any where [he is found as a thief].

E.   If so, why does Scripture say, "Breaking in"?

F.   It is because most thieves are found in a break-in [through a wall].

G.   A further Tannaite teaching:

H.   "[If a thief be found] breaking in" (Ex. 22:1);

I.   I know only that the rule applies to a break-in [through one's walls]. How do I know that the same rule applies to a break-in through one's roof, courtyard, or outer buildings?

J.   Scripture says, "If the thief be found" -- wherever he is found [as a thief].

K.   If so, why does Scripture state, "Breaking in"?

L.   It is because the act of breaking in on his part itself constitutes the admonition [not to do so].

VII.

A.   Said R. Huna, "In the case of a minor who is pursuing one, it is permitted to kill him and so to save him at the cost of his own life."

B.   He maintains that it is not necessary to give an admonition to a pursuer, and there is no distinction between an adult and a minor.

C.   R. Hisda objected to R. Huna, <u>The woman who is in hard labor -- they chop up the child in her womb and they remove it limb by limb, because her life takes precedence over his life. If its greater part has gone forth, they do not touch him, for they do not set aside one life on account of another life [M. Oh. 7:6].</u> Now why should that be the case? He is in the status of a pursuer [thus a threat to life]."

D.   That case is different, for the threat to life derives from the action of heaven.

E.   May I say that the following supports him:

F.   In the case of one who was pursuer in pursuit of his fellow to kill him, one says to him, "See that he is an Israelite, a member of the covenant, and the Torah has said, 'Whoever sheds the blood of man, [to save that man] his own blood shall be shed,' which means that one must save the blood of this party at the cost of the blood of that party."

G.   That statement accords with the view of R. Yose b. R. Judah.

H.   For it has been taught on Tannaite authority:

I.   R. Yose b. R. Judah says, "In the case of an associate [of sages], there is no need for admonition, for admonition applies only so that the court may distinguish inadvertent from deliberate crime [but an associate knows the law and whatever he does is deliberate, by definition]."

J.   Come and take note: "In the case of one who was in pursuit of his fellow to kill him, one says to him, "See that he is an Israelite, a member of the covenant, and the Torah has said, 'Whoever sheds the blood of man, [to save that man] his own blood shall be shed' (Gen. 9:6), which means that one must save the blood of this party at the cost of the blood of that party."

K.   If [the pursuer] then said, "I know that that is how matters are," he is exempt [from being put to death, having desisted].

L.   But if he said, "It is on that very condition that I act," then he is liable [T. San. 11:4B-E]. [This shows that one has to give an admonition to the pursuer, contrary to the view of Huna].

M.   No, the rule at hand applies to a case in which one party was on one side of the canal, the other on the other said, in which case [the one who gives the warning] cannot save the other party.

N.   What can one do? He has to bring him to court!

O.   But if he were to bring him to court, there would have to be advance admonition.

P.   If you want, I shall propose the following:

Q.   R. Huna may say to you, "I rule in accord with the Tannaite authority in the matter of the break-in, who has said, 'The act of breaking in constitutes ample admonition [against doing so, and no further admonition is required. The same rule applies here.]"

Unit I provides a clarification of the reasoning of the rule at hand. Unit II cites Tosefta's complement and glosses it. Unit III is continuous with the foregoing. Unit IV then takes up the exposition of the verse of Scripture on which the Mishnah's rule rests, and the same exercise occupies units V, VI. Only unit VII undertakes an independent analysis, this with reference to the requirement of admonition in the case of pursuit. The whole is an orderly and cogent composition.

8:7

A. [73A] And these are those who are to be saved [from doing evil] even at the cost of their lives:

B. he who pursues after his fellow in order to kill him --

C. after a male, or after a betrothed girl;

D. but he who pursues a beast, he who profanes the Sabbath, he who does an act of service to an idol -- they do not save them even at the cost of their lives.

I.

A. Our rabbis have taught on Tannaite authority:

B. How do we know that in the case of one who pursues his fellow to kill him, it is permitted to save [such a person from sinning] at the cost of his life?

C. Scripture says, "You shall not stand by the blood of your neighbor" (Lev. 19:16).

D. Does that verse serve the present purpose? It is needed, rather, in accord with that which is taught on Tannaite authority:

E. How do we know that, if one sees his fellow drowning in a river, or being dragged off by a wild beast, or mugged, he is liable to save him?

F. Scripture says, "You shall not stand by the blood of your neighbor" (Lev. 19:16).

G. That indeed is the case [that the verse cited earlier serves the present purpose].

H. How, then, do we know that it is permitted to save such a person [from sinning] even at the cost of his life?

I. We establish an argument a fortiori, on the basis of the case of a betrothed girl.

J. Now if, in the case of a betrothed girl, in which case the attacker comes only to inflict damage, the Torah has said that it is permitted to save her at the cost of his life,

K. if one pursues his fellow to kill him, all the more so!

L. But do we inflict penalties merely on the basis of the outcome of a logical argument?

M. A member of the house of Rabbi stated on Tannaite authority:

N. It is on the basis of an argument of analogy.

O. "For when a man rises against his neighbor and kills him, even so in this matter" (Deut. 22:26) [in the setting of the rape of a betrothed girl].

P. But what lesson is to be derived from the case of the murderer? [Freedman, p. 496, n. 4: For the simile itself is superfluous, since the Torah explicitly states that the maiden is not punished. Hence it implies that a certain feature of the law of a murderer holds good here too and vice versa.]

Q. "Lo, this comes to teach a lesson but turns out to be the subject of a lesson.

R. "There is then an analogy to be drawn between the murderer and the betrothed girl.

S. "Just as in the case of the betrothed girl, it is permitted to save her at the cost of the attacker's life, so the murderer may be saved [from sin] at the cost of his life."

T. And how do we know that the rule just now stated in fact applies to the betrothed girl herself?

U. It is in accord with the statement of the Tannaite authority of the house of R. Ishmael.

V. For the Tannaite authority of the house of R. Ishmael [taught], "'[The betrothed girl cried,] but there was none to save her' (Deut. 2:27).

W. "But if there had been someone there to save her, then, in any means by which one may save her, one does so."

II.

A. Returning to the body of the cited passage:

B. How do we know that if one sees his fellow drowning in a river, or being dragged off by a wild beast, or mugged, he is liable to save him?

C. Scripture says, "You shall not stand by the blood of your neighbor" (Lev. 19:16).

D. Does that proposition derive from the present passage? Lo, it derives from the following passage:

E. How do I know that one must save his neighbor from the loss of himself?

F. "'Then you shall restore him to him" (Deut. 22:2). [Freedman, p. 496, n. 7: The passage refers to restoring a neighbor's lost property. This interpretation extends it to his own person, that is, if he has lost himself, he must be helped to find his way again. Hence it also applies to rescuing one from danger].

G. If proof derives from that passage, I might have maintained that that rule applies only to saving another as one's personal obligation, but one need not take the trouble of going out and hiring [others to do so].

H. So we are informed that the rule applies even to engaging others to do son.

III.

A. Our rabbis have taught on Tannaite authority:

B. All the same are the cases of one who pursues his fellow to kill him, a male, a betrothed girl, other sorts of deeds punishable by death inflicted in the court, and those punishable by death inflicted as extiration, people save [such persons committing these cries] at the cost of their own lives.

C. But if it was a widow married to a high priest, or a divorcee or a woman who had performed the rite of removing the shoe married to an ordinary priest, they do not save him at the cost of his life.

D. If the [betrothed girl] had previously been the object of the commission of a transgression, they do not save such a girl at the cost of the rapist's life.

E. If there is another way of saving her, they do not save her at the cost of his life.

F.   R. Judah says, "If she herself had said, 'Let him be,' lest he kill her [they do not save him at the cost of his life,] [T.: even though by leaving him, he gets involved with a capital crime]" [T. San. 11:11C-F].

G.   What is the source of the foregoing?

H.   Scripture has said, "But the girl [read naarah but written naar, boy] you shall do nothing, there is in the girl no sin worthy of death" (Deut. 22:26).

I.   [Since the word for girl, while read as girl, is written as boy, we understand that] when the word is written as "boy" it refers to a case of sodomous rape, and when it is read as "girl" it refers to the rape of a betrothed girl.

J.   "Sin" refers to the category of crimes for which one is liable to extirpation.

K.   "Death" refers to crimes in the classification of those punishable by death at the hand of a court.

L.   Why do I require the specification of the several items [rather than deriving all of the cases from a single example]?

M.   It was necessary to make explicit reference to each one of them [in the verse just now cited].

N.   For if the All-Merciful had made reference only to the case of homosexual rape, I might have supposed that one saves the sinner at the cost of his life in that case only, because it is not the natural way of having sexual relations.

O.   But in the case of a girl, in which case it is the natural way, I might have said one does not do so.

P.   And if the All-Merciful had made explicit the case of the girl alone, it might have been argued that in that case one takes extraordinary measures, because it inflicts injury on her [by destroying her virginity], but in the case of a boy, in which there is no injury, I might have said that is not the case.

Q.   And if the All-Merciful had made explicit these two items, [73B], I might have argued that in the one case it is because it is not natural, and in the other because it inflicts injury [by destroying virginity], but in the other matter of forbidden sexual relations, in which case the form of sexual relations is natural and the consideration of inflicting injury through destroying virginity is uncommon, I might have said that that is not the case.

R.   Accordingly, the All-Merciful wrote, "...sin...."

S.   And if, furthermore, the All-Merciful had written the word, "...sin...", I might have reached the conclusion that that word encompasses even cases in which one is liable only for violating a negative commandment.

T.   So the All-Merciful wrote, "...death...."

U.   And if the All-Merciful had written the word, "...death...," I might have concluded that the rule applies to cases in which the court inflicts the death penalty, but it does not apply to cases in which the penalty is extirpation at the hand of heaven.

V.   Accordingly, the All-Merciful wrote the word, "...sin..."

W.   But then why should the All-Merciful not have written the words, "...sin worthy of death...," and it would not then have been necessary to make explicit reference to the case of the boy or the girl?

X.   That indeed is the case, but the explicit reference to the boy and the girl serve, in the one case, to eliminate [from the list of those who are saved from sin at the cost of their lives] one who is about to commit an act of idolatry, and, in the other case, to eliminate the cases of one who proposes to have relations with a beast and one who is about to violate the Sabbath.

Y.   But in the view of R. Simeon b. Yohai, who has held that, in he case of one about to commit an act of idolatry, it is permitted to save such a one at the cost of his life, for what purpose are the references made.

Z.   One serves to eliminate the case of a person about to commit bestiality [one who is not saved at the cost of his life from sin], and the other to eliminate the case of one about to violate the Sabbath.

AA. [How so?] It might have entered your mind that one would encompass Sabbath violation on the analogy of the matter of idolatry, since the word "profanation" applies to both.

BB. And in the view of R. Eleazar b. R. Simeon, who has said that in the case of one who profanes the Sabbath, it is permitted to save him at the cost of his life, on the basis of the analogy drawn between the Sabbath and idolatry on the basis of the appearance of the word "profanation" in both cases, what is to be said?

CC. One reference serves to eliminate the case of bestiality, and, as to the other, since the All-Merciful made reference to the boy, it made reference all also to the girl [but it is not a redundancy, so Freedman, p. 498, n. 6: for though "boy" is written the context demands that "girl" be read, since the entire passage refers to a girl].

IV.

A.   **R. Judah says, "Even if she herself had said, 'Let him be,' lest he kill her [they do not save him," etc.]:**

B.   What is at issue?

C.   Said Raba, "It is in a case in which while the girl is concerned about her virginity, she nonetheless lets him do as he wishes, so that he will not kill her.

D.   "Rabbis take the view that the All-Merciful focuses upon the matter of the girl's virginity, and lo, the girl is concerned about her virginity, [so one may kill the rapist].

E.   "R. Judah takes the view that the reason that the All-Merciful has said that one may kill the rapist is that the girl herself is prepared to be killed [for the sake of her honor]. But since in this case she is not prepared to be killed, [one does not kill on account of her being raped]."

F.   Said R. Pappa to Abayye, "As to the case of a widow married to a high priest, there too is a consideration of dishonor [since the woman can no longer marry any other priest]."

G.   He said to him, "The All-Merciful takes account of a major form of dishonor, but as to a minor form of dishonor, the All-Merciful does not take account."

V.

A.   **Sin -- this refers to the violation of rules the penalty of which is extirpation:**

B.   An objection was raised:

C.   These are the girls invalid for marriage to an Israelite who nonetheless receive a
      fine paid as a penalty by the man who seduces them: ...he who has sexual relations
      with his sister [M. Ket. 3:1A,D]: [Freedman, p. 499, n. 4: Even his sister, though
      "And she shall be his wife" of Deut. 22:28 is inapplicable. But if she might be saved
      by his life, he should not be fined. In the case of the death penalty, this principle
      holds good even if the offender is not actually executed or, as in this case, slain by
      the rescuers.]

D.   Rabbis stated before R. Hisda, "It is at the moment at which sexual relations begin
      that he is exempt from being slain [to save him at the cost of his life from
      committing a sin]. But the penalty of paying money does not apply until the
      completion of the act of sexual relations."

E.   That explanation serves the one who maintains that the beginning of sexual relations
      comes with the first "kiss" [meeting of the sexual organs], but in the view of him
      who says that the beginning of the first stage of sexual relations takes place at the
      point of entry of the crown of the penis into the vagina, what is there to be said?

F.   Rather, said R. Hisda, "We deal with a case in which the man first had sexual
      relations through the anus, and then went and had sexual relations through the
      vagina. [Freedman, p. 499, n. 8: Since she has been unnaturally violated before,
      whether by her brother or another, she may not be saved now by his life. Therefore
      he is fined for destroying her virginity. Otherwise she can be saved.]

G.   Raba said, "The rule applies where the girl permits him [to rape her], so that he will
      not kill her, and it represents the position of R. Judah."

H.   [74A] R. Pappa said, "It represents the case in which he has seduced her and the
      position of all authorities."

I.   Abayye said, "It applies in a case in which one could save her by cutting off one of
      his limbs [so the objection that he is liable to the death penalty does not apply]."

J.   "It stands within the position of R. Jonathan b. Saul."

VI.

A.   For it has been taught on the strength of Tannaite authority:

B.   R. Jonathan b. Saul says, "If there is one in pursuit, who was pursuing his fellow so
      as to kill him, and one can save him [from the sin] at the cost of one of his limbs
      [rather than by killing him] and one did not do so, he is put to death on his account."

C.   What is the scriptural basis for the position of R. Jonathan b. Saul?

D.   It is because it is written, "If men strive [and hurt a woman], he shall surely be
      punished ... [and pay as the judges determine. And if any mischief follow, then you
      shall give life for life]" (Ex. 21:22ff).

E.   And [in this connection] R. Eleazar said, "Scripture speaks of attempted murder [of
      one against the other], for it is written, 'And if any mischief follow, then you shall
      give life for life' (Ex. 21:22) [Freedman, p. 500, n. 8: though the murder of the
      woman is unintentional, thus the extreme penalty is explicable only on that
      assumption].

F.   "And even so, Scripture has said, 'If no mischief follows, he shall surely be punished.'

G.   "Now if you maintain that if one can save [the pursuer from committing sin] by taking away one of his limbs, it is not permitted to save him at the cost of his life,

H.   "Then you can find a case in which one is going to be punished [as Scripture here says], in a case in which one can have saved the man from sin at the cost of one of his limbs.

I.   "But if you maintain that, even if one can save [the pursuer from sin] by taking away one of his limbs, one nonetheless has the right to save him at the cost of his life, how would you find such a case in which one might _ever_ be punished along the lines of Scripture's statement? [Accordingly, we have Jonathan b. Saul's scriptural foundations.]"

J.   But the present case is to be distinguished, since here, there is death to be inflicted on account of one victim, and a monetary compensation to be paid on account of the other. [Freedman, p. 500, n. 10: He is liable to be put to death because he seeks to slay his combatant, but the monetary liability arises through his injury to the woman. Where, however, these liabilities are incurred on account of two difference persons, it may be that the one does not cancel the other.]

K.   The present case indeed is _not_ to be distinguished, for Rabbah has said, "If one was pursuing his fellow and broke utensils, whether they belong to the one who is being pursued or to any other man, [the pursuer] is exempt from having to pay compensation.

L.   "What is the reason? The pursuer is at risk of being put to death.

M.   "But if the one who was being pursued broke utensils, if they belong to the pursuer, he is exempt from having to pay compensation.

N.   "If they belong to anybody else, he is liable.

O.   "If they belong to the pursuer, he is exempt, so that the victim's property is not treated as more valuable to him than his person [since if the victim were able to kill the pursuer, he would not be liable to the death penalty].

P.   "If they belonged to anyone else, he is liable, because he is in the situation of saving his life at the cost of someone else's property.

Q.   "And as to one who was pursuing so as to save the life of his victim and broke utensils, whether they belonged to the pursuer, the pursued, or anyone else, he is exempt from having to make compensation.

R.   "That in point of fact is not logical.

S.   "But if you maintain the contrary position, it will turn out that no one will ever try to save his fellow from a pursuer [since he will undertake risks he cannot afford]. [At any rate the proposition of K is proved.]

VI.

A.   But he who pursues a beast [profanes the Sabbath or does an act of service to an idol -- they do not save them even at the cost of their own lives] [M. 8:7D]:

B.   It has been taught on Tannaite authority:

C. R. Simeon b. Yohai says, "If one performs an act of service to an idol, it is permitted even at the cost of his own life to save him from sin.

D. "This is by an argument a fortiori: Now if on account of an offense to an ordinary person [e.g., the rape of a betrothed girl], it is permitted to save the offender even at the cost of his own life, on account of an offense to the Most High, is it not all the more so [that one should kill such a person in order to save him from sin]?"

E. But are penalties to be inflicted merely because of logical reasoning?

F. He indeed takes the view that penalties are to be inflicted because of the results of logic.

G. It has been taught on Tannaite authority"

H. R. Eleazar b. R. Simeon says, "One profaning the Sabbath may be saved from sin at the cost of his own life."

I. He takes the view of his father, who has said that penalties are to be inflicted because of the results of logic.

J. And the case of the Sabbath derives from the case of idolatry by an analogy resting on the common use of the word "profanation" in respect to both sorts of actions [in regard to the Sabbath at Ex. 31:14, and in regard to idolatry at Lev. 18:21].

VIII.

A. Said R. Yohanan in the name of R. Simeon b. Yehosedeq, "They took a vote and decided in the upper room of the house of Nitzeh in Lod, as follows: 'In the case of all transgressions that are listed in the Torah, if people say to a person, "Commit a transgression and so avoid being executed," one should commit a transgression and avoid execution, except for the matters of idolatry, sexual immorality, and murder.'"

B. And may not commit an act of idolatry [to save his life]?

C. And lo, it as been taught on Tannaite authority:

D. Said R. Ishmael, "How do we know on the basis of Scripture that if people should say to someone, 'Commit an act of idolatry and do not suffer death,' that he should commit an act of idolatry and not suffer death?

E. "Scripture says, 'You shall live by them' (Lev. 18:5) -- and not die by them.

F. "May I suppose that one may do so even in public?

G. "Scripture says, 'Do not profane my holy name, for I shall be sanctified' (Lev. 22:32)."

H. Those who hold to the contrary [at Nitza's house in Lydda] accord with the view of R. Eliezer.

I. For it has been taught on Tannaite authority:

J. R. Eliezer says, "[Scripture states], 'And you shall love the Lord your God with all your heart, with all your soul, with all your might.' (Deut. 6:5) If it is said, 'With all your soul (Deut. 6:5),' why is it also said, 'With all your might'? And if it is said, 'With all your might,' why is it also said, 'With all your soul'?

K. "But if there is someone who places greater value on his body than on his possessions, for such a one it is said, 'With all your soul.'

L.   "And if there is someone who places greater value on his possessions than on his life, for such a one it is said, 'With all your might.'"

M.   And as to the matter of sexual immorality and murder?

N.   It is in accord with the view of Rabbi.

O.   For it has been taught on Tannaite authority:

P.   Rabbi says, "'For as when a man rises against his neighbor and slays him, even so is this matter' (Deut. 22:26).

Q.   But what lesson is to be derived from the case of the murderer [as above]? Lo, this comes to teach a lesson but turns out to be the subject of a lesson.

R.   There is an analogy to be drawn between the murderer and the betrothed girl. Just as in the case of the betrothed girl, it is permitted to save her at the cost of the attacker's life, so the murderer may be saved from sin at the cost of his life.

S.   "And an analogy is further to be drawn between the case of the betrothed girl and that of the murderer.

T.   "Just as in the matter or of murder, one should be killed and not commit murder, so as to a betrothed girl, let her be slain but not violate the law.

U.   "How do we know that there is the case for the murderer himself?

V.   "It is a matter of reasoning."

W.   That is in line with the case of one who came before Raba and said to him, "The master of my town has said to me, 'Go and kill so-and-so, and if you do not do so, I shall kill you.'"

X.   He said to him, "Let him kill you, but do not kill. Who will say that your blood is redder than his. Perhaps the blood of that man is redder [than yours]."

IX.

A.   When R. Dimi came, he said R. Yohanan said, "[The cited rule about having to give up one's life on account only of the three sins listed] applies solely in the time in which there is no royal decree [to violate the Torah]. But if there is a royal decree, then even on account of the most inconsequential religious duty, one should be put to death and not violate the law."

B.   When Rabin came, he said R. Yohanan said, "Even in the time in which there is no royal decree [to violate the Torah], one may not apply the cited rule except in private. But as to an action to be done in public, then even on account of the most inconsequential religious duty, one should be put to death and not violate the law."

C.   What would be a minor religious duty?

D.   Raba, son of R. Isaac, said Rab said, "[74B] Even to change one's shoe lace [from what Jews regularly wore to what gentiles wore]."

E.   And how many people constitute a public?

F.   Said R. Jacob said R. Yohanan, "A public audience is not less than ten."

G.   It is self-evident that we require the "public" to be made up of Israelites, for it is written, "But will I be sanctified among the children of Israel" (Lev. 22:23).

H.   R. Jeremiah raised the question, "If nine are Israelites and one a gentile, what is the law?"

I.   Come and take note of the following:

J.   R. Yannai, brother of R. Hiyya bar Abbar, repeated on Tannaite authority, "The meaning of the word 'among' in two passages supplies the answer.

K.   "Here it is written, 'I will be sanctified among the children of Israel (Lev. 22:23) and elsewhere, 'Separate yourselves from among this congregation' (Num. 16:21).

L.   "Just as, in the latter passage, the ten are all Israelites, so, here too, the ten must all be Israelites."

M.   And lo, there is the case of Esther, who violated the law in public (by marrying a gentile].

N.   Said Abayye, "Esther was merely in the status of the soil of the earth [and not an active sinner]."

O.   Raba said, "A case in which [a violation of the law] is on account of the benefit accruing to the [persecutors and not spite] is different, for if you do not hold that view, then how can we hand over to them our braziers and coal shovels [Freedman].

P.   "Rather, a case in which [a violation of the law] is on account of the benefit accruing to the persecutors is different, and the same principle applied there [to Esther]."

Q.   Raba accords with a view of his expressed elsewhere, for Raba said, "In the case of an idolator who [out of spite] said to an Israelite, 'Cut grass on the Sabbath and throw it to cattle, and if not, I shall kill you,' the Israelite should be killed and cut it.

R.   "[If he said], 'Cut it and toss it into the river,' he should be killed and not cut it.

S.   "What is the reason? It is the pagan's wish to make the Israelite transgress a teaching of the faith."

X.

A.   The question was addressed to R. Ammi, "Is a son of Noah commanded to accept martyrdom in the sanctification of God's name, or is he not commanded to accept martyrdom in the sanctification of God's name?"

B.   Said Abbaye, "Come and take note: The sons of Noah were given seven commandments. But if it were the case [that martyrdom was demanded of them], there should be eight, [not seven]."

C.   Said Raba to him, "Those seven and whatever pertains to keeping those seven [including martyrdom, if need be]."

D.   What is the rule?

E.   Said R. Adda bar Ahbah said members of the house of Rab said, "It is written, 'In this thing, the Lord pardon your servant, that when my master goes into the house of Rimmon to worship there, and he leans on my hand, and I bow myself in the house of Rimmon' (2 Kgs. 5:18).

F.   "And it is written, 'And he said to him, Go in peace' (2 Kgs. 5:19).

G.   [75A] "Now if it were so [that a Noahide has to sanctify God's name], he should not have said such a thing to him."

H.   The one was in private [in which it was permitted], the other in public [when one must be martyred and not commit idolatry.

XI.

A. Said R. Judah said Rab, "There was the case of a man who gazed upon a woman and whose heart become sick with desire for her. They came and asked physicians, who said, 'He has no remedy unless he has sexual relations with her.'

B. "Sages ruled, 'Let him die but not have sexual relations with her.

C. "[The physicians proposed,] 'Let her stand nude before him.'

D. "[Sages ruled,] 'Let him die, but let her not stand nude before him.'

E. "'Let her talk with him behind a wall.'

F. "'Let him die and let her not talk with him behind a wall.'"

G. There is a dispute on this case between R. Jacob bar Idi and R. Samuel bar Nahmani. One said, "The reason is that she was a married woman."

H. The other said, "She was unmarried."

I. Now if she was a married woman, that is why the rulings were as they were.

J. But in the view of him who said that she was unmarried, why so strict a set of rulings?

K. R. Pappa said, "Because of the insult to her family."

L. R. Aha, son of R. Iqa, said, "It was so that an Israelite woman should not be licentious."

M. And why not let him marry the woman?

N. Marriage would not settle his mind, in accord with what R. Isaac said,

O. For R. Isaac said, "From the day on which the Temple was destroyed, the pleasure of sexual relations was taken away [from Israelites] and handed over to transgressors.

P. "For it is said, 'Stolen waters are sweet, and bread eaten in secret is pleasant' (Prov. 9:17)."

As usual, we begin, at unit I, with scriptural proof for the proposition of the Mishnah, M. 8:7A. Unit II continues the foregoing. Units III-V then complement the Mishnah-paragraph with Tosefta's treatment of the same subject. Unit VI concludes the foregoing. Unit VII moves on to M. 8:7D. From unit VIII to the end we consider the matters for which one must accept martyrdom rather than violate the Torah. So, as usual, the entire composition serves the interests of the Mishnah-paragraph, either directly or indirectly.

INDEX

Abayye
13, 20, 22, 28, 29, 34, 57, 65-67, 73,
74, 80, 92, 97, 98, 100-105, 124, 134,
146, 176, 177, 179, 181-83, 186, 188,
190, 198, 200, 203, 212, 216, 222,
237, 242, 249, 250, 254

Abbahu
18, 22, 30, 47, 49, 57, 96, 146, 172,
174, 232, 237

Abbaye
138, 139, 142, 143, 146, 149, 160,
182, 254

Abia
161

Abin bar Hiyya
192

Abin bar Kahana
192

Abraham
49, 80, 94, 166, 170, 226

Aha
30-33, 37, 39, 41, 48, 64-68, 73, 93,
96, 135, 139, 156, 159, 160, 173, 178,
179, 199, 210, 255

Aha bar Hanina
33, 64-66, 96

Aha bar Jacob
32, 39, 93, 159, 173

Aha of Difti
65, 135, 179, 210

Ahadboi bar Ammi
149

Aibu bar Nigri
216

Amram
165, 230

Aqiba
12, 15, 21, 22, 42, 44, 63, 87, 125,
126, 137, 138, 145-47, 164, 165, 175,
189-92, 201-203, 205, 206, 209, 214,
215, 217-19

Ashi
12-14, 17, 21, 30, 65-67, 72, 86, 98,
127, 149, 182, 199, 216, 222

Assi
14, 20, 30, 64-66, 68, 76

Ben Zakkai
12, 53, 61, 62

Dimi
50, 80, 155, 160, 166, 191, 221, 223,
230, 253

Dosa
192

Eleazar
13, 25, 29, 42, 44, 48, 49, 58, 76, 78,
80, 85, 107, 128, 130, 131, 154, 160,
166, 167, 172, 191, 192, 195, 198,
200, 216, 217, 236, 249, 250, 252

Eliezer
12, 43, 82, 87-90, 119, 120, 122-24,
164-66, 179, 209, 217-19, 252

Hamnuna
14, 15, 150, 161, 180

Hanan
60, 68, 177-79, 228, 229, 235

Hanan bar Moledah
228, 229

Hanania
12

Hananiah b. Gamaliel
154

Hanina
11, 19, 24, 25, 33, 41, 48, 50, 64-66,
73, 76, 80, 96, 107, 123, 124, 160,
162, 166-70, 196, 198, 200, 205, 216,
229, 230, 235, 238, 243

Hanina b. Gamaliel
168

Hanina bar Kahana
229

Hezekiah
30, 36-38, 59, 95, 173, 174, 195, 222

Hisda
15, 16, 24, 25, 38, 61, 62, 72, 86, 89,
90, 101, 102, 104, 147, 155, 166, 221,
222, 225, 231, 245, 250

Hiyya
14, 17, 18, 22, 24, 37, 38, 72, 174,
192, 216, 217, 221, 225, 233, 254

Hiyya bar Abba
17, 18, 216, 233

Huna
30, 67, 72, 73, 77, 111, 158, 166, 167,
171, 211, 223, 224, 228, 229, 235,
244, 245

Huna bar Manoah
67

Idi
64, 139, 143, 255

Iqa
67, 139, 159, 178, 255

Isaac
15, 25, 32, 43, 49, 50, 62, 89, 120,
138, 153-55, 158, 162, 170, 173, 194,
226, 229, 232, 253, 255

	DATE DUE		
9/13/02			
MAY 1 4 2018			